THIRD EDITION

SCHOOL LAW AND THE PUBLIC SCHOOLS

A PRACTICAL GUIDE FOR EDUCATIONAL LEADERS

Nathan L. Essex

University of Memphis

PEARSON

Boston ■ New York ■ San Francisco
Mexico City ■ Montreal ■ Toronto ■ London ■ Madrid ■ Munich ■ Paris
Hong Kong ■ Singapore ■ Tokyo ■ Cape Town ■ Sydney

Vice President: *Paul A. Smith*
Senior Editor: *Arnis E. Burvikovs*
Editorial Assistant: *Megan Smallidge*
Senior Marketing Manager: *Tara Whorf*
Production Coordinator: *Pat Torelli Publishing Services*
Editorial Production Service: *Argosy Publishing, Inc.*
Manufacturing Buyer: *Andrew Turso*
Cover Administrator: *Joel Gendron*

For related titles and support materials, visit our online catalog at www.ablongman.com.

Between the time website inforamtion is gathered and then published, it is not unusual for some sites to have closed. Also, the transcription of URLs can result in unintended typographical errors. The publisher would appreciate notification where these errors occur so that they may be corrected in subsequent editions.

Library of Congress Cataloging-in-Publication Data
Essex, Nathan L.
  School law and the public schools : a practical guide for educational leaders / Nathan L.
  Essex.—3rd ed.
    p. cm.
    Inclues index.
    ISBN 0-205-41205-X
    1. Educational law and legislation—United States. 2. School management and
organization—Law and legislation—United States. I. Title.

KF4119.E84 2004
344.73'071—dc22

2004043738

To my mother and father, the late Bertha Essex and Nathan Essex, for their unconditional love, nurturing, guidance and personal sacrifices from my earliest years that enabled me to achieve my professional goals. I will always cherish their memories and feel the beauty of their love in my heart. I am thankful to have been blessed with such wonderful parents. It is to their memory that I dedicate this third edition.

CONTENTS

CHAPTER 1

Legal Framework Affecting Public Schools   **1**

CHAPTER 2

Religion and the Public Schools   **12**

CHAPTER 3

Students, the Law, and Public Schools   **43**

CHAPTER 6

School Personnel and School District Liability   135

CHAPTER 7

Liability and Student Records   168

CHAPTER 9

Discrimination in Employment   214

CHAPTER 12
School Desegregation   **308**

APPENDIX A

APPENDIX B

List of Cases

PREFACE

How do educational leaders respond to the legal challenges facing their organizations in a highly litigious society? How do they ensure that their organizations are achieving their mission without unduly restricting the constitutional rights and personal freedoms of their students and staff? How do leaders know when they are operating within the law? How can they build and foster an organizational culture that places high value on the personal rights and uniqueness of each individual? These are issues this book addresses.

School Law and the Public Schools: A Practical Guide for Educational Leaders, Third Edition, is based on the premise that educational leaders and policy makers must know the law that governs the operation and conduct of their organizations as they face a highly litigious society. Increasingly, educational leaders will need to exercise discretion in making sound and legally defensible decisions that affect students and school personnel under their authority. They will need to guide the development and execution of sound, well-developed policies, rules, and regulations governing many aspects of their operation. Educational leaders must ensure that they possess the legal knowledge necessary to accomplish these important administrative tasks successfully.

The goal of the third edition is to provide comprehensive and practical knowledge of relevant and contemporary issues that affect the organization and administration of schools. **This edition includes three new chapters involving** *instructional programs, school desegregation, due process, and school safety.* It also includes the No Child Left Behind Act of 2001, legal aspects of personnel recruitment, Homeland Security, the Gun-Free School Act, the recent landmark U.S. Supreme Court decision regarding affirmative action and college admissions policies, and the Ninth Circuit Court's ruling on the Pledge of Allegiance, among other topics. One important dimension of this text is the addition of exercises at the end of each chapter that provide meaningful application experiences for educational leaders. Expanded discussion of legal issues supported by charts and tables are integrated throughout the text to amplify topics under discussion. Practicing and prospective educational leaders, students of educational leadership, teachers, prospective teachers, and policymakers at all educational levels will gain knowledge that will help them effectively perform their professional duties within the boundaries of constitutional, statutory, and case law.

This book is organized and written in a style that facilitates ease of reading even for those individuals who have little or no legal background. Significant court cases that address the issues most relevant to effective practice have been carefully selected. The text begins with an in-depth focused discussion of major legal issues followed by relevant constitutional, statutory, and case law. Legal citations are used to support and enhance the discussion of these issues. Legal references are found on each page supporting the topics under discussion, thus enabling the reader to easily ascertain the legal sources of authority related to those particular topics.

One unique and salient feature of this text is the administrative guides that relate to major issues discussed in each chapter. These guides provide readers with pertinent information to direct their day-to-day decisions and actions as they encounter a wide array of legal challenges within their organizations. No attempt was made to review or include a significant number of state statutes or interpretations, because there are numerous variations from state to state. The primary focus of this text involves legal sources or developments that have significant implications for effective educational leadership throughout public schools in the United States.

Finally, the appendices include relevant constitutional provisions, and carefully federal statutes as well as an expanded glossary of important legal terms to assist the reader and provide relevance to the body of the text. *School Law and the Public Schools* provides a practical and useful resource guide for educational leaders aimed at increasing their knowledge and awareness of the complex legal issues that impact their organizations. It will enable them to perform their legal duties more effectively and meet the requirements of reasonableness as they move their organization toward their mission.

ACKNOWLEDGMENTS

I would like to express my heartfelt appreciation to my administrative secretary, Carol Brown, for the countless hours she spent preparing this document. Her energy, enthusiasm, encouragement, and support far exceeded my expectations. For her untiring efforts, I am eternally grateful.

I would also like to express my appreciation to my wife, Lorene, and my children, Kimberly, Jarvis, and Nathalie, for their love, support, and encouragement during the writing of this text. Their support provided me inspiration to persevere through the completion of this project.

I express gratitude to my daughter, Nathalie, a second-year law student at St. Louis University, for her editorial research and technical assistance, which aided me greatly in the production of this book.

Last, I express appreciation to my administrative team, friends, and colleagues for their support and encouragement during the writing of this third edition, and to the following reviewers: Genniver Bell, Fayetteville State University; Veronica Jones, Northern Arizona State; Scott McLeod, University of Minnesota; and Carol Anne Pierson, St. Bonaventure University.

To my staff, colleagues, and family, I am immensely grateful.

N.L.E.

ABOUT THE AUTHOR

Nathan L. Essex is professor of Educational Law and Leadership at the University of Memphis and President of Southwest Tennessee Community College. He received a B.S. in English at Alabama A&M University, an M.S. in Educational Administration at Jacksonville State University, and a Ph.D. in Administration and Planning at the University of Alabama.

Essex's interests include law, educational policy, and personnel administration. He has served as consultant for more than 100 school districts and numerous educational agencies. He served as a policy consultant with the Alabama State Department of Education for 12 years and received numerous awards in recognition of his contributions in the field of education. He is the recipient of the Truman M. Pierce Award for Educational Leadership, for outstanding contributions which advanced the direction of education in the state of Alabama; the Academic Excellence Award in recognition of professional achievement and academic excellence in the research, service, and teaching of education, Capstone College of Education Society, The University of Alabama; Teaching Excellence Award; Distinguished Service Award—*Who's Who in the State of Tennessee*; The University of Memphis Distinguished Administrator of the Year 1995–1996, "Educator on the Move," the University of Memphis; Phi Delta Kappa, the President's award for leadership and service to the community, Youth Services, Inc.; *Who's Who in Corporate Memphis*, *Grace* Magazine; and President Bush's Community Service Award, just to name a few. Essex has published numerous articles, book chapters, and newsletters on legal issues. Many of his works appear in *The Administrator's Notebook, The Horizon, Compensation Review, The Clearinghouse, The American School Board Journal, American Management Association, Community College Review, Education and Law,* and many other professional journals. He is highly sought by educators at all levels to share his knowledge and expertise regarding legal issues that impact public schools.

CHAPTER 1

LEGAL FRAMEWORK
AFFECTING PUBLIC SCHOOLS

SOURCES OF LAW

Bill of Rights and the Fourteenth Amendment

The Bill of Rights represents the primary source of individual rights and freedoms under the U.S. Constitution. The first ten amendments to the Constitution are viewed as fundamental liberties of free people because they place restrictions on the government's powers to intrude on the fundamental rights of all citizens. These restrictions simply mean that the government cannot exercise certain powers in relationship to free people. For example, the government cannot pass laws prohibiting the freedom of speech. Consequently, citizens can speak freely within the boundaries of the Constitution without undue interference by the government. At its inception, the Bill of Rights limited only the federal government's powers and not those of state government, which meant that states relied on their own Bill of Rights to limit state powers.

However, this all changed with the adoption of the Fourteenth Amendment in 1868. The Fourteenth Amendment, which guarantees due process of law and fundamental fairness, was applied to the states. The Fourteenth Amendment stipulates, "No state shall make or enforce any law which shall abridge the privileges or immunities of citizens of the United States; nor shall any state deprive any person of life, liberty, or property without due process of law; nor deny to any person within its jurisdiction the equal protection of the laws." Fourteenth Amendment provisions are enforced by state or federal courts operating within their proper jurisdiction, since they are considered federal law. Prior to the adoption of the Fourteenth Amendment, there were very few controls placed on state governments if they failed to abide by their own Bill of Rights. Relief could be sought only in the state courts without any certainty that these courts would enforce their own Bill of Rights. Federal courts had no authority to enforce a state Bill of Rights that was solely under the jurisdiction of state courts. By virtue of the Fourteenth Amendment, that authority is now vested in the federal courts.

Along with due process and equal protection provisions, the most formidable freedom contained in the Bill of Rights include freedom of speech, press, assembly, and religion, as well as freedom from unreasonable searches and protection against self-incrimination. Thus, the first ten amendments now apply to encroachment by state government. Since public schools are agents of the state, they are subject to the provisions of the Bill of Rights, which means that school officials must recognize and respect the constitutional rights of students and school personnel. Failure to do so will result in infringement of their constitutionally protected rights and possible legal challenges through the courts.

The Federal Constitution

The Constitution of the United States is the basic law of the land. It provides a framework of law in which orderly governmental processes operate. The Constitution thus becomes the primary source of law. All statutes enacted at the federal, state, and local levels as well as state constitutions, local regulations, and ordinances are subordinate to the Constitution. The federal Constitution is distinguishable in its provision to protect fundamental rights of all citizens of the United States. Inherent among these rights are those involving personal, property, and political freedoms. Although the Constitution does not make reference to education, it does impact the operation and management of schools, particularly with respect to amendments, which protect the individual rights of students, faculty, and staff.

One salient feature of the Constitution is the provision that calls for the separation of powers involving the executive, judicial, and legislative branches of government. The precept of separated powers provides each branch with the proper checks and balances on the powers of other branches.

State Constitutions

Based on the Tenth Amendment to the federal Constitution, powers not delegated to the United States by the Constitution, nor prohibited by it to the states, are reserved to the states respectively. Since education is not mentioned in the Tenth Amendment, it is left to states to control. Therefore, state constitutions represent the basic source of law for individual states and generally require legislative bodies to perform various functions, including establishing systems of public education. They prescribe funding and operational schemes for public schools. State constitutions also restrict the powers legislative bodies may exercise.

State constitutions very often address the same subject matter found in the federal Constitution, such as due process, individual rights and freedoms, as well as separation of church and state. State constitutions may exceed coverage granted by the federal Constitution but may not fail to meet the basic requirements of the Constitution or contradict it in any manner. Thus, a state statute may be in direct conflict with both federal and state constitutions or may violate one and be in compliance with the other. In all cases, federal and state constitutions prevail.

Statutes

Statutes represent an act of the legislative branch of government. The word *statute* is derived from the Latin term *statutum*, meaning "it is decided." Statutes are the most abundant source of law affecting public schools. School district policy, rules, and regulations are generally based on statutory law. Since education is considered a state function by virtue of the Tenth Amendment, courts tend to support the view that state legislatures should exercise power over public schools. It is only when statutes conflict with the federal Constitution, federal law, or state constitutions that a challenge is brought to the courts. In short, statutes are always subject to review by the judicial branch of government to determine their constitutionality. Statutes represent the most effective means of developing new law or changing old laws.

State legislators grant local school boards the authority to adopt and enforce reasonable rules and regulations necessary for the operation and management of schools. When challenged, school officials must be able to demonstrate that a legitimate state interest is met by enforcing a particular rule or regulation, especially in cases where individual freedoms are restricted.

Court or Case Law

Case law is generally reflected in judge-made or common law, as distinguished from statutory law. Common law consists of the judgments, opinions, and decisions of courts adopting and enforcing preceding usages and customs. Frequently, case law relies on past court decisions, which are called *precedents.* This practice is derived from the rule of law known as *Stare decisis*, a Latin term meaning "let the decision stand." This doctrine requires courts to observe legal precedents established in previous cases in the same jurisdictions in making future decisions involving the same or similar subject matter and factual circumstances. Although courts generally rely on precedent, they are not absolutely bound by it in rendering a decision. Factual circumstances may be sufficiently different to warrant a different decision, even when the subject matter is similar. Moreover, the rationale used in reaching the decision may not be viewed as applicable to the particular case under review. Federal courts, in their rulings, have contributed to a significant body of case law, which impacts the development of educational policies governing the administration and operation of public schools.

Case law is sometimes viewed as unsettled law because occasionally courts render conflicting rulings within their jurisdictions. Consequently, a ruling by a federal, district, or appellate court only affects educational policymakers in that particular jurisdiction. The Supreme Court is the single court whose decisions affect the organization and administration of public schools across the nation. Even so, there are many instances in which state and federal appellate decisions are not followed due, in large measure, to the fact that the Supreme Court has no ability to hear every conceivable issue relating to schools.

State Agencies

State legislatures in virtually all states have created administrative agencies to execute various laws and policies governing public schools. One of these agencies typically includes state boards of education. The legislature generally prescribes the duties and scope of authority delegated to state boards. Members of the state board of education are either appointed by the governor or elected by popular vote by citizens within the state. Conflicts frequently arise with state boards of education based on the separation of the executive, legislative, and judicial branches of government. The legislature is prohibited from delegating its powers to an administrative agency.

For example, the legislature in the state of Illinois commanded the superintendent of public instruction to prepare specifications for minimum requirements to conserve the health and safety of students. The specifications developed by the superintendent of instruction were challenged by the board of education under a claim that they were unconstitutional. The board sought injunctive relief against their enforcement. The circuit court granted relief. The superintendent appealed the decision. The State Supreme Court of Illinois held that the statute was a proper delegation of administrative authority to the superintendent. However, the superintendent's specifications, which preempted the entire field of school safety and purported to strike down all local codes and ordinances relating to school safety, were invalid. Only the legislature had the power to preempt local codes and ordinances regarding school safety.

The state board of education may exercise broad or limited powers, based on legislative authorization. Public schools are generally placed under the control of the state board of education. In this capacity, the state board of education becomes a policy-making body that functions immediately below the legislature.

In general, most state boards have six legal powers in common. They (1) establish certification standards for teachers and administrators, (2) establish high school graduation requirements, (3) establish state testing programs, (4) establish standards for accreditation of school districts and preparation programs for teachers and administrators, (5) review and approve the budget of the state education agency, and (6) develop rules and regulations for the administration of state programs.*

State boards of education may not abrogate responsibilities delegated to them by state statutes. The courts are reluctant to impose their judgment regarding decisions which are made within the state board of education's designated authority unless there is evidence of arbitrary and capricious acts or a violation of an individual's constitutional rights. In such cases, the courts will intervene to determine whether the evidence supports constitutional violations. In reviewing the action of an administrative board, one court has held that it will go no further than to determine (1) whether the board acted within its jurisdiction; (2) whether it acted according to law; (3) whether its action was arbitrary, oppressive, or unreasonable and represented its will rather than its judgment; and (4) whether the evidence was such that it might reasonably make the order or determination in question.[1]

In addition to state boards of education, each state has a state department of education, which is headed by a state superintendent or chief state school officer. State departments are the professional arm of the chief state school officer. These departments consist of specialists in virtually all areas relating to education. They provide consultation and advice to local school districts, the state board, and the chief state school officer. State departments are generally depositories for massive amounts of research data and strategic reports collected from local school districts. Much of these data consist of reports necessary to ensure that the state is in compliance with federal and state mandates and to facilitate education planning at the state and local levels.

School Board Policies

School board policies represent a basic source of law for school personnel as reflected in the rules and regulations governing the total operation of schools. School board policies are legally defensible as long as they do not conflict with the federal or state constitutions, federal and state statutes, or case law. Once these legal requirements are met, the school board as the delegated policy-making body at the local level may not violate its own policies. A school board is legally required to adhere to its own policies. Failure to do so may result in legal challenges by those adversely affected by the board's actions.

*Reprinted with permission from 2003 Education Commission of the States, "Helping State Leaders Shape Education Policy," 700 Broadway, #1200, Denver, Colorado 80203-3460.

THE U.S. SYSTEM OF COURTS

The judicial system consists of federal and state courts. The organization of the courts at both levels is essentially the same: trial courts, intermediate courts of appeal, and the highest court, which is the Supreme Court. State constitutions usually prescribe the powers of state courts as well as their jurisdiction. Irrespective of the level, courts are limited only to cases or legal conflicts presented to them for resolution. Courts cannot take it upon themselves to decide on the constitutionality of a statute or a policy unless a suit is brought challenging the legality of that particular statute or policy.

The courts usually perform three types of judicial functions when they are called on to act. They (1) settle controversies through applying basic principles of law to specific factual circumstances, (2) interpret legislative enactments, and (3) determine the constitutionality of legislative or administrative mandates. When applying principles of law to specific situations, the courts may find that principles of law are vague or ambiguous. In such cases, the courts must rely on legal precedent for direction.

In interpreting statutes, the courts, through their analogies and rulings, may actually affect the definition of the legislation by assigning meaning to it. When determining the constitutionality of statutes, courts make the presumption that such statutes are constitutional. Consequently, those who challenge the legality of the statute must assume the burden of proof to demonstrate otherwise. The Supreme Court in Florida addressed this issue when it stated:

> We have held that legislative acts carry such a strong presumption of validity that they should be held constitutional if there is any reasonable theory to that end. . . . Moreover, unconstitutionality must appear beyond all reasonable doubt before an act is condemned. . . . If a statute can be interpreted in two different ways, one by which it will be constitutional, courts will adopt the constitutional interpretation.[2]

Federal Courts

Federal courts typically deal with cases involving federal or constitutional issues ("federal questions") or cases in which the parties are residents of different states ("diversity of citizenship"). The federal court system includes district courts, appellate courts, and the Supreme Court. There are 95 federal district courts in the United States. At least one federal court is found in each state. Larger states, such as New York and California, have as many as four federal courts. Federal courts usually hear cases between citizens of different states and cases involving litigation of federal statutes.

Federal appellate courts are represented by circuit courts of appeal. There are 13 federal circuit courts, including 11 with geographic jurisdiction over a number of states and territories, one for the District of Columbia, and another involves three specialized federal courts. Table 1.1 and Figure 1.1 identify the geographic areas associated with each circuit. There are many judges on the various courts of appeals; for example, the Sixth Circuit Court of Appeals has 14 judges and 8 "senior" judges available to sit in panels of 3 judges. The primary function of the appellate court is to review the proceedings of lower courts to determine whether errors of law (as opposed to facts) were committed, such as procedural irregularities, constitutional misinterpretations, or inappropriate application of rules of evidence. Panels of judges for appellate courts hear oral arguments from the appellant and the

TABLE 1.1   Jurisdiction of Federal Circuit Courts of Appeal

CIRCUIT	JURISDICTION
1st	Maine, Massachusetts, New Hampshire, Puerto Rico, Rhode Island
2nd	Connecticut, New York, Vermont
3rd	Delaware, New Jersey, Pennsylvania, Virgin Islands
4th	Maryland, North Carolina, South Carolina, Virginia, West Virginia
5th	Louisiana, Mississippi, Texas
6th	Kentucky, Ohio, Michigan, Tennessee
7th	Illinois, Indiana, Wisconsin
8th	Arkansas, Iowa, Minnesota, Missouri, Nebraska, North Dakota, South Dakota
9th	Alaska, Arizona, California, Guam, Hawaii, Idaho, Montana, Nevada, Northern Mariana Islands, Oregon, Washington
10th	Colorado, Kansas, New Mexico, Oklahoma, Utah, Wyoming
11th	Alabama, Florida, Georgia
DC	Washington, DC
Federal	Washington, DC (specialized courts)

appellee, examine written arguments, vote, and render a ruling. The appellate court may also, based on its finding, remand the case to be retried by the lower court.

State Courts

State courts are a part of each state's judicial system, with the responsibility of hearing cases involving issues related to state constitutional law, state statutes, and common law. Many education cases are heard in state courts, because they do not involve a federal question. The structure of state courts is similar to those found in the federal courts: courts of general jurisdiction, courts of special jurisdiction, courts of limited jurisdiction, and appellate courts. There are variations in the names of these courts among the 50 states but all states have at least three to four tiers of courts.

Courts of General Jurisdiction.   Courts of general jurisdiction are often referred to as district or circuit courts. Their jurisdiction covers most cases except those held for special courts. In many instances, decisions may be appealed from these courts to intermediate appellate courts or even to the state supreme court. Areas adjudicated by these courts include civil, criminal, traffic, and juvenile issues.

Courts of Special Jurisdiction.   Courts of special jurisdiction were established to hear legal disputes in special matter areas. They are generally referred to as trial courts with *limited* jurisdiction and may be called municipal, justice of the peace, probate, small claims, or traffic court.

Intermediate Appellate Courts.   Intermediate appellate courts have emerged over the past three decades to hear appeals from trial courts or certain state agencies. Their primary role involves reviewing proceedings from trial courts to determine whether substantive or procedural errors occurred in applying the law. In a sense, their duties are similar to the highest

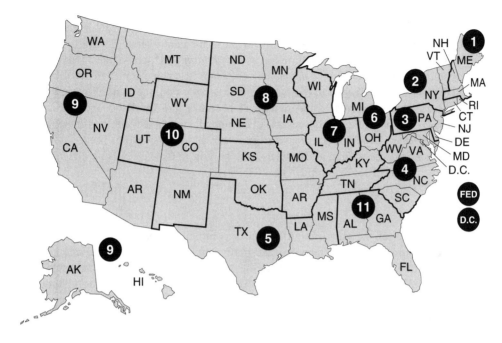

FIGURE 1.1   Federal Circuit Courts of Appeal

court within the state. However, the primary difference between the two is discretion. The intermediate court has less discretion in accepting cases than does the highest or state supreme court. Many, but not all, of the cases heard by the intermediate courts are mandatory.

Appellate Courts.   Appellate courts represent the highest courts within the state. They are considered courts of last resort. In 44 states, these are referred to as the state supreme courts. These courts have some discretion in accepting cases, but must hear mandatory cases based on appeal and decide on the merits of each case. State statutes generally prescribe the types of cases that must be heard by the various courts within a state. Discretionary jurisdiction involves cases in which a party files a petition to the state supreme court, seeking redress. It is then left to the court to use its discretion in deciding to accept or reject the case. It is important to understand that state courts play a vital role in addressing many issues involving the administration of public schools.

ANALYSIS OF AN APPELLATE COURT OPINION

Court proceedings are concluded with a written opinion setting forth the decision of the court on an issue under review by the court. These opinions consist of a set of components designed to facilitate an understanding of the court's ruling. The most common elements include the name of the case, the year in which the case was decided by the court, the appellant's contention, the appelle's defense, the procedure by which the case reached the court, the facts giving rise to the case, the ruling of the court, the court's rationale for the ruling, and the final disposition on the issue.

Case (Citation)

Cases are usually named for parties involved in the controversy. The party initiating the suit at the trial court level is referred to as the *plaintiff.* The party against whom the suit or action is brought is called the *defendant.* The plaintiff's name comes first, followed by the defendant's (e.g., *Baker v. Owen*). If the case is appealed, the party initiating the appeal who was not supported at the first level becomes the appellant, and the other party becomes the appellee. In this instance, the appellant is listed first and the appellee last (e.g., *Owen v. Baker*). Even though it may take as long as several years before all legal remedies are exhausted in a particular case, the year in the case citation indicates the time in which the decision was rendered.

Procedure

The initiator of the suit (plaintiff) files a complaint seeking relief by the courts for alleged improper actions taken by the defendant or failure on the defendant's part to meet certain legal standards. In either case, the plaintiff contends that an indefensible act has been attributed to the defendant. The party against whom a complaint is filed responds to the complaint with a rationale as to why certain actions were taken or were not taken. The defendant attempts to justify its actions regarding the plaintiff. In appellate decisions, an explanation may be given as to how the case reached the appellate level. An appeal or a petition for a writ of *certiorari* is the most common means used to bring a case to a higher court level. At the U.S. Supreme Court level and in some states courts of appeals, the writ of *certiorari* is used to remove a case from a lower court to a higher court for review.

Facts

The facts of a case describe the specific details leading to the conflict or controversy that resulted in the case reaching the court. The facts will describe the nature of the conflict as determined by the evidence presented during the actual proceeding. The facts are only at issue at the lower trial court level, not at the appeals stage. Appellate courts apply the law to the facts as determined by the trial.

Ruling and Justification

The ruling of the court, made manifest in the form of the written decision or opinion of the court, represents the court's response to the issue presented for its review. The ruling is usually accompanied by a justification detailing the basis on which the ruling was made. The ruling usually includes statements covering primary facts and the major conclusions reached by the courts. *Stare decisis,* or following precedents, is an important component in all court decisions.

Disposition

The disposition follows the ruling of the case that determines whether the plaintiff or the defendant was supported by the courts in the dispute. Once the victor is determined, the court reaches a conclusion and orders that some action be taken consistent with its ruling. If the plaintiff wins, the court will prescribe a remedy for the damages suffered by the plaintiff. It may be in the form of an order compelling the defendant to compensate the plaintiff for damages or an injunction prohibiting the defendant from continuing a certain practice deemed to be unjust. If the defendant is upheld, the case may be dismissed with an order that the plaintiff pay court fees and other legal fees associated with the case. In some instances, the case may be passed to an appellate court to determine the proper remedy. The appellate court may uphold the lower court decision, reverse the lower court decision, or modify the decision in some manner. The court may also remand the case back to the lower court for further proceedings based on its review of the case.

THE SUPREME COURT

The Supreme Court is the highest court in the land. Unlike lower courts, there is no appeal beyond the decision of this court. The Supreme Court's ruling can be overturned only by an amendment to the federal Constitution. Nine justices, including a Chief Justice, comprise the high court. To avoid political infringement, they are appointed to life terms.

Interestingly, the Supreme Court first convened in New York in 1790 and adjourned because it had nothing to do. It decided only 56 cases over a ten-year period, with very few of the cases having any real significance. Cases reach the Supreme Court primarily in two ways: on appeal and by *writ of certiorari*. The Supreme Court's review occurs in the following manner:

ON APPEAL (A REVIEW BY RIGHT)

From State Courts
1. Where a state court has held a federal statute or treaty provision unconstitutional
2. Where a state court has upheld a state law or state constitutional provision arguably in conflict with the federal Constitution, laws, or treaties

From Federal Courts of Appeals
1. Where a federal law or treaty is held unconstitutional
2. Where a state law or state constitutional provision is held invalid because it conflicts with a federal law, treaty, or constitutional provision

From Federal District Courts (direct appeal to Supreme Court)
1. Where a federal statute having a criminal penalty is held unconstitutional
2. Where judgment has been rendered to enforce antitrust laws, the Interstate Commerce Act, or Title II of the Federal Communications Act
3. Where a three-judge district court grants or denies an injunction restraining enforcement of state statutes or federal statutes, or orders of certain federal agencies

ON CERTIORARI (A DISCRETIONARY REVIEW GRANTED OR DENIED BY VOTE OF THE SUPREME COURT)

From State Courts
1. In cases involving federal questions where the decision supported a federal claim made under federal law or constitutional provisions

From Federal Courts of Appeals
1. Where a decision interpreted or applied the Constitution or various federal laws

   or
2. Where state laws or state constitutional provisions have been challenged in conflict with federal law where the court of appeals upheld the state provisions.[3]

Decisions reached by the Supreme Court are group decisions, which are thought to produce stability. Justices work collectively but independently to arrive at decisions. The high court meets for 36 weeks, commencing on the first Monday of each October and ending during the week of July 7th. The justices spend their time listening to lawyers' arguments, discussing court business, writing or studying opinions, and reading briefs submitted by attorneys. Each justice works six days a week, eight to ten hours each day. Court is open four days each week from Mondays through Thursday. During this time, the justices listen to oral arguments four hours each day. Each case is given only one hour to argue its position, with the plaintiff and the defendant receiving one half hour each to make their point. The Court recesses for two weeks to allow the justices to perform their important duties relating to the business of the Court.

Supreme Court Ritual

On Fridays at 11:00 A.M., the justices meet in a conference room (which is lined with books from floor to ceiling at a marble fireplace). They meet under a painting of Great Chief Justice Marshall, the fourth Chief Justice of the United States, and shake hands, showing harmony of aims. Justices are called to chamber by a buzzer five minutes before 11:00 A.M.

Seated at the head of the table is the Chief Justice, directly across from him at the other end of the table sits the Senior Associate Justice. The rest sit on either side of the table according to rank in seniority, descending in seniority away from the Chief Justice. The most recently appointed justice serves as a "messenger," carrying messages in and out of the conference room. Discussion of issues passes from justice to justice according to seniority. After discussion, there is a call for a vote—four votes bring a case to the Court; five votes dispose of it. If a justice disqualifies himself or herself and the vote is four to four, the lower court decision stands. Justices vote in reverse order, from least senior to most senior.

After voting, the case is assigned a justice for opinion. Writing is assigned by the Chief Justice if he voted with majority; if not, then the next most senior justice performs this task. When the opinion is written, it is disseminated to other justices for their concurrence or dissention. They also look for weaknesses. Frequently, the opinion is rewritten by the original author, sometimes as many as 25 times. It is then filed in Open Court.

U.S. Supreme Court Decisions

Supreme Court decisions include three citations that are often referred to as *parallel citations,* which means that the same case can be found in three different sets of documents. These sources are as follows:

1. *United States Reporter* (U.S.), the official reports of Supreme Court Decisions
2. *Supreme Court Reporter* (Sup. Ct. or S.Ct.), published by West Publishing Company

3. *United States Supreme Court Reporter* (L. Ed.), published by Lawyers Cooperative Publishing Company.

Parallel citations are illustrated in the following example: *Baker v. Carr,* 369 U.S. 186, 82 S.Ct. 691, 7 L. Ed. 2d 663 (1992). In the first citation, 369 refers to the volume in the *United States Reporter;* 186 refers to the page in which the case can be found. The second citation, 82, refers to the volume of the *Supreme Court Reporter;* 691 refers to the page in which the case can be found. In the third citation, *Lawyer's Edition, 7* refers to the volume; 2d refers to the second edition and 633 refers to the page in which the case can be found; and 1992 refers to the year in which the decision was rendered. Either of these three sources may be used to locate a U.S. Supreme Court case.

■ ■ ■ ■ ■ ▬▬▬▬▬▬▬▬▬▬▬▬▬▬▬▬▬▬▬▬▬▬▬▬▬▬▬▬▬▬▬

ADMINISTRATIVE GUIDE

LEGAL FRAMEWORK

1. The U.S. Constitution is the fundamental law of the land. State laws and school district policies or administrative practices may not conflict with any constitutional amendments.
2. When developing school policies, the U.S. Constitution should be considered the primary source of law. Statutes should be considered the second primary source of law if they are consistent with the Constitution. If not, case law becomes the second primary source, with statutes becoming the third primary source.
3. Since education is a state function, state statutes create local school districts and establish all requirements that school districts must meet. Statutes are subject to review by the judicial branch of government to determine their constitutionality.
4. With the exception of U.S. Supreme Court decisions, school leaders must adhere to court rulings affecting their respective states and circuits for administrative guidance.
5. The courts will not permit school boards to violate their own policies once they are determined to be legally defensible.

ENDNOTES

1. *Board of Education of the City of Rockford v. Page,* 211 N.E. 2d 361 (Ill. 1965).
2. *Hobbs v. County of Moore,* 267 N.C. 665, 149, S.E. 2d 1 (1966).
3. Arval A. Morris, *The Constitution and American Education* (St. Paul, MN: West Publishing, 1974).

CHAPTER 2

RELIGION AND THE PUBLIC SCHOOLS

The Fourteenth Amendment, a key component of the U.S. Constitution, focuses on the rights and privileges of citizens of the United States in the provision that states:

> All persons born or naturalized in the United States are subject to the jurisdiction thereof, are citizens of the United States and of the state wherein they reside. No state shall make or enforce any law which shall abridge the privileges or immunities of citizens of the United States; nor shall any state deprive any person of life, liberty, or property without due process of law; nor deny to any person within its jurisdiction the equal protection of the law.

While the Fourteenth Amendment prohibited infringement on the rights of U.S. citizens, the Constitution as a whole made virtually no reference to religious liberties of U.S. citizens when it was ratified by the states. The only exception was a religious-test provision that prohibited states from imposing religious tests for federal offices. This provision became the last clause of Article VI of the Constitution. The omission of religious liberties in the Constitution was defended by Madison, which led Jefferson to convince him that a religious provision in the Bill of Rights was needed. The uncertainty of whether religious rights were implied in the Constitution was sufficient enough to justify the need for a Bill of Rights protecting religious freedoms. Madison then introduced a series of proposals that included amendments aimed at preventing encroachment by government into the rights and liberties of all citizens. These proposals, presented to the House of Representatives, eventually became the Bill of Rights. Noticeably among these rights was the separation of church and state, which guarantees religious freedoms and prohibits the establishments of religion by the government.

Although religious freedoms are addressed in the Bill of Rights, conflicts involving church and state interactions have intensified over the past decade, as numerous challenges have been levied against public schools regarding certain questionable religious practices. Courts increasingly have been called on to determine the constitutional validity of these practices.

The tension between church and state issues relates to the requirement that the government maintains a neutral position toward religion. In 1879, the Supreme Court in the landmark *Reynolds v. United States* invoked Thomas Jefferson's view that there be a wall of separation between church and state.[1]

The First Amendment serves as the basis for delineating certain individual religious rights and freedoms, as well as governmental prohibitions regarding religion. The First

Amendment to the United States Constitution states, "Congress shall make no laws respecting an establishment of religion or prohibiting the free exercise thereof; or abridging the freedom of speech, or of the press; or the right of the people peaceably to assemble and to petition the government for a redress of grievances."

While the initial intent of the First Amendment prohibited Congress from making laws supporting religion or prohibiting the rights of individuals to exercise their religious rights, the United States Supreme Court, in a compelling decision, *Cantwell v. Connecticut,* held that this prohibition aimed at Congress also applied to the states.[2] The Fourteenth Amendment made the First Amendment applicable to state action, thus providing the same constitutional guarantees to citizens against state infringement of their religious rights by prohibiting the establishment of religious practices in public schools.

The First Amendment contains two essential clauses regarding religion: the establishment clause and the free exercise clause. The *establishment clause* prohibits the state from passing laws that aid a religion or show preference of one religion over another; the *free exercise clause* prohibits the state from interfering with individual religious freedoms. The combined effect of these two clauses compels public schools as state agencies to maintain a neutral position regarding religious matters in their daily operations. This means that the state can neither aid nor inhibit religion—it must adhere to the principle of neutrality. The intent of the establishment clause was clearly enunciated in the famous *Everson* case in which the United States Supreme Court stated:

> The "establishment of religion" clause of the First Amendment means at least this: Neither a state nor the Federal Government can set up a church. Neither can pass laws which aid one religion, aid all religions, or prefer one religion over another. Neither can force nor influence a person to go to or to remain away from church against his will or force him to profess a belief or disbelief in any religion. No person can be punished for entertaining or professing religious beliefs or disbeliefs, for church attendance or non-attendance. No tax in any amount, large or small, can be levied to support any religious activities or institutions, whatever they may be called, or whatever form they may adopt to teach or practice religion. Neither a state nor the Federal Government can, openly or secretly, participate in the affairs of any religious organizations or groups and vice versa. In the words of Jefferson, the clause against establishment of religion by law was intended to erect "a wall of separation between Church and State."[3]

Since the *Cantwell* decision, which held that the Fourteenth Amendment makes the First Amendment applicable to state action, the establishment clause has significant implications for the administration of public schools.

The *Establishment Clause* essentially raises concerns in instances where school personnel act as government officials. When school officials are not acting in this capacity, the *Establishment Clause* does not restrict their religious freedom. Freedom of speech, association, and religion protects school personnel just as it protects the religious activities of other citizens.

SCHOOL-SPONSORED PRAYER

The issue of prayer in public schools was addressed in a landmark case in the early 1960s by the United States Supreme Court. Prior to this time, prayer was routinely offered in public schools across the nation and generally supported by the courts. In spite of the landmark *Engle* decision banning prayer in public schools, school prayer continues to be challenged by Congress, state legislatures, and citizens as they persist in seeking creative ways to support prayer in the nation's schools. For example, a Republican congressman in 1996 prepared an amendment to the Constitution designed to allow prayer in public schools. Representative Ernest Istook of Oklahoma indicated that he introduced a 52-word "Religious Freedom Amendment" before Congress. Americans United for Separation of Church and State and other opponents were strongly opposed to such a measure and cited the harmful impact it would have for minority religions. This proposal represents just one example of congressional efforts to return prayer to public school. Prayer will continue to be a hotly contested issue, as it has quickly become one of the most highly debated topics in the United States today.

The United States Supreme Court first addressed prayer in public schools in the famous *Engle* case. In 1962, the New York Board of Regents required the reading of a school-sponsored, nondenominational, voluntary prayer, which was to be recited by each class in the presence of the classroom teacher. This prayer was composed by the State Board of Regents and read as follows:

> Almighty God, we acknowledge our dependence upon thee and we beg thy blessings upon us, our parents, our teachers and our country.

Those students who did not wish to recite the prayer were excused from participation. This practice was challenged by parents on the grounds that it violated the establishment clause of the First Amendment and was in conflict with the beliefs and religious orientation of some students. The U.S. Supreme Court held for the parents, ruling that the prayer was religious in nature and did in fact violate the establishment clause of the First Amendment.

In holding that the state's support of prayer recitation in the public schools was illegal, the Court stated, "In this country, it is no part of the business of government to compose official prayers for any group of the American people to recite as part of a religious program carried on by the government."[4] Although this ruling has been consistently reinforced by numerous court decisions since 1962, it still remains a highly controversial issue as persistent lawmakers in many states continue their efforts to reinstate some form of prayer in public schools, as illustrated by the following case.

In November of 1996, the U.S. Supreme Court refused to revive a 1994 Mississippi statute that authorized voluntary student prayer at assemblies, sports events, and other school activities. The high court, without comment, allowed the lower court ruling to stand, which found the law unconstitutional and disallowed its implementation. Interestingly, the state did not, in its appeal to the Supreme Court, address the merits of the law itself but rather argued that the plaintiffs who challenged the law had no legal standing to do so. The state further argued that the law should not have been barred before it was actually enforced.

The lower court rejected both arguments, holding that the law violated the establishment clause of the First Amendment. This law was enacted by legislators after Bishop Knox, a high school principal, defied his superiors by permitting students to pray daily over the school's public address system. As a consequence, Knox was fired by the school board, but this was later reduced to a suspension due to widespread public support for his actions. The Mississippi law called for nonsectarian and nonproselytizing student-initiated prayer and voluntary prayer during school activities and events. This practice was challenged by the American Civil Liberties Union. Both the district court and the U.S. Court of Appeals for the Fifth Circuit barred this practice on the grounds that the state was endorsing a religion. However, the lower court let stand a previous ruling that allowed student-led voluntary prayer at graduation ceremonies.

The *Jones v. Clear Creek Independent School District* case (discussed later in this chapter) represented a major step for school prayer proponents. The Fifth Circuit Court held that nonschool-sponsored, student-initiated prayer at graduation ceremonies did not offend the First Amendment prohibition regarding separation of church and state. The court viewed this practice as an exercise of students' First Amendment rights to free speech, which did not create excessive entanglement between the church and state.[5]

SCHOOL-SPONSORED BIBLE READING

In 1963, the U.S. Supreme Court addressed the constitutionality of the practice of Bible reading in public schools. Two similar cases reached the Supreme Court during the same period of time. *Abington School District v. Schempp* involved a challenge regarding the validity of a Pennsylvania state statute that required the reading of ten verses of the Bible without comment at the opening of each school day. A companion case, *Murray v. Curlett,* challenged the actual practice of daily Bible reading in the schools.

In the former case, several members of the Unitarian Church brought suit against the state to prohibit the state from enforcing the statute, as it was contrary to their religious beliefs and in violation of the First Amendment. The legislature attempted to defend its practice by making provisions for students to be excused with parental consent, if the practice offended them.

The facts surrounding the *Murray* case were similar to those in the *Schempp* case, with the exception that no state statute was involved. The Supreme Court, in addressing both cases, ruled in an 8–1 decision that these Bible-reading practices were unconstitutional. The Court found these practices to be an advancement of religion and a clear violation of the separation of church and state. Justice Clark, speaking for the majority, stated, "It is no defense to urge that the religious practices here may be a relatively minor encroachment on the First Amendment. The breach of neutrality that is today a trickling stream may all too soon become a raging torrent and, in the words of Madison, 'It is proper to take alarm at the first experiment on our liberties.'"[6]

The Supreme Court invoked the *primary effect* test to determine the impact of the statute and practice relating to each case. The primary effect test raises the question of whether the primary purpose of a law or practice has the effect of advancing or inhibiting religion and creating excessive entanglement between church and state. If the response to these questions is affirmative, the principle of neutrality has been breached and the act is considered to be an impermissible establishment of religion and a violation of the First Amendment. The Court did, however, indicate in the *Schempp* case that the use of the Bible as a historical, literary, ethics, or philosophical document is permissible if a secular purpose is clearly served.

SILENT PRAYER AND MEDITATION

In recent years, attempts also have been made by state legislatures to support some form of state-sponsored voluntary prayer or meditation in public schools. Their efforts, however, have been largely unsuccessful. Numerous challenges to these types of statutes or practices have been led by opposing parents and citizens. Their challenges cover a full range of school activities, such as meditation and prayer at school-sponsored athletic events and graduation ceremonies, both of which will be discussed later in this chapter.

The United States Supreme Court, in 1985, responded to the silent meditation and prayer issue by ruling in the *Wallace v. Jaffree* case that a period of silence set aside for meditation or voluntary prayer in the public school is in violation of the First Amendment. This case reached the Supreme Court when an Alabama federal district court invalidated two state statutes but supported another. The first of two statutes addressed by the district court involved § 16-1-20, enacted in 1978, which authorized a one-minute period of silence in all public schools in Alabama for meditation. The second statute involved § 16-1-20.1, enacted in 1981, which authorized a period of silence for meditation or voluntary prayer. The last statute, § 16-1-20.2, enacted in 1982, authorized teachers to lead willing students in a state-prescribed prayer that read, "Almighty God . . . the creator and supreme judge of the world. . . ." The district court held that there was nothing wrong with § 16-1-20 but that § 16-1-20.1 and § 16-1-20.2 were both invalid because their sole purpose was to encourage religious activities in the schools. After the trial on the merits, the district court did not change its interpretation of these two statutes but held that they were constitutional because, in its opinion, Alabama has the power to establish a state religion if it so chooses.

The Court of Appeals agreed with the district court's initial interpretation of the purpose of both § 16-1-20.1 and § 16-1-20.2 and held both statutes to be unconstitutional. This case arose when appellee Ishmael Jaffree, a resident of Mobile County, Alabama, filed a complaint on behalf of three of his minor children. Jaffree sought a declaratory judgment and an injunction against the state, restraining it from maintaining or allowing the maintenance of religious prayer services or other forms of religious observances in the schools. His complaint further alleged that two of his children had been subjected to various forms of religious indoctrination and were exposed to ostracism from class members when they refused to participate in a teacher-led prayer. The record further revealed that Jaffree repeatedly requested that devotional services be discontinued. Jaffree filed a complaint on June 4, 1982, challenging the constitutionality of the three Alabama statutes. State Senator Donald Holmes testified that § 16-1-20.1, enacted in 1981, was designed to return voluntary prayer to the public schools.

The district court concluded, after extensive review, that the establishment clause does not prohibit the state from establishing a religion, and dismissed Jaffree's challenge of the three statutes for failure to state a claim for which relief could be granted. However, in consolidating the two cases, the court of appeals reversed the district court's ruling. The state appealed to the U.S. Supreme Court, arguing that, at best, § 16-1-20.1 was a permissible accommodation of religion. The Supreme Court, in its ruling against the state of Alabama, concluded that no secular purpose was identified by the state, and that the Alabama legislature intended to establish prayer in the schools, which violates the principle of neutrality and the separation of church and state. Thus, these practices were held to be unconstitutional.[7]

AID TO PAROCHIAL SCHOOLS

Public aid to parochial schools has created numerous legal questions and conflicts. School districts have been challenged on issues involving the awarding of free textbooks, transportation, tax credits, and auxiliary services. Many of these issues have received mixed reviews by the courts.

In cases where evidence reveals that the aid directly benefited the child rather than the parochial school, courts have been permissive in allowing certain types of aid under the *child benefit theory*. This theory is valid if parochial children are the primary beneficiaries of a public-supported service provided for all children. Conversely, if the aid serves to benefit primarily parochial schools, it will be deemed impermissible and a violation of the First Amendment. When state activities cannot be clearly separated from religious activities, excessive entanglement occurs, thus preventing a clear line of separation between the two.

The issue of aid to parochial schools continues to be contested, as there are strong advocates as well as opponents involved in the debate. Advocates have requested the U.S. Supreme Court to reverse its 1985 decision that disallows public school teachers from providing Title I remedial instruction in parochial schools. The New York City Public Schools and Roman Catholic parents sought reconsideration of the high court decision in the *Aguilar v. Felton* case[8] in which the court held in a 5–4 decision that it was an unconstitutional establishment of religion for public school teachers to provide remedial classes in religious schools. This ruling created enormous costs incurred by the district through the purchase of mobile classrooms and leasing land to house the mobile classes. These groups charged that these funds, roughly $14 million used to purchase mobile classrooms and lease land, could be better spent to support the Title I program.

An appeal in the *Agostini v. Felton*[9] case arose when the New York City School Board filed a motion asking a federal judge to be relieved from the 1985 *Felton* ruling. The National Committee for Public Education and Religious Liberty argued that it would be more feasible for the district to send private school students to Title I school sites for instruction. There was no dispute that private school students are eligible for Title I services. What was in dispute is how can they be best served.

The district judge upheld the use of mobile classes and ruled that the U.S. Supreme Court's decision could not be overturned. The U.S. Court of Appeals for the Second Circuit heard the board's appeal, agreeing with the district court's ruling that the Supreme Court's decision could not be overturned. However, on need, the case was readdressed by the Supreme Court. In a rather rare and surprising move, the Court revised its previous decision in *Aguilar* by ruling in a 5–4 decision that the Constitution does not prohibit Title I from serving eligible religious school students on their premises. The legal significance of the Supreme Court's decision is that church-state barriers to Title I services no longer exist. These services can be provided to parochial students without offending church-state constitutional prohibitions.

The *Lemon v. Kurtzman* and *Early v. Dicenso* cases are perhaps the most significant early cases involving state aid to parochial schools. These cases arose when Rhode Island and Pennsylvania laws providing assistance to parochial schools, their students, and their teachers were challenged by various citizens and taxpayers. Rhode Island implemented an educational assistance program designed to assist private and parochial schools. This program provided supplemental teacher salaries for teachers who taught secular instruction in parochial schools. Pennsylvania enacted a similar statute but included assistance in purchasing supplies and textbooks in secular subjects.

Citizens in both states sought declaratory relief regarding practices that violated the First Amendment. The Pennsylvania District Court dismissed the complaint, while the Rhode Island court ruled that the practice was unconstitutional. The U.S. Supreme Court subsequently held that a law providing a state subsidy for nonpublic school teachers' salaries is unconstitutional, even when the funds are paid only to teachers of secular subjects. The high court also struck down a state law that reimbursed nonpublic schools for expenses incurred in teaching secular subjects. Justice Burger, speaking for the majority, stated, "The First Amendment not only prohibits the passing of laws establishing religion but it also prohibits passing of a law respecting such establishment."

This ruling referenced the famous Lemon Test (which is discussed later in this chapter) in deciding on the constitutionality of certain practices involving public and parochial schools. Based on the *Lemon* standards, it was determined that a law must meet the following criteria to be legally valid regarding religion:

1. It must have a secular purpose.
2. It must neither advance nor inhibit religion.
3. It must not create excessive entanglement.[10]

As aid to parochial school continues to be challenged, the following examples illustrate the courts' responses to certain practices:

1. Tuition reimbursement to parents of parochial school children is deemed unconstitutional.[11]
2. Shared time and community education programs for parochial school students violate the First Amendment.[12]
3. State financing of auxiliary services and direct loans for instructional equipment and materials for parochial schools is a violation of the First Amendment.[13]
4. Tax deductions for parents of parochial school children do not violate the First Amendment.[14]
5. Free public transportation for parochial school students does not violate the First Amendment.[15]
6. Free textbooks for parochial school students at state expense does not violate the First Amendment.[16]

Aid to students in religious schools received major impetus in a recent development in *Mitchell v. Helms,*[17] in which the U.S. Supreme Court ruled that a federal program that placed computers and other instructional equipment in parochial school classrooms did not violate the constitutional separation of church and state. Reversing an appeals court decision in a Louisiana case, the justices upheld, 6–3, a federal program that has distributed educational equipment and other materials to public and private schools since 1965. This practice was challenged by respondents who argued that direct nonincidental aid to religious schools is always impermissible. They further argued that the purpose of the direct/indirect distinction is to prevent subsidization of religion.

Concluding for the majority justices, Thomas, Scalia, and Kennedy supported the view that Chapter II, as applied in Jefferson Parish, is not a law respecting an establishment of religion simply because many of the private schools receiving Chapter II aid in the parish are religiously affiliated. Furthermore, Chapter II does not define its recipients by reference to religion. Aid is allocated on the basis of neutral, secular criteria that neither favor nor disfavor religion and is made available to both religious and secular beneficiaries on a nondiscriminatory basis.

Also, Chapter II does not result in governmental indoctrination of religion. It determines eligibility for aid neutrally, making a broad array of schools eligible without regard to their religious affiliations or lack thereof. Thus, it is not problematic that Chapter II could be fairly described as providing "direct" aid. Finally, the Chapter II aid provided to religious schools does not have an impermissible content. The statute explicitly requires that such aid be secular, neutral, and nonideological.

Religious Symbols

Public schools may not display religious exhibits or other visual materials. It may be appropriate, however, for public school teachers to acknowledge and explain the various holidays of all cultural and religious groups as a unit in cultural heritage or some other related subject, as long as a secular purpose is served.

Public school teachers should refrain from the use of religious symbols or pictures, even in conjunction with discussing the various holidays. A case could be made that the presence of the crucifix creates a religious atmosphere in the classroom. The presence of any type of religious symbol or picture would violate the principle of neutrality. Pictures of religious events may also create a religious atmosphere.

Religious Displays

Religious displays are prohibited in public school settings. To illustrate, a Michigan secondary school displayed a picture of Jesus Christ in a hallway near the gymnasium. This picture had been in place for more than 30 years. A student filed a lawsuit seeking an order to have it removed, based on a violation of the establishment clause to the First Amendment. The court held for the student by ordering that the picture be removed. The school appealed to the U.S. Court of Appeals for the Sixth Circuit.

The school argued that the plaintiff had graduated and the issue was moot. The court disagreed, finding that the student did, on occasion, visit the school for various sports events and other school activities. Further, the picture had the potential to offend others. The court, in its ruling, relied on the three-pronged test found in the *Lemon* case. In finding that the display served no secular purpose, it served to advance religion and created excessive entanglement—all violations of the First Amendment. The order was affirmed.[18]

It would be permissible, however, to employ seasonal decorations, such as snow, pine trees, wreaths, eggs, or bunny rabbits. These are considered merely reflections of the joy and merriment associated with various holidays, so long as they are not used to meet a sectarian purpose.

Public schools may not erect any type of religious display on school property. However, in 1963, one such display was held by a district in New York to be a mere passive accommodation of religion.[19] This court supported the erection of a nativity scene on school grounds. The posture of the courts today would not support such a finding. It is indisputable that the presence of a nativity scene on school property violates the separation of church and state by demonstrating preference of one religion over another and is in clear violation of the establishment clause of the First Amendment.

Ten Commandments

Two early court decisions, one at the federal district level and the other by the U.S. Supreme Court, held that posting of the Ten Commandments in a public school is unconstitutional. North Dakota passed a law requiring the display of a placard that contained the Ten Commandments of the Christian and Jewish religions. The statute called for this display to be located in a conspicuous place in every classroom in public schools. The district court ruled that this practice violated the *Establishment Clause* of the First Amendment.[20] Interestingly, the State Supreme Court of Kentucky in *Stone v. Graham*[21] reached a tie decision regarding a statute that required posting the Ten Commandments in public school classrooms. The tie proved to be insignificant, when the U.S. Supreme Court in a 5–4 decision held that this practice was unconstitutional and a violation of the *Establishment Clause* of the First Amendment.

PRAYER AT SCHOOL EVENTS

Student-Led Prayer at Public School Events

In a significant development, a federal court of appeals held that the U.S. Supreme Court ruling in the *Santa Fe* case does not prevent students in Alabama from discussing religion in public schools or praying publicly, so long as such activities are voluntary. This ruling is significant in that it represents the first interpretation by an appeal's court of the Supreme Court's *Santa Fe* decision. The recent Circuit Court ruling upholds its earlier decision permitting voluntary student-led prayer at public school events. In earlier action, the Eleventh Circuit Court overturned a federal district court ruling that limited religious expression by students in Dekalb County, Alabama. The U.S. Supreme Court asked the Circuit Court of Appeals to reassess its decision based on its ruling in the *Santa Fe* case. The Circuit Court has stated in its most recent ruling that its decision was not in conflict with the high court's ruling in *Santa Fe* based on voluntary prayer in Alabama as contrasted with school-sanctioned, student-led prayer in Texas.

The Eleventh Circuit ruling was an outgrowth of a suit filed by the plaintiff Chandler in Alabama, who challenged the practice of offering prayer at school-sponsored events. He specifically objected to the practice of offering student-led prayer at athletic contests. The *Santa Fe* and *Chandler*[22] cases appear to represent opposite sides of the same constitutional coin. For example, *Santa Fe* prohibits school-sponsored prayer, whereas *Chandler* condemns school censorship of prayer.

The Alabama case was initially filed by the American Civil Liberties Union on behalf of Dekalb County educator, Michael Chandler, who challenged religious practices in public schools. The essence of the recent Eleventh Circuit ruling is that students do not shed their religious rights when they enter the schoolhouse door. The Circuit Court rejected the argument that prayer is forbidden by the First Amendment and supported the concept of free speech as guaranteed by the First Amendment. What does this ruling really mean? For now, it means that any student-led group in the Eleventh Circuit may engage in voluntary prayer at school events. However, school personnel may not direct or supervise students who initiate religious expression.

In its ruling, the appeals court interestingly adopted the Supreme Court's language in stating that there is nothing in the Constitution that prohibits prayer. In the aftermath of the Eleventh Circuit ruling, what are the implications? Although this ruling affects only public schools in Alabama, Florida, and Georgia, it means that in those states, at least for now, school valedictorians, regardless of their belief or faith, may voluntarily pray at graduation ceremonies. It also allows student athletes to voluntarily engage in prayer at an athletic contest so long as school officials remain completely neutral. The Eleventh Circuit Court ruling reopens the debate on the legality of voluntary prayer by students at school-sponsored events. At issue are the free expression rights of students and the free exercise of their religious beliefs versus the *Establishment Clause* of the First Amendment. The First Amendment does not prohibit student-initiated private prayer. Based on the free exercise clause, students have the right to pray voluntarily any time and any place so long as it is private and strictly voluntary. However, what is prohibited by the First Amendment is institutionally sponsored public prayer, which is an obvious violation of the *Establishment Clause* of the First Amendment. School officials should clearly understand this important distinction. This debate will likely persist as states continue to seek ways to address religion in public schools.

Athletic Contests

Any type of school-sponsored prayer at athletic contests is deemed to be a violation of the First Amendment. The principle of neutrality mandates that public schools remain neutral in all matters relating to religion. For a number of years, there was a prevailing view that prayer could be offered at athletic events so long as attendance was not compulsory. If attendance was voluntary, with prior knowledge that prayer would be offered, the offended person could simply avoid attending the event during the short time period in which prayer was to be offered. This view has not been accepted or supported by the courts in recent years, however. When public schools allow prayer to be offered at school events, they are placing the weight and influence of the school in support of a religious activity—an impermissible accommodation to religion and an obvious violation of the establishment clause. Courts in recent years have been fairly consistent in holding that prayer at football games and other athletic events violates the *Establishment Clause* of the First Amendment. The following case reflects the sentiment of the courts regarding prayer at athletic events.

The *Jager* case arose in Georgia when a high school student complained to his principal about invocations at home football games. The student indicated that invocations were in conflict with his religious beliefs. Invocations were delivered, in large part, by Protestant Christian clergy and had been practiced since 1947. The school had adopted an "equal access" plan that provided for the random selection of the invocation speaker by the student government.

The student filed suit against the district, seeking declaratory relief regarding the selection process and to prohibit the offering of invocations at home football games, as both practices were in violation of the First Amendment clause. The district court held for the school district. The student appealed to the U.S. Court of Appeals for the Eleventh Circuit.

The court of appeals applied the Lemon Test to determine whether the invocations violated the establishment clause, based on a case involving aid to parochial schools, which was discussed earlier in this chapter. According to the Lemon Test, for such practices to be held constitutional, they need to have a *secular purpose* that *neither advances nor inhibits religion,* and they *do not create excessive entanglement between the state and religion.*[23] The court held that the equal access plan had no secular purpose and did, in fact, promote religion in violation of the establishment clause, even though it did not involve excessive entanglement with religion. The circuit court reversed the district court's decision, holding for the student.[24]

Based on the ruling in the *Jager* case, public school officials are well advised to refrain from the use of prayer at any school-sponsored event.

Prayer at Athletic Contests

Prohibition of prayer at school events was given a major thrust when the U.S. Supreme Court in a 6–3 ruling in *Santa Fe Independent School District v. Jane Doe*[25] banned student-led prayer at athletic contests, graduations, and other school-sponsored events. This ruling challenged previous lower court decisions permitting student-led prayer at graduation exercises in *Jones v. Clear Creek Independent School District* and *Adler v. Duval County School Board in Florida,* which will be discussed later in this chapter.

The U.S. Supreme Court decision stemmed from a case that was initiated in Santa Fe, Texas. Santa Fe's high school implemented a policy that allowed the school's student council chaplain to deliver a prayer over the public address system before each home varsity football game. This practice was challenged by respondents, Mormon and Catholic students, under the *Establishment Clause* of the First Amendment. While the suit was pending, petitioner school districts adopted a different policy, which authorized two student elections, the first to determine whether invocations should be delivered at home games and the second to select the spokesperson to deliver them. After students held two elections authorizing such prayers and selecting a spokesperson, the district court entered an order modifying the policy to permit only nonsectarian, nonproselytizing prayer. Before the revised policy was implemented, the Fifth Circuit held that even as modified by the district, the policy was invalid because it violated the *Establishment Clause* of the First Amendment. The district argued, unpersuasively, that the messages, delivered at football games, are private student speech, not public speech. The district also argued that it did not coerce students to participate in religious observances.

In its ruling against the district, the U.S. Supreme Court stated, "The delivery of a message such as an invocation on school property at school sponsored events over the public address system by a speaker representing the student body under the supervision of school faculty based on school policy that implicitly encourages public prayer is not properly characterized as private speech."[26]

Various district and circuit courts rendered decisions that made it possible prior to the recent U.S. Supreme Court ruling in the *Santa Fe* case for states to decide if they wanted to support student-led prayer at graduation ceremonies. With this landmark *Santa Fe* ruling, states no longer may decide if voluntary student-initiated prayer may be offered at school events. According to the High Court's ruling, this is an impermissible act that violates the *Establishment Clause* of the First Amendment.

The Court noted further that this case demonstrates that student views are not unanimous on the issue of prayer and that the establishment clause's purpose is to remove debate over this kind of issue from governmental supervision and control. Although the ultimate choice of student speakers is attributable to students, the district's decision to hold this constitutionally problematic election is clearly a choice attributed to the state. The argument by the district that no coercion is involved lacks merit. Students who participate in band, cheerleading, and football are sometimes mandated to attend the athletic events for class credit. The Constitution demands that schools not force on students the difficult choice between whether to attend these games or risk facing a personally offensive religious ritual.

ADMINISTRATIVE GUIDE

PRAYER, BIBLE READING, AND SILENT MEDITATION

1. School-sponsored prayer is illegal and cannot be justified based on First Amendment prohibitions.
2. School-sponsored Bible reading in public school is an illegal activity. However, the Bible may be used as an instructional document to meet a secular purpose.
3. Silent meditation or any other type of devotional activity sanctioned by schools will not be supported by the courts.
4. Invocations at school-sponsored athletic activities violate the establishment clause of the First Amendment.
5. Private voluntary prayer by a student is permissible under the free exercise clause of the First Amendment.

VOLUNTARY PRAYER AT COMMENCEMENT EXERCISES

As previously discussed, the constitutionality of prayer in public schools was seriously challenged in 1962 in the landmark *Engel v. Vitale* case in which the U.S. Supreme Court struck down the daily recitation of prayer over a school's public address system. This landmark ruling banned prayer in any form in all school activities across the nation, based on a violation of the establishment clause of the First Amendment. In spite of this 1962 ruling, prayer at graduation ceremonies has continued to be controversial.

For example, in a leading case in California, two taxpayers challenged the inclusion of religious invocations, benedictions, and other religious rituals at the public high school graduation ceremonies. The invocations and benedictions were delivered by a Protestant minister or a Catholic priest, all of which contained religious content. Summary judgment was granted on behalf of the taxpayers. The district appealed to the California Court of Appeals. The appellate court reversed the trial court's ruling, which resulted in an appeal by the taxpayers to the California Supreme Court.

The court ruled that the practice of including religious invocations and benedictions at high school graduation ceremonies conveyed a powerful message that the district approves of the content of prayers offered and favored one religion over others. Since there are vast areas of Christian denominations and non-Christians, respect for all of these groups requires that the state not place its stamp of approval on any particular practice. The court further stipulated that public school graduation ceremonies involving prayer cannot be in harmony with the First Amendment's command for neutrality. Therefore, the court of appeal's judgment was reversed.[27]

However, in another significant development, the U.S. Supreme Court let stand a stunning appeals court decision permitting student-initiated, student-led prayer at the Clear Creek Independent School District's graduation ceremonies in Texas. In this decision, a federal appeals court ruled that a Texas school district's policy of allowing each high school senior class to decide whether to offer student-initiated and student-led prayers at its graduation ceremony does not violate the First Amendment ban on the government's establishment of religion.

Prayer at graduation ceremonies will continue to be a highly sensitive and controversial issue. During the last several years, courts have become increasingly active in responding to issues involving religion in public schools. School officials no longer enjoy the freedom they once had in planning school programs based solely on community values and standards. During the 1950s, religious controversies were not viewed primarily in terms of constitutional rights but rather in terms of community sentiment. However, the courts in recent years have abandoned community sentiment in favor of constitutionality. The Supreme Court's position in *Jones v. Clear Creek Independent School District,* however, may provide an opportunity for communities to decide if they wish to have students assume the decision-making role. For now, at least, under certain conditions, voluntary student-led prayer at graduation ceremonies may be permissible. This is a major victory for proponents of prayer and perhaps an end to some of the controversy involving graduation ceremonies.

Landmark Rulings

Prior to the U.S. Supreme Court ruling in the *Santa Fe* case, a three-judge panel of the U.S. Court of Appeals for the Fifth Circuit ruled that the Clear Creek Independent School District's Policy did not violate the *Establishment Clause* of the First Amendment, nor did it conflict with the Supreme Court's ruling in a 1992 Rhode Island case in which the high court ruled that a Providence Middle School principal violated the establishment clause by inviting a rabbi to deliver a prayer at a promotion ceremony.[28] From the Court's view, the administrator's involvement suggested that the school was compelling students to participate in a religious exercise. However, the significance of the more recent *Jones v. Clear Creek Independent School District* case in Texas is that it creates a way to include prayer in graduation ceremonies without creating conflict with the Supreme Court's previous decisions.

In the Rhode Island case (*Lee v. Weisman*) the three-part establishment clause test set forth in the *Lemon* case[29] was used by the Supreme Court in ruling against the school district. Under the Lemon Test, a state practice that is challenged as unconstitutional must meet the criteria that it has a secular purpose, that its practices neither advance nor inhibit religion, and that it does not foster excessive entanglement between the state and religion. The student-initiated prayer in the *Clear Creek* case obviously met the Lemon Test, since the school played no role in offering the program and had no influence on the student who led the prayer.

The *Clear Creek* case reached the court in 1987, when the district's policy was challenged in federal court by two students. The Federal District Court and the Fifth Circuit Court of Appeals upheld the district's policy. The two students appealed to the U.S.

Supreme Court. The Supreme Court vacated the Fifth Circuit Court's original ruling and asked the court of appeals to reconsider the case in light of the *Lee v. Weisman* decision. The three-judge panel unanimously concluded that the Clear Creek policy allowing for student-initiated prayer did not fail the so-called Coercion Test set forth in the Rhode Island case. The Supreme Court declined to review the federal court of appeal's decision, thus allowing student-initiated voluntary prayer at graduation ceremonies to be considered constitutionally permissible in the Fifth Circuit.[30]

The clear distinction between these two cases lies in the difference between student-initiated and school-initiated prayers. When the school initiates a prayer, it creates excessive entanglement and advances religion, both of which violate the basic tenets of the First Amendment. When students voluntarily do so without involvement of the school, excessive entanglement is not evident.

Impact of Ruling

An earlier decision of the U.S. Supreme Court to let stand the U.S. Court of Appeals for the Fifth Circuit decision created opportunities for every state in the country to make an independent judgment regarding student-led graduation prayers, although the Fifth Circuit ruling affects only Texas, Louisiana, and Mississippi. In the Texas case, the district's policy did not mandate prayer but merely made provisions for one should the seniors agree. The prayer, if supported by students, would be led by a student volunteer and be nonsectarian and nonproselytizing in nature. The reality of the Texas decision is that students could do what the school officials could not. It was not surprising to observe other states following the Texas decision.

In fact, a case arose in Florida during the same year in which a ruling was handed down by the Fifth Circuit Court in the *Clear Creek* case. In *Adler v. Duval County School Board,* a Florida school board revised its graduation exercise policy by allowing the graduating class discretion to choose opening and closing remarks of two minutes or less to be delivered by a student volunteer selected by the class. The policy required that the student volunteer prepare the message without supervision or review by the school board. Senior classes at ten schools voted for prayer; seven other senior classes voted for a secular message or no message.

A group of graduating seniors and their parents filed suit against the board in the district court of Florida, alleging violation of their rights under the First Amendment. The court applied the familiar Lemon Test and held that the policy did not violate the Lemon criteria of having the primary effect of advancing religion or excessively entangling the school district with religion. Evidence revealed that the policy had a secular purpose of safeguarding the free speech rights of students participating and refraining from content-based regulations. The policy was held to be neutral, involving no coercion of students by school officials.[31] These two cases may very well serve as precedents for other states, as they approach the legalities of prayer at graduation ceremonies.

Prayer at School Board Meetings

School boards that open their meetings with prayer are violating the Constitution's First Amendment establishment clause. The Sixth Circuit Court of Appeals relied on a series of prayer cases in rendering its decision. A school board started a practice of inviting clergy to offer prayer at its meetings. Later, one of the board members who was a minister began offering prayers at subsequent meetings. This practice was challenged by a student and a teacher who frequently attended board meetings. The Federal District Court upheld the board's practice, finding that the meetings resembled legislative sessions rather than school events and relied on the 1983 U.S. Supreme Court ruling that allowed official prayers at the beginning of a state legislative session. The student and teacher appealed to the Sixth Circuit, which ruled that board meetings were held on school property, were regularly attended by students, and did not resemble legislative sessions. The court further emphasized that board meetings had a function that was uniquely directed toward students and school matters, making it necessary for students to attend such meetings on many occasions. The Sixth Circuit Court stated that prayer at school board meetings was potentially coercive to students in attendance. The Circuit Court reversed the District Court's ruling, holding that prayer has the tendency to endorse Christianity while excessively entangling the board in religious matters.[32]

ADMINISTRATIVE GUIDE

PRAYER AT SCHOOL EVENTS

In light of the court rulings regarding prayer at graduation ceremonies, it would be prudent for administrators to develop carefully drawn guidelines to minimize legal challenges in this area, such as the following:

1. Develop legally defensible guidelines that are supported by the U.S. Supreme Court decision addressing student-initiated prayer at athletic contests and other school events.
2. Do not rely on customs and community expectations when encouraging student-initiated prayer at school events.
3. Student-initiated prayer is probably permissible at school events when not endorsed by school officials.
4. School officials should respond judiciously if alerted that school personnel are encouraging students to offer voluntary prayer at school-sponsored events.
5. Voluntary student-led prayer will likely pass court scrutiny when it is initiated solely by students without involvement of school personnel.
6. Prayer at school board meetings violates the establishment clause and creates excessive entanglement and cannot be justified on the basis that such meetings are similar to legislative sessions rather than school events.

USE OF SCHOOL FACILITIES BY RELIGIOUS STUDENT GROUPS

The use of school facilities by student religious groups continues to create friction between students and school officials. Considerable tension has mounted in recent years between administrators and student religious groups regarding access to school facilities during the school day. At issue is the growing debate regarding the viability of the *Equal Access Act*. Does it, in fact, provide free access to student religious groups? Are students' First Amendment rights violated when access is denied? Under what circumstances may student religious groups be denied access?

Congress attempted to address these issues when it passed the Equal Access Act in 1984 for the expressed purpose of providing student religious clubs equal opportunities to access high school facilities as enjoyed by other noncurricula clubs. Under federal statute, it is unlawful for any public secondary school that receives federal financial assistance that has created a "limited open forum" to deny access to student-initiated groups on the basis of religion, political, or philosophical content of their speech. A limited open forum exists when an administrator allows one or more noncurricula-related student groups to meet on school premises during noninstructional time.[33]

Before the passage of this act, the U.S. Court of Appeals for the Second, Fifth, Tenth, and Eleventh Circuits had routinely denied access to student religious clubs. With the passage of this act, controversy still exists regarding its interpretation. For example, do school administrators have the right to deny students access and do students have a constitutional right to be provided access? Based on the intent of the act, it would be unlawful for a student religious group to be denied use while other noncurricula student groups were not. If the school claims not to have an open forum, there likely would not be an infringement of students' personal rights. Perhaps the most controversial issue to date is the question of exactly what constitutes a limited open forum. With increasing frequency, administrators appear to be taking the position that limited open forums do not exist in their schools as a means of disallowing free access to student religious clubs.

In summary, then, if a school official allows any noncurricula student club to use school facilities, then student religious groups also must be allowed equal access. The viability of the Equal Access Act has been debated across the nation, including cases in Texas, Nebraska, Washington, Pennsylvania, and Virginia.

Legal Precedents

As administrators deal with student religious clubs, their actions should be guided by a sense of fundamental fairness and respect for the First Amendment rights of others. The U.S. Supreme Court earlier bypassed an opportunity to set an important precedent in this area in 1986 when it declined on technical grounds to review a Bible-study case, *Bender v. Williams Sport.*[34] By failing to hear this case, the Supreme Court left the issue to be decided by the lower courts, thereby failing to create uniform compliance across the country and addressing the constitutionality of the law itself. However, the Supreme Court did address the issue in 1990. Between 1986 and 1990, a number of lower court decisions were rendered in various states across the country. Following is a brief description of those decisions.

In a 1988 case, *Mergens v. Board of Education of the Westside Community Schools,*[35] the district judge ruled that an Omaha district did not create an open forum for student speech, and thus need not allow a Bible student club to meet at the high school.

In a 1987 case, *Garnett v. Renton School District,*[36] a U.S. district judge ruled that the Seattle district did not have to accommodate a prayer club at the high school. The judge held that the Equal Access Act did not apply in Washington State because the state's constitution contained stricter language regarding separation of church and state than was found in the First Amendment. Attorneys for the plaintiff argued unsuccessfully that Congress intended the Equal Access Act to supersede state legal and constitutional provisions. This case was appealed to the appellate courts, which unanimously affirmed the lower court's findings that officials at Charles Lindberg High School were not required to accommodate the prayer club because the school did not provide a limited open forum and thus was not bound by the 1984 law's requirements. The three-judge panel also ruled that school officials did not violate the students' free speech rights because the district had not created a public forum.

In yet another case, *Clark v. Dallas Independent School,*[37] in 1992, a U.S. district judge ruled against a prayer group whose meetings grew into loud revivals involving proselytizing of other students. In his ruling, the judge indicated that the Equal Access Act may, in fact, violate the First Amendment *Establishment Clause.*

To avoid the label of limited open forums under the Equal Access Act, many districts either have refused to permit any extracurricula clubs access or have created extremely broad definitions of precisely what is *curriculum related.* This, then, allows schools to maintain school-based clubs without recognizing religious clubs.

On appeal, the Supreme Court addressed the equal access issue in the *Board of Education of Westside Community Schools v. Mergens.* The Supreme Court was faced with deciding whether the Equal Access Act prohibited Westside High School from denying a student religious group access to school facilities, and, if so, whether the act violated the *Establishment Clause* of the First Amendment.

Students at Westside were provided more than thirty clubs from which to choose, all of which met after school. Membership was voluntary and a club sponsor was required for each club based on board policy. Board policy further stipulated that no club or organization shall be sponsored by any political or religious organization or by any organization that denies membership based on race, color, creed, gender, or political belief. Mergens, a student, petitioned Westside High for permission to conduct a religious meeting on school premises. Her request was denied on the basis that the meeting would violate the establishment clause. A suit subsequently filed by Mergens contended that the denial violated the Equal Access Act. The school responded by indicating that the act was unconstitutional and did not apply to the school. The district court held for Westside in supporting the denial. However, the court of appeals reversed the district court's decision, holding that the act was constitutional and that Westside was in violation of the act.

The case reached the Supreme Court when the district appealed. Justice O'Connor, speaking for the majority, affirmed the court of appeals' ruling by stating that the Equal Access Act constitutionally prohibits a limited open forum from denying a student group's request to use school facilities based on the religious content of their meeting. The act intended to grant equal access to secular and religious speech. Since the meeting occurs at noninstructional time and limits school official participation, the Equal Access Act creates no substantial risk of excessive entanglement. The court of appeals' ruling was affirmed.

Based on the Supreme Court ruling, schools that provide a limited open forum may not permit certain groups to use school facilities while denying others. Once a limited forum is established, it must be equally accessible among all student groups and it may not be restricted based on religious, political, or philosophical ideologies. Schools may bar such clubs if those schools have a closed forum in which no clubs are allowed to use school facilities during noninstructional hours. Whether the school district maintains a limited open forum or a closed forum is left to the discretion of the school district, unless otherwise determined by state statute. Once the decision is reached regarding either of these options, consistency and fairness must prevail, as the option chosen is executed by the district.

The Equal Access Act continues to be a stormy issue. Issues involving religious freedom are highly charged emotionally, and there is no indication that this will change in the foreseeable future. As administrators deal with student religious clubs, their actions should be guided by a sense of fundamental fairness and respect for the First Amendment rights of others. These actions should not be taken simply because the courts mandate them, but rather because fair administration is right and proper.

Administrators should ensure that criteria, rules, and regulations governing student clubs be carefully drawn and communicated to all students. Ideally, student representatives should be involved in the policy development process. All efforts should be made to provide equal protection for all groups, regardless of philosophical ideology. The only way this can be achieved is through a strong conviction and commitment to fairness for all students irrespective of differences that might exist regarding their religions or moral beliefs.

ADMINISTRATIVE GUIDE

EQUAL ACCESS

1. Do not allow some student clubs with similar noncurricula functions to meet on school premises while denying other religious clubs this same privilege, especially where there are ideological differences between the administration and the student groups.
2. Avoid denying religious clubs access based on personal or philosophical disagreement with the clubs objectives.
3. Do not establish extremely broad definitions as to what is considered curriculum related in an effort to ban religious clubs.
4. Avoid classifying all other clubs as curriculum related irrespective of function, and disallowing the same classification for religious clubs.
5. School authorities should consult the district's legal counsel regarding any questionable religious activities in their schools.
6. High school student religious clubs may be allowed to use school facilities if the school supports a limited open forum. They cannot be denied use if other noncurricular groups are permitted to use facilities before or after the school day.

Use of School Facilities by Outside Religious Groups

Many local school districts, in an effort to be responsive to their communities, provide access to school facilities for various public organizations during noninstructional hours. This accommodation is typically viewed as a positive gesture and one that is consistent with the view that schools serve as centers for community activities. In most instances, there is minimal conflict between local school officials and community organizations over the use of school facilities.

One area, however, that often creates controversy, friction, and even legal challenges involves the use of school facilities by community-based religious groups. Legal challenges by these groups usually involve allegations that school officials' denial of access to district facilities amounts to a violation of their freedom of expression and equal protection rights under the law. School officials respond that the district must maintain a clear separation between religious activities and state activities based on First Amendment prohibitions.

When *denying* access to religious groups, are school officials, in fact, infringing on the group's free exercise and freedom of expression rights? How far can school districts go to accommodate religious organizations? How do district officials respond to the needs of religious groups without violating First Amendment prohibitions involving church-state relations? How do they respond to challenges by other citizens who contend that the use of school facilities by religious groups offends the community? School district officials find themselves in a precarious position when they attempt to make reasonable accommodations to religious groups without offending the establishment clause of the First Amendment, which prohibits staff support of religious activities.

Relevant Cases.   The following cases illustrate the court's position on the use of school facilities by religious groups. A community church, through its minister, requested the use of a school facility for regular Sunday services and was told that district policy prohibited the use of school facilities for any religious purpose. The policy stated that district facilities shall be open to public, literary, scientific, recreational, or educational meetings or for discussions on matters of public interest. Although the portion of the policy dealing with religious activity was later removed, the church was denied access. The church contended that an open forum existed based on the language in the policy and that their denial violated their right to free speech and assembly.

The court did find that the district's community use policy created an open forum. *However, it held that the practice of excluding religious organizations from holding religious services in its facilities was justified. The court ruled that religious services held on a regular basis would violate the establishment clause.*[38] This violation provided a compelling reason to justify the content-based restriction of the open forum.

In contrast, the court supported a religious organization in the *Gregoire v. Centennial* case (1988)[39] when the Centennial School District developed a facilities use policy prohibiting religious activities within its buildings. A district court enjoined the policy, thus allowing the plaintiff to use a school auditorium to hold a magic show after which an evangelical message was given. The school district then altered its policy to include a list of organizations that were allowed to use school facilities. This new policy also included a prohibition on religious services as well as the distribution of religious materials. The plaintiff requested to use the facility again if it were open to the public, claiming that facilities are open forums and prohibitions against religious activities violated equal protection, free speech, and the exercise clause of the First Amendment. The court held that the new policy still created a prohibition against religious activity and a violation of the plaintiffs free speech and free exercise rights. The court noted that the list of other groups who could use facilities created an open forum. Once created, the plaintiff cannot be denied access based on content of speech.

In a recent landmark case, *Bronx Household of Faith v. Community School District No. 10* (1997),[40] involving use of school facilities by a religious group, the U.S. Supreme Court rejected an appeal from an Evangelical Christian Church that had sought to use a middle school gymnasium in New York for religious services. This religious group contended that the school district should not be permitted to ban the use of the gym by religious groups while allowing other community groups to use it. According to the plaintiffs, this amounted to discrimination.

By policy, the New York City Board of Education permits rental of schools for a variety of community purposes, including religious discussions, but prohibits their use for religious services. The Bronx Household of Faith challenged this rule in federal district court. The district court ruled for the school district. On appeal, the U.S. Court of Appeals also ruled for the school district. In its ruling, the appeals court indicated that the use of school facilities by community groups created an open forum rather than a traditional public forum. Under First Amendment freedoms, government restrictions on speech in a public forum are held to very strict scrutiny. However, in a limited open forum, such as a public school, the government can restrict speech if it makes reasonable and *viewpoint-neutral* distinctions among speakers. Further, public school officials reasonably might wish to avoid the appearance of sponsoring religious services. Since the U.S. Supreme Court rejected an appeal, the appeal court's decision stands.

Finally, in the *Lamb's Chapel v. Center Moriches School District* case (1993)[41] involving a closed forum, an Evangelical Christian Church applied on four occasions for approval to use public facilities of a local high school for various nonsecular functions, including family-oriented films with a Christian perspective. Each request was denied by school officials because the proposed functions were church related and had religious connotations. School officials relied on a New York State law that bars the use of district facilities for religious purposes. The minister of the church brought legal action against the district, claiming First and Fourteenth Amendment violations—freedom of speech and equal protection of the law, respectively. The Second Circuit Court of Appeals held that the facilities were not deemed open forums; therefore, the church's First and Fourteenth rights were not abridged. However, the U.S. Supreme Court unanimously ruled that the district's rule was unconstitutional as applied to the film series. The Court acknowledged that the district, like a private owner of property, could have preserved its property for the use to which it was dedicated and need not have permitted any after-hours use of its property. However, once the district voluntarily made its facilities available for use by after-hours groups, it could not enforce rules designed to exclude expression of specific points of view. The Court further concluded that to permit Lamb's Chapel to use the facilities would not violate the establishment clause, because it would have neither the purpose nor primary effect of advancing or inhibiting religion and would not foster excessive entanglement with religion.

Use of School Facilities by Community Groups

Local school boards, either through implied powers or specific authority, have the capacity to formulate policies governing the use of school facilities within their districts. By policy or practice, school officials may permit public groups to use school facilities during noninstructional hours so long as their activities do not interfere with normal school operations. Unless otherwise prescribed by state statute, districts are not required to provide facilities to community groups. It is within the discretion of school boards to determine if the district will support an "open forum." An open forum is present when the district allows community groups to use its facilities during noninstructional hours. If supported, the district may not discriminate against any community group based on philosophical or ideological differences. The district must remain *viewpoint neutral* in accommodating these groups. However, if the district chooses a closed forum, then no community groups are allowed to use facilities. Under an open forum, districts may prescribe certain policies regarding the use of their facilities with respect to maintenance, safety, and overall operations. Reasonable fees may also be imposed to cover costs associated with opening, closing, cleaning, and generally maintaining facilities during use by community groups.

Right to Deny Access

School districts may deny access to community groups even when an open forum exists in instances where there is evidence of abuse or destruction of property. Willful violation of district policy or local or state laws also may result in denial of use. If the facility is used for subversive activities aimed at carrying out unlawful objectives, access may be justifiably denied. Additionally, criminal charges may be levied against guilty parties depending on the circumstances surrounding each case. Activities conducted in school facilities that pose a threat to public safety may also be curtailed. The district should have approved written policies that address all aspects of facility use by community groups. All approved policies governing the use of district facilities must be applied fairly and consistently with all groups, including religious groups.

When conflict arises over denial of school facilities by school officials, it will usually involve either freedom of association, freedom of expression, or equal protection challenges. School districts will normally be supported by the courts in cases involving denial based on issues pertaining to unlawful acts, threats to health or safety, and destruction of school property. They generally will not be supported in matters involving free speech and association or equal protection violations. When challenges arise, the courts will examine all relevant facts surrounding the particular case and determine if a substantive right is in question.

■ ■ ■ ■ ■

ADMINISTRATIVE GUIDE

USE OF FACILITIES BY OUTSIDE RELIGIOUS GROUPS

1. School districts must allow religious groups access to their facilities if other nonreligious groups are permitted to use them.
2. School officials are not expected to allow religious groups to use facilities for regular religious services, even when an open forum is established by the district.
3. School districts are not required to accommodate religious groups under a closed forum policy.
4. In the absence of religious services, school officials must remain *viewpoint neutral* in permitting religious groups to use facilities under an open forum.

RELIGIOUS ACTIVITIES AND HOLIDAY PROGRAMS

The observance of holy days by public schools is clearly an unconstitutional activity if conducted in a devotional atmosphere. The First Amendment prohibits states from either aiding religion or showing preference of one religion over another. Public schools may not celebrate religious holidays. There should be no worship or devotional services nor religious pageants or plays of any nature held in the school. However, certain programs may be conducted if a secular purpose is clearly served.

For example, the district court upheld a school's Christmas program in South Dakota when certain parents challenged the religious content of a Christmas program that was sponsored, based on school district policy. The district's policy was challenged on the grounds that it violated the *Establishment Clause* of the First Amendment. The U.S. District Court of South Dakota held for the school district in ruling that the performance of music containing religious content does not within itself constitute a religious activity, as long as it serves an educational rather than a religious purpose.[42]

Schools, however, are prohibited from the use of sacred music that occurs in a devotional setting. This type of music may be sung or played as a part of a music appreciation class, as long as a secular purpose is served. School choirs and assemblies may be permitted to sing or play holiday carols, as long as these activities are held for entertainment purposes rather than religious purposes.

Released Time for Religious Instruction

Releasing public school students for religious instruction has not been a major issue in recent years. Public school officials are aware that a very fine line separates church and state relationships. Landmark rulings prohibiting prayer, Bible reading, and financial aid to parochial schools have heightened awareness among public school officials of the need to adhere to the principle of neutrality regarding their role in religious matters affecting the operation of public schools.

Prior to these landmark decisions in the 1960s, it was not an uncommon practice in some districts to observe teachers of religious instruction entering public schools to teach religious classes for students whose parents granted consent. This practice involved virtually all denominations. Since no public school funds were involved in teaching these classes, there was a commonly held view that such practices were an acceptable accommodation to parents and students who wished to participate in religious instruction.

However, in a leading Illinois case, the U.S. Supreme Court held that offering religious instruction on a released-time basis in public schools was unconstitutional. The case arose when the board of education initiated a program that permitted representatives of various religious groups to provide religious instruction during the school day on a voluntary basis. McCollum, a private citizen and a parent, challenged this practice as a violation of the establishment clause of the First Amendment and sought declaratory relief.

The school district stressed the point that no school resources were involved and those students who did not wish to participate in religious instruction were allowed to move to some other location in the building for secular instruction. Class attendance records were maintained by religious instructors. However, the facts revealed that school property was utilized for religious instruction and a close relationship emerged between the school and religious organizations. The state trial court upheld this practice. The state supreme court affirmed the trial court's ruling.

However, the U.S. Supreme Court reversed that decision, holding that "the state may not permit religious teaching on tax-supported public school property during regular school hours." This practice aids religion through the implementation of compulsory attendance laws and was deemed to be a violation of the First Amendment, which created a wall of separation between church and state that must be respected.[43]

In a later case with a slightly different twist, the U.S. Supreme Court upheld a released-time program involving religious instruction. This case involved a New York City program that permitted public schools to release students during the school day to attend religious instruction at religious centers at locations around the city. All administrative activities were coordinated by the religious organization, which assumed full responsibility for transportation and attendance reporting.

Zorach, a citizen of New York, filed suit, challenging this practice as a violation of the First Amendment's ban on separation of church and state. Zorach further charged that normal school activities ceased while students were transported to religious centers and that public school teachers were required to monitor students released to attend these centers.

The U.S. Supreme Court upheld this practice by stating that the city may permit public school students to attend religious centers during school hours, since no compulsion is involved and no public school resources are expended. Parents decide whether their children will attend religious centers. Since this program is voluntary, public schools do no more than make a mere scheduling accommodation. The Court held that this practice did not violate First Amendment prohibitions.[44]

Although both programs were voluntary in nature, the obvious difference in these two cases rests on one important fact. In the *McCollum* case, the school utilized resources in the form of classrooms during the school day, whereas in the *Zorach* case, no public tax-supported resources were involved. In a more recent development, the U.S. Court of Appeals for the Tenth Circuit held a released-time program unconstitutional that allowed students to attend religious seminars and receive public school credit for classes that were viewed as denominational in nature.[45]

Posting Religious Mottos and Expressions

In recent developments, state boards of education across the country are developing resolutions supporting the posting of the Ten Commandments in public school buildings. These resolutions are strongly opposed by the American Civil Liberties Union. The view held by opponents of this practice is that such postings amount to a government endorsement of religion. State officials respond by suggesting that such postings teach civility as well as proper moral and ethical values badly needed by children.

Some state officials are supporting policies calling for posting the words *In God We Trust* in public schools as a motto that has been in use on U.S. currency since 1864. These efforts will undoubtedly result in legal battles as they are embraced by other school districts across the United States. For example, Colorado's State Board of Education voted to urge schools to post *In God We Trust* in buildings throughout the state as a means of celebrating national heritage, traditions, values, and civic virtue.

Opponents are charging that the board is attempting to use a familiar and generally accepted phrase to inject religion into public schools. The resolution calls for the Colorado State Board of Education to encourage the appropriate display of this national motto in school buildings. Congress approved this phrase during the nineteenth century in response to a request from the clergy. The U.S. Supreme Court has never addressed this issue. However, several appeals courts have allowed its use on coins, suggesting that it does not amount to a government endorsement of religion. These developments point to the ongoing tension that exists between issues relating to separation of church and state and the level of emotions surrounding these issues. Only time will reveal how the courts will address these emerging conflicts.

Distribution of Religious Materials

Public school personnel are not permitted to distribute religious materials on school premises. Such practice would be a clear violation of the establishment clause. Public school officials also may not allow religious groups to distribute religious materials on school grounds. Support of such practices would suggest that the school embraces religion and could suggest preference of one religion over another. Again, the principle of neutrality commands that schools assume a neutral position, neither supporting religion nor prohibiting individual students from exercising their religious rights. Two cases illustrate the courts' posture regarding the distribution of religious materials.

One case involving the distribution of religious material arose in Florida when an elementary student brought religious pamphlets to distribute to her classmates. The school district's policy vested the superintendent with power to restrain the distribution of any materials unrelated to school courses in the public schools. When the elementary student requested, through her teacher, to be allowed to distribute the pamphlets, they were confiscated and carried to the principal, who subsequently destroyed them, indicating that he could not permit the distribution of religious material at school.

The student and her mother filed suit in the U.S. District Court, seeking a preliminary injunction against enforcement of the policy. The court held that the motion was premature and that the policy had never been applied by the school. The Eleventh Circuit Court affirmed the district court's decision. The district court then addressed the student's request for a permanent injunction against enforcing the policy. The court discerned that the policy was a content-based prior restraint ban on free speech that could be justified only with a showing that the literature would materially or substantially disrupt the operations of the school or infringe on the rights of other students.

In the absence of this showing, the school district's policy, as expected, could not be supported under the law. The First Amendment to the U.S. Constitution prohibits the government from inhibiting the free exercise of religion. There was no evidence that the distribution of the religious pamphlets interfered *materially* or *substantially* with school operations. The court held for the student by issuing a permanent injunction against the enforcement of the policy and also awarded nominal damages and attorney fees.[46]

The other leading case, *Tudor v. Board of Education,*[47] arose in New Jersey, where the highest court in New Jersey struck down an attempt by Gideons International to distribute the Gideon Bible throughout the public schools. Distribution of the Bible was expressly approved by the board of education. Approval was based on parental requests that Bibles be distributed to their children. The court, in assessing this practice, determined that the Gideon Bible was sectarian, based on testimony of representatives of various faiths, many of whom did not accept part or all of the Gideon Bible. The court also considered testimony from psychologists and educators who affirmed that the distribution of permission slips for parental consent would create subtle pressure on all children to accept the slips. Furthermore, the distribution of the Bible, as embraced by the school, would signify that school officials had given the Bible their stamp of approval, thus creating increased tension among other religious groups.

The court, in its ruling, found the practice to be unconstitutional in that it showed preference of one religion over others, thus violating the establishment clause. The Fifth Circuit Court of Appeals unanimously agreed with the New Jersey district court's ruling in the related *Meltzer v. Board of Public Instruction of Orange County.*[48]

In yet another case involving the distribution of the Bible, a Nebraska school board member withdrew his son from school and resigned from his position on the board when his son was given a Gideon Bible in the school's hallway. The distribution was clearly in violation of unwritten district policy, which permitted distribution of Bibles to fifth-graders on the sidewalk and off school premises once per year. The school employed an open forum policy, which made sidewalks available to any group after school hours. The facts revealed that distribution was voluntary, as students were reminded over the school's public address system that they were not required to accept a Bible. On the following day, students received Bibles in the hallway. Although there was no evidence that the district played any role in this activity, the board member filed suit in the U.S. District Court under 42 U.S.C. § 1983.

The court held that the district played no role in the hallway distribution and that its open forum was valid, since it had a neutral purpose that neither advanced or inhibited religious groups. It further noted that no groups had ever been denied access to the sidewalk and that no district resources were involved. The court granted summary judgment for the district.[49]

Pledge of Allegiance

Emerging Landmark Case.   A landmark case challenging the daily ritual of reciting the pledge of allegiance has emerged in the Ninth Circuit Court in California regarding the constitutionality of the inclusion of the words *under God.* The final outcome of the ruling in this case will have a profound affect on public schools, on state and federal governments, and on American citizens in general. Forty-nine states have filed briefs supporting the Pledge of Allegiance.

This case arose when Michael R. Newdow, an atheist, filed a suit on behalf of his eight-year-old daughter challenging the inclusion of *under God* in the pledge. A panel of the U.S. Court of Appeals for the Ninth Circuit in San Francisco created quite a controversy when it ruled 2–1 that the inclusion of *under God* was an unconstitutional establishment of religion by the government.

While Newdow does not have legal custody of his daughter, the court held that he has legal standing to raise the challenge on behalf of his daughter, who has not been named in court papers. The defendants are the Elk Grove Unified School District, the State of California, the U.S. Congress, and President George W. Bush. The eight-year-old girl's mother, Sandra Banning, has publicly confirmed that her daughter has no religious objection to reciting the pledge in school. Newdow and Banning, the child's parents, have never been married. Both held informal custody of their daughter until February 2003, after which time sole custody was awarded to Ms. Banning. A California Superior Court barred Newdow from naming his daughter as defendant.

U.S. Circuit Judge Alfred T. Goodwin wrote the original opinion against the constitutionality of the pledge and also stated that the mother had no power as sole legal custodian to insist that her child be subjected to unconstitutional state action. U.S. Circuit Judge Ferdinand F. Fernandez, who dissented, agreed only on the issue of legal standing. Subsequently, a larger panel of Ninth Circuit judges heard this case and supported the decision of the three judge panel. This case has been appealed to the Supreme Court.

The Bush Administration has defended the words "under God" in the Pledge of Allegiance and asked the Supreme Court to uphold the daily recitation of the pledge. The Administration's rationale is that reciting the Pledge of Allegiance is a patriotic exercise and not a religious testimonial. In addition, the Administration said that the reference to "a nation under God" in the Pledge of Allegiance is an official acknowledgement of what all students may properly be taught in school regardless of their religious affiliation. Jay Sekulow, Chief Counsel of the American Center for Law filed court appeal or court papers on behalf of members of Congress. The Ninth Circuit Court of Appeals has delayed implementing its decision until the Supreme Court rules on the case.[51]

While it is difficult to predict the outcome of this case, it appears that the U.S. Supreme Court will presumably address criteria similar to that used in the *Lemon* case:

Does the pledge have a secular purpose?
Does it advance or inhibit religion?
Does it create excessive entanglement?

In addition, the court will likely consider that reciting the pledge is optional, as decided in 1943 in *West Virginia State Board of Education v. Barnette,* in which the U.S. Supreme Court held that public school officials may not require students to salute and pledge allegiance to the flag.[50] After the events of September 11, 2001, America has become strongly united around patriotism, which will no doubt have some impact on the ultimate ruling. Added to these developments is the fact that *In God We Trust,* found on U.S. coins, has been held to be a national slogan and not the government's endorsement of religion. It will be interesting to observe the outcome and impact of this case.

■ ■ ■ ■ ■

ADMINISTRATIVE GUIDE

RELIGIOUS ACTIVITIES

1. School-sponsored holiday programs are permitted if they are not conducted in a religious atmosphere.
2. Released time for religious instruction may be allowed if evidence reveals that no public school resources are involved. Use of public school resources violates the establishment clause of the First Amendment.
3. School districts may find it difficult to justify the posting of the Ten Commandments or other references to God as meeting a purely secular purpose.
4. Religious pageants, displays, or symbols will not meet the constitutional requirements of neutrality by school officials. Statues or pictures may be used to teach art form if taught as a secular activity.
5. The distribution of religious material by external groups is illegal if the distribution occurs on school premises. However, a student may be allowed to distribute religious pamphlets if the distribution does not interfere with normal school activities or create material or substantial disruption.
6. School authorities must respect the free exercise rights of students, unless the exercise of those rights violates the rights of others or disrupts the educational process.
7. School authorities must refrain from any activity that would create an unclear line of separation between school activities and religious activities.
8. School authorities should consult the district's legal counsel regarding any questionable religious activities in their schools.
9. Aid to students attending religious school in the form of computers and equipment is permissible as part of a general program designed to enhance overall educational opportunities of all students.
10. Students may not be compelled to recite the Pledge of Allegiance based on their right to freedom of expression.

RELIGION AND STUDENT EXPRESSION

Jean Riley is the principal of a small elementary school in a metropolitan school district. One of her best teachers asked her first graders to make a poster depicting things for which they were thankful. One student made a poster expressing thanks for Jesus. Posters were displayed in the school's hallway. The student's poster was removed but later returned in a less prominent place. The next year, the student was chosen to read a story to the class. The student selected an adaptation of a Biblical story.

■ ■ ■ ■ ■
DISCUSSION QUESTIONS

1. Should the student be permitted to read his Biblical story? Why or why not?
2. What is the legal issue surrounding both the poster and the Biblical story?
3. What legal risks does the school incur (if any) if it permits both of these activities?
4. What legal risks does the school incur if it denies both of these practices?
5. How would the courts likely rule on this case? Provide a rationale for your response.

RELIGION AND TEACHER FREEDOM

Karen White, a kindergarten teacher, informed her parents and students that she could no longer lead certain activities or participate in certain projects because they were religious in nature according to her newly acquired affiliation with Jehovah's Witnesses. This meant that she could no longer decorate the classroom for holidays or plan for gift exchanges during the Christmas season. She also could not sing "Happy Birthday" or recite the Pledge of Allegiance. Parents protested and Bill Ward, the school principal, recommended her dismissal based on her ineffectively meeting the needs of her students.

■ ■ ■ ■ ■
DISCUSSION QUESTIONS

1. Is there a justifiable basis for Karen's dismissal?
2. If so, What grounds does Bill Ward have to recommend dismissal? Are these valid grounds? Why or why not?
3. If Karen White is an otherwise competent and effective teacher, how defensible can the principal's recommendation for dismissal be?
4. Is the school in violation of Karen's religious rights? Why or why not?
5. How do you think the courts would rule in this case? Provide a rationale for your response.

STUDENT ASSIGNMENT AND GRADING

Norma Davis, a tenth-grade English teacher, assigned her class a research paper. She was specific regarding the number of sources from which information should be obtained. Each topic was subject to her approval and had to be interesting, researchable, decent, and familiar to the student. Susan Chandler submitted an outline for a paper, without prior approval of Ms. Davis, entitled "The Life of Jesus Christ." Davis rejected the outline. Susan refused to select another topic. When the paper was due, Susan received a grade of zero. Susan's parents filed suit on her behalf alleging that her First Amendment right was violated.

■ ■ ■ ■ ■ ▬▬▬▬▬▬▬▬▬▬▬▬▬▬▬▬▬▬▬▬▬▬▬▬▬▬▬▬▬▬▬▬▬▬▬

DISCUSSION QUESTIONS

1. Is a grade of zero justified for Norma? Why or why not?
2. Did Ms. Davis have the right to reject Susan's paper? Why or why not?
3. Did Susan have a right to research a topic that contained religious content? Why or why not?
4. Does rejection by the teacher amount to a First Amendment infringement? Why or why not?
5. As principal, how would you resolve this matter?
6. How do you think the court would rule in this case? Provide a rationale for your response.

USE OF FACILITIES BY RELIGIOUS GROUPS

Gayle Dixon is the principal of a midsize metropolitan high school. The school maintains an open forum, thereby allowing noncurricular groups to use facilities during noninstructional times, including student religious groups. A Bible club has requested the use of school facilities, but Dixon learned that the club's charter allows only Christians to be club officers. In her mind, this provision of the charter is discriminatory. Based on this provision, she rejected the club's request to use school facilities. The club filed suit.

■ ■ ■ ■ ■ ▬▬▬▬▬▬▬▬▬▬▬▬▬▬▬▬▬▬▬▬▬▬▬▬▬▬▬▬▬▬▬▬▬▬▬

DISCUSSION QUESTIONS

1. Does the club have legitimate grounds to file suit? Why or why not?
2. Is Dixon justified in rejecting the club's request to use school facilities? Why or why not?
3. Does the Bible club have the right to specify that only Christians may be club officers? Why or why not?
4. If you were the principal, would you handle this situation any differently?
5. How do you think the court would rule in this case? Provide a rationale for your response.
6. What are the administrative implications of this case?

USE OF FACILITIES BY THE COMMUNITY

A Midwestern school district approved a policy allowing open access to its facilities by the public so long as public use did not interfere with school activities. A group of graduating seniors and their parents arranged for a baccalaureate ceremony sponsored by the community. The ceremony was to be held in a school gymnasium. Verbal authorization was granted by school district officials. One month later, the district approved a new policy, which prohibited the group from using the gym.

■ ■ ■ ■ ■ ▓▓

DISCUSSION QUESTIONS

1. Does the board's action constitute a breach of duty to honor its verbal authorization? Why or why not?
2. Does the district have a right to change its policies after giving verbal authorization for use of the gym? Why or why not?
3. Does the district's action amount to a breach? Why or why not?
4. What is the legality of reversing a policy that has been approved and executed for an extended period of time?
5. Would the district's action constitute discrimination against the students, their parents, and the community?
6. What might the district's defense be in this situation?
7. How would the court likely rule on this issue? Provide a rationale for your response.
8. What are the administrative implications?

Note: The board is the legal body for the district.

Student Response Sheet

Professor _____   Student _____

Course _____   Date _____

Title of In-Basket Exercise _____

Reaction:

_____

_____

_____

_____

_____

_____

_____

_____

_____

_____

_____

_____

_____

_____

_____

_____

_____

_____

_____

_____

_____

_____

ENDNOTES

1. *Reynolds v. United States,* 98 U.S. (8 OTTO) 145 (1879).
2. *Cantwell v. Connecticut,* 310 U.S. 296 (1940).
3. *Everson v. Board of Education of the Township of Ewing,* 330 U.S. 1, 15 (1947).
4. *Engel v. Vitale,* 370 U.S. 421, 82 S.Ct. 1261 (1962).
5. *Ingebretsen v. Jackson Public School District,* 864 F. Supp. 1473 (S.D. Miss. 1994).
6. *School District of Abington Township v. Schempp; Murray v. Curlett,* 374 U.S. 203, 83 S.Ct. 1650 (1965).
7. *Wallace v. Jaffree,* 472 U.S. 38, 105 S.Ct. 2479 (1985).
8. *Aguilar v. Felton,* 473 U.S. 402 (1985).
9. *Agostini v. Felton,* 473 U.S. 402, 105 S.Ct. 3232, 87 L. Ed. 2d 290 (1985).
10. *Lemon v. Kurtzman and Early v. Dicenso,* 403 U.S. 602, 91 S.Ct. 2105 (1971).
11. *Sloan v. Lemon,* 413 U.S. 825 93 S.Ct. 2982 (1973).
12. *School District of the City of Grand Rapids v. Ball,* 473 U.S. 373, 195 S.Ct. 3216 (1985).
13. *Meek v. Pittenger,* 421 U.S. 349, 95 S.Ct. 1753 (1975).
14. *Mueller v. Allen,* 463 U.S. 388, 103 S.Ct. 3062 (1983).
15. *Everson v. Board of Education,* 330 U.S. 1, 67 S.Ct. 504 (1947).
16. *Cochran v. Louisiana State Board of Education,* 281 U.S. 370 (1930).
17. *Mitchell v. Helms,* 120 S.Ct. 2530; 147 L. Ed. 2d 660; 68 (2000).
18. *Washegisic v. Bloomingdale Public Schools,* 33 F. 3d 679 (6th Cir. 1994).
19. *Lawrence v. Buchmuller,* 40 Misc. 2d 300, 243 N.Y.S. 2d 87, 91 (Sup. Ct. 1963).
20. *Ring v. Grand Forks School District No. 1,* 483 F. Supp. 272 (N.D. 1980).
21. *Stone v. Graham,* 599 S.W. 2d 157 (Ky 1980).
22. *Chandler v. Siegelman,* 230 F. 3d 1313 (11th Cir. 2000).
23. *Lemon v. Kurtzman,* 403 U.S. 602 (1971).
24. *Jager v. Douglas County School District,* 862 F. 2d 824, 11th Cir. (1989).
25. *Santa Fe Independent School District v. Jane Doe,* 120 S.Ct. 2266; 147 L. Ed. 2d 295 (2000).
26. Ibid.
27. *Sands v. Morongo Unified School District,* 809 P. 2d 809 (Cal. 1991).
28. *Lee v. Weisman,* 505 U.S. 577 (1992).
29. *Lemon v. Kurtzman,* 403 U.S. 602 (1971).
30. *Jones v. Clear Creek Independent School District,* 977 F. 2d 963 (5th Cir. 1992).
31. *Adler v. Duval County School Board,* 851 F. Supp. 446 (M.D. Fla. 1994).
32. *Coles v. Cleveland Board of Education,* 1999, WL 144262 (6th Cir. 1999).
33. 20 U.S.C. § 4071 (1988).
34. *Bender v. Williams Sport,* 106 S.Ct. 1326 (1986).
35. *Mergens v. Board of Education of the Westside Community Schools,* 496 U.S. 226 (1990).
36. *Garnett v. Renton School District,* 675 F. Supp. 1268 (W.D. Wash. 1987).
37. *Clark v. Dallas Independent School,* 806 F. Supp. 116 (N.D. Texas 1992).
38. *Wallace v. Washoe County District* (1988).
39. *Gregoire v. Centennial School District,* 907 F. 2d 13; 66 1378-70, 1382 (3rd Cir. 1990).
40. *Bronx Household of Faith v. Community School District No. 10,* 127 F. 3d 207 (2nd Cir. 1997).
41. *Lamb's Chapel v. Center Moriches School District,* 508 U.S. 384, 124 L. Ed. 2d 352, 113 S.Ct. 2141 (Sup. Ct. 1993).
42. *Florey v. Sioux Falls School District,* 464 F. Supp. 911 (D.S.D. 1979).
43. *People of State of Illinois ex rel. McCollum v. Board of Education of District No. 71, Champaign County, Illinois,* 333 U.S. 203, 68 S.Ct. 462 (1948).
44. *Zorach v. Clauson U.S. Supreme Court,* 343 U.S. 306, 72 S.Ct. 679.
45. *Lanner v. Wimmer,* 662 F. 2d 1349 (10th Cir. 1981).
46. *Johnson-Loehner v. O'Brien,* 859 F. Supp. 575 (M.D. Fla. 1994).
47. *Tudor v. Board of Education of Borough of Rutherford,* 14 N.J. 31,100 A. 2d 857 (1953), cert. den., 348 U.S. 816, 75 S.Ct. 25, 99 L. Ed. 664 (1954).
48. *Meltzer v. Board of Public Instruction of Orange County,* U.S. Court of Appeals, 5th Cir. (1978), 577 F. 2d 311, cert. denied, 439 U.S. 1089 (1979).
49. *Schanou v. Lancaster County School District No. 160,* 863 F. Supp. 1048 D. Neb. (1994).
50. *West Virginia State Board of Education v. Barnette,* 319 U.S. 624, 63 S.Ct. 1178, 1943.
51. *Newdow v. United States,* 315 F. 3d 495 (C.A. 9, 2002).

CHAPTER 3

STUDENTS, THE LAW, AND PUBLIC SCHOOLS

School officials are granted broad powers to establish rules and regulations governing student conduct in the school setting. These powers, however, are not absolute. They are subject to the standard of *reasonableness*. Generally, rules are deemed to be reasonable if they are necessary to maintain an orderly and peaceful school environment and advance the educational process. The courts—in determining the enforceability of policies, rules, and regulations—require evidence of *sufficient justification* by school authorities of the need to enforce the policy, rule, or regulation. Since students enjoy many of the same constitutional rights as adults, courts have been very diligent in ensuring that their constitutional rights be protected.

While school rules are necessary to ensure proper order and decorum, they should not be so broad and nebulous as to allow for *arbitrary and inconsistent interpretation.* Fundamental fairness requires that students know what behavior is required of them by school officials. They should not be expected to conform to rules that are vague and ambiguous in meaning or application. Rules should be sufficiently definite in providing students with adequate information regarding expected behavior. They should be stated in such a manner that students of average intelligence are not necessarily required to guess at their meaning. *It is important to remember that a fair and reasonable exercise of administrative authority will withstand court scrutiny.*

Further, in determining whether policies or regulations are fair and reasonable, it is necessary to assess them in the context of their application. Whether a rule or regulation is legally defensible depends on the fact situation.

The concept of *in loco parentis* (in place of parent) has permitted school officials to promulgate rules that allow them to exercise a reasonable degree of control over students under their supervision. This concept, however, is not without limits. School authorities and teachers do not fully occupy the place of the parent. *Their control or jurisdiction is limited to school functions and activities.* Although *in loco parentis* is considered a viable concept, it does require prudence on the part of school officials and teachers. Prudence in this instance implies that school authorities' actions must be consistent with those of the average parent under the same or similar circumstances. Generally, if administrative actions conform to this norm, they are judged to be reasonable. Although children are subject to reasonable rules and regulations promulgated by school officials, they do enjoy personal rights that must be recognized and respected by school officials.

In the landmark 1960s *Tinker* case, the U.S. Supreme Court for the very first time held that *students possess the same constitutional rights as adults and that these rights do not end at the schoolhouse door.* This ruling by the high court significantly altered the relationship between school officials and students. The *Tinker* ruling clearly mandated that professional educators respect the civil rights of students in the school. In cases where student rights are restricted, school officials must demonstrate a *justifiable or legitimate reason* for doing so. In these instances, the burden of proof justifiably rests with school officials. For example, school officials may restrict the rights of a student if they are able to demonstrate that such a restriction is necessary to maintain order and proper decorum in the school. A student's rights also may be restricted if the exercise of those rights infringes on the rights of others. In short, no rights are absolute but, rather, are subject to reasonable restrictions that must be justified by school officials.

The development of a legally defensible code of student conduct represents one method of ensuring that the rights of students are protected. The student code should be developed through the involvement of school personnel, parents, citizens, and even students, where appropriate. A final step should include a review by the school district's attorney to validate the code's legality. Once approved and adopted, policies should be disseminated, periodically reviewed, and revised as needed.

FREEDOM OF EXPRESSION

Freedom of expression is derived from the First Amendment to the U.S. Constitution, which provides, in part, "Congress shall make no law . . . abridging the freedom of speech, or of press or of the rights of peoples to peacefully assemble." The *Tinker* case confirmed that students are entitled to all First Amendment guarantees, subject only to the provision in which the exercise of these rights creates material and substantial disruption in the school. An excerpt from *Tinker* pointed out the following:

> School officials do not possess absolute authority over their students. Students in school as well as out of school are "persons" under our Constitution. They possess fundamental rights which the State must respect. . . . In our system, students may not be regarded as closed-circuit recipients of only that which the state chooses to communicate. They may not be confined to the expression of those sentiments that are officially approved. In the absence of a specific showing of constitutionally valid reasons to regulate their speech, students are entitled to freedom of expression of their views.[1]

Stated differently, the First Amendment to the Constitution guarantees the right to freedom of speech to U.S. citizens, including students in public schools. This freedom, however, does not include a license to exercise such rights in a manner that creates *material or substantial disruption to the educational process.* These were the criteria applied by the Supreme Court in determining whether regulations prohibiting student expression were constitutionally valid.

The *Tinker* case is viewed as the leading case in addressing speech as symbolic expression. This case emerged in December of 1965, when a group of adults and students in Des Moines, Iowa, met to oppose the involvement of the United States in the Vietnam war. They decided to reveal publicly their opposition and their support for a truce by wearing black armbands during the holiday season.

Principals of the Des Moines schools became aware of the plan and adopted a policy that stated that any student wearing an armband would be asked to remove it. Those students who refused to obey would be suspended from school until they returned without the armbands.

On December 16, Mary Beth Tinker and Christopher Eckhardt wore black armbands to school. John Tinker wore his armband the next day. Since they refused to remove the armbands, all three were sent home. The students, through their parents, then brought suit to enjoin the board of education from enforcing the regulation.

The Supreme Court, having granted certiorari, began its hearing of the *Tinker* case. By a final vote of 7–2, the high court invalidated the rule barring the wearing of black armbands. The Supreme Court, in rendering its decision, stated:

> School officials banned and sought to punish petitioners for a silent, passive expression of opinion, unaccompanied by any disorder or disturbance on the part of petitioners. There is no evidence whatever of petitioners' interference, actual or nascent, with the school's work or of collision with the rights of other students to be secure and to be let alone. Accordingly, this case does not concern speech or action that intrudes upon the work of the school or the rights of other students.[2]

As one can see by the court's ruling in the *Tinker* case, students are entitled to express their views in an orderly fashion. Since the wearing of armbands was totally divorced from disruptive or potentially disruptive conduct by those participating, they were afforded the protection of the First Amendment.

To gain a clearer view of the nature of the litigation involving freedom of expression in the *Tinker* case, a contrasting Fifth Circuit Court of Appeals case, *Blackwell v. Issaquena County Board of Education,* emerged in Mississippi when a principal banned the wearing of political buttons in response to a disturbance by students noisily talking in the corridor when they were scheduled to be in class. Those students wearing the buttons were found pinning them on other students who objected. Class instruction deteriorated into a state of general confusion and a breakdown in discipline. Students were warned during an assembly program not to wear the buttons. This warning was repeated on the following day. Violators were subsequently suspended. As the suspended students left campus, they attempted to influence other nonviolators to leave with them. The court held for the board of education, upholding the principal's action as reasonable, based on the factual circumstances surrounding these incidents. The Fifth Circuit justices reasoned that it is always within the province of school authorities to provide by regulation for the prohibition and punishment of acts calculated to undermine the school's routine. "This is not only proper in our opinion, but it is necessary."[3]

As illustrated by this case, evidence of material and substantial disruption forms sufficient grounds to limit freedom of expression. The significant difference, however, in viewing these two cases is that there was no evidence of disruption in *Tinker,* but considerable evidence of disruption in *Blackwell.* Consequently, the principal's action was not justified in the former case but well justified in the latter. The importance of this distinction is evident when a valuable constitutional right is involved. In these instances, decisions must be made on a case-by-case basis.

A landmark case involving freedom of expression by students was heard by the U.S. Supreme Court in 1986.[4] This case arose when a male student at Bethel High School delivered a speech nominating a fellow student for elective office before an assembly of over 600 peers, many of whom were 14-year-olds. Students were required to attend the assembly or report to study hall. In his nominating speech, the student referred to his candidate in terms of an elaborate, explicit sexual metaphor, despite having been warned in advance by two teachers not to deliver it. During the speech, a counselor observed students' reactions, which included laughter, graphic sexual gestures, hooting, bewilderment, and embarrassment. One teacher reported that she had to use class time the next day to discuss the speech. The morning after the assembly, the student was called into the assistant principal's office and notified that he had violated a school rule prohibiting obscene language or gestures. When he admitted to the assistant principal that he had deliberately used sexual innuendo in his speech, he was informed that he would be suspended for three days and that his name would be removed from the list of candidates for student speaker at the school's commencement exercises.

The student brought suit against the school in a U.S. district court, claiming that his First Amendment right to freedom of speech had been violated. The district court agreed and awarded him $278 as compensation for deprivation of his constitutional rights based on two days of suspension and $12,750 in litigation costs and attorney's fees. The court also ordered the school district to allow the student to speak at commencement. The U.S. Court of Appeals, Ninth Circuit, rejected the school district's appeal and held that the district had failed to prove that the speech had interfered with or disrupted the educational environment. On further appeal by the school district, the U.S. Supreme Court ruled that while public school students have the right to advocate unpopular and controversial views in school, that right must be balanced against the schools' interest in teaching socially appropriate behavior. A public school, as an instrument of the state, may legitimately establish standards of civil and mature conduct. The Court observed that such standards would be difficult to convey in a school that tolerated the "lewd, indecent and offensive" speech and conduct that the student in this case exhibited. Consequently, the school district's action was upheld.

■ ■ ■ ■ ■ ▬▬▬▬▬▬▬▬▬▬▬▬▬▬▬▬▬▬▬▬▬▬▬▬▬▬▬▬▬▬▬▬▬▬▬▬▬

ADMINISTRATIVE GUIDE

FREEDOM OF EXPRESSION

1. School officials may restrict freedom of expression where there is evidence of material and substantial disruption, indecent or offensive speech, violation of school rules, destruction of school property, or disregard for authority. In each case, students must be provided minimal due process before any punitive action is taken.
2. Buttons, pamphlets, and other insignia may be banned if the message communicated is vulgar or obscene, or mocks others based on race, origin, color, sex, or religion. They may also be banned if their content is inconsistent with the basic mission of the school. School policies that address these issues should be developed and communicated to students and parents.
3. To justify the prohibition of a particular form of expression, there must be something more than a mere desire to avoid the discomfort and unpleasantness associated with an unpopular view. Such action is arbitrary, capricious, and indefensible.
4. The time, place, and manner of the distribution of pamphlets, buttons, and insignia may be regulated by school officials. Prohibiting distribution in class during regular school hours or in the corridors between classes is considered reasonable.
5. Unsubstantiated fear and apprehension of disturbance are not sufficient grounds to restrict the right to freedom of expression.

Protests and Demonstrations

Protests and demonstrations are considered forms of free expression. Thus, students are afforded the right to participate in these activities under certain conditions. As long as these activities are peaceful, do not violate school rules, and do not result in destruction of school property, protests and demonstrations are allowed. Because school officials are charged with the responsibility to protect the health and safety of all students and to provide an orderly school environment, they may regulate the time, place, and manner of conducting these activities. Such regulations however, are considered to be mere conditions rather than prohibitions.

School officials should anticipate that minor disruption may occur when there is disagreement or opposite points of view regarding various issues in schools. The courts concur that *minor disruption must be tolerated by school officials.* Only when school officials demonstrate that a particular form of expression has caused or will likely cause material and substantial disruption can they justifiably restrict students' rights to free speech.

■ ■ ■ ■ ■ ▬▬

ADMINISTRATIVE GUIDE

PROTESTS AND DEMONSTRATIONS

1. Demonstrations that deprive other students of the right to pursue their studies in an orderly and peaceful environment can be disallowed.
2. Students engaged in demonstrations and protests cannot obstruct the corridors or prevent free movement among students who are not participants in these activities.
3. Any activities associated with demonstrations and protests that result in disrespect for authority, destruction of property, violation of school rules, or any other unlawful activities may be banned.
4. An activity involving students' right to freedom of expression cannot be banned because it creates discomfort or conflicts with the views of school officials.

School-Sponsored Newspapers

Courts generally hold that a school publication has the responsibility for providing a forum for students to express their ideas and views on a variety of topics of interest to the school community. While the newspaper is intended to represent a forum for student expression, those responsible for its production should be mindful of their obligation to embrace responsible rules of journalism. The school newspaper should reflect editorial policy and sound judgment of student editors who operate under the guidance of a faculty advisor.

Although faculty advisors are generally assigned the responsibility to monitor material written for the student newspaper, in reality, their primary responsibility should involve advice with respect to form, style, grammar, and appropriateness of material recognizing that *the final decision for printed material rests with student editors.*

Thus, student editors under the guidance of their advisors, should be free to report the news and to editorialize, but at all times adhere to the rules of responsible journalism. A faculty advisor may not be punished, demoted, or dismissed for allowing constitutionally protected material to be printed that may prove distasteful to school officials. When justified, school administrators may exercise *limited review* of school-financed publications so long as they spell out, in policy, the reason for the review, the time frame involved, the person(s) responsible for reviewing the material, and specifically what material will be reviewed. Administrators should not abuse the review process by employing unreasonable time frames and unnecessary time delays to suppress material deemed to be personally objectionable. Students are afforded the right to express their views and ideas that do not materially and substantially affect the operation of the school. The review process, if employed, should always be guided by a sense of fairness and openness. Broad censorship by school officials is not permitted and is in violation of the free speech rights of students. In light of these precautions, however, students' free speech rights are not without limits. *Material that is libelous, vulgar, obscene, or mocks others on the basis of race, origin, sex, color, or religion is impermissible.* In cases where the newspaper is produced by students as a part of their school curriculum, school officials may regulate content that is inconsistent with the basic educational mission of the school.

A newspaper produced as a part of the school's curriculum may not enjoy the same privileges as one that is produced outside of the school's curriculum. While in both cases, the paper is intended to serve as a forum for student expression, more latitude is extended when the paper is not considered to be a part of the school's curriculum. For example, if the newspaper is not deemed part of the curriculum, then greater freedom should be granted to student editors in reporting the news, when there is no evidence of disruption or defamation. Also, school authorities would likely incur less risk of lawsuits if the school's paper is not considered to be a part of the curriculum. However, if it is considered part of the curriculum, then school authorities must be allowed to exercise *reasonable control* over newspaper content because they may be subject to liability for defamation involving libel.

Although administrators may exercise greater authority in monitoring student press, particularly school-sponsored newspapers, care should be taken not to violate student rights in the process. The *Hazelwood* decision, discussed later in this chapter, does not mean that administrators may arbitrarily suppress or censor student speech. For example, there should be sufficient evidence to demonstrate that the content of the publication does in fact create a disruptive influence on the school's program and is inconsistent with the mission of the school. In the absence of such evidence, censorship would be inappropriate and unjustified.

While the U.S. Supreme Court's decision in *Hazelwood* provides greater latitude for administrators, courts generally still accept the notion that a school publication has the responsibility for *leading opinions, provoking student dialogue, and providing a forum for a variety of student opinions.* Administrators must be mindful of the intended purpose of student publications and be guided by respect for the freedom of expression rights of students.

In a leading case, the U.S. Supreme Court in the *Hazelwood School District v. Kuhlmeier* reached a landmark decision. The *Kuhlmeier* case originated in the spring of 1983 when a high school principal in a suburban St. Louis district prevented the school publication *Spectrum* from running articles that profiled three pregnant students. The publication also quoted other students on the reasons for their parents' divorces. The principal was concerned that the identity of three pregnant girls might be revealed through the feature in the paper. He also believed that the article's reference to sexual activity and birth control were inappropriate for some of the younger students at the school. Finally, he felt that the divorced parents of the students who were identified in the article should have been provided an opportunity to respond to the remarks made by their children or to consent to the publication of the article.

Student editors claimed that the principal's actions amounted to prior restraint of free press and a denial of due process, both First and Fourteenth Amendment violations. In May 1985, a federal district judge ruled that because the paper was produced as part of the school's journalism curriculum, it was not a public forum entitled to the same degree of First Amendment protection accorded to student speech carried out independently of any school-sponsored program or activity. This court held that the principal needed only a reasonable basis for his action. However, the U.S. Court of Appeals for the Eighth Circuit reversed the federal district court's ruling in a 2–1 decision, stating that the *Spectrum* was a public forum intended to be a marketplace for student expression and not simply a part of the school's journalism curriculum. Since the paper was considered a public forum, the principal's actions were subject to the same free speech standards established by the Supreme Court in the *Tinker* case in which the U.S. Supreme Court enumerated:

> To justify a prohibition of a particular expression of opinion, school officials must be able to show that their action was caused by something more than a mere desire to avoid the discomfort and unpleasantness that always accompany an unpopular viewpoint. There must be facts that might reasonably lead school authorities to forecast substantial disruption of or material interference with school activities.[5]

In reviewing all circumstances related to this particular case, the U.S. Supreme Court reversed the Eighth Circuit Court of Appeals in ruling that the principal did not violate students' free speech rights by ordering certain material removed from an issue of the student newspaper. The Court concluded by stating the following:

> We cannot reject as unreasonable Principal Reynolds' conclusion that neither the pregnancy article nor the divorce was suitable for publication in the *Spectrum*. Reynolds could reasonably have concluded that students who wrote and edited the article had not sufficiently mastered those portions of the Journalism II Curriculum that pertained to the treatment of controversial issues and personal attacks, the need to protect the privacy of individuals whose most intimate concerns are to be revealed in the newspapers and "the legal, moral and ethical restrictions imposed upon journalists within the school community" that includes adolescent subjects and readers.[6]

The *Hazlewood* ruling has important implications for student newspapers that are part of the school's curriculum in that restrictions may be placed on them based on reasonable grounds.

ADMINISTRATIVE GUIDE

STUDENT NEWSPAPERS
In light of the courts' posture, school authorities would be well advised to consider these suggestions to avoid legal challenges regarding school-sponsored student newspapers:

1. Through the involvement of representative students, teachers, and other interested persons, formulate a set of legally defensible policies governing publication of the school's newspaper.

(continued)

■ ■ ■ ■ ■ ▬▬▬▬▬▬▬▬▬▬▬▬▬▬▬▬▬▬▬▬

ADMINISTRATIVE GUIDE (*continued*)

2. Choose responsible student editors who will exercise high standards of responsible journalism.
3. Be aware that administrative prerogatives vary based on whether the student newspaper is considered to be an open forum or a curriculum-based publication.
4. Emphasize to student editors that they have primary responsibility to see that the newspaper is free of libelous statements and obscenity. Additionally, they should be reminded that newspapers are subject to the law of libel.
5. Develop regulations that prescribe procedures to be followed in the event that prior review is warranted. These should include:
   a. A definite period of time in which the review of materials will be completed
   b. The specific person to whom the materials will be submitted
   c. What specific materials are included for review
6. Do not impose policy restrictions on school-sponsored publications that cannot be defended on reasonable grounds.
7. Consult the school district's legal advisor in cases where there is uncertainty regarding the appropriate administrative action to be taken when controversial subject matter is proposed by students.

Nonschool-Sponsored Newspapers

Nonschool-sponsored newspapers are those not endorsed by the school but printed at students' expense away from school premises. These publications may not be totally prohibited by school officials. Restrictions, however, may be imposed regarding the time, place, and manner of distribution. Such restrictions are recognized as conditions affecting freedom of press, not prohibitions. Students also may be required to remove any debris in the area after papers are distributed. Thus, students have the right to distribute underground newspapers so long as the distribution does not interfere with normal school activities or create material disruption. The school assumes no responsibility to assist with the publication or distribution of such newspapers and is not generally held liable for the content of the newspapers. Students who are responsible for producing the newspapers are held accountable for any libelous material printed in the newspaper.

Generally, broad censorship of nonsponsored newspapers is not permitted, but *material that is libelous, is clearly obscene, or would lead school officials to forecast a material and substantial disruption of the educational process or violate the rights of others may be suppressed.* This point was illustrated in *Bystrom v. Fridley High School Independent School District* in which the Eighth Circuit Court of Appeals supported a school rule that prohibited publication of material that was pervasively indecent and vulgar, even though there was some subjectivity involved in the interpretation of content in the newspaper.[7]

One should be mindful, however, that the courts require stricter standards to be met when school officials attempt to restrict free speech before it actually occurs. In all instances, legitimate and defensible reasons for suppressing material must be clearly demonstrated. For example, in the *Burch v. Barker* case, which involved an underground newspaper, the Ninth Circuit Court of Appeals held that the school rule involved was too broad and vague so as to give school officials unlimited discretion in exercising prior restraint. Further, such policy was unconstitutional for lack of specificity for distribution and approval procedures. Most significant, however, was that the school policy was unduly broad concerning the content-based requirements for exercising prior restraint.[8]

■ ■ ■ ■ ■ ▬▬

ADMINISTRATIVE GUIDE

NONSCHOOL-SPONSORED STUDENT PUBLICATIONS

1. Defensible policies should be developed that cover all aspects of student publications. These policies should be carefully crafted and communicated to students and their parents. Fundamental fairness should be the guiding principle in developing these policies.
2. School policies regarding nonschool-sponsored publications should not be written using broad and vague language so as to provide unlimited discretion in exercising prior restraint measures by school officials.
3. School officials must establish proof of disruption of a material and substantial nature before they can initiate disciplinary action against students. Disciplinary actions must meet the standards of fundamental fairness.
4. Actions by school officials are justified when there is evidence that the publication encourages disregard for school rules and disrespect for school personnel.
5. If the publication contains vulgar or obscene language, ridicules others, or violates policies on time, place, and conditions for distribution, disciplinary action by school officials is generally supported by the courts.
6. School officials may not be held accountable for content in a nonschool-sponsored newspaper. Student editors are responsible for their own acts of libel.

Censorship

Limited review of school-sponsored publications may be permitted, but *broad censorship* is not. School officials' commitment to sponsor a student publication should reflect a commitment to respect personal rights associated with freedom of expression. School officials have the option to decide whether they wish to finance a school-sponsored publication. Once a decision is made to support an open forum for student ideas, broad censorship powers may not be imposed. School officials must be mindful that students are afforded the right to express their ideas and criticisms when these expressions do not materially and substantially interfere with proper decorum in the school. However, as previously stated, material that is vulgar, libelous, or indisputably obscene may be prohibited. The U.S. Supreme Court defined *obscenity* as material that describes or portrays hard-core sexual conduct specifically described by state law and that lacks serious literary artistic, political, or scientific value.

As one may discern, obscenity matters are typically influenced by state and local community standards. The courts generally hold that constructive criticism of school policy or practice is permitted but material that falls in the area of personal attacks on school personnel is not.

ADMINISTRATIVE GUIDE

CENSORSHIP

1. Courts are in disagreement regarding the extent to which school officials may examine and make judgments on student publications prior to their distribution.
2. If prior restraint is invoked, there should be a demonstrated and compelling justification for doing so.
3. School officials must be able to demonstrate that the distribution of a student publication will create a material and substantial disruption.
4. If limited review is legally justified, the following safeguards should be included:
   a. A brief review process
   b. An explanation of the person(s) vested with the authority to approve or disapprove the material
   c. The form in which the material is to be submitted
   d. A clear and specific explanation of the types of items that are prohibited, with a rationale as to why they are prohibited
   e. An opportunity for students to appeal the decision if they feel that it is unjust

DRESS AND APPEARANCE

There seems to be a prevailing view that issues involving dress should be left to the decisions of state courts. The U.S. Supreme Court has consistently declined to address this issue. Student dress as a form of free expression is not viewed as significant as most other forms of free expression. There is, however, a First Amendment freedom associated with it.

Dress may be regulated if there is a defensible basis for doing so. However, school regulations that violate students' rights by being vague, ambiguous, and failing to demonstrate a connection to disruption will not meet court scrutiny. Dress regulations based on fashion or taste as a sole criterion will not survive court scrutiny. School officials, however, may within reason prescribe rules governing student dress and appearance with an emphasis on *reasonableness*. Emphasis on reasonableness centers around well-established facts that (1) students have protected constitutional rights and (2) students' rights must be weighed against a compelling need to restrict their rights. In fact, the courts are now requiring school officials to demonstrate the reasonableness of their rules before the courts will even elect to decide whether constitutional rights of students are violated.

Dress is generally viewed as a form of self-expression reflecting a student's values, background, culture, and personality. Thus, a student must be provided opportunities for self-expression. Therefore, restrictions on student dress are justified only when there is evidence of material or substantial disruption of the educational process. Violation of health and safety standards or cases where unusual attention is drawn to one's anatomy are also justifiable reasons to restrict certain types of dress. In most cases, courts tend to respond favorably when there is expressed community sentiment regarding dress standards.

The following restrictions have been upheld by the courts regarding dress and appearance:

1. School regulations necessary to protect the safety of students (e.g., wearing of long hair or jewelry around dangerous equipment in laboratories)
2. School regulations necessary to protect the health of students (e.g., requiring students to keep hair clean and free of parasites)
3. Rules prohibiting dress that does not meet standards of the community (e.g., dressing in a manner that calls undue attention to one's body)
4. Dress that results in material and substantial disruption to the orderly administration of the school (e.g., wearing T-shirts containing vulgar, lewd, or defamatory language based on race, color, gender, national origin, or religion)

■ ■ ■ ■ ■ ▬▬▬▬▬▬▬▬▬▬▬▬▬▬▬▬▬▬▬▬▬▬▬▬▬▬▬▬▬▬▬▬▬
ADMINISTRATIVE GUIDE

DRESS AND APPEARANCE

1. Local school dress codes developed by the school should be approved by the board of education. Faculty, students, parents, and citizens should be involved in the formulation of such regulations.
2. Policies and regulations governing dress should be communicated and discussed with students and parents.
3. Dress codes will be supported by the courts only when there is evidence that they are reasonable.
4. Dress and appearance restrictions based on taste, style, and fashion rather than health, safety, and order will not pass court scrutiny.
5. Appearance that does not conform to rudiments of decency may be regulated.
6. Dress that is considered vulgar or that mocks others on the basis of race, gender, religion, color, or national origin may be prohibited.

Health and Safety Issues

Schools are vested with broad and implied powers designed to protect the health, safety, and welfare of students. Therefore, school officials may promulgate reasonable rules and regulations necessary to address health and safety concerns of students. Thus, situations involving certain types of dress that pose a threat to the safety and well-being of students may be regulated. For example, if students are wearing excessively long hair in vocational shop classes or other laboratory situations that pose a threat to their safety, school officials may take appropriate steps to regulate hair length. Similarly, if fancy jewelry is worn that poses a potential threat to safety when students are engaged in shop, activity-oriented classes, or physical education classes, similar measures may be taken to regulate the type of jewelry worn.

Students may be required to wash long hair, for hygienic purposes. For example, if certain types of fungus are associated with dirty, long hair, a student may be required to take appropriate steps to rectify the problem. Other hygienic issues related to dress where there is clear evidence that a problem exists may be addressed by school officials. In every case, efforts should be made to ensure that the dignity and personal rights of students are protected. If there is evidence that reasonable dress codes are developed using these standards, the courts are less inclined to intervene, particularly when representatives of the community have been included in the development of dress codes.

Controversial Slogans

Slogans worn on T-shirts, caps, and other items that are in direct conflict with the school's stated mission may be regulated. Those expressions that violate standards of common decency and contain vulgar, lewd, and otherwise obscene gestures also may be regulated. In instances where disruption occurs or where there is a reasonable forecast that disruption might occur, school officials may take appropriate action to rectify the situation. These actions are particularly relevant when the content of such expressions mocks others based on race, gender, color, religion, language, sexual orientation, or national origin.

A leading case emerged in the U.S. District Court in Massachusetts. Two minor high school students in *Pyle v. The South Hadley School Committee* sued the school committee, challenging a school policy that prohibited them from wearing on school premises either of two T-shirts, one offering a suggestive sexual slogan and the other bearing slang references to male genitals. They sought injunctive relief, alleging that their First Amendment rights were violated with respect to freedom of expression. They further declared that T-shirts are not horribly offensive when compared to other influences in society.

Female students had frequently commented to their English teachers about the sexual harassment environment in the school and how a lack of sensitivity to harassment adversely affected their ability to learn. One T-shirt bore the following: "Coed Naked Band" and "Do It To The Rhythm." The other included the slogan, "See Dick Drink, See Dick Die, Don't Be A Dick." These slogans were deemed to be suggestive and vulgar, based on the school committee's findings. Further, these statements interfered with the school's mission and were demeaning to women. The district court upheld school official's position, based on the findings of the committee.[9]

In short, banning controversial slogans will generally be upheld if there is sufficient evidence of disruption or the message is offensive to others based on race, gender, color, religion, or national origin. As in this case, the school should have policies that address these issues as well as an impartial committee to review these incidents on a case-by-case basis.

SEARCH AND SEIZURE

The Fourth Amendment to the U.S. Constitution provides protection of all citizens against unreasonable search and seizure. This amendment provides, in part, that "the right of people to be secure in their persons, houses, papers and effects against unreasonable searches and seizures, shall not be violated, and no warrants shall be issued, but upon probable cause."

Since students enjoy many of the same constitutional rights as adults, they are granted protection against unreasonable search and seizure. The major challenge facing school officials involves the task of delicately balancing a student's individual right to Fourth Amendment protection against their duty to provide a safe and secure environment for all students.

To search or not to search a pupil's locker, desk, purse, and automobile on school premises presents a perplexing problem for educators. Basic to this issue is the question of precisely what constitutes a *reasonable search*. The reasonableness of the search becomes the critical issue in cases where students claim personal violations based on illegal searches.

Most authorities point out the distinction between searches of a student's person and searches that involve lockers and desks. The major distinction, of course, is that lockers and desks are considered to be school property. Consequently, school officials are provided greater latitude in searching lockers and desks than they are a student's person.

The underlying command of the Fourth Amendment is that searches and seizures be deemed reasonable. Thus, if students are to be searched, the search must be reasonable. What, then, constitutes a reasonable search? A reasonable search is one that clearly does not violate the constitutional rights of students. What is reasonable will depend on the context within which a search takes place.

Reasonable Suspicion

School officials need only reasonable suspicion to initiate a search. This standard is less rigorous than the requirement of probable cause. What exactly constitutes reasonable suspicion? *Reasonable suspicion* is based on information received from students or teachers that is considered reliable by school officials. As long as the informant is known rather than anonymous and the information provided seems credible, courts will generally find little difficulty supporting administrative actions based on reasonable grounds.[10, 11, 12, 13]

Consequently, school officials may search if reasonable suspicion is established as the primary basis for the search. The courts have declared that *in loco parentis* cannot stand alone without reasonable suspicion. One court stated: "A school teacher, to a limited extent at least, stands *in loco parentis* to pupils under her charge. The *in loco parentis* doctrine is so compelling in light of public necessity and as a social concept antedating the Fourth Amendment, that any action including a search taken thereunder upon reasonable suspicion should be accepted as necessary and reasonable."[14]

From the courts' view, reasonable suspicion is the key ingredient in legalizing school searches. When an educator is operating under reasonable suspicion in school-related searches, no constitutional violation is in question. This issue was settled in the landmark *New Jersey v. T.L.O.* case in 1985, when the Supreme Court reaffirmed that searches conducted by school authorities are indeed subject to standards of the Fourth Amendment; however, the warrant requirement in particular is unsuited to the school environment. According to the high court, requiring a teacher to obtain a warrant before searching a child suspected of an infraction of school rules would unduly interfere with the maintenance of the swift, informal disciplinary procedures needed in the schools. This is the only case involving school searches in which the U.S. Supreme Court has made a ruling.

On March 7, 1980, a teacher at Piscataway High School discovered two girls smoking in a lavatory. One of the two girls was the respondent T.L.O., who at that time was a 14-year-old high school freshman. Because smoking in the lavatory was a violation of a school rule, the teacher took the two girls to the principal's office, where they met with Assistant Vice Principal Theodore Choplick. In response to questioning by Mr. Choplick, T.L.O.'s companion admitted that she had violated the rule. T.L.O., however, denied that she had been smoking in the lavatory and claimed that she did not smoke at all.

Mr. Choplick asked T.L.O. to come into his private office and demanded to see her purse. Opening the purse, he found a pack of cigarettes, which he removed from the purse and held before T.L.O. as he accused her of having lied to him. As he reached into the purse for the cigarettes, Mr. Choplick also noticed a package of cigarette rolling paper. In his experience, possession of rolling paper by high school students was closely associated with the use of marijuana. Suspecting that a closer examination of the purse might yield further evidence of drug use, Mr. Choplick proceeded to search the purse thoroughly. The search revealed a small amount of marijuana, a pipe, a number of empty plastic bags, a substantial quantity of money in one-dollar bills, an index card that appeared to be a list of students who owed T.L.O. money, and two letters that implicated T.L.O. in marijuana dealing.

The student's parents moved to have the evidence suppressed, claiming that the search was unlawful due to the absence of a search warrant. The Supreme Court, in upholding the school administrator, did not require that the search be based on the higher standard of "probable cause" necessary for obtaining a search warrant, reasoning that to do so "would unduly interfere with the maintenance of the swift and informal disciplinary procedures needed in the schools." Thus, the court struck a balance between the pupil's "legitimate expectations of privacy" and the need of the school to preserve a proper learning environment.

A search of a student by a teacher or school official must be both "justified at its inception" and "reasonably related in scope to the circumstances which justified the interference in the first place." School officials are, accordingly, neither vested with the broad authority of a parent, nor subject to the restrictions of police in searching students to enforce school policies and discipline. In sum, school officials should have reasonable grounds to believe a search of a particular student is necessary to provide pertinent proof that the student has violated a particular policy, rule, or law. Further, the scope of the search must be limited to the incident at hand. In other words, a sweep search of all students in hope of turning up evidence of contraband or violation of rules would be illegal. Neither may a particular student be searched because he or she created a reasonable suspicion of violation of some unparticular rule. Nor could any student be searched because of a particular violation by an unknown person. There should be *individualized* suspicion, referring to both the individual student and the individual violation.[15]

Student Desks

Student desks are subject to search if school officials meet the standard of reasonableness. Desks should never be searched based on a mere "hunch"; rather, reliable information must lead school officials to believe that school rules have been violated or that the health or safety of students is threatened. In all cases, searches should be based on clearly written policies that inform students that desks are subject to search if reasonable suspicion is established. School policies should spell out the conditions and circumstances under which desk searches will occur. Again, wider discretion is provided school officials in searches involving school property.

Student Lockers

School officials must meet the same standard of reasonableness here as previously mentioned regarding the search of student desks. Because student lockers provide privacy for students, oftentimes there is a greater tendency to expect students to harbor items that violate school rules or items that involve criminal activity. *This view alone does not justify an indiscriminate search.* Again, students should be informed that lockers will be searched if reasonable suspicion is established to justify a need to search. If a search of a student's locker becomes necessary, the student and at least one other school official should be present to ensure that proper procedures are followed. The student affected should open the locker in the presence of school officials. This student may also request the presence of another student if he or she wishes. In no cases except extreme emergencies, such as a bomb threat, should an indiscriminate search be initiated. Barring an emergency, indiscriminate searches of students' lockers are *indefensible* and *illegal.*

Book Bags

Searches involving book bags tend to be extremely complex, due to the intrusive nature of the search itself. A more extensive and intrusive search will likely require stronger evidence to establish reasonable suspicion. At least one court has stated that "we are also of the view that as the intrusiveness of the search intensifies, the standard of Fourth Amendment reasonableness approaches probable cause, even in the school context."[16]

In a New Jersey case, *Desilets v. Clearview Regional Board of Education,* involving book bag searches of students engaged in a field trip, the Superior Court of New Jersey held that the search of students' hand luggage was justified under the Fourth Amendment, based on a legitimate interest of school administrators and teachers in preventing students from taking contraband on field trips. This case arose when the parents of a junior high school student sued the board, superintendent, and principal, alleging that search of their child's book bag before he boarded the bus violated his Fourth Amendment rights. Brian was a tenth-grader participating in a voluntary field trip. Permission slips were sent to parents, indicating that hand luggage would be searched based on board policy. Brian's mother testified that she read the slip before signing it. Based on prior knowledge of the search, students had an opportunity to remove any items, while not illegal, but personal to the student.

The court held for the school board by stating that the search was justified at its inception by the unique burden placed on school personnel in the field trip context and that the search limited to hand luggage was reasonably related to the school's duty to provide discipline, supervision, and control.[17] This decision reflects a more liberal view by the court regarding search but it should not be viewed as a license to conduct unwarranted and more intrusive searches.

Automobiles

School officials may search student automobiles parked on school property if the standards of reasonable suspicion are met. Students and parents should be informed by school or district policy that automobiles are subject to reasonable search if there is a legitimate basis for doing so. For example, if a school official receives information from a reliable source who indicates that a student's automobile contains illegal items in violation of school rules, the official may request that the automobile be searched. Similar procedures should be followed as suggested earlier in the search of student lockers—that is, having the student and another witness available during the actual search.

If the student's automobile is parked on nonschool property, *probable cause* must be established, involving law enforcement officials who are required to present a warrant prior to the initiation of a search. Again, parents should be informed of the impending search so as to allow them the opportunity to initiate any steps they deem necessary in this situation. If illegal items such as drugs or weapons are discovered, they are admissible in a court of law. In one compelling case involving search of a student's automobile for drugs, the assistant principal observed that the student had glassy eyes, a flushed face, slurred speech, the smell of alcohol, and an unsteady gait. These observations formed the basis to search the student's automobile under the concept of reasonable suspicion. The court found ample evidence to support reasonable suspicion.[18]

Personal Searches

Personal searches are strongly discouraged unless there is overwhelming evidence to support the need for the search. Even then, there should be a sense of urgency based on a belief that the student has in his or her possession some dangerous item that could pose a serious threat to the health and safety of the student or others in the school. Whether a search of this nature is considered reasonable will be based on the individual facts surrounding the case. The courts will generally establish the standard based on the facts presented to determine reasonableness. In doing so, they will attempt to balance the student's privacy rights against the interest of school officials to conduct the search.

Personal searches of an intrusive nature should be avoided except under extremely serious circumstances. The more intrusive the search, the closer it triggers the need for probable cause. Students should be protected from intrusive body cavity searches if at all possible. When facts reveal that a personal search is necessary, every precaution should be taken to conduct the search in a private setting with persons of the same gender present. The student should be afforded the greatest amount of protection to privacy as possible under the circumstances. If the search involves removal of the student's garment, the student should be allowed to remove, in privacy, any garments or items of clothing the search warrants. He or she should be provided alternative clothing during the search process.

Only school personnel of the same gender should be involved in this type of search, and extreme caution should be taken to ensure, as much as possible, that the student is not demeaned or embarrassed during this process. Unless there is an extreme sense of urgency, it might be advisable to isolate the student, keeping him or her under observation, and consult with the student's parents or legal guardian. Under any circumstances, parents should be advised of the type of search conducted, the evidence that gave rise to the need to conduct the search, specifically who was involved in conducting the search, and expressly what was discovered during the search process. Personal searches should be considered searches of *last resort* and should be handled based on school or district policy. Searches of this nature should never be calculated to cause embarrassment or mental distress for the student.

For example, when money was missing from a classroom in Alabama, a teacher searched the books of two students and subsequently required the students to remove their shoes. The court held that the fact that both students were in the room alone when the money disappeared was sufficient to give rise to reasonable suspicion, which was necessary to conduct the limited search.[19]

A more intrusive search will require *significant evidence to establish reasonable suspicion and a justification to conduct the search.* When an assistant principal observed a boy with an odd bulge in his pocket, the principal searched and found a small calculator case and marijuana. The court held that the mere notice of a bulge did not form a sufficient basis to establish reasonable suspicion. Reasonable suspicion must be based on clearly articulated facts from which rational inferences can be drawn in order to reach the conclusion of reasonable suspicion. The court noted that without having prior knowledge of the student's involvement with drugs, the mere observation of a bulging calculator was insufficient to warrant the need to search.[20]

Strip Searches

Strip searches should be avoided except under extreme circumstances involving the health and safety of other students. Historically, courts have not viewed strip searches by school officials very favorably because they are considered the most intrusive forms of all searches. There should be a strong sense of urgency accompanying a strip search that involves an immediate threat to health, safety, and order in the school. Remember, as one court previously stated, "We are of the view that as the intrusiveness intensifies, the standard of the Fourth Amendment reasonableness approaches probable cause even in the school context."[21] Thus, when a teacher conducts a highly intrusive invasion, such as strip search, it is reasonable to approach the probable cause requirement.

Although probable cause should be closely linked with strip searches, courts in recent years seem more inclined to allow strip searches in certain situations. Among these are a reasonable suspicion that the student is in possession of something that is illegal, against school regulations, or harmful to the health and safety of other students.

An example of the lack of sufficient information to justify a strip search is found in *Cales v. Howell Public School,* in which a female student was forced to remove her jeans and submit to a visual inspection of her brassiere. The court ruled that the fact that the student had ducked behind a car and had given a school security guard a false name was insufficient to establish reasonable suspicion. The court held that without further specific information, the school had no more reason to believe that the girl was hiding drugs than to believe that she was skipping class, stealing hub caps, or anything else illegal.[22]

In one of the more revealing cases involving strip search, the court held for school officials. In *Cornfield by Lewis v. School District No. 230,* a student who was subjected to a strip search brought action against the school district, teachers, and dean, alleging violation of his constitutional rights. The lower court granted summary judgment in favor of the teacher and dean. The student appealed. The Court of Appeals for the Seventh Circuit held that the strip search was reasonable under the Fourth Amendment.

This case arose when Brian, a student enrolled in a behavior disorder program at the high school, was observed outside the building, in violation of school rules. Further, he was reported by an aide and corroborated by another teacher to have been well endowed by virtue of an unusual bulge in his crotch area.

Brian was boarding the bus when he was taken aside by the teachers and the dean, who believed that the bulge was drugs. When asked to accompany them to the office, Brian became agitated and yelled obscenities. Permission was sought from Brian's mother to conduct the search. The parent refused to grant permission. The search was, in fact, conducted in the locker room by requesting that Brian strip and put on a gym uniform. Visual inspection took place but no body cavity search occurred. No drugs were found.

The court held that "privacy rights of students versus the need of the school to maintain order does not require strict adherence to probable cause standards." However, a nude search by an official of the opposite sex would violate the standard of excessive intrusion. The court held for the school district.[23] This case represents a rare exception to the traditional views held by the courts. School officials should *not* view this case as a license to arbitrarily initiate a strip search.

Involvement of Law Enforcement Officials

When law enforcement officials enter the school to conduct a search, the search must be preceded by a *warrant*. If a warrant is issued, strong evidence involving probable cause should be established. Reasonable suspicion would not apply in a search involving law enforcement officers unless officers were assisting school officials with disciplinary action. In such a case, reasonable suspicion will likely be adequate. Typically, when law enforcement officers are involved in a school search, there are facts and circumstances based on trustworthy information that are sufficient in themselves to warrant a person of reasonable caution to believe that some type of illegal activity or crime has been committed.

Before police officers initiate a search of a student, parents or legal guardians should be contacted immediately by school officials and informed of the situation. Parents may wish to be present during the search process. In any case, parents should always be informed prior to any action taken by law enforcement officials. When parents cannot be reached, there should be documented evidence verifying that a bona fide effort was made to reach them. Documentation should include, at a minimum, time of day, the number(s) called, and witnesses to verify that an effort was made to reach the parents.

If parents cannot be reached or elect not to be present during the search, a school official should accompany the officer(s) and serve as a witness during this process. Details of this activity should be communicated to parents immediately so that they are knowledgeable of the circumstances involving the search and the resulting action taken by law enforcement officials based on the search. Students and their parents have consistently challenged searches by police officers on school property.

In a recent case involving search, a group of high school students brought action through their parents against the city of Slidell, Louisiana and its police officers, alleging a Fourth Amendment violation based on an incident in which students were called out of class for questioning about a rumored after-school fight. The district court dismissed the claim against the city but found that the officers violated students' Fourth Amendment rights. The students were awarded nominal damages but the district court refused to award attorney fees. The officers and students appealed. The Court of Appeals held that detention of students for questioning did not violate their Fourth Amendment rights.[24]

In another case involving search, action was brought on behalf of high school students against the school board, school officials, the sheriff, and a law enforcement officer alleging violations of the students' Fourth Amendment rights with respect to search and seizure of their persons during a drug sweep of the school. On the defendants' motions for summary judgment, the district court held that a reasonable suspicion standard rather than a probable cause standard applied to the assessment of the legality of the student search under the Fourth Amendment and that a strip search of a student who was in the vicinity where drugs were found was reasonable under the Fourth Amendment. Even if the strip search was unreasonable, individual defendants were entitled to qualified immunity from the student's Fourth Amendment claim. The district court held that the officer's search of the student was reasonable. The sheriff could not be held liable under § 1983 for an alleged illegal search of the student on the basis that he failed to adequately train and supervise his officers. A strip search of a student in the school's parking lot was based on individualized suspicion. Although the search was not reasonably related to the objects of the search and was excessively intrusive, school officials and the school board cannot be held liable for officers' illegal search of student in a parking lot. Also, the sheriff had no duty, under the

Fourth Amendment, to intervene in an illegal search of a student in the parking lot. The officers did not use excessive force when they allegedly choked a student in the parking lot to prevent him from swallowing evidence and/or a potentially harmful substance. The sheriff was entitled to qualified immunity from the student's excessive force claims based on failure to intervene. The school district's motion for summary judgment was granted.[25]

In another case, students who were seized, handcuffed, transported, and detained at a municipal building in response to a threatening letter found on school premises brought suit against the school district and the city alleging deprivation of their Fourth and Fourteenth Amendment rights. Defendants moved to dismiss for failure to state a claim of action. The district court held that students' Fourth Amendment protections against unreasonable search and seizure were not violated, given the magnitude of the potential threat posed by the letter. This fact, coupled with school authorities' apparent belief that the students were associated with the suspected letter writer because they congregated in the same area of the school, was sufficient to justify the action taken by the school district.[26]

Use of Canines

The use of canines by school officials has received mixed reviews by the courts. The courts appear to be almost evenly divided on this issue. However, with the growing incidence of drugs and violence in schools, the courts may eventually reach some level of consensus regarding this issue.

The Seventh Circuit Court in *Doe v. Renfrow* held in a questionable decision that school officials stood *in loco parentis* and had the right to use dogs to seek out drugs. In this particular case, school officials, in cooperation with local police, detained 2,700 junior and senior high school students in their classrooms while canines walked through classroom aisles and sniffed students. When the dogs alerted their trainers to a student, that particular student was searched. Fifty students were searched. One student was subjected to a strip search after the initial search produced no drugs. The court held that school officials had a reasonable basis for believing that students had drugs in their possession when the canines led them to a particular student.[27]

In a similar ruling, the Tenth Circuit Court of Appeals in *Zamoro v. Pomeroy* held for the school in its use of dogs in exploratory sniffing of lockers. The court noted that the school gave notice at the beginning of the school year that lockers may be periodically inspected and furthermore that lockers were jointly possessed by both students and the school. Since school officials are charged with the responsibility to maintain a safe and orderly school environment, it was necessary for them to inspect lockers even though a slight Fourth Amendment infringement was involved.[28]

In a different ruling, the Federal District Court in *Jones v. Latexo Independent School District* held that the use of dogs was too intrusive in the absence of individual suspicion. In this case, dogs were used to sniff both students and automobiles. Since students did not have access to their cars during the school day, school officials' interest in using dogs to sniff cars was minimal and unreasonable.[29]

In a related case, *Horton v. Goose Creek Independent School District,* the court held that the use of canines to sniff lockers and cars did not constitute a search. Further, school officials may employ canines to search students if there is reasonable cause, but intrusion on the dignity and personal security that accompanies this type of search cannot be justified by the need to prevent alcohol and drug abuse when there is no individualized suspicion.

Therefore, such a search is unconstitutional.[30] This court seems to support the use of canines, if there is a legitimate basis to do so, but ruled that such measures cannot be justified in the absence of individualized suspicion involving canines. In short, mass searches are not permitted.

In a more recent case, a challenge to a canine search arose when a former high school student brought § 1983 action against the school district, school officials, and law enforcement officers, alleging that a dog sniff at school violated his Fourth Amendment right to be free from unreasonable search and seizure. The U.S. District Court for the Eastern District of California entered summary judgment for the school district. The student appealed. The court of appeals held that the plaintiff lacked the standing to seek injunctive relief. The student also failed to support official capacity claims against defendants, which included an inability to establish that a dog sniff of high school students was a Fourth Amendment search and that a random and suspicionless dog sniff search of a student was unreasonable under the circumstances. The plaintiff was a former high school student. Since he was no longer a student at high school or at any other school in the school district subsequent to the time of dog sniffing incident, he was not supported by the court. Summary judgment was granted to the school district.[31]

In a related canine case, an expelled high school student filed a suit against various school defendants alleging that his constitutional rights had been violated. The basis for this challenge involved a search of his truck that revealed the presence of a knife on school grounds, resulting in his expulsion. The student alleged that his substantive rights were violated. In determining the reasonableness of the search, the court made a two-fold inquiry: first, whether the search was justified at its inception and second, whether it was reasonably related in scope to the circumstances that justified the search in the first place. The court held that where a school official has reasonable grounds to believe a search will disclose evidence that a student has violated a school rule, the initiation of a search is justified. The court further held that a search of the student's truck was permissible after a canine duly trained and certified in exploratory sniffing alerted officials to the truck. The alert, while not a search, gave school officials reasonable grounds to suspect that a search of the truck would uncover evidence of a rule violation. The court held for the district.[32]

■ ■ ■ ■ ■ ▬▬▬▬▬▬▬▬▬▬▬▬▬▬▬▬▬▬▬▬▬▬▬▬▬▬▬▬▬▬▬▬▬▬▬▬

ADMINISTRATIVE GUIDE

SEARCH AND SEIZURE

1. A student's freedom from unreasonable search should be carefully balanced against the need for school officials to maintain order, maintain discipline, and protect the health, safety, and welfare of all students.
2. Factors such as the need for the search, the student's age, history, and record of behavior, the gravity of the problem, and the need for an immediate search should be considered before initiating a search.
3. A school search should be based on reasonable grounds, for believing that something contrary to school rules or significantly detrimental to the school and its students will be produced by the search.
4. The information leading to school searches should be independent of law enforcement officials. Searches involving law enforcement officials must be accompanied by probable cause and a search warrant.

■ ■ ■ ■ ■ ▬▬▬▬▬▬▬▬▬▬▬▬▬▬▬▬▬▬▬▬▬▬▬▬▬▬▬▬▬▬▬▬▬▬▬▬▬▬

ADMINISTRATIVE GUIDE (*continued*)

5. Although the primary purpose for the search should be to secure evidence of student misconduct for school disciplinary purposes, it may be contemplated under certain circumstances that criminal evidence may be made available to law enforcement officials.
6. Strip searches should be avoided except where imminent danger exists. Such searches can be justified only in cases of extreme emergency where there is an immediate threat to the health and safety of students and school personnel. In such cases, school authorities should be certain that their actions are fully justified with convincing information to support this more intrusive search.
7. School personnel should conduct the search in a private setting. At best, a search is a demoralizing experience; care should be taken to minimize embarrassment to the student as much as possible.
8. The magnitude of the offense, the extent of the intrusiveness, the nature of the evidence, and the background of the student involved should be considered before a search is initiated.
9. A "pat-down" search of a student, if justified, should be conducted by a school official of the same sex and with an adult witness of the same sex present, if possible. Personal searches conducted by persons of the opposite sex can be very dangerous.
10. Arbitrary searches or mass shakedowns cannot be justified as reasonable and are illegal.
11. The use of canines should be avoided unless there is sufficient evidence to justify the need to employ these methods. Serious incidents that pose an imminent threat to students' safety should form the basis for such action.

"NO PASS, NO PLAY" RULE

A number of school boards across the nation have implemented policies that bar student athletes from participating in competitive athletics unless they earn a certain number of course credits during a designated period of time. The intent of these policies is to emphasize academics over athletics and to encourage students to concentrate on their studies. Since most athletes enjoy participating in competitive athletics, these policies were viewed by school boards as excellent incentives for athletes to maintain good grades and remain in school.

School boards in California and Texas were among the leaders in implementing "no pass, no play" policies. Since their implementation, these policies have received mixed reviews. Many students who have struggled to earn course credit and lost their eligibility have dropped out of school. Consequently, many school boards are reexamining their policies with a view on easing standards and reducing the length of time students remain ineligible. Other districts have implemented tutorial programs and study halls for ineligible students as well as second-chance opportunities. Most "no pass, no play" policies require that eligible students earn and maintain a grade-point average of 2.0 to participate in competitive athletics. There are written procedures that serve as checks and balances to ensure that the student is meeting academic requirements. School board policies vary in their degree of restrictiveness. In some instances, student athletes must present weekly reports signed by each teacher indicating that the student is making satisfactory progress in each class. If the student is not making satisfactory progress, the teacher indicates where the deficiencies are and what the student has to do to remove the deficiency. The student is not allowed to participate until the deficiency is removed.

"No pass, no play" affects other areas aside from competitive athletics, such as marching band, debate teams, pom-pom squads, and other extracurricular activities. Although "no pass, no play" policies have received mixed reviews, the perceived advantages and disadvantages of such policies are summarized as follows:

ADVANTAGES	DISADVANTAGES
1. Students will be more inclined to attend class.	1. Students who experience academic difficulty may drop out of school when eligibility is lost.
2. Students will assume greater responsibility for academic achievement in school.	2. Good students sometime struggle in difficult courses.
3. Students will take school work more seriously.	3. Some students will opt to take less demanding classes.
4. Parents will become more involved in academic progress of their children.	4. If no extra support is provided for failing students, they may drop out of school.
5. Students will remain in school and graduate with a diploma.	5. Too much of the teacher's time is spent on issuing weekly reports on student progress.
6. Academics are stressed over extracurricular activities.	6. The program has not proven to be effective.

ADMINISTRATIVE GUIDE

NO PASS, NO PLAY

1. Involve parents and students in the development of "no pass, no play" policies.
2. Make certain that policies are fair, reasonable, and legally defensible.
3. Provide strong remedial support for students who experience academic difficulty in classes.
4. Closely monitor policy implementation and maintain the necessary flexibility to modify the policy as the need arises.

USE OF PAGERS AND CELLULAR PHONES

The use of pagers and cellular phones by public school students has increased in frequency and popularity in recent years. Students find these devices to be affordable and convenient sources of communication both on and off school premises. Although no legal challenge has reached the courts regarding the school district's authority to restrict or prohibit their use, the courts would likely support school officials' decision to do so unless there is evidence that a First Amendment right is in jeopardy, which is unlikely.

It is well established that school officials may prohibit any practice that creates material or substantial disruption to the educational process. School districts may minimize legal challenges where there is evidence that the use of pagers and cellular phones creates disruption or that they are used for improper purposes. School officials are given the authority to maintain a safe and orderly environment to facilitate teaching and learning. Consequently, they may prohibit any practice that affects proper order and decorum, since learning cannot occur in a disruptive environment. When school officials provide evidence that pagers and cellular phones create a disruptive influence in the school and are abused by students, they will likely succeed in prohibiting student possession of these devices on school premises. This prohibition will not likely offend the personal rights of students.

However, school boards, through district policy, may allow special exceptions in cases where such devices are needed for medical emergencies involving students with a chronic illness or other special circumstances that warrant their use. School officials should examine the need for these devices on a case-by-case basis and demonstrate flexibility in allowing students to use them under special and justifiable circumstances. Such exceptions should be reflected by school district policy, requiring proper documentation by parents or medical experts that these devices are necessary and essential under certain conditions.

If pagers and cellular phones are prohibited by policy, all allowable exceptions should be filed and readily available should school officials need to retrieve them if challenged by parents who may raise questions regarding preferential treatment. In the absence of compelling evidence that pagers and cellular phones are needed by students, school officials will likely succeed without court intervention, so long as they consistently adhere to their own policies and demonstrate no evidence of disparate treatment among students regarding permission to use these devices. A number of states has currently formulated policies prohibiting the use of pagers and cellular phones in public schools and stated expected consequences for policy violators and exceptions granted for special use. School officials, however, appear to be moving toward relaxing policies that prohibit the use of cellular phones.

ADMINISTRATIVE GUIDE

PAGERS AND CELLULAR PHONES

1. Do not arbitrarily ban the use of pagers and cellular phones by students unless there is sufficient evidence of disruption or improper use.
2. If permitted, develop specific guidelines governing the conditions under which these devices may be used.
3. If not permitted for general use, allow for exceptional cases involving medical emergencies or other special circumstances that warrant the use of these devices.
4. Policies or guidelines should always be guided by a sense of fairness and due consideration for the unique and personal needs of students.

CORPORAL PUNISHMENT

Corporal punishment is a highly controversial topic in the United States today. Perhaps no other legal issue in education has drawn as much criticism as the use of physical punishment in public schools. Those who support corporal punishment contend that it will cause changes in student behavior, teaching students self-discipline and respect for authority. Those who oppose corporal punishment view it as a legalized form of child abuse, which conveys to students that violence is an acceptable method of resolving problems or disagreements. Irrespective of the views supporting or opposing corporal punishment, the courts still view corporal punishment as an acceptable form of discipline when administered in a reasonable manner. While corporal punishment is considered to be an acceptable form of discipline by the courts, school personnel increasingly are facing charges of assault and battery, prosecution, and even termination of employment for abusive acts against students.

Corporal punishment usually involves the use of physical contact for disciplinary purposes. As a disciplinary tool, this type of discipline is not uncommon within school systems in the United States. In fact, 23 states currently allow corporal punishment to be used as a means of discipline. Interestingly, the courts, under the concept of *in loco parentis,* have sanctioned reasonable corporal punishment by school personnel, but no laws except those in one state protect school personnel who administer it.*

Every industrialized country in the world—except the United States, Canada, and one state in Australia—now prohibits school corporal punishment. Table 3.1 depicts a sample of the trend toward the elimination of corporal punishment in schools, dating as far back as the 1700s. Figure 3.1 shows those states in the United States that have banned corporal punishment. Table 3.2 depicts the top ten states, based on the percentage of students struck by educators, that currently administer corporal punishment. As can be seen, southern states have the highest percentage of students receiving corporal punishment over those states in other regions of the country. However, the overall number of students struck each year has declined during the past 20 years, with the most dramatic decline occurring in 1997–1998, where school paddlings dropped by 27 percent from the year before, as educators have sought other methods of disciplining students in public schools.

The question of the constitutionality of corporal punishment was reaffirmed in the landmark case, *Ingraham v. Wright,* where the U.S. Supreme Court ruled that even severe corporal punishment may not violate the Eighth Amendment prohibition of cruel and unusual punishment. This case arose when Ingraham and another student from the Dade County, Florida, public schools filed suit after they had been subjected to paddling. State law allowed corporal punishment if it was not "degrading or unduly severe" and if it was done after consultation with the principal or other teacher in charge of the school. Paddling was considered a less drastic form of punishment than suspension. For violating a teacher's instructions, Ingraham had received 20 licks while he was held over a table in the principal's office. He required medical attention and missed school for several days.

Because this paddling was probably "unduly severe," the high court hearing the evidence and appeals found no constitutional violation. According to Justice Powell, "The schoolchild has little need for the protection of the Eighth Amendment." It is more appropriately applied in the case of the criminally convicted and thereby involuntarily confined. A student is always free to leave the premises and return home at the end of the day. "The child brings with him the support of family and friends and is rarely apart from teachers and other pupils who may witness and protest any instances of mistreatment."[33]

---

*The Alabama legislature passed a teacher immunity bill, Act #95-53, that provides immunity for teachers to use corporal punishment or otherwise maintain order when exercising such authority within their local boards.

While the court declined to declare corporal punishment as used in the context of public schools to be a violation of the cruel and unusual proscription or due process under federal law it did state that paddling students deprived them of liberty interests protected by the Constitution. Although not required by law, but in the spirit of fairness, *rudimentary due process* should be applied before corporal punishment is administered. However, there is no requirement that there be a formidable load placed on school officials in administering corporal punishment. Thus, state and local school districts are left to decide for themselves what is required. When corporal punishment is approved by state law or local rules, only a brief explanation of the wrong charged and an opportunity to hear the student's comments are probably all that are necessary to comply with due process requirements prior to paddling a student. Again, a prudent policy would require that an adult witness be present and that parents' wishes concerning this form of punishment be considered, if not respected.

In addressing the issue, the U.S. Supreme Court referred to traditional common law.

TABLE 3.1 Facts About Corporal Punishment Worldwide
Worldwide Bans on Corporal Punishment

Every industrialized country in the world now prohibits school corporal punishment, except the United States, Canada, and one state in Australia. The following list shows a sample of the trend toward the elimination of corporal punishment in schools, dating back to the 1700s.

YEAR	COUNTRY	YEAR	COUNTRY
1783	Poland	1970	Germany
1820	Netherlands	1970	Switzerland
1845	Luxembourg	1982	Ireland
1860	Italy	1983	Greece
1867	Belgium	1986	United Kingdom**
1870	Austria	1990	New Zealand
1881	France	1990	Namibia
1890	Finland	1996	South Africa
1900	Japan	1998	England*
1917	Russia	1998	American Samoa
1923	Turkey	1999	Zimbabwe
1936	Norway	2000	Zambia
1949	China	2000	Thailand
1950	Portugal	2000	Trinidad and Tobago
1958	Sweden	2001	Kenya
1967	Denmark	2002	Fiji
1967	Cyprus		

*This ban solidifies a ban imposed in 1986, extending the ban to *all* private schools.

**Includes England, Scotland, Wales, and Northern Ireland.

Source: U.S. Department of Education, Office for Civil Rights, 2000 Elementary and Secondary School Civil Rights Compliance Report. Compiled by the National Coalition to Abolish Corporal Punishment in Schools: Columbus, Ohio: 614/221-8829. http://www.stophitting.com

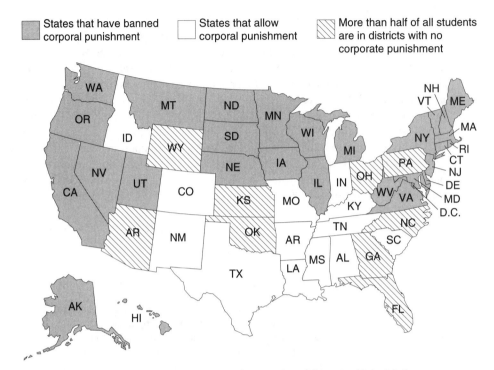

These 27 states have now banned corporal punishment, with legislation underway in many more:

Alaska	Michigan	Oregon
California	Minnesota	Rhode Island**
Connecticut	Montana	South Dakota***
Hawaii	Nebraska	Utah*
Illinois	Nevada	Vermont
Iowa	New Hampshire*	Virginia
Maine	New Jersey	Washington
Maryland	New York*	West Virginia
Massachusetts	North Dakota	Wisconsin

* Banned by state regulation
** Banned by every school board in the state
*** Banned by law rescinding authorization to use

FIGURE 3.1   U.S. States Banning Corporal Punishment

Source: U.S. Department of Education, Office for Civil Rights, 1998 Elementary and Secondary School Civil Rights Compliance Report. State and national totals are statistical projections made by the U.S. Department of Education. Compiled by the National Coalition to Abolish Corporal Punishment in Schools, Columbus, Ohio 614/221-8829.

The use of corporal punishment in this country as a means of disciplining schoolchildren dates back to the colonial period. It has survived the transformation of primary and secondary education from the colonials' reliance on optional private arrangements to our present system of compulsory education and dependence on public schools. Despite the general abandonment of corporal punishment as a means of punishing criminal offenders, the practice continues to play a role in the public education of schoolchildren in most parts

TABLE 3.2   Corporal Punishment in U.S. Public Schools 1999–2000 School Year: Data released February, 2003

In the United States as a whole, **342,038** students were subjected to corporal punishment. This is a drop of 7 percent from the previous survey two years earlier [taking enrollment increases into account], continuing a steady trend. Total U.S. public school enrollment was 46,306,355 students in 1999–2000. Twenty-seven states and the District of Columbia now have prohibited all corporal punishment in public schools. Data for the remaining 23 states are listed below.

STATE	NUMBER OF STUDENTS HIT	PERCENT OF TOTAL STUDENTS
Alabama	39,197	5.4
Arizona	632	< 0.1
Arkansas	40,437	9.1
Colorado	260	< 0.1
Delaware	65	0.1
Florida	11,405	0.5
Georgia	25,189	1.8
Idaho	23	< 0.1
Indiana	2,221	0.2
Kansas	99	< 0.1
Kentucky	2,797	0.4
Louisiana	18,672	2.6
Mississippi	48,627	9.8
Missouri	9,223	1.0
New Mexico	2,205	0.7
North Carolina	5,717	0.5
Ohio	1,085	0.1
Oklahoma	17,764	2.9
Pennsylvania	407	< 0.1
South Carolina	3,631	0.5
Tennessee	38,373	4.2
Texas	73,994	1.9
Wyoming	8	< 0.1
U.S. Total	**342,038**	**0.7**

Source: U.S. Department of Education, Office for Civil Rights, 2000 Elementary and Secondary School Civil Rights Compliance Report. Compiled by the National Coalition to Abolish Corporal Punishment in Schools: Columbus, Ohio: 614/221-8829. http://www.stophitting.com

of the country. Professional and public opinion is sharply divided on the practice, and has been for more than a century. Yet we can discern no trend toward its elimination. The Eighth Amendment does not apply to the administration of discipline through corporal punishment to public school teachers and administrators.[34]

In spite of this ruling, federal courts have subsequently ruled that excessive corporal punishment violates the substantive due process clause of the Fourteenth Amendment. The courts, however, have fallen short of determining exactly when corporal punishment becomes excessive.

Although the *Ingraham* case upholds the legality of corporal punishment as an acceptable means of controlling student behavior, local school district policy in many cases has seriously limited its use. Nevertheless, according to a recent survey conducted by the National Center for the Study of Corporal Punishment and Alternatives in Schools, at least two million U.S. schoolchildren are physically punished each year.

Reasonable Punishment

Poor decisions regarding the use of corporal punishment by school officials may result in civil damage suits or even criminal prosecution for assault and battery. Corporal punishment, when permitted, should be used only as a *last resort* measure. Every reasonable method should be employed prior to its use. Working very closely with teachers, parents, or guardians to resolve a child's deviant behavior is viewed as a more positive alternative.

If corporal punishment is employed, students should be informed beforehand of specific infractions that warrant its use. When administered, the punishment should be reasonable and consistent with the gravity of the infraction. Corporal punishment should never be administered *excessively or with malice.*

In the past, there have been numerous suits alleging that children were struck with double belts, lacrosse sticks, baseball bats, electrical cords, bamboo rods, hoses, and wooden drawer dividers. Other suits have alleged that children were kicked, choked, and forced to eat cigarettes. Such acts by school personnel are totally indefensible. None of these practices meets the test of reasonableness established by today's courts. The right to discipline students is subject to the same standards of reasonableness as would be expected by the average parent.

The courts have advanced two standards governing corporal punishment of students: The first is the reasonableness standard—punishment must be exerted within bounds of reason and humanity. The second is the good faith standard—the person administering the punishment must not be motivated by malice and must not inflict punishment wantonly or excessively.[35]

In a rather interesting case, *Baker v. Owen,* the U.S. Supreme Court affirmed the judgment of a three-judge panel of the U.S. District Court in North Carolina, which upheld the administration of corporal punishment over a parent's objection. In this case, Russell Baker, a sixth-grade student, was paddled for violating an announced rule against throwing kick balls except during the designated play period. Russell's mother had requested that her son not receive corporal punishment because she was opposed to it. Despite her objection, Russell was corporally punished for his disobedience. In her suit, the parent alleged violations of the child's right to procedural due process and that the paddling amounted to cruel and unusual punishment, thus violating the Eighth Amendment. The court held for the teacher.

The court identified procedural safeguards that should be invoked to meet minimal standards of due process: (1) Specific warning must be given about what behavior would result in corporal punishment and evidence must exist that other measures attempted had failed to bring about desired behavioral modifications, (2) administration of corporal punishment must take place in the presence of another school official, and (3) upon request, a written statement must be given to parents regarding reasons for the punishment and the name of the official witness.

Further, it was held that the two licks administered by the teacher with an instrument that was somewhat longer and thicker than a foot ruler involved no lasting effect or discomfort and was not in violation of the Eighth Amendment involving cruel and unusual punishment.[36] Interestingly, another court has ruled that there is no constitutional violation when a school district complies with a minor's wish for corporal punishment rather than follow the parent's preference for suspension.[37]

Minimal Due Process

Before corporal punishment is administered, school officials should have formulated rules that provide students with adequate notice that specific violations may result in the use of corporal punishment. These rules should be published and disseminated to parents and students. Further, the student who is to be punished should be informed of the rule violation in question and provided an opportunity to respond. A brief but thorough *informal hearing* should be provided so as to allow the student the opportunity to present his or her side of the issue. Upon request, parents or guardians must be provided a written explanation of the reasons for the punishment and the name of the school official who was present to witness the punishment. These conditions would satisfy minimal due process requirements. Since the student's property rights are not involved, an extensive, full due process procedure is not warranted.

Excessive Punishment

School officials must exercise extreme care to ensure that corporal punishment is not deemed excessive. Excessiveness occurs when the punishment is inflicted with such force or in a manner that is considered to be *cruel and unusual.* Excessiveness also occurs when no consideration is given to the *age, size, gender, and physical condition, or the student's ability to bear the punishment.*

Assault and battery charges are normally associated with allegations of excessive punishment. Both are classified as intentional torts. An assault involves "an overt act or an attempt to inflict immediate physical injury to the person of another. The overt act must be a display of force or menace or violence of such a nature as to cause reasonable apprehension of immediate bodily harm."[38] The person accused of an assault must have the ability to execute it. All of the elements found in this definition must be present to sustain an assault charge. An assault occurs when a person has been placed in fear for his or her immediate safety. A battery, on the other hand, is a successful assault that involves actual physical contact.

From the school official's perspective, when corporal punishment is administered in a rude and malicious manner, using poor judgment regarding the excessive nature of the punishment, assault and battery charges may be eminent, especially if there is a view that the official *intended* to harm the student. Intent is an important element involving a battery. The person who inflicts the harm must be perceived as purposely doing so. Stated differently, the official's contact with the student must be intentional. Of course, once corporal punishment is administered, school personnel may find it difficult to refute that this form of punishment was not inflicted in an excessive manner intended for and directed at the student. Although *in loco parentis* allows school officials to administer corporal punishment, their actions must be considered reasonable and necessary under the circumstances.

An example of excessive, rude, and malicious punishment is demonstrated in one of the most blatant cases involving the use of corporal punishment. This case arose in Georgia when a 14-year-old freshman varsity football player, Durante Neal, alleged that his teacher and coach violated his right under the due process clause to be free from excessive corporal punishment.

During football practice, Royonte Griffin, another football player, slapped Neal in the face. Neal reported the incident to Coach Ector, who allegedly told him that he needed to learn how to handle his own business. Neal then picked up a weight lock and placed it in his gym bag. After practice, he was again approached by Griffin. Neal pulled the weight lock out of his bag and hit Griffin in the head and then placed the lock back in his bag. Both then began to fight. During the fight, Coach Ector and the principal, Herschel Robinson, were in the immediate area. Neither attempted to stop the fight. Coach Ector dumped the contents of Neal's bag on the ground shouting repeatedly, "What did you hit him with?" Ector told Neal that he would be hit with the same object he used to hit Griffin. Ector took the same weight lock and struck Neal in his left eye. As a result of the blow, Neal's eye was knocked completely out of its socket leaving it destroyed and dismembered. Neal's eye was hanging out of his head as he experienced severe pain, but neither Ector or Robinson stopped the fight.

Neal sued Ector, Robinson, Superintendent Dolinger, and the Fulton County School Board under 42 U.S.C. § 1983, claiming that Ector's use of corporal punishment was so excessive as to shock the conscience and violate his Fourteenth Amendment substantive due process rights. Neal further charged that the school board, superintendent, and principal were liable for failing to properly train, instruct, and supervise Coach Ector. The district court held for the school district.

On appeal, the board's motion for summary judgment was declined by the Eleventh Circuit Court of Appeal. The Eleventh Circuit Court held that Ector's conduct did constitute corporal punishment. The court then addressed the issue of whether corporal punishment, regardless of its severity, rose to the level of a substantive due process claim. In doing so, the court referred to the leading corporal punishment case, *Ingraham v. Wright,* and disagreed with the district court's interpretation of it. The Fifth Circuit ruling in *Ingraham* declined to suggest that corporal punishment could not rise to the level of a constitutional violation. It further held that the facts in both cases were too different to arrive at the same conclusion. The court of appeals examined (1) the need for the punishment, (2) the relationship between the need and amount of punishment administered, and (3) the extent of the injury inflicted. The court concluded that the plaintiff had stated a claim of action and that Ector went too far in using an obviously excessive amount of force that presented a reasonably foreseeable risk of serious bodily injury. The Circuit Court ruled that the plaintiff had adequately alleged a violation of his right under the Fourteenth Amendment to be free from excessive corporal punishment. The district court's judgment dismissing the case was reversed and remanded for further proceedings consistent with the court's opinion.[39]

■ ■ ■ ■ ■ ▬▬▬▬▬▬▬▬▬▬▬▬▬▬▬▬▬▬▬▬▬▬▬▬▬▬▬▬▬▬

ADMINISTRATIVE GUIDE

CORPORAL PUNISHMENT

1. Corporal punishment should not be used except for acts of misconduct that are so anti-social and disruptive in nature as to shock the conscience.
2. School officials should not expect the courts to support malicious and excessive physical punishment of students.
3. The punishment must not be inflicted with such force or in such manner as to be considered malicious, excessively cruel, or unusual.
4. Reasonable administration of corporal punishment should be based on such factors as the gravity of the offense and the age, size, gender, and physical ability of the child to bear the punishment.
5. If a student professes a lack of knowledge regarding the rule violation or innocence of the rule violation, a brief but adequate opportunity should be provided to explain the rule and to allow the student to speak on his or her behalf.
6. Whenever possible, students should be provided punishment options for deviant behavior. Corporal punishment should never be administered when the child is physically resisting.
7. Attempts should be made to comply with the parent's request that corporal punishment not be administered on the child with the understanding that the parent assumes responsibility for the child's behavior during the school day.

CLASSROOM HARASSMENT

Harassment is a form of sexual discrimination. The Supreme Court, in a stunning 5–4 decision, ruled that public schools may be sued for failing to deal with students who harass their classmates.[40] This landmark decision, hailed as a victory by sexual harassment protection groups, raises a number of interesting questions: How will it affect the operation and management of schools? Will it create insurmountable problems of supervision for teachers and principals? Will every adolescent gesture made against a classmate trigger a need for the school to respond? Has the High Court invoked a federal code of conduct that regulates behavior typically associated with adolescence? These are complex issues facing school leaders as they attempt to address harassment issues in their schools.

The Supreme Court's Decision

Justice Sandra Day O'Conner, writing for the majority, attempted to clarify these complex issues by indicating that lawsuits are valid only when the harassing student's behavior is so severe, pervasive, and objectively offensive that it denies the victim equal access to an education guaranteed by federal law. She further suggested that harassment claims are valid only when school administrators are clearly unreasonable and deliberately indifferent toward the alleged harassing conduct, which obviously means that they must have been aware of such conduct and did nothing to address it. However, liability charges may be made even if a teacher is the only one aware of the harassing behavior. An excerpt from the High Court's majority opinion states the following:

We consider here whether a private damages action may lie against the school board in cases of student-on-student harassment. We conclude that it may, but only where the funding recipient acts with deliberate indifference to known acts of harassment that are so severe and pervasive and objectively offensive that they effectively bar the victim's access to an educational opportunity or benefit. . . .

We stress that our conclusion . . . does not mean that recipients can avoid liability only by purging their schools of actionable peer harassment or that administrators must engage in particular disciplinary action. . . . School administrators will continue to enjoy the flexibility they require. . . .

Courts . . . must bear in mind that schools are unlike the adult workplace and that children may regularly interact in a manner that would be unacceptable among adults.

A Dissenting Opinion

Based on the majority ruling, school leaders need not fear lawsuits unless they are deliberately indifferent to reported cases of harassment. The High Court's decision is not intended to restrict administrative flexibility in managing schools. Since this case resulted in a 5–4 ruling, there were obviously dissenting opinions.

Dissenting Justice Anthony Kennedy stated that the majority's decision will result in the diversion of scarce resources from educating children and that many school districts, desperate to avoid Title IX peer harassment suits, will adopt whatever federal code of student conduct and discipline the Department of Education sees fit to impose on them.

Justice Kennedy held a sympathetic view of the impact that future sexual harassment litigation will have on schools that are already financially overburdened. He also expressed concern over the federal government's attempt to regulate classrooms, which he felt would conflict with the traditional states' role of regulating their schools. Dissenting Justice Kennedy further pointed to the Court's inability to make meaningful distinctions between elementary schools, secondary schools, and universities in addressing the issue of harassment.

Danger Signals

Nonetheless, it appears that school leaders are not liable unless they knew of the harassing behavior and failed to take reasonable steps to respond. One issue, however, that might complicate this finding is whether evidence suggests that school leaders should have known of the harasser's conduct. For example, if it is common knowledge among students and teachers that harassing behavior is occurring in specific situations, it may be increasingly difficult for school leaders, when challenged, to claim to be unaware of it. There are instances in which they are expected to know of improper conduct and take appropriate steps to respond to it. Failure to do so may result in liability charges.

School leaders may receive notice of harassment in a variety of ways. According to the Office for Civil Rights (OCR), school officials should know of alleged sexual harassment when a student files a grievance or complains to a teacher about classmate's behavior. They should also pay attention when a student, parent, or other individual contacts the principal or teacher regarding allegations of harassment. In these instances, the student who has been subjected to harassing conduct has met the notice requirement under OCR guidelines. It then becomes the responsibility of the principal or a designee to respond appropriately.

The Pivotal Case

This case decided by the Supreme Court arose in Georgia in 1992 when LaShonda Davis alleged that a classmate sexually harassed her on repeated occasions. Over a period of several months, these incidents of harassing behavior were reported each time to teachers and subsequently to the principal. Davis, who is black, accused the school of taking no action against the offending student when the incidents were reported, but later disciplining that student when he harassed a white student. Davis filed a suit in the U.S. District Court for the Middle District of Georgia, alleging Fourteenth Amendment violations by the teacher, principal, county board of education, and school board members. The school district filed a motion for dismissal.

The district court took a conservative view in stating that the Constitution limits conduct of state officials and does not protect citizens from the actions of private parties. According to the court, liability extends only to governmental entities that hold a special relationship to the complaining party, and to government officials who place the party in a position of danger. The court held that since neither of these conditions applied in this case, school officials were protected by qualified immunity from constitutional complaints.

The district court also ruled that there was no merit to Davis's contention that the school board should be liable for failing to enact a sexual harassment policy. Because she was unable to demonstrate that the offensive conduct resulted from an absence of board policy, the case was dismissed. Davis's mother appealed the district ruling to the U.S. Court of Appeals for the Eleventh Circuit, which also held for the district. The case was then appealed to the U.S. Supreme Court, which ruled that school administrators were liable in such cases.

Courts are fairly consistent in ruling that harassment suits are only valid when harassing students' behavior is so severe, pervasive, and objectionably offensive that it denies the victim equal access to an education. Further, school officials must be clearly unreasonable and deliberately indifferent toward the harassing conduct.

In a recent case, the parents and guardians of three second-grade students brought action against the school board under Title IX, alleging that their daughters were victims of sexual harassment by another second-grade student. The U.S. District Court of the Middle District of Florida granted summary judgment for the school board. The plaintiffs appealed. In ruling for the school district, the court of appeals held that the alleged behavior was not severe enough to have a systemic effect of denying the girls equal access to an educational program or activity as required to support a Title IX claim against the school district.[41]

■ ■ ■ ■ ■ ▬▬▬▬▬▬▬▬▬▬▬▬▬▬▬▬▬▬▬▬▬▬▬▬▬▬▬▬▬▬▬▬▬▬

ADMINISTRATIVE GUIDE

CLASSROOM HARASSMENT

1. Formulate district policies and procedures to address sexual harassment for employees and students. Be certain that everyone—faculty, students, and staff—understands these policies and the consequences for violating them.
2. Establish a zero tolerance policy so that everyone understands the school's position on issues involving harassment.

(continued)

ADMINISTRATIVE GUIDE (*continued*)

3. Provide staff development programs periodically for faculty and staff to familiarize them with all aspects of harassment and specific behavior considered to fall in the harassment category.
4. Encourage faculty and students to report all violations through a well-defined, developed, and publicized grievance procedure.
5. Provide educational programs for students on classroom harassment and school sanctions associated with harassment conduct.
6. React swiftly and judiciously to complaints filed by students, faculty, and staff so that everyone knows that the institution takes harassment seriously.
7. Create an environment where students and school personnel feel comfortable in honestly reporting complaints of harassment free of any form of reprisal.
8. Protect the confidentiality of those filing complaints to the greatest degree possible. Professional reputations can be damaged if charges prove to be false.
9. Create and maintain a school climate characterized by mutual respect and consideration of others.
10. Based on a recent Supreme Court decision in the *Gebser* case, students who are sexually abused by teachers cannot recover monetary damages from school officials unless officials knew of the harassment and were in a position to act and failed to do so.

PREGNANT STUDENTS

The courts have generally held that pregnant students may not be denied the opportunity to attend school. The basis for the court's position is that pregnant students must be afforded equal protection under the law, as well as due process of the law.

School officials have attempted to withdraw pregnant students from school based on knowledge that such students have become pregnant, whereas others have specified a particular time for withdrawal. Many of these rules have been successful in the past. However, the courts have become increasingly amenable to declaring these rules invalid. The commonly acceptable practice is that the student's physician may prescribe the time at which the student should withdraw for health and safety reasons. Upon withdrawal, school officials must provide appropriate home-based instruction. When cleared by the attending physician after childbirth, she may return to school and be entitled to the same rights and privileges afforded other students. She cannot be denied participation in school activities, events, or organizations during her pregnancy or after her pregnancy, unless participation is disallowed by her physician or school officials can demonstrate a legitimate reason to limit her participation.

The fact that a student is pregnant is not a sufficient ground to deny attendance in a public school, even if she is unwed. However, the school may develop rules that are necessary for the student's health, safety, and well-being. These will generally be viewed as reasonable if there is no evidence of arbitrary or capricious application. The following case is an example of arbitrary and capricious actions by school officials.

In a Kansas case, the board of education attempted to exclude a married student from school. This student married after discovering her pregnancy, before the child was born. She was abandoned by her husband shortly after their marriage. After giving birth, she attempted to reenter school. The court ruled that the board had acted in an arbitrary and capricious manner in attempting to exclude the student from school, stating that the student should not be prevented from securing an education that would better prepare her to meet the challenges of life.[42]

MARRIED STUDENTS

Married students have the right to attend public schools. Any rules designed to exclude married students from attending school are invalid and in violation of their Fourteenth Amendment rights—namely, equal protection under the law. School board rules that prohibited married students from permanently attending public schools were invalidated by the courts during the late 1920s and early 1930s. They suggested even then that there must be a showing of immorality, misconduct, or a deleterious effect on other students.[43] School rules that required students to withdraw from school for a one-year period after marriage were invalidated by the court.[44] Further, the court established the position that a 16-year-old married student has the right to attend public school, even when she has a child.[45]

Married students are considered to be *emancipated* and not subject to compulsory attendance laws. Thus, a married or minor student cannot be coerced to attend school. These students attend as they wish to do so. *Emancipation* means that the student is free of parental authority and control and free to make independent decisions.

There has been debate over the extent to which married students should be permitted to participate in extracurricular activities endorsed by the school. While extracurricular activities have frequently been viewed as privileges that may or may not be granted by the board, this view has been invalidated on the basis that denying such privileges would violate equal protection and due process provisions of the Fourteenth Amendment. Further, extracurricular activities are considered to be mere extensions of the regular academic program. How, then, could school officials allow married students to participate in the regular academic programs yet deny them the opportunity to participate in an extension of that program? To do so would be arbitrary, capricious, and entirely indefensible.

■ ■ ■ ■ ■

ADMINISTRATIVE GUIDE

PREGNANT AND MARRIED STUDENTS

1. Pregnant and married students are afforded the same rights as all other students enrolled in public schools, and they may not be prohibited from attending school.
2. There must be compelling evidence to demonstrate that the presence of married or pregnant students creates disruption or interference with school activities or a negative influence on other students to justify any attempt to restrict their attendance.
3. The pregnant student's physician is authorized to determine when the student should withdraw from school and when it is feasible for her to return.
4. Homebound instruction should be offered for students who have withdrawn from school due to pregnancy.
5. A heavy burden of proof rests with school officials in instances where attempts are made to exclude either pregnant or married students from participating in regular and extracurricular activities.
6. The courts are unanimous in invalidating school rules that prohibit married or pregnant students from attending school.

STUDENT PROTEST FOR POOR TREATMENT

A group of students in Cloverdale School has staged a protest regarding the general treatment of students by both teachers and administration. They have camped out on the school lawn.

■ ■ ■ ■ ■

DISCUSSION QUESTIONS

1. Under what conditions would such action be considered legal?
2. Under what conditions would such action be considered illegal?
3. What action should school officials take in both cases described in 1 and 2?
4. Write a set of defensible guidelines that should be followed by school personnel in dealing with student protest and demonstration.

STUDENT NEWSPAPER AS A FORUM FOR STUDENT EXPRESSION

Daisy Robinson is the principal of a midsize high school in a rural community. She has been quite liberal in recognizing that the school's newspaper is a forum for students to address issues of interest to students. However, in one instance, she determined that information contained in the student newspaper was inappropriate. Based on her judgment, she seized all copies of the newspaper because of a threatening letter falsely attributed to the football team and a libelous letter about the school's counselor. The editors filed suit, alleging violation of their First Amendment rights.

■ ■ ■ ■ ■

DISCUSSION QUESTIONS

1. Does the editor have a legitimate claim? Why or why not?
2. Can Robinson legally seize all copies of the newspaper? Why or why not?
3. Would the principal be in greater jeopardy in the absence of specific policies/guidelines governing the student newspaper?
4. What factors would the court consider in ruling in this case?
5. Write a defensible policy statement addressing undesirable content in the student newspaper.

STUDENT PUBLICATION AND CENSORSHIP

Brian Dickerson, a student editor in a northeastern upper-middle-class school district, wrote a review in the student newspaper on a movie that was rated "R." The review did not contain any vulgar or offensive language. School officials censored the review on the basis that it might pose a danger to students' health. Brian's parents sued on his behalf claiming First Amendment violations.

DISCUSSION QUESTIONS

1. Do Brian's parents have a legitimate cause of action? Why or why not?
2. Can school officials censor material that they believe is harmful to students?
3. What evidence is needed to justify censorship? (Be specific.)
4. How do you think the court would rule in this case?
5. Provide a rationale to support your response to question 4.
6. What are the administrative implications suggested by this case?

IMMUNIZATION AND RELIGION

Tom Banks is the principal of a large elementary school in an urban district. The school includes students from kindergarten through sixth grade. The district requires all students to be immunized before enrolling in school. Two kindergarten children whose parents hold sincere and genuine religious beliefs against immunization were not allowed to enroll. The parents who were Jewish, based their belief on a passage from the Bible which they interpreted as forbidding immunization. The parents requested an exemption. Based on information Banks received from a local rabbi, nothing in Jewish teaching prohibits immunization for children.

DISCUSSION QUESTIONS

1. Is the request by parents reasonable? Why? Why not?
2. How should Banks respond to the parents' request?
3. The parents have a sincere and genuine religious beliefs against immunization for their children. Should the school or district respect their beliefs?
4. What is the relative weight of parental rights versus the powers of the school or district?
5. If you were facing this issue how would you respond?
6. How do you think the court would view this issue?
7. What is the solution?

SEARCH OF STUDENT INVOLVING PROTRUDING OBJECT

Jim Robinson is a tenth-grade teacher. While walking down the hall, he spotted a suspicious object protruding from a student's pocket. He asked the student to empty his pocket but the student refused.

DISCUSSION QUESTIONS

1. Does the teacher have grounds to make such a request?
2. Does the student have a right to refuse to obey the teacher's request?
3. Should physical force be used to identify the object?
4. Would such a search be legal?
5. What guidelines would you suggest school personnel follow in matters involving student search in situations such as this one?

SEARCH ON SCHOOL'S PARKING LOT

Bruce Johnson is a first-year principal at Atwood Middle School in an urban district. One of his security guards spotted a student ducking behind a parked automobile in the campus parking lot. She was ordered to empty her purse, which contained several readmittance slips that she should not have had in her possession. The security officer telephoned Johnson and verbally informed him of the incident. Johnson told the security officer to initiate a thorough search of the student.

DISCUSSION QUESTIONS

1. Was there a reasonable basis to initiate a search in this case? Why or why not?
2. Did the student's behavior give rise of the need to be searched? Why or why not?
3. Can reasonable suspicion be clearly established and justified in this case? Why or why not?
4. As principal, would you have handled this situation differently? If so, describe your approach. If not, defend your position.
5. How would the court likely rule in this case?
6. What are the administrative implications of conducting a search under the circumstances described in this case?

CORPORAL PUNISHMENT OVER STUDENT'S OBJECTION

Carl Palmer, principal of Carbondale Middle School, became very upset with Walter Johnson for being disrespectful to several of his teachers. Palmer explained to Walter that because of his actions, he, Palmer, must administer corporal punishment based on school policy. As the principal proceeded to get his instrument to administer the punishment, Walter told him that he was not going to hit him with anything. Other students, faculty, and staff in the outer office heard him say this.

DISCUSSION QUESTIONS

1. What is the dilemma facing Palmer?
2. Should Palmer proceed with his plan to administer the punishment? Why or why not?
3. Does the student have the right to decide his punishment?
4. Is the principal creating a problem maintaining respect and discipline when others heard Walter refuse to accept punishment?
5. If the principal decides to administer punishment, what steps should he follow to ensure legal defensibility?
6. What should the principal's decision be in this situation?
7. What should be the basis for his decision?

ENDNOTES

1. *Tinker v. Des Moines Independent Community School District*, 393 U.S. 503, at 511, 89 S.Ct. 733, 21 L. Ed. 2d 731 (1969).
2. Ibid.
3. *Blackwell v. Issaquena County Board of Education*, 366 F. 2d 749 (5th Cir. 1966).
4. *Bethel School District v. Fraser*, 478 U.S. 675, 106 S.Ct. 3159, 93 L. Ed. 2d 549 (1986).
5. *Tinker*, op. cit.
6. *Hazelwood School District v. Kuhlmeier*, 484 U.S. 260, at 276; 108 S.Ct. 562; 98 L. Ed. 2d 592 (1987).
7. *Bystrom v. Fridley High School Independent School District No. 14*, 822 F. 2d 747 (8th Cir. 1987).
8. *Burch v. Barker*, 861 F. 2d 1149 (9th Cir. 1988).
9. *Pyle v. South Hadley School Committee*, 861 F. Supp. 157 (D. Mass. 1994), 55 F. 3d 20 (1st Cir. 1995).
10. *In re Gault*, 387 U.S. 1; 875 S.Ct. 1428; 18 L. Ed. 2d 527 (1967).
11. *Goss v. Lopez*, 419 U.S. 565; 955 S.Ct. 729; 42 L. Ed. 2d 725 (1975).
12. *Dixon v. Alabama State Board of Education*, 186 F. Supp. 945; reversed 294 F. 2d 15; cert. denied, 368 U.S. 930, 825 S.Ct. 368 (1961).
13. *Wood v. Strickland*, 420 U.S. 308; 95 S.Ct. 992; 43 L. Ed. 2d 214 (1975).
14. *People v. Jackson*, 65 Misc. 2d 909, 319 N.Y.S. 2d 731 (1971).
15. *New Jersey v. T.L.O.*, 469 U.S. 809; 105 S.Ct. 68; 83 L. Ed. 2d 19 (1984).
16. *Bellnier v. Lund*, 438 F. Supp. 47 (N.D. N.Y. 1977).
17. *Desilets v. Clearview Regional Board of Education*, 137 N.J. 585, 647 A. 2d 150 (1994).
18. *Shamberg v. State*, 762 P. 2d 488 (Alaska App. 1988).
19. *Wynn v. Board of Education of Vestavia Hills*, 508 So. 2d 1170 (Ala. 1987).
20. *In re William G.*, 211 Cal. Rptr. 118 (1985).
21. *M. M. v. Anker*, 607 F. 2d 588 (2d Cir. 1979).
22. *Cales v. Howell Public Schools*, 635 F. Supp. 454 (E.D. Mich. 1985).
23. *Cornfield by Lewis v. Consolidated School District No. 230*, 991 Vol. II F. 2d 1316 (7th Cir. 1993).
24. *Milligan v. City of Slidell*, 226 F. 3d 652 (La. 2000).
25. *Rudloph v. Lowndes County Board of Education*, 242 F. Supp. 2d 1107.
26. *Stockton v. City of Freeport, Texas*, 147 F. Supp. 2d 642 (2001).
27. *Doe v. Renfrow*, 475 F. Supp. 1012 (N.D. Ind. 1979).
28. *Zamaro v. Pomeroy*, 639 F. 2d 662 (10th Cir. 1981).
29. *Jones v. Latexo Independent School District*, 499 F. Supp. 223 (E.D. Tex. 1980).
30. *Horton v. Goose Creek Independent School District*, 690 F. 2d 470 (5th Cir. 1982).
31. *B.C. v. Plumas Unified School District*, 192 F. 3d 1260, 138 Ed. Law Rep. 1003 (Cal. 1999).
32. *Bundick v. Bay Independent School District*, 140 F. Supp. 2d 735, 154 Ed. Law Rep. 183 (S.D. Texas 2001).
33. *Ingraham v. Wright*, 430 U.S. 651; 97 S.Ct. 1401; 51 L. Ed. 2d 711 (1977).
34. Ibid.
35. Ibid.
36. *Baker v. Owen*, 395 F. Supp. 294 (M.D. N.C. 1975).
37. *Woodward v. Los Fresnos Independent School District*, 732 F. 2d 1243 (5th Cir. 1984).
38. *State v. Ingram*, 237 N.C. 197, 74 S.E. 2d 532 (1953).
39. *Neal v. Fulton County Board of Education*, 229 F. 3d 1069; U.S. App. (2000).
40. *Davis v. Monroe County Board of Education*, 526 U.S. 629; 119 S.Ct. 1661; 143 L. Ed. 2d 839 (1999).
41. *Hawkins v. Sarasota County School Board*, 322 F. 3d 1279 (2003).
42. *Nutt v. Goodland Board of Education*, 128 Kan. 507, 278 P. 1065 (1929).
43. *McLeod v. State*, 122 So. 77 (Miss. 1929).
44. *Board of Education of Harrodsburg v. Bentley*, 383 S.W. 2d 287 (Tex. 1967).
45. *Alvin Independent School District v. Cooper*, 404 S.W. 2d 76 (Tex. 1966).

■ ■ ■ ■ ■

CHAPTER 4

DUE PROCESS AND
STUDENT SAFETY

HOMELAND SECURITY

Due to the events of 9/11, there is increasing concern regarding safety across the nation. The United States has initiated a terrorist alert system based on guidelines formulated by the Department of Homeland Security which was created by HR 5005 in the 107th Congress and signed into law on November 26, 2002 by President Bush. Since the alert system was created, the United States has vacillated between orange (high risk) terror alert and yellow (an elevated) terror alert condition.

Under the No Child Left Behind Act, school safety also has become a major priority for local school districts, which must provide assurances that plans are on file regarding steps schools will initiate to maintain safe and drug free environments. In March 2003, Secretary of Education Rod Paige announced that $30 million is available in fiscal 2003 to assist school districts in improving and strengthening emergency response and crises management plans. Additionally, the National School Safety Center (NSSC) was created to provide assistance in combating school safety problems so that schools can be free to focus on the primary job of educating the nation's children. The NSCC was established by presidential directive in 1984 as a partnership between the U.S. Department of Justice and the U.S. Department of Education. It has since become a private, nonprofit organization serving school administrators, teachers, law officers, community leaders, government officials, and others interested in creating safe schools throughout the United States and internationally.

The NSCC has developed guidelines for each of the groups identified above to enhance safety. Minimal guidelines pertaining to the roles of schools in Homeland Security are listed below. Schools are free to develop guidelines that exceed those suggested by the safety center. The guides are as follows:

1. **In the school's mission statement, identify the context for which the school wishes the academic learning to take place**, using phrases like "to learn in a safe and secure environment free of violence, drugs and fear." Such phrases enhance the school's legal position to create and enforce policies that promote a safe, caring, and disciplined school climate. A statement of this nature can have a powerful effect on the validity and credibility of the school's efforts to create and preserve a safe environment.

2. **Identify a specific procedure for evaluating and responding to threats.** Every campus should have a series of threat assessment protocols so that school officials can effectively work with mental health and law enforcement professionals in handling circumstances that could result in potential violence or harm. School officials should make certain students are involved in the planning process. For the most part, students are the best information resources for inside threats. Recent studies by the Secret Service revealed that in the vast majority of student shootings, other students on the campus were aware that the event might occur. Having a tip line or safe reporting mechanism in place for students is critical.

3. **Identify the potential disasters that could occur based on the school's setting and climate.** Such disasters may include

   – Civil unrest/demonstrations/rioting
   – Bomb threats/explosions
   – Intruders/unauthorized visitors
   – Hostage takings
   – Sniper attacks
   – Extortion
   – Assault/battery/rape
   – Weapons possessions
   – Drug abuse/trafficking
   – Gang-related violence/drive-by shootings
   – Kidnappings/abductions
   – Child abuse/neglect/molestation
   – Life-threatening illness
   – Accidental injury or death
   – Intentional injury or death
   – Utility failures
   – Chemical spills
   – Automobile accidents
   – Natural disasters: earthquake, flood, tornado, fire, hurricane, tsunami
   – Mass transit disasters: falling aircraft/train derailment/bus accidents

4. **Control campus access.** Minimize the number of campus entrance and exit points used daily. Access points to school grounds should be limited and supervised on a regular basis by individuals who are familiar with the student body. Campus traffic, both pedestrian and vehicular, should flow through areas that can be easily and naturally supervised. Delivery entrances used by vendors also should be checked regularly. Parking lots often have multiple entrances and exits, which contribute to vandalism and defacement of vehicles and school property. Vehicular and pedestrian access should be carefully controlled. Perimeter fencing should be considered. Bus lots should be secured and monitored. Infrequently used rooms and closets should be locked. Access to utilities, roofs, and cleaning closets should be secured.

5. **Identify specifically assigned roles and responsibilities.** Specific policies and procedures that detail staff members' responsibilities for security should be developed. These responsibilities may include monitoring hallways and restrooms, patrolling parking lots, and providing supervision at before-school and after-school activities.

Specific roles and responsibilities should also be assigned for times of crisis, including the appointment of a crisis team.

6. **Identify whom to call in a crisis.** Maintain an updated list of whom to call in case of various kinds of crises. Develop a close working partnership with these emergency responders. When a crisis occurs, school officials do not have the time or luxury to determine who handles chemical or biological disasters or who handles bomb threats. Know the extent of services offered by these agencies. Determine what to do when an emergency responder is not immediately available. Develop a close working partnership with law enforcement officials. If available, get to know the school security before there is a crisis. Develop a memorandum of understanding as to the role of a police officer on campus. Determine in advance who will lead, who will follow, and how searches, interrogations, and other issues will be handled. Create a close working partnership with mental health professionals who can assist school officials in evaluating and assessing potentially dangerous students who may threaten or intimidate others. The counselor or psychologist also can be an important partner in the aftermath of a crisis.

7. **Provide training for all members of the school community regarding cultural awareness and sensitivity.** It is important to consider the impact of cultural influences on a school community's ability to create and maintain safe, secure, and peaceful schools. Cultural influences will directly affect the information, strategies, and resources that will be used in safe school planning. Sensitivity to cultural influences also apply to creating a plan to manage and respond to a crisis.

8. **Establish an emergency operation communication system.** In addition to campus intercoms and two-way radios, it is important for school officials to be able to communicate with law enforcement and outside telephone providers. This includes the use of cell phones.

9. **Implement a uniform school crime-reporting and record-keeping system.** When school administrators know what crimes are being committed on their campus, when they are committed, where a crime is committed, and who is involved. This knowledge becomes extremely useful in determing the types of strategies and supervision that should be implemented. In addition, it is important to conduct some level of crime analysis to determine what, if any, links exist among various aspects of criminal activity on the campus.

Preparing for National Emergencies

Schools should begin a process of learning and staying informed about potential national security threats, preparing for emergencies, and responses during an attack. In addition to the following recommendations, visit the U.S. Department of Homeland Security Web site at www.dhs.gov/dhspublic/ for more information.

1. **Identify potential and reliable sources of information to be accessed once a crisis situation develops.** Prepare a plan that identifies the first and subsequent contacts you will make to access credible information and appropriate direction for action.

2. **Perform an assessment of your school's risk during a national crisis.** This includes

   - Evaluating health and medical on-site preparedness
   - Checking the availability and accessibility of local emergency services, including HAZMAT (hazardous materials), fire, emergency medical, law enforcement, and local and federal emergency management agencies
   - Identifying potential terrorist targets in your local community
   - Identifying and taking inventory of potential informal contacts in the community who could provide food, water, shelter, medical aid, power sources, and other forms of emergency support
   - Reviewing viable communications plans, such as phone chains and parent contact information

3. **Be observant of the activities transpiring on campus.** During periods of high alert, an additional level of vigilance must be in place. Everyone who comes onto the campus must have a legitimate purpose. It is important to have a uniform screening policy for all visitors, including vendors and delivery/service personnel. All visitors should be required to sign in at the school office, state their specific business, and wear or visibly display a visitor's badge. All school employees should be advised to greet visitors or any unidentified persons and direct them to the main office to ensure that these persons have legitimate business at the school. Teachers and staff should be trained to courteously challenge all visitors. "May I help you?" is a kind, non-threatening way to begin.

   Confirm the identity of service personnel and anyone seeking access to operational systems such as heating/air conditioning units, gas or electric utilities, telephone systems, security systems, maintenance areas, and other related locations. Maintain accurate records of service and delivery personnel, including a log of dates and times of service delivery, types of services, full names of service personnel, company represented, and vehicle information.

   Develop procedures for identifying and keeping track of volunteer workers on campus. Enforce sign-in/sign-out procedures for volunteers.

   During periods of high alert, be on the watch for suspicious people, packages, and activities on or near your campus. Notify authorities of these observations. Activities that should be observed include someone photographing or videotaping on or near your campus, unidentified or unfamiliar vehicles parked on or near campus for extended periods of time, unclaimed packages or backpacks left unattended, or unfamiliar people seeking information that is out of the ordinary.

4. **In view of Homeland Security recommendations, it is especially important to pay added attention to the possibility of the following kinds of disasters. Review and revise your crisis plans accordingly.**
   - Bomb threats/explosions
   - Suicide bombings
   - Intruders/unauthorized visitors
   - Biological/radiological attacks

– Utility failures
– Mass transit disasters: falling aircraft/train derailment/bus accidents

HANDLING GANG VIOLENCE IN SCHOOLS

While the nation faces threats of terrorism that affect the health and safety of all citizens, U.S. schools also face safety threats that affect the welfare of students. Maintaining safe schools has become a major challenge for school officials during the past decade. School shootings in Pearl, Mississippi; West Paducah, Kentucky; Jonesboro, Arkansas; Edinboro, Pennsylvania; Springfield, Oregon; and Littleton, Colorado have increased pressures on school leaders to provide a safe learning environment where teachers can effectively perform their instructional duties. A survey conducted in the late 90's by Howard-Met Life revealed a general climate of anger and violence around the nation's schools. A large minority of the student body appears to have a predisposition toward violence based on their inability to control anger. Bullying, insulting, or disrespectful behavior oftentimes resulted in fights. If access to guns is added, there is a greater probability of violent outcomes. Another major threat to school safety is the presence of youth gangs in many schools.

Gang presence in public schools appears to be decreasing (Figure 4.1). According to a recent report, the percentage of students who reported the presence of street gangs in their schools decreased from 28 percent in 1989 to 17 percent in 1999. Although gang presence has decreased, it still poses a major challenge for school leaders.

With the presence of gangs in schools, school leaders are encountering pressures from parents, citizens, and school boards to provide a safe environment where teachers can teach and students can learn. Added to these pressures is the view of the courts that schools are "safe places" based on the assumption that children are supervised by licensed and

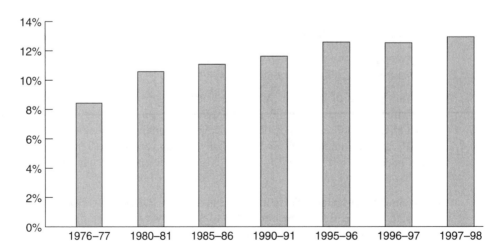

FIGURE 4.1 Percentage of students ages 12 through 18 who reported that street gangs were present at school during the previous six months, by race/ethnicity: 1989, 1995, and 1999.

Source: U.S. Department of Justice, Bureau of Justice Statistics, School Crime Supplement to the National Crime Victimization Survey, January–June 1989, 1995, and 1999.

well-trained teachers and administrators. Since schools are presumed to be safe, failure to provide a safe environment can prove costly when evidence reveals that school leaders failed to act responsibly in protecting students when they knew or should have known of impending danger.

School leaders are expected to be able to foresee that certain activities in their school may result in harm to others. Once potential danger is determined, reasonable and prompt action must be taken to prevent harm. A safe school environment has to be a high priority among school leaders.

Gang Characteristics and Membership

Gangs are best described as groups of individuals involved in unusually close social relationships. They share a common collective identity expressed through a gang name. Gangs adopt certain symbols or signs and claim control over a certain turf or territory. These organized groups are often involved in drugs, weapons trafficking, and other forms of criminal activity. They can create fear among other students and increase the level of violence in schools.

Gang members are typically young teenage males of similar ethnic or racial backgrounds. Loyalty is expressed through adherence to a strict gang code. Camaraderie is solidified through participation in group activities that are often antisocial, illegal, violent, and criminal. Goals, identified roles, and responsibilities are clearly established and defined, often unspoken but understood. The chain of command is hierarchical and respected by members. In recent years, gangs have attracted younger members (as young as 8 and 9 years old) and have also shown a growth in the number of female members.

Youths join gangs for various reasons, including the desire for excitement; peer pressure; neglect; economic reward; the need for recognition, identity, and acceptance; and lack of appropriate involvement. They show strong loyalty to their gang and will do whatever is necessary to be initiated into the gang, including committing violent crimes.

Gangs are forces that are challenging schools and communities across the nation. School leaders, however, have an especially important role to play, since gang violence has quickly become a part of public schools' vocabulary.

Gang Dress

Gang members tend to wear specific apparel or colors to convey gang affiliation. Where gang activity has been prevalent in the school or community and there is clear knowledge that certain types of dress are associated with disruptive gang activity, school officials may prohibit such dress. In all cases, this prohibition should be preceded by school policies that clearly communicate the need to regulate certain types of dress.

In most cases, the pattern or style of dress is generally chosen by gang leaders. As pressure is exerted by parents, law enforcement officers, and school officials, gangs will often change their appearance to become less recognizable. Today, many gang members wear professional sports team jackets, caps, and T-shirts, making it difficult to identify them. Since school officials are responsible for protecting students from potential danger, they may take reasonable steps to minimize gang presence in school. On the other hand, school officials should provide opportunities for all students to succeed in school and feel that they are important members of the school's family. In many cases, the lack of success in school and a feeling of alienation contribute to gang affiliation.

■ ■ ■ ■ ■

ADMINISTRATIVE GUIDE

GANG VIOLENCE

1. Efforts should be made to ensure that school personnel have knowledge of gang identification strategies as well as gang management techniques.
2. Policies and procedures should be established to address gang violence in the school.
3. A system should be implemented to report suspected gang involvement and activity to proper law enforcement gang units.
4. Dress related to gang activity may be banned by school officials.

SCHOOL UNIFORM DRESS POLICIES, SCHOOL SAFETY, AND STUDENTS' FREEDOM OF EXPRESSION RIGHTS

Many school officials in their desire to create and maintain safe schools have developed uniform dress code policies for students. These policies are intended to provide easy identification of students, eliminate gang dress, promote discipline, deter theft and violence, prevent unauthorized visitors from intruding on campus, and foster a positive learning environment. Although there is no consensus regarding the effectiveness of school uniforms, their use is increasing in schools across the nation as part of an overall program to improve school safety and discipline. For example, school districts in Georgia, Indiana, Louisiana, Maryland, Tennessee, Utah, and Virginia have enacted school uniform regulations. Many large public school systems, including Baltimore, Cincinnati, Detroit, Los Angeles, Miami, and New York, have schools with either voluntary or mandatory uniform policies, generally in elementary and middle schools. In addition, many private and parochial schools have required uniforms for several years.

As school uniform policies are drawn by school leaders, it is prudent that they be mindful of the freedom of expression rights of students. Policies that do not recognize these rights are risky at best and may result in legal challenges and unnecessary legal costs to school districts. School officials should be assured, within limits, that the First Amendment rights of students are protected as they strive to create and maintain safe schools. As discussed in Chapter 3, students' rights must be recognized and respected.

Early Legal Challenges

With frequent acts of violence in public schools, schools are moving swiftly and aggressively to enforce uniform dress policies. Early legal battles have already surfaced over dress codes and religious freedoms in Mississippi involving the rights of students to wear clothing with religious symbols to school. Officials in Harrison County, Mississippi, backed off on the same day of enforcing a regulation that prohibited a Jewish student from wearing a Star of David necklace to class based on its policy of prohibiting students from wearing anything that could be viewed as a gang symbol. A similar case arose in Van Cleave, Mississippi, when a local board of education banned students from wearing clothing with Christian symbols based on the school's mandatory uniform policy. In this case, two students wore T-shirts stamped with the words "Jesus loves me." The basis for imple-

ADMINISTRATIVE GUIDE

UNIFORMS

1. Involve parents, teachers, community leaders, and student representatives in drafting school uniform policies.
2. Make certain that students' religious expressions are preserved in relation to uniform dress codes.
3. Make certain that students' freedom of expression rights are protected within reasonable limits as uniform dress standards are established.
4. Make financial provisions for economically disadvantaged students regarding mandatory uniforms.
5. Enforce school uniform policies fairly and consistently.
6. Implement school uniform policies as a component of an overall school safety program.
7. Uniform policy drafts should be presented to legal counsel for review.
8. School uniform policies should be reviewed and revised as the need arises.

menting the mandatory uniform policy was safety. After an unsuccessful appeal to the school board, parents of the two students filed a suit in the U.S. District Court challenging the legality of a policy that prohibits free expression of their children's religious beliefs. These early legal cases may suggest a lack of some degree of sensitivity to the First Amendment rights of students as school uniform policies are drafted.

ZERO TOLERANCE AND SCHOOL SAFETY

School safety has become a leading priority for school leaders as they respond to a wave of violence that has struck public schools throughout the United States, resulting in 348 deaths between 1992 and 2003. (See Table 4.1.) Although schools are still considered safe places, limiting violence has become a part of public schools' agenda. Many districts have initiated a zero tolerance policy in an effort to reduce school violence. Opponents are raising questions as to whether school leaders are going too far and moving too swiftly with a "one strike, you're out" approach. They also are questioning whether school leaders' actions are reasonable and legally defensible.

Zero Tolerance

Zero tolerance is not new. It emerged during the 1990s, aimed primarily at students who concealed weapons and drugs on school grounds. In fact, President Clinton provided a major boost when he signed the Gun Free School Act of 1994 that mandates expulsion of students who bring a weapon to school. This federal statute affects each state that receives federal funds and requires local educational agencies to expel from school for a period of not less than one year any student who is found to have brought a weapon to school under the jurisdiction of the local school district. However, the statute does provide the chief administrator of the district the latitude to modify the expulsion requirement for students on a case-by-case basis.

TABLE 4.1   Deaths by School Types

SCHOOL YEAR	ELEMENTARY SCHOOL	MIDDLE SCHOOL	HIGH SCHOOL	ALTERNATIVE SCHOOL	OTHER
1992–1993	3	7	42	2	2
1993–1994	12	7	32	2	
1994–1995	1	3	17		
1995–1996	1	8	22	4	1
1996–1997	4	3	18	1	
1997–1998	5	10	28	1	
1998–1999		5	24	2	
1999–2000	5	6	17		4
2000–2001	3	3	15	1	1
2001–2002			2	2	
2002–2003		2	4		
Totals	34	54	221	15	8

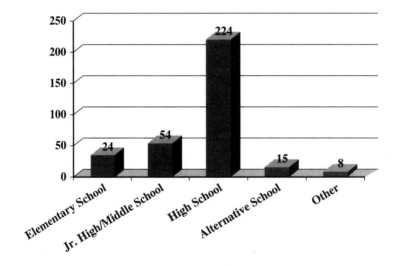

Source: The National School Safety Center, 141 Duesenberg Drive, Suite 11, Westlake Village, CA 91362.

Even though this statute is a version of a "one strike, you're out" strategy, it does provide flexibility based on administrative discretion. Thus, in the strictest sense, it is not absolute zero tolerance. In contrast, the controversy in Decatur, Illinois is an example of "one strike, you're out" that failed to provide administrative discretion. Seven students involved in a brawl at a football game in which no weapons were involved and no serious injuries occurred were expelled for two years based on the district's zero tolerance policy. Their expulsions were later reduced to one year as a result of strong protests from segments of the community. Critics expressed concern that the penalty was unduly harsh and not proportional to the offense committed by these students. Due to the escalating controversy, the governor finally bent the rules to allow these students to attend an alternative school.

In a leading case involving zero tolerance, a suspended middle school student brought action under 42 U.S.C. § 1983 alleging denial of due process and other rights. The complaint was dismissed for failure to state a claim. The student appealed. The court of appeals held that there was no evidence that school officials failed to provide the student constitutionally sufficient due process in various notices and hearings it accorded him.

Benjamin Ratner, age 13, was a student in the eighth grade. On October 8, 1999, a schoolmate told Ratner that she had been suicidal the previous evening and had contemplated killing herself by slitting her wrists. She also told Ratner that she unintentionally brought a knife to school in her binder that morning. Ratner had known her for two years, was aware of her previous suicide attempts, and feared for her safety. Consequently, he took the binder from her and placed it in his locker. He did not inform school authorities about the knife, but intended to tell both his and her parents after school.

By lunchtime that day, the assistant principal had learned that the girl might have given a knife to Ratner. The dean of the school called Ratner to her office and inquired about the knife. Ratner admitted that he had it, and at her direction he went alone to his locker, retrieved the binder, and gave it to her. The dean acknowledged that she believed Ratner acted in what he saw as the girl's best interest and that at no time did Ratner pose a threat to harm anyone with the knife.

Nonetheless, Ratner was suspended by the assistant principal for ten days for possessing a knife on school grounds in violation of school board policy. Four days later, the school's principal affirmed Ratner's suspension with written notice. Two days after that, the divisional superintendent issued written notice informing Ratner that he was being suspended indefinitely pending further action by the school board and informing Ratner that he was recommending to an administrative hearing panel that Ratner be suspended for the remainder of the school term, which ended February 1, 2000. The administrative hearing panel met on October 29, 1999, and recommended Ratner be suspended for the remainder of the term. Ratner was given written notice of his long-term suspension. Ratner's mother requested and received a hearing before the school district's discipline committee to appeal, but that committee unanimously approved Ratner's long-term suspension.

Ratner, through his mother, filed suit against the school district and four of its employees under 42 U.S.C. § 1983. Ratner alleged that his suspension under what is called a zero tolerance policy amounted to a violation of his Fourteenth Amendment rights to due process and equal protection and his Eighth Amendment right to be free from cruel and unusual punishment. He also asserted several other causes of action. He sought compensatory and punitive damages, fees and costs, and other relief. Ratner's complaint charged that the school employs a zero tolerance policy regarding weapons, a policy that precludes officials from considering the circumstances of a particular case when meting out punishment.

The district court dismissed Ratner's complaint for failure to state a claim of action. In its memorandum opinion, the district court concluded Ratner's claim was, in essence, a claim of due process violations. The district court also concluded, correctly, that the school officials provided Ratner a constitutionally sufficient, even if imperfect, process in the various notices and hearings it accorded him. "However harsh the result in this case, the federal courts were not properly called upon to judge the wisdom of a zero tolerance policy.

Instead, the inquiry here was limited to whether Ratner's complaint alleged sufficient facts which if proven would show that the implementation of the school's policy in this case failed to comply with the United States Constitution." The district court concluded that the facts alleged in this case did not support his claim. The judgment of the district court was affirmed.[1]

A contrasting zero tolerance case arose on the morning of February 20, 1998, when Liliana Cuesta and eight other students at Killian Senior High School distributed an anonymous pamphlet, entitled "First Amendment," on school grounds. The pamphlet's cover featured a graphic of Dawson, the school's principal, with a dart through his head. The pamphlet included several poems, cartoons, and essays. Among the essays was one in which the author "wondered what would happen" if he shot the principal, the school's teachers, or other students. The same essay made reference to "an African disease" and "immigrants who can't talk a f____ word of English." Cartoons in the pamphlet depicted violent and sexual activity.

The zero tolerance policy contained three provisions of the school board rules and was supplemented by the code of student conduct. Under the rules, school police are responsible for "providing assistance" in "the prevention and detection of crime and the enforcement of the penal laws of this state as the violation occurs on or to the properties of the Dade County Public Schools." The rules also stated that "all employees are under an affirmative duty to report any criminal act, and/or disruptive, and/or inappropriate behavior. . . . All violations of law and incidents of disruptive and/or inappropriate behavior are to be reported in accordance with administrative procedures established by the Superintendent of Schools." Finally, the rules state that "the Board endorses a zero tolerance policy toward school related violent crime." The code of student conduct describes the zero tolerance policy as requiring "school districts to invoke the most severe consequences provided for in the Code of Student Conduct in dealing with students who engage in violent criminal acts. . . ." The consequences provided for in the code of student conduct direct individuals to "refer criminal acts to the Miami-Dade County Public Schools Police and the local police agency for appropriate legal action."

Cuesta, who was over 18 years old, was booked and strip-searched pursuant to a Metro-Dade County policy requiring the strip search of all newly arrested felons. The strip search, conducted by a female corrections officer in a closed room, required Cuesta to completely disrobe; to lift her breasts exposing the area underneath, and to squat down and cough while exposing her buttocks. After the strip search was completed, Cuesta was placed in a holding cell with several other women until she was released on bond.

Four days after the arrests, the state attorney's office decided not to prosecute any of the students who had participated in creating and distributing the pamphlet. The state attorney issued a press release indicating that the decision not to file criminal charges was made because "recent decisions of the United States Supreme Court . . . render the statute in question unconstitutional and unenforceable."

Cuesta later filed suit under 42 U.S.C. § 1983 against the Dade County School Board and the police officer, for violating her First and Fourth Amendment rights by unlawfully arresting her, and against Miami Dade County, for violating her Fourth Amendment rights by subjecting her to an unconstitutional strip search. The district court granted a motion to dismiss the officer based on qualified immunity. The district court then granted summary judgment for both the county and the school board. Cuesta appealed those grants of summary judgment.

In this appeal, the court considered two issues: whether a school board is liable for an allegedly unlawful arrest stemming from a zero tolerance policy toward school-related violent crime and whether a county is liable for an allegedly unconstitutional strip search of the arrestee. With respect to the first issue, the court concluded that a school board cannot be held liable for allegedly unlawful arrests that result from a policy that merely calls on school officials to report criminal behavior. With respect to the second issue, the court concluded that there was reasonable suspicion to strip search the arrestee, and therefore the search was constitutional. Accordingly, the court affirmed the district court's grant of summary judgment to both defendants.[2]

Recent Zero Tolerance Practices

Since zero tolerance has emerged in a number of districts, students have been affected in ways that raise questions regarding the legal defensibility of these approaches. For example, a 16-year-old female student in Washington was met by police and expelled for using her finger to make a gun and jokingly saying, "Bang." She has since been reinstated. A high school senior in Virginia was suspended for ten days and required to attend a substance abuse seminar for using mouthwash on campus, thus violating the school alcohol policy. A 13-year-old male student in Texas was arrested and spent five days in jail awaiting a hearing for writing a spooky story about killing classmates. He subsequently received home schooling. An 18-year-old male student in Georgia wrote a story in his journal about a deranged student who goes on a rampage at school, which resulted in his expulsion and arrest with no opportunity to graduate. Another student in Georgia was suspended for two weeks for giving his French teacher a gift-wrapped bottle of French wine. Other accounts involve a 7-year-old student who was suspended for bringing nail clippers to school in Illinois and a 15-year-old in Virginia who was suspended for dying his hair blue. A photo of an army enlistee in the senior class, who posed on top of a cannon outside a Veterans of Foreign Wars post in Minnesota, was censored because it violated Nevis High School's zero tolerance weapons policy. After a month-long battle, a compromise was reached that involved covering the barrel with a flag. Unquestionably, school officials are relatively uneasy about school safety based on past incidents of violence in schools. However, their concerns are expected to be tempered with sound reason and a regard for the rights of students. Most of the incidents cited earlier did not reach the courts, but the case involving the account of a deranged student did. In this case, the judge ruled that the student's journal entry did not, in fact, constitute a threat. Even with the judge's ruling, the student had to attend another school in the district. Prosecutors were still weighing a case against him.

As school officials move toward implementing zero tolerance, they are expected to do so in a thoughtful and deliberate fashion, ensuring that their approach is fundamentally fair and legally defensible. Policies that do not weigh the severity of the offense, the student's history of past behavior, due process, and alternative education for students involved in long-term expulsion are at best highly risky. School officials are expected to strike a delicate balance between safety in their schools and the rights of students under their supervision. Anything less could result in undesirable outcomes, significant legal challenges, and mounting legal expense to the school district.

ADMINISTRATIVE GUIDE

ZERO TOLERANCE

1. Do not use zero tolerance solely to rid the school of disruptive students.

(continued)

■ ■ ■ ■ ■ ▬▬▬▬▬▬▬▬▬▬▬▬▬▬▬▬▬▬▬▬▬▬▬▬▬▬▬▬▬▬▬▬▬▬

ADMINISTRATIVE GUIDE (*continued*)

2. Involve teachers, parents, community leaders, and student representatives in the formulation of zero tolerance policies.
3. Draft policies with recognition that students possess constitutional rights
4. Do not move too swiftly with the assumption that zero tolerance is a cure-all for student misconduct.
5. When it becomes necessary to expel students for an extended period of time, seek alternative educational opportunities.
6. Consider the student's history of behavior in school, the seriousness of the offense, and the immediate need to act before determining punishment.
7. Make certain that the student's substantive and procedural process rights are addressed in all disciplinary matters.

SCHOOL SUSPENSION

School suspension is a legal form of discipline for students who violate school or district policy often involving issues relating to school safety. In-school suspensions are used by 91 percent of the school districts in the United States, whereas out-of-school suspensions are used by 95 percent of the districts. Race, ethnicity, and socioeconomic status are often factors that have an impact on school suspensions. There appears to be a close relationship between socioeconomic status, race, and ethnicity and the rate of suspensions. A larger number of minority students of lower socioeconomic status are suspended yearly than other students.

School suspensions require that *substantive and procedural* provisions of due process are met. Due process of law is a fundamental right guaranteed to citizens of the United States under the Fourteenth Amendment of the Constitution. This amendment provides, in part, that "no State shall . . . deprive any person of life, liberty or property, without due process of law." Basically, due process is a course of legal proceedings following established rules that assure enforcement and protection of individual rights. The guarantees of due process require that every person be entitled to the protection of a fair trial. The essential element of due process is *fundamental fairness*, which means a fair hearing, a fair trial, and a fair judgment.

■ ■ ■ ■ ■ ▬▬▬▬▬▬▬▬▬▬▬▬▬▬▬▬▬▬▬▬▬▬▬▬▬▬▬▬▬▬▬▬▬▬

ADMINISTRATIVE GUIDE

SUSPENSION

1. Adequate notice must be provided to students and parents regarding the existence of rules governing student behavior. These should be clearly communicated to all affected by their implementation.
2. A record should be compiled that includes the following information:
   a. The infraction allegedly committed
   b. The time of the alleged infraction
   c. The place the alleged infraction occurred

■ ■ ■ ■ ■

ADMINISTRATIVE GUIDE (*continued*)

    d. Those person(s) who witnessed the alleged act

    e. Previous efforts made to remedy the alleged misbehavior

3. Students facing suspension should, at minimum, be provided some type of notice followed by a brief informal hearing.

4. Students should be provided either oral or written notice of charges against them, the evidence school authorities have to support the charges, and an opportunity to refute the charges.

5. Since permanent removal is not intended, no delay is necessary between the time notice is given and the time of the actual hearing. In most instances, school officials may informally discuss alleged misconduct with students immediately after it is reported.

6. During the hearing, the school official should listen to all sides of the issue. There should be adequate time provided for students to present their side of the issue without interruption.

7. Parents or guardians should be informed of the hearing and provided written notification of the action that results from the hearing. At a minimum, the written notice should include

    a. The charge(s) brought against the student

    b. A description of the available evidence used to support the charge(s)

    c. The number of days suspended

    d. A determination of whether suspension is an in-school or out-of-school suspension

    e. A list of other conditions that must be met before the student returns to school (e.g., a conference with parent or guardian)

    f. A statement that informs parents or guardians that the suspension can be appealed to the district's pupil personnel director or a designee

8. Parents or guardians should be informed by phone of the suspension, followed by written notification, which should be promptly mailed, preferably by registered mail on the day of the hearing.

Procedural and Substantive Due Process

Due process consists of two essential aspects: substantive and procedural. Students as citizens are entitled to rights associated with both aspects. *Substantive due process* deals with the student's individual or personal rights, whereas *procedural due process* requires that certain legal procedures be followed to ensure fundamental fairness and to avoid arbitrary and capricious actions by school officials.

Substantive due process suggests that when students' rights are restricted, a valid reason must be demonstrated to justify such restriction and the actual means employed to deny the student's right must be reasonably calculated. Procedural due process requires that a *legally defensible procedure* be followed to ensure that proper safeguards are available to protect the rights of those whose rights are in jeopardy. The significance of substantive and procedural requirements is that both provisions must be met by school officials to succeed in meeting the basic requirements of the Fourteenth Amendment.

An example of a procedural due process violation is illustrated in the *Gault* case, which occurred in Arizona in 1967. Gerald Gault, a juvenile, had been found guilty of making an obscene phone call. The typical punishment for an adult committing the same offense would have been a $50 fine. But since Gerald was considered a juvenile, he was remanded by the court to the state reform school for a period of up to six years.

The U.S. Supreme Court held that Gault had been committed to the industrial school without the benefit of procedural due process. The high court also noted that the Arizona law regarding juveniles contained several deficiencies: (1) no appeal of the conviction was provided, (2) no written charges of the alleged crime were presented during the hearing, and (3) protection against self-incrimination had been denied.

In overturning the verdict, the Supreme Court stated the following: "Where a substantial penalty is involved, a juvenile, like an adult, is entitled to due process of law."[3] The impact of the *Gault* ruling was significant in its broad and liberal application. This decision defined how school officials must respond to students in disciplinary hearings and guaranteed that no student shall be denied personal rights under the Fourteenth Amendment.

Another leading U.S. Supreme Court case, *Goss v. Lopez*, determined that students facing suspensions of up to ten days or less were entitled to oral or written notice of charges, an explanation of the evidence to be used against them, and an opportunity to present their side of the issue. This case arose when Lopez, a high school student in Columbus, Ohio, was suspended from school with at least 75 other students who were connected to a disturbance in the school cafeteria. The disturbance followed a disagreement with school administrators regarding which community leaders would be permitted to speak during the school's assembly program. Polarization rapidly deteriorated into a disturbance, which resulted in suspensions during Black History week. The suspensions were to last ten days.

There was no hearing prior to or after the suspension. Consequently, Lopez had no opportunity to affirm or deny his participation in the disturbance. A state law required the principal to notify parents within 24 hours of a suspension for up to ten days, and such notice must provide the reason(s) for the suspension. No other forms of due process were required. No notice of charges, no opportunity to be heard, no chance to confront witnesses, or no right to further appeal were required. Lopez filed suit. His case, along with others, was heard by a three-judge federal district court, which found the state's law unconstitutional. The administrators appealed to the Supreme Court, where the lower court's decision favoring the students was upheld.

The administrators had sought to have the Court affirm their contention that since there is no federal constitutional right to a free public education, there is no corresponding federal constitutional right requiring the application of due process procedures to suspensions from public schools. Justice White, writing for the Court, said that since the state had extended the right to attend public schools to students, including Lopez, that right is a legitimate property interest protected by the due process clause of the Constitution, and the state "may not withdraw that right on grounds of misconduct, absent fundamentally fair procedures to determine whether the misconduct has occurred." At the least, students facing a short suspension from school, not exceeding ten days, and thereby facing loss of "a protected property interest must be given some kind of notice and afforded some kind of hearing." White's statement noted, in part, that although Ohio may not be constitutionally obligated to establish and maintain a public school system, it has nevertheless done so and has required its children to attend. Those young people do not "shed their constitutional rights" at the schoolhouse door.

The Supreme Court also noted the existence of a liberty interest stemming from charges of misconduct leveled against the students involved. The Court stated:

If charges are sustained and duly recorded, they could seriously damage students' standing in the school as well as interfere with future opportunities to pursue an education or employment. It is apparent that the right claimed by the state to determine unilaterally without due process that misconduct has occurred collides with the requirements of the Constitution.[4]

The implications of this decision for practitioners suggest that, for school suspensions of up to ten days, a student must be given notice of the misconduct, as well as an opportunity for a hearing regarding the misconduct. Such notice and hearing may occur almost immediately after the infraction, and only "rudimentary" procedures are required. The hearing need only be an explanation of the evidence against the student after he or she is told the nature of the charges and is provided an opportunity to tell his or her side of the story. In case the student's presence on the premises poses a continuing threat or danger, the student may be immediately removed from school, with the notice and hearing following whenever practicable.

For suspensions of more than ten days (and expulsions), obviously more than rudimentary due process procedures must be observed. However, the Supreme Court has not currently addressed this situation, and case law precedents are conflicting among the various circuit courts of appeals. A prudent school leader, however, should err on the side of providing students an opportunity for full protection of due process, including, but not limited to the following:

1. Notice of charges
2. Prior notice of hearing
3. Right to legal counsel at all appropriate stages
4. Hearing before impartial party
5. Right to compel supportive witnesses to attend
6. Right to confront and cross-examine adverse witnesses, and/or to view and inspect adverse evidence prior to hearing
7. Right to testify in their own behalf
8. Right to have a transcript of proceedings for use on appeal

EXPULSION

Unlike suspension, expulsion is considered one of the more severe forms of discipline because it involves long-term separation from the school district or, in some instances, permanent separation. Expulsion usually involves more serious offenses or rule violations than does suspension. In recent years, a significant number of expulsions has been linked with weapons violations. With continued gang presence in school and frequent incidents of violence school officials will be challanged to maintain safe schools.

Expulsion is typically used by school districts as a form of discipline for students who commit serious infractions. Since expulsion is considered to be a form of discipline that deprives the student of the right to attend school, it must be preceded by a formal hearing in which the student is afforded full Fourteenth Amendment rights involving due process and equal protection privileges.

Because of the threat of expulsion is so serious, students and parents should be aware of the types of infractions that may result in expulsion. These infractions should be identified by school and district policy. Additionally, they should be clearly communicated to students and parents to ensure that there is no misinterpretation regarding the intent and substance of expulsion policies. Parents, students, citizens, and school personnel should be involved in the development of expulsion policies, recognizing that the board of education has the ultimate authority for approving such policies.

In virtually every state, the board of education is the only body with legal authority to expel students. The board is responsible for holding the expulsion hearing and meeting all rudiments of due process consistent with the Fourteenth Amendment. Any errors along procedural or substantive grounds usually will result in the student being supported by the courts. The *Dixon v. Alabama State Board of Education* case, involving expulsion of higher education students, illustrates how students' Fourteenth Amendment rights were violated by school officials.

The *Dixon* case involved a group of higher education students who were expelled without due process provisions. Although this case involved expulsion in a higher education institution, it has application to due process rights of all public school students. Students at Alabama State University in early 1960 engaged in off-campus sit-in demonstrations in a privately owned cafeteria in the county courthouse. The students were expelled by the university without opportunity to appear at a hearing, on the basis that they had violated their "contract" with the university to adhere to certain standards of conduct. University officials failed to consider that the students involved had a constitutional interest in attending the state school. According to tradition, discipline involving students, even behavior off campus, was permitted without regard to whether the students had a constitutional interest that could not be deprived without due process of law. This tradition was based on the theory that students should properly behave as ladies and gentlemen, and their conduct should not reflect adversely on the reputation of the institution. During this time, this view was consistent with the *in loco parentis* concept widely used in K–12 schools, both public and private, where school officials could act as arbitrarily as parents in meting out discipline.

The court decision held that, contrary to the contract theory tradition, as students in a state-supported college or university, students do hold a constitutional right not to be expelled without some appropriate and fair due process, such as notice of charges and the opportunity for some form of hearing.[5] *Dixon* is significant for K–12 public school officials because it represents the first time public school administrators were challenged for arbitrarily enacting and enforcing rules without consideration to act with some degree of fairness toward students.

Wood v. Strickland is another significant case where school officials failed to observe procedural guidelines. The outcome resulted not only in a ruling on behalf of the students but also one in which individual board members were informed that they could be liable for damages resulting from the violation of students' constitutional rights. This case involved three female high school students, all sophomores, 16 years of age. All three girls admitted mixing three bottles of 3.2 beer into a soda pop punch, bringing it to a school function, and serving the mixture, apparently without noticeable effect, to parents and teachers.

Following the spread of rumors, the students were called in and confessed to what they had done. The board of education thereafter held a meeting to which neither the students nor their parents were invited. Despite a plea for clemency by the school's principal, the board decided to expel the girls for the remainder of the year—a period of three months.

The board did not attempt to prove that the particular mixture involved was "intoxicating," stating that its prohibition had been meant to include *any alcoholic beverage*. At a second board meeting two weeks later, at which time the students were represented, the board refused to withdraw its action "because the rule prescribed a mandatory expulsion for the offense." The students, through their parents, brought action to block the board's decision. Their petition was later amended to include financial damages against the board members as individuals under the Civil Rights Act of 1871 (42 U.S.C. Sec. 1983).

The district court originally favored the school board on the grounds that the board members were immune from damages, but the court of appeals reversed, holding that the board's failure to present any evidence that the punch was, in fact, "intoxicating" was a violation of the plaintiffs' constitutional rights.

On appeal, the Supreme Court, by a 5–4 vote, stated that malicious intent was not always required to hold a public official liable for damages:

> Ignorance of what a student's constitutional rights are *will not always* serve as a defense in such cases. . . . School officials are entitled to a "qualified" privilege against damages for wrongful acts while *acting in good faith*. However, school board members will not be considered *absolutely immune* to such payment if they *knew*, or *reasonably should have known*, that the actions they took would violate the constitutional rights of a student, just as if they took the action with *malicious intention* to cause deprivation of some right to which the student is *entitled*.[6]

As one can see, a lack of awareness of students' constitutional rights will not pass court scrutiny, especially when it is evident that school authorities should have been aware of these rights.

■ ■ ■ ■ ■ ▬▬▬▬▬▬▬▬▬▬▬▬▬▬▬▬▬▬▬▬▬▬▬▬▬▬▬▬▬▬▬▬▬▬▬▬
ADMINISTRATIVE GUIDE

EXPULSION
These steps, if implemented correctly, will meet the standards of due process and fundamental fairness while ensuring that the constitutional rights of students are protected.

1. Students, parents, or legal guardians should be informed based on school or district policy of specific infractions that may result in expulsion. They should also be informed of their Fourteenth Amendment rights regarding substantive and procedural due process.
2. In cases of serious misconduct for which serious disciplinary measures may be imposed, the student is entitled to written notice of the charges, and a right to a fair hearing. Written notice must be furnished to the students, parent, or guardian well in advance of the actual hearing.
3. At a minimum, the following procedural steps should be considered:
   a. Written notice of charges
   b. Right to a fair hearing
   c. Right to inspect evidence
   d. Right to present evidence on student's behalf
   e. Right to legal counsel
   f. Right to call witnesses
   g. Right to cross-examination and to confrontation
   h. Right against self-incrimination
   i. Right to appeal

METAL DETECTORS

Metal detectors have grown in use and popularity as school officials seek to maintain a safe and orderly school environment. To date, there has been no legal challenge reaching the Supreme Court regarding the use of detectors. However, several cases have emerged at the district court level. In *Thompson v. Carthage School District*, a school bus driver noticed fresh cuts in a seat cushion and reported such to the principal, who ordered that all male students in grades 6 through 12 be searched, based on school policy. There also was information indicating that drugs were present in the school. The students were searched using metal detectors. If the detector sounded, the student was patted down. One student was searched and crack cocaine was found. He was subsequently expelled. That student filed suit, alleging wrongful expulsion. The district court ruled for the student. However, the appeals court reversed the district court's decision by indicating that the exclusionary rule compromises school safety and held that the search was justified from its inception, based on reasonable suspicion and inferences.[7]

A number of other cases involving metal detector screening arose through challenges by plaintiffs regarding the legality of this practice in public schools. In one case, *In re F.B.*, a student was found to be in possession of a knife in a Philadelphia school. He was later arrested based on metal detection screening. A motion was filed by the student, attempting to suppress the evidence that had been seized. He claimed that the search was unreasonable and that no individual suspicion existed to justify the search at its inception. The court applied the reasonable factor found in the *T.L.O.* case and held that the search was justified at its inception based on the high incidents of violence in Philadelphia schools. The court ruled further that the search was reasonable and legally defensible because school officials had no way of knowing whether students had weapons prior to entering the building.[8]

A similar case, *People v. Pruitt*, arose in Chicago involving a metal detector screening conducted in the public schools by city police of Chicago. During the screening process, it was discovered that a student was in possession of a loaded 38-caliber pistol. He was subsequently arrested. The validity of the search was deemed appropriate by the court. The court again referred to the Fourteenth Amendment test of reasonableness established in the *T.L.O.* case. The court held that the action was justified at its inception based on a record of violence in the schools.[9]

In another case, *People v. Dukes*, the New York City Board of Education formulated guidelines regarding the use of metal detectors in a high school to be used by a special task force that included police officers. Scanning posts were established in the main lobby of the school based on guidelines. All students who entered the building were randomly subject to search, based on the length of waiting lines. During the screening process, a student was found to be in possession of a switchblade knife and subsequently charged with a misdemeanor. The student challenged the charge and attempted to have the evidence suppressed. The court held that the administrative action was reasonable. In so finding, the court assessed the degree of intrusion versus the severity of damages and the need to conduct the screening at its inception. The court concluded that the search was reasonable and that the school had a compelling interest to provide a safe and secure school.[10]

The use of metal detectors, like other intrusive methods, must be justified as reasonable and necessary to meet a legitimate school objective. In these cases, maintaining a safe and orderly school environment was considered a legitimate school objective. There should be, in all cases, *significant* or *compelling* evidence to suggest that metal detectors be used. If a school has a chronic history of drug use and violence involving the use of weapons, the courts will likely support the use of metal detectors as a means of combating these problems. If metal detectors are employed by the school officials, students should be informed before the procedure is implemented that they are subject to this type of screening. Such information should be included in school or district policy and clearly communicated to students and parents. In no instance, except extreme emergencies, should students be surprised by the use of metal detectors. Also, if detectors are used, the methods employed in using them must be reasonable and not designed to degrade students.

ADMINISTRATIVE GUIDE

METAL DETECTORS

1. Metal detectors should be used only when there is evidence of student behavior that poses a threat to the health and safety of students in the school. Students and parents should be informed beforehand that metal detectors will be employed and informed of the reasons for employing this method, barring an emergency situation.
2. If metal detectors are used to achieve a legitimate school interest, then use will likely be supported by the courts.
3. Students and parents should be informed through a legally defensible school policy regarding the use of metal detectors.
4. Students and parents should not be surprised by the use of metal detectors, except in unusual circumstances.
5. If school officials' acts are reasonable regarding the use of metal detectors, they will generally receive minimal resistance from parents.

DRUG TESTING

Drug use affects the health and safety of a significant number of students across the United States. Many are beginning to use drugs at a younger age than did their peers in previous years. For example, in 2000, the use of marijuana on a trial basis rose by 3 percent among students in grades 4 through 7, representing an increase from 250,000 children to roughly 480,000 who experimented with drugs. Because of this steady increase in drug use among students, the courts have become more lenient in their rulings supporting school authorities. Controlling drug and alcohol use by students presents a formidable challenge for school authorities, thus leading a number of districts to consider seriously or actually implementing drug testing programs.

Drug testing programs have already been initiated in the private sector and by state and federal governmental agencies as well. These programs were designed to combat drug use and promote safety and personal health.

The U.S. Supreme Court ruled on two drug testing cases in 1989. One case involved the testing of railway employees; the other involved testing of customs service employees. The High Court ruled that a drug test, irrespective of the method, constitutes a search. While the Court recognized that these programs constituted a search, both searches were upheld, based on the government's compelling interest in promoting public safety through minimizing rail accidents and protecting the public against certain agents who carried firearms. In neither case was individual suspicion necessary nor required to justify the testing program.

Until the mid nineties, no case involving drug testing in public schools had been litigated by the U.S. Supreme Court. *Vernonia School District v. Acton*, however, reached the Supreme Court when the Ninth Circuit Court reversed the district court's holding for the school district. School officials in Oregon formulated a district policy based on the belief that some athletes had been smoking marijuana and using other drugs. They also believed that drugs were a major factor in the formulation of rowdy student groups carrying such names as "Big Elk" and "Drug Cartel." Under the district's policy, all student athletes were required to provide a urine sample at the beginning of the season for the particular sport in which they participated. Random tests were conducted among selected athletes. Athletes who tested positive were offered the choice between counseling and weekly testing or suspension from athletics for the current and subsequent season.

James Acton, a seventh-grade student who wished to join the football team at Washington Grade School, challenged the policy. Since his parents refused to sign the consent form for drug testing, he was suspended from athletics. There was absolutely no evidence that James used drugs. The district court rejected the family's claim of unreasonable intrusion in 1992, but the Ninth Circuit reversed the district court's decision. The school district based its decision on the landmark *New Jersey v. T.L.O.* case, in which the court ruled that school officials had greater latitude to search students in the school environment in order to maintain orderly conduct. The Supreme Court held for the school district.

Supreme Court Justice Scalia, writing for the majority, stated that the Vernonia School District's program was reasonable and constitutionally permissible for three reasons. First, students, especially student athletes, have low expectations for privacy in communal locker rooms and restrooms where students must produce their urine samples. "School sports are not for the bashful," Scalia wrote. He stated further that it was clear from the court's earlier cases that school officials could generally exercise a degree of supervision and control over students that could not be exercised over free adults. Second, Justice Scalia said the testing program was designed to be unobtrusive, with students producing their samples in relative privacy and with the samples handled confidentially by an outside laboratory. Finally, the program served the district's interest in combating drug abuse. "It seems self-evident to us that drug use, of particular danger to athletes, is effectively addressed by making sure that athletes do not use drugs."[11]

The Supreme Court, in this case, adopted a sympathetic view of the problems encountered by school districts with respect to drug use by student athletes. Additionally, the Court placed great importance on the "role model" image of the student athletes. It also emphasized that student athletes should not expect complete privacy—a price that must be paid to participate in athletic programs.

■ ■ ■ ■ ■ ▬▬▬▬▬▬▬▬▬▬▬▬▬▬▬▬▬▬▬▬▬▬▬▬▬▬▬▬▬▬▬▬▬▬

ADMINISTRATIVE GUIDE

DRUG TESTING STUDENT ATHLETES

1. Initiate a district-wide program on drug education, stressing the harmful effects of drugs and the benefits of abstaining from the use of drugs.

ADMINISTRATIVE GUIDE (*continued*)

2. Develop school and district policies prohibiting the use and/or possession of drugs on school grounds, indicating specific actions that will be taken when students are found guilty of violating school and district policy.
3. Develop a full due process procedure to ensure that there is a fair and impartial opportunity for student athletes to present their side of the issue if accused of drug use.
4. Involve teachers, parents, student athletes, health officials, and community citizens in formulating school and/or district policies regarding drug testing programs that are reasonable and legally defensible.
5. Provide support in cases where students are found guilty of drug use. This is a time when students need as much support as possible.
6. Develop and maintain open relationships with parents so that frequent communication can occur, especially in cases where there is a suspicion that a student may be involved with drugs.
7. Do not use the recent Supreme Court decision as a license to treat students unfairly. If a drug-testing program is adopted for athletes, be certain that there is a need to adopt such a program.

GANG AND STUDENT DRESS

A large high school in the northeastern United States initiated a policy prohibiting the wearing of gang symbols such as jewelry, emblems, earrings, and athletic caps. This policy was developed based on gang activities that were prevalent in the school. Bill Foster, who was not involved in gang activity, wore an earring to school as a form of self-expression and a belief that the earring was attractive to young ladies. He was suspended for his act. Consequently, he filed suit.

DISCUSSION QUESTIONS

1. Were Bill's freedom of expression rights violated in this case? Why or why not?
2. Was his suspension justified? Why or why not?
3. Should Bill have been permitted to wear the earring, since he was not involved in gang activity?
4. As principal, what factors would you weigh in determining whether Bill would be permitted to wear an earring? (Be specific.)
5. Would the court support Bill? Why or why not?
6. Would the court support school officials? Why or why not?
7. What are the administrative implications suggested by this case?

EXPULSION FOR ASSAULT OF A STUDENT

Larry Smith, principal of Farley Middle School in an upscale community, recently recommended to his superintendent that a student, Susan Brown, be expelled for the remainder of the year for various acts of misconduct including disrespect for authority and physically attacking a student who refused to loan her money.

■ ■ ■ ■ ■

DISCUSSION QUESTIONS

1. What type of evidence is needed to sustain a recommendation of expulsion?
2. Outline a legally defensible procedure that should be followed in this situation, including the rights to which Susan is entitled.
3. If the student's parents challenge the expulsion, how do you think the courts would respond to the procedure you outlined?
4. Provide a rationale for your response to question 3.
5. How does expulsion differ from suspension with respect to due process consideration? (Be specific.)

ENDNOTES

1. *Ratner v. Loudoun County Public Schools* *;534 U.S. 1114; 122 S.Ct. 922; 151 L. Ed. 2d 886 (2002).
2. *Cuesta v. School Board of Miami-Dade County*, 285 F. 3d 962 (2002).
3. *In re Gault*, 387 U.S. 1; 875 S.Ct. 1428; 18 L. Ed. 2d 527 (1967).
4. *Goss v. Lopez*, 419 U.S. 565; 955 S.Ct. 729; 42 L. Ed. 2d 725 (1975).
5. *Dixon v. Alabama State Board of Education*, 186 F. Supp. 945; reversed 294 F. 2d 15; cert. denied, 368 U.S. 930; 825 S.Ct. 368 (1961).
6. *Wood v. Strickland*, 420 U.S. 308; 95 S.Ct. 992; 43 L. Ed. 2d 214 (1975).
7. *Thompson v. Carthage School District*, U.S. App. Lexis 15461 (8th Cir. 1996).
8. *In re F.B.*, 658 A. 2d 1378 (Pa. Super. 1993).
9. *People v. Pruitt*, 662 N.E. 2d 540 (Ill. App 1 Dist. 1996).
10. *People v. Dukes*, 580 N.Y.S. 2d 850 (NY City Crim. Ct. 1992).
11. *Vernonia School District v. Acton*, 115 S.Ct. 2386; 132 L. Ed. 2d 564 (1995).

CHAPTER 5

INDIVIDUALS WITH DISABILITIES

In 1975, Congress enacted *P.L. 94-142, the Education for All Handicapped Children Act,* based on findings that supported the need for the act. Congress discerned that there were more than eight million children in the United States with disabilities whose needs had not been fully met. Roughly four million of these same children had not been provided appropriate educational services that allowed them to receive an equal educational opportunity. Even more startling was the realization that over one million children with disabilities had not received any type of public educational opportunity. Many of those who did receive some form of public education were not able to receive the full benefits of an educational experience because their disabilities had not been discovered. In many instances, parents were forced to seek assistance for their children outside the public school arena, oftentimes at great expense and inconvenience to the families.

Based on these findings, Congress realized that it was in the nation's best interest for the federal government to intervene and work collaboratively with states in addressing the needs of children with disabilities throughout the country. This intervention was presented in the form of P.L. 94-142. The Education for All Handicapped Children Act (EAHCA) has undergone a number of amendments since its inception. As of 1990, it is currently referred to as *Individuals with Disabilities Education Act (IDEA).* Although the act has been amended on a number of occasions, its primary purpose has remained intact.

There has been a steady increase in the number of children who have been classified as disabled, as shown in Table 5.1. This growth trend highlights the importance of improving services to meet the needs of these children and providing equal access to educational opportunities.

Individuals with disabilities are protected by three significant federal statutes: Individuals with Disabilities Education Act of 1990 (IDEA), Americans with Disabilities Act of 1990 (ADA), and the Rehabilitation Act of 1973, Section 504. These statutes were enacted to protect individuals with disabilities from discrimination and to provide them equal access to educational opportunities, facility utilization, and employment opportunities in public school settings.

Two leading cases focused major attention to the needs of children with disabilities during the early 1970s: *The Pennsylvania Association for Retarded Children v. Commonwealth* and *Mills v. Board of Education.* In the *Pennsylvania* case, a district court ruled that the state's children with mental retardation were entitled to a free public education and, whenever possible, should be educated in regular classrooms rather than classrooms that were isolated from the normal school population. The court stated:

TABLE 5.1 Students with Disabilities

In 1998–1999, six million children (ages 0 to 21), or about 13 percent of public school children, were enrolled in special education programs. Slowly increasing numbers and proportions of children are being served in programs for the disabled. During the 1990–1991 school year, 11 percent of students were served in these programs, compared with 13 percent in 1998–1999. Some of the rise since 1990–1991 may be attributed to the increasing proportion of children identified as learning disabled, which rose from 5 percent of enrollment to 6 percent of enrollment in 1998–1999.

	PERCENT OF ALL STUDENTS SERVED BY FEDERALLY SUPPORTED PROGRAMS FOR STUDENTS WITH DISABILITIES[1]						
TYPE OF DISABILITY	1976–1977	1980–1981	1990–1991	1995–1996	1997–1998	1998–1999	1999–2000
All disabilities	**8.32%**	**10.14%**	**11.43%**	**12.43%**	**12.80%**	**13.01%**	**13.22%**
Specific learning disabilities	1.80	3.58	5.17	5.75	5.91	5.99	6.05
Speech or language impairments	2.94	2.86	2.39	2.28	2.30	2.29	2.30
Mental retardation	2.17	2.03	1.30	1.27	1.28	1.28	1.28
Serious emotional disturbance	0.64	0.85	0.95	0.98	0.98	0.99	1.00
Hearing impairments	0.20	0.19	0.14	0.15	0.15	0.15	0.15
Orthopedic impairments	0.20	0.14	0.12	0.14	0.15	0.15	0.15
Other health impairments	0.32	0.24	0.13	0.30	0.41	0.47	0.54
Visual impairments	0.09	0.08	0.06	0.06	0.05	0.06	0.06
Multiple disabilities	—	0.17	0.23	0.21	0.23	0.23	0.24
Hearing impaired–blindness	—	0.01	(2)	(2)	(2)	(2)	(2)
Developmental delay	—	—	—	—	0.01	0.03	0.04
Autism and traumatic brain injury	—	—	—	0.09	0.12	0.14	0.17
Preschool disabled[3]	0.44	0.57	0.95	1.21	1.22	1.22	1.24

Notes: Counts are based on reports from the 50 states and District of Columbia. Increases since 1987–1988 are due in part to legislation enacted in fall 1986, which mandates public school special education services for all handicapped children ages 3 through 5. Because of rounding, details may not add to totals.

[1] Based on the enrollment in public schools, kindergarten through twelfth grade, including a relatively small number of prekindergarten students. Includes students ages 0 to 21.

[2] Less than .05%.

[3] Includes preschool children 3 to 5 years and 0 to 5 years served under Chapter I of the Elementary and Secondary Education Act and the Individuals with Disabilities Education Act (IDEA). Prior to 1987–1988, these students were included in the counts by handicapping condition. Beginning in 1987–1988, states were no longer required to report preschool handicapped students (0–5 years) by handicapping condition.

Source: U.S. Department of Education, National Center for Education Statistics, *Digest of Education Statistics 2001.*

A free public program of education and training appropriate to the child's capacity, within the context of a presumption that, among the alternative programs of education and training required by statutes to be available, placement in a regular public school class is preferable to placement in a special public school class. Further, placement in a special public school class is preferable to placement in any other type of program of education and training.[1]

The *Mills* case challenged the exclusion of children with disabilities from the District of Columbia public schools, which resulted in the denial of a publicly supported education. In rendering summary judgment for the plaintiff, the court stated:

No child eligible for a publicly supported education in the District of Columbia shall be excluded from a regular public school assignment by a rule, policy or board policy unless such child is provided adequate alternative educational services consistent with the child's needs which may include special education or tuition grants. Further, if the child is to be reassigned or provided other alternatives, procedural due process shall be required.[2]

These two cases, coupled with political pressures nationwide regarding children with disabilities, resulted in the passage of federal legislation by the Congress, which culminated in the adoption of the Rehabilitation Act of 1973 and the subsequent passage of the EAHCA. The Education for All Handicapped Children Act provided federal funds and extensive regulations designed to provide equal access and a free, appropriate education for children with disabilities. With the passage of new laws and amendments, numerous modifications and extensions have resulted in major improvements for these children.

INDIVIDUALS WITH DISABILITIES EDUCATION ACT OF 1990 (IDEA)

Mandatory Requirements

As stated previously, IDEA succeeded Public Law 94-142, the Education of All Handicapped Children Act of 1975. Congress passed the IDEA to define clearly the responsibilities of school districts regarding children with disabilities and to provide a measure of financial support to assist states in meeting their obligations.

The IDEA essentially guarantees children with disabilities, ages *3 to 21,* the right to a free, appropriate education in public schools. This act also establishes *substantive* and *procedural due process rights,* which will be discussed later in this chapter. To meet eligibility requirements, a state must develop a plan to ensure a free, appropriate education for all children with disabilities within its jurisdiction. Additionally, each state must formulate a policy that ensures certain due process rights for all children with disabilities. The state's plan should include its goals and a timetable for meeting these goals, as well as the personnel, facilities, and related services necessary to meet the needs of children with disabilities. The state's plan also must include a well-designed system for allocating funds to local school districts. In turn, each local district must submit an application to the state, demonstrating how it will comply with the requirements of IDEA. District plans must be on file and available for review by citizens upon request.

An earlier challenge reached the U.S. Supreme Court regarding a free, appropriate education in the *Rowley* case.[3] In New York, parents of a child who was nearly totally deaf brought suit against school administrators for failing to provide their child a qualified sign language interpreter for all her academic classes. The school district had provided the child a hearing aid as well as additional instruction from a tutor. A U.S. district court, in a decision upheld by the U.S. Court of Appeals, Second Circuit, ruled that even though the child was performing better than average in her class and was advancing easily from grade to grade, she was not performing as well academically as she would have without her disability. Because of the disparity between her achievement and her potential, the court held that she was not receiving a free, appropriate public education as provided by the Education for All Handicapped Children Act. However, the lower courts' decisions were reversed by the U.S. Supreme Court, which held that the EAHCA is satisfied when the state provides personalized instruction with sufficient support services to allow the child with disabilities to receive educational benefits from that instruction. The High Court held that the individualized educational program required by the EAHCA should be reasonably calculated to enable the child to achieve passing marks and advance from grade to grade. The act does not require the school to provide a sign language interpreter as requested by this child's parents. The act was not intended to guarantee a certain level of education but merely to open the door of education to children with disabilities by means of special educational services. Additionally, the decision noted that a state is not required to maximize the potential of each child who is disabled commensurate with the opportunity provided children who are not disabled. This landmark decision established the standard for determining the proper interpretation of free, appropriate education.

The IDEA requires each state to allocate federal funds first to children with disabilities who are not receiving any type of education and subsequently to children with the most severe disabilities within each disability category. The IDEA further stipulates that, to the fullest extent possible, children with disabilities must be educated with children who are not disabled. In principle, no child with disabilities may be excluded from receiving a free, appropriate public education. The statute does not require such a child to demonstrate that he or she will benefit from special education, as a condition to receiving educational services. With the wide array of disabilities, the IDEA does not require equality of results; it merely requires that children with disabilities benefit from instruction.

In another leading case, *Timothy W. v. Rochester, New Hampshire School District,*[4] the court addressed the issue of whether a district may require a child to demonstrate a benefit as a condition prior to participation in special education. Timothy had multiple physical handicaps and was profoundly mentally retarded. He suffered from complex developmental disabilities, cerebral palsy, cortical blindness, and a seizure disorder. Appropriate services were requested by his mother and refused by the Rochester School District on the grounds that Timothy's disability was so severe that he could not benefit from an education. Since the district felt that the child could not benefit from special education, Timothy was not entitled to one.

After seven years of proceedings, evaluations, and expert testimony, there was difference of opinion regarding Timothy's ability to benefit from any educational program. The district court ruled for the school district, based on its review of materials, reports, and testimony that Timothy was incapable of benefiting from special education. The district court relied quite heavily on *Board of Education of Hendrick Hudson Central School v. Rowley*[5] in concluding that a child is not entitled to a public education unless he or she can benefit from it. The district court, however, misjudged *Rowley,* which focused on the *level* and *quality* of programs and services rather than the actual criteria for access to programs.

The First Circuit Court, in reversing the district court's ruling, observed that the Individuals with Disabilities Education Act specifically recognizes that education for children with severe physical disabilities is to be broadly defined to include basic functional life skills as well as traditional academic skills. The primary question facing the school district, according to the Circuit Court, was to determine, in conjunction with Timothy's parent, what constitutes an appropriate individualized educational program for Timothy.

The judgment of the district court was reversed, and the case was remanded to the district court, which retained jurisdiction until a suitable individualized education program was developed. Timothy was entitled to an interim placement until the final individualized educational program (IEP) was developed and agreed on by all parties. The district court also was instructed to address the question of damages that were assessed against the school district.

As this case illustrates, no child with disabilities may be excluded from receiving a free, appropriate public education. Furthermore, no child with disabilities may be required to demonstrate that he or she will benefit from special education as a condition precedent to receiving appropriate services.

NATIONAL COUNCIL ON DISABILITY

On January 25, 2000, the National Council on Disability (NCD), an independent federal agency of 15 members appointed by the president and confirmed by the Senate, released its report entitled "Back to School on Civil Rights." The council's purpose is to promote policies, programs, practices, and procedures designed to assure equal opportunity for individuals with disabilities irrespective of the nature and severity of their disability. Based on NCD's finding, every state was out of compliance with the Individuals with Disabilities Education Act to some degree. More than half of the states failed to ensure compliance in five of the seven key compliance areas (see Table 5.2). These findings point to a significant failure by most states in addressing the needs of students with disabilities and meeting the intent of IDEA.

TABLE 5.2 IDEA State Compliance Rate

DISABILITY COMPONENT	COMPLIANCE FAILURE RATE OF ALL STATES
1. General supervision ensures that local educational agencies are carrying out their responsibilities to ensure compliance with IDEA.	90%
2. Transition services ensure that schools promote appropriate transition activities for students with disabilities when they leave school for postsecondary study or employment.	88%
3. Free appropriate education ensures that every child with a disability is provided an opportunity to receive a free appropriate education.	80%
4. Procedural safeguards ensure that all due process rights of disabled students and their parents are met.	78%
5. Least restrictive environment ensures that all disabled children are placed in an appropriate learning environment with the least amount of restrictions based on their disability.	72%
6. IEP protection ensures that the goals and objectives established for meeting the educational needs of disabled children are appropriate and evaluated yearly.	44%
7. Protection in evaluation ensures that parents receive written notice explaining the proposed evaluation and reasons for such evaluations as well as their rights relating to the evaluation process.	38%

Source: National Council on Disability.

Functional Exclusion of Disabled Children

Two practices tend to create additional challenges for children with disabilities: exclusion from educational programs and misclassification based on improper assessment. Both practices may result in functional exclusion of disabled children. *Functional exclusion* occurs when disabled children receive a highly inappropriate placement that denies them the opportunity to receive an appropriate education. Both of these practices generally result in legal challenges. In recent years based on IDEA, considerable progress has been made regarding inclusion of disabled students. Unfortunately, errors continue to occur regarding proper classification and placement. Consequently, school officials should exercise caution to ensure that classification and placement of disabled children are executed properly.

Interpretation and Identification of Children with Disabilities

The term *children with disabilities* is defined by the IDEA as those who meet the following conditions:

> Mental retardation, hearing impairments which include deafness, speech or language impairment, visual impairment including blindness, learning disabilities, brain injury, emotional disturbance, orthopedic impairments, autism, traumatic brain injury, specific learning disabilities and other impairments who by reason of such conditions need special education and related services.[6]

Prereferral Intervention

Regular classroom teachers have the responsibility of identifying students who may need special services in order to receive the full benefits of an education. This function should be executed before any formal assessment or special programming occurs. In short, the teacher must raise the question after carefully working with the student over a reasonable period of time and examining the student's work to determine whether he or she needs special assistance beyond that which is provided in the regular classroom. This question should emerge after continuous and multiple efforts have failed to meet the needs of the student through the regular classroom program.

Deficiencies in academic performance, as well as those related to social and interpersonal behavior, may be evident during the teacher's work with and observation of the student. After the regular classroom teacher has worked with a student and appears convinced that the student needs special assistance, a request should be made in the form of a *referral*. Virtually all school districts have well-developed policies and procedures regarding referrals. Although the procedures vary from district to district, usually there is some type of referral form used by the regular teacher when a student is deemed to need special services. This form should be as inclusive as possible in providing relevant information needed to conduct a formal assessment of the student if needed. Data requested on the referral form may include the student's name, present grade level, age, gender, standardized test scores, local test data, strengths and weaknesses in key subject areas, reading ability, behavior and relationships with fellow students, pertinent family data, and teaching methods or strategies that have been successful, as well as those that have been unsuccessful.

If a formal assessment procedure is contemplated, the student's parent must grant consent to do so and must be informed of personal rights under due process procedures. Teachers should approach the referral process with great care, since it affects the student's education, consumes time and district resources, and may result in stigmatizing a student. It is not uncommon for districts to hold prereferral conferences to discuss concerns regarding the student's academic and social performance. These meetings will usually involve the referring teacher, a special education professional, the principal, the counselor, and, in many instances, the parent. Such meetings might be used as an intermediate measure to discuss the implementation of new and different strategies regarding the student's academic and social performance. During this time, an evaluation period should be established to assess the student's progress before a formal assessment is contemplated and decisions made regarding the need for special services. It is highly desirable to employ some type of intervention prior to implementing a formal assessment process. This measure, if implemented appropriately, may reduce *overreferrals and misclassifications* and result in the best education program for the student, particularly when new strategies and interventions are implemented and evaluated over a reasonable period of time.

In each case, school officials should ensure that the school's review process is consistent with state and federal regulations and that whatever action is taken is in the best interest of the student. If it is determined that the student's problem stems from a disability, a classification is agreed on during the conference in which the parent is present. Once there is agreement on the classification, this information is passed on to a committee, which, along with the parent, will engage in developing the student's individualized educational program. The parent must sign the IEP and approve any placement outside of the regular classroom.

Thus, school districts are required to evaluate every child with disabilities to determine the nature of the disability and the need for special education and related services. Prior to this evaluation, each district must forward to the child's parent a written notice, in the parent's native language, describing the proposed evaluation process. Parental consent must be sought prior to the actual evaluation. If consent is not provided, the district must initiate an impartial hearing through a hearing officer to secure approval to conduct the evaluation.

Once approval is granted, the evaluation must be fully objective and free of any form of bias. The meeting should be conducted, in the child's native language, by a multidisciplinary team qualified to assess a wide range of skill areas. Every effort must be made to ensure that only validated tests designed to assess specific areas of need are utilized. This evaluation process should occur in a timely fashion and address each area of the child's suspected disability.

No single test should be used as the sole criterion for determining disabilities; rather, a battery of appropriate tests designed to assess areas of suspected disabilities should be used. The child's strengths and weaknesses should be identified during this process, since these will determine, to a large extent, the nature of his or her individualized program. A parent or legal guardian who is dissatisfied with the evaluation may secure an independent evaluation at the school district's expense, unless the hearing officer agrees with the district's assessment. In either case, reevaluation of each child with disabilities should minimally occur every three years.

Individualized Educational Program Requirement

When the evaluation results are produced, an individualized educational program must be designed for each child with disabilities. This process usually involves one or more meetings in which the child's teacher, parent, and special education representative for the district are present to review and discuss evaluation results. It is also recommended that a representative from the evaluation team be present to respond to questions and interpret results. If feasible, this person may be represented by the child's teacher or the special education supervisor. At a minimum, each IEP should include the following:

1. A statement detailing the child's present level of educational performance
2. A statement of annual goals, as well as short-term instructional objectives
3. A description of specific educational services to be provided and a determination as to whether the child is able to participate in regular educational programs
4. A description of transitional services to be rendered if the child is a junior or senior in high school, to ensure that necessary services are provided when the child leaves the regular school environment
5. A description of services to be provided and a timetable for providing these services
6. An explanation of relevant criteria and procedures to be employed annually to determine if instructional objectives are or have been achieved

Equal Access to Assistive Technology for Students with Disabllities

The Technology-Related Assistance for Individuals with Disabilities Act Amendments of 1994 provides financial assistance to states to support systems changes that assist in the development and implementation of technology-related support for individuals with disabilities. The act further ensures timely acquisition and delivery of *assistive technology devices,* including equipment and product systems commercially acquired, modified, or customized that are used to increase, maintain, or improve functional capabilities of a child with disabilities.

Technology assistive services are also included in this act and involve any service that directly assists a child with a disability in the selection, acquisition, or use of an assistive technology device. These services may include (1) purchasing, leasing, or otherwise providing for the acquisition of assistive technology by the child; (2) selecting, designing, fitting, customizing, adapting, applying, maintaining, repairing, or replacing assistive technology devices; (3) coordinating and using other therapies, interventions, or services with assistive technology devices, such as those associated with existing education and rehabilitation plans and programs; (4) training or technical assistance for the child or, where appropriate, the family of such child; and (5) training or technical assistance for professionals (including individuals providing education and rehabilitation services), employers, and other individuals who provide services to, employ, or are otherwise substantially involved in the major life functions of the child.

As a part of assistive technology service, training for teachers, employers, administrators, and/or any other persons who are dealing directly with student disabilities must be accommodated. Training needs may include:

1. An understanding of federal law—Section 504, ADA, and/or IDEA
2. An understanding of their responsibilities in providing accommodations
3. An understanding of the rights of the child with disabilities
4. An understanding of how accommodations and modifications should be provided

Program Review and Changes

Each IEP must be reviewed and revised annually, if necessary, to ensure that the continuing needs of the child are met. If changes are contemplated, the child's parent or legal guardian must be notified. If either objects to the proposed changes, an impartial hearing must be held to resolve the conflict. If this process proves unsuccessful, the parent or guardian may appeal to the state agency and subsequently to the courts if a resolution is not reached at the state level. This appeals process is designed to ensure fundamental fairness and to meet the requirements of due process, as spelled out in the disabilities act.

Education-Related Service Requirement

A related service is viewed as one that must be provided to allow the child with disabilities to benefit from special education. A related service may be a single service or an entire range of services or programs needed to benefit the child. Examples of such services include, but are not limited to, transportation, medical services, counseling services, psychological services, physical therapy, speech pathology, audiology, and occupational therapy.

Interestingly, litigation has challenged precisely what is considered to be a related service. A challenge was brought by a school district in the *Irving Independent School District v. Tatro* regarding the difference between a medical service and a related service. Amber Tatro, 8 years old, was born with spina bifida. Due to a bladder condition, she was unable to urinate properly. Her condition required a clean, intermittent catheterization (CIC) every three or four hours to empty her bladder and to avoid injury to her kidneys. This procedure was not considered to be a complex one. In fact, her parents, babysitter, and teenage brother were all trained to perform this simple procedure in a matter of minutes. The record shows that Amber will soon be able to perform this procedure herself. When Amber reached school age, her parents requested that school personnel perform this procedure as needed during the school day. The district refused, arguing that this service was a medical, rather than a related service, and did not serve the purpose of diagnosis or evaluation.

A suit was filed on Amber's behalf, challenging the decision of the district and requesting that the district be required to administer this procedure. The district court held for Amber by stating that the Education for All Handicapped Children Act required that such services be provided. This decision was affirmed by the court of appeals and granted review by the U.S. Supreme Court. The Supreme Court sided with the two previous courts by holding that school authorities must provide clean, intermittent catheterization to students requiring such a procedure. The Court further enumerated that there can be no question that the EAHCA mandates states to provide programs for children with disabilities, which include special education and related services necessary to achieve the act's objectives. The Court stated:

There is no question that CIC is a related service under the provisions of the act and one that is necessary for the child to benefit from special education services. While it is recognized that the act technically excludes complex medical services that may not be within the competency level of school personnel, CIC is viewed as a simple procedure capable of being performed by a nurse or a lay person with minimal preparation. The court concluded that CIC must be provided by public schools to children in need of this service.[7]

As illustrated by this case, school districts will be required to provide simple medical procedures under the category of related services, when such procedures do not require complex mastery and the services are necessary for the child to benefit from an appropriate special education program.

Least Restrictive Environment

The IDEA embraces the notion that children with disabilities be placed in educational settings that offer the least amount of restrictions, when appropriate. This view is supported by the philosophy that children with disabilities should be educated with children who are not disabled under normal classroom conditions. The primary objective is to provide children with disabilities an opportunity to interact, socialize, and learn with "regular" students, thus minimizing the tendency to become stigmatized and isolated from the school's regular program. There is also inherent value in providing nondisabled students an opportunity to increase awareness of the many challenges faced by children with disabilities and to sensitize them to their unique needs. Thus, the least restrictive provision of the act mandates the inclusion of students with disabilities into regular classrooms. This provision is clearly established in the regulation that states:

> To the maximum extent possible handicapped children in public, private or other institutions should be educated with children who are not handicapped and that separate schooling or other removal of handicapped children from the regular educational environment should occur only when the nature or severity or the handicap is such that education in regular classes with the use of supplementary aids and services cannot be achieved satisfactorily.[8]

This regulation is designed to ensure that students with disabilities be provided the broadest range of opportunities, based on the least restrictive environment provisions. The interpretation of precisely what constitutes *the least restrictive environment* has led to conflicts as well as litigation. Generally, when a child with disabilities is not involved in regular classroom instruction, the district must demonstrate through the evaluation and IEP process that a segregated facility would represent a more appropriate and beneficial learning environment. Since the law indicates a strong preference for inclusion, the burden of proof rests with educators to demonstrate that their decisions are not arbitrary or capricious regarding the placement of a child with disabilities. The statute does not mandate inclusion in each case involving such a child, but it does require that inclusion be used to the fullest extent possible and as appropriate based on the unique needs of the child with disabilities.

The least restrict environment (LRE) is a relative concept. What constitutes the least restrictive environment for one child might be totally inappropriate for another. For example, a regular classroom placement might be restrictive and inappropriate if the child's instructional and social needs cannot be adequately met. Because there is such wide variation of needs among students with disabilities, there is no ideal way to provide appropriate educational services to such children. Given the variations among these students, a range of placement options must be provided, which might include but are not limited to the following possibilities:

- Regular class with support from regular classroom teachers
- Regular class with support instruction from special teachers
- Regular class with special resource instruction
- Full-time special education class in regular school
- Full-time special school
- Residential school
- Homebound instruction

The particular placement options should be determined by the needs of the child who has disabilities and the type of environment that will best meet his or her educational and social needs.

One challenge involving placement occurred in this case.[9] Beth is a 13-year-old girl with Rett Syndrome. This neurodevelopmental disorder affects only one in ten thousand girls and does not affect boys. It is characterized as a form of autism, resulting in severe to profound disabilities to motor functioning, communication, and cognition. Beth's motor skills are estimated at between five- and seven-months old. She can only walk with one-on-one assistance and uses a wheelchair almost exclusively. These limitations, combined with her inability to speak, make traditional communication and cognition tests inappropriate. Beth primarily communicates through eye gaze, looking at or away from a person to indicate "yes" or "no," respectively, or looking at one item or picture from among several choices. She can sometimes manipulate a switch with her hand, although her motor skills may deteriorate as the disorder progresses to its next stage.

Beth began receiving services from the North Suburban Special Education School District, a special educational cooperative to which Lake Bluff belongs, in 1990, at age two, and was diagnosed with Rett Syndrome in 1991. She participated in the Co-op's early childhood program from 1991 through 1994. The Co-op provided Beth with a one-on-one aide, adaptive physical education, speech/language therapy, occupational therapy, and physical therapy. To begin the 1994–1995 school year, at her parents urging, Beth was placed in a regular kindergarten class, with a continuation of those services offered in the early childhood program. The district convened a conference annually to review and update Beth's IEP. In June 1997, at the IEP conference following Beth's second-grade year, the district recommended Beth be placed in the Co-op's self-contained education life skills (ELS) program. For most of the school day Beth would be in a classroom with five to seven other students, many of whom also have forms of autism. The special education teachers are specifically trained and experienced in dealing with students with severe cognitive and communicative disabilities.

Beth's parents rejected this placement, demanded a due process review, and invoked the IDEA's "stay put" provision, 20 U.S.C. § 1415. The impartial hearing officer, on May 26, 2000, ruled in favor of the district. Beth's parents sought review by the district court. While the due process hearing was pending, Beth continued in regular education, progressing with her peers through sixth grade.

Beth's parents brought action against the school district and superintendent, alleging that the defendants failed to provide their daughter with a free appropriate public education

(FAPE) under IDEA, and they requested a review of the administrative decision upholding district's decision to place Beth in a special education program. On cross-motions for summary judgment, the district court held that the standard that the impartial hearing officer used to determine whether the school district complied with the IDEA in its proposed placement of Beth was appropriate. This decision required that the school perform a careful and competent analysis, including reasonable efforts to obtain relevant information needed to develop a beneficial placement. The court held that the school's efforts were appropriate and that the district acted reasonably under the IDEA in determining appropriate placement for Beth. The district was not required under the IDEA to pay for private therapy for Beth. Further, the district did not intentionally discriminate against her in violation of the Americans with Disabilities Act (ADA) and the Rehabilitation Act when it determined that appropriate placement for the student was in a special education program, rather than the regular classroom. The court held for the district.

Beth B. v. Lake Bluff School District, 211 F.Supp. 2d 1020, 168 Ed. Law Rep. 212, (N.D. Ill. 2001).

Inclusion of Children with Disabilities

Inclusion is a mere extension of the traditional concept of *mainstreaming.* Its intent is to ensure, as much as possible and when appropriate, that children with disabilities are placed in regular classrooms. Inclusion is seen as one mechanism designed to ensure that all children receive a free, appropriate education in an effort to maximize their learning potential.

Implicit in this concept is the notion that some educational benefit is conferred on students with disabilities when they attend public schools. A child's evaluation results, which are used to develop the IEP, would ultimately determine the nature of the placement. Since the IEP is tailored specifically to meet the needs of the child with disabilities, it must be reasonably calculated to enable the child to receive the benefit of instruction.

Inclusion also is valuable in integrating children with disabilities into the regular school program. Many educators feel that all children—disabled and nondisabled—benefit from this arrangement. Although many educators support inclusion as a way of placing children with disabilities in the most ideal educational environment, there are many others who feel that inclusion places these children in nonsupportive environments, eliminating valuable time from their learning activities. This may be particularly critical in environments where the classroom teacher is not properly trained to work with children who have disabilities. The preparation of teachers to meet the needs of these children is critical, since inclusion is an important component of the IDEA that supports equal access for children with disabilities.

Under the concept of inclusion, regular classroom teachers in schools across the country are challenged to meet the needs of students with disabilities. In many instances, teachers are unprepared to do so. Since the IDEA specifies that students with disabilities be provided a free, appropriate public education in the least restrictive environment based on each student's individualized educational program, there is an affirmative obligation placed on schools to serve the needs of these students. If teachers are not prepared to meet these needs, a legal issue may emerge regarding both *academic injury* as well as *physical injury* to the student.

With increasing frequency, regular classroom teachers are called on to meet the academic needs and perform related services such as catheterization, suctioning, colostomy, and seizure monitoring when students with disabilities are placed in regular classrooms. If teachers are unable to perform these vital services effectively, resulting in injury to the child, liability charges may be forthcoming, depending on the nature of the injury and factors leading to such injury. Thus, not only are classroom teachers expected to meet the academic needs of children with disabilities but they may also be expected to provide special education services during the inclusion period.

School districts, then, have the responsibility of ensuring that a *reasonable standard of care* is met when regular teachers work with students who have disabilities. This means that districts must be properly prepared to meet the diverse needs of such students, which may be accomplished through systematic and continuous training as well as appropriately developed policies and procedures regarding the teacher's role in relation to students with disabilities. These procedures should be monitored on a systematic basis and altered as the need arises. Failure to adhere to these precautions may form the grounds for liability suits for physical injury, as well as threats of educational malpractice if parents of children with disabilities allege that academic injury resulted from the teacher's lack of skill or fidelity in performing professional duties.

Length of School Year

Numerous lawsuits have emerged regarding the adequacy of the length of the school term in relationship to the needs of children with disabilities. There appears to be some evidence that supports the view that these children regress more quickly when they are without education and services than do students without disabilities. Based on this view, the courts have been quite liberal in granting requests for continuous or year-long schooling for children with disabilities, as illustrated by the following case.

The mother of a child with severe disabilities requested his school district to provide a summer program for him, including transportation. Her request was denied. The mother appealed the district's decision to the Texas Education Agency. A hearing examiner ruled on her behalf. The school district then filed suit, seeking review in U.S. district court. The court found that the student, having been without a structured summer program, suffered significant regression of the knowledge gained and skills learned during the school year. The U.S. Court of Appeals agreed with the district court's decision in holding that if a child with disabilities experiences severe or substantial regression during the summer months in the absence of an appropriate summer school program, the child is entitled to year-round services. Since the child in this case would suffer significant regression, he was entitled to summer instruction. The court further found that the request for transportation was reasonable because the mother was a full-time employee, and it would not create an undue burden on the school district to provide transportation.[10] Also, attorney's fees were awarded to the parent, based on the *Handicapped Children's Protection Act,* which makes this provision if parents or guardians are successful in their litigation against state or local agencies.

Residential Placement

The issue regarding whether a child with a disability should be placed in a residential facility tends to draw controversy between parents and school district officials. Residential facilities are typically expensive and, in most cases, more restrictive for the child.

However, IDEA requires such placements where there is sufficient evidence that residential placement is necessary to provide special education and related services to the child with disabilities. In such cases, the costs related to residential placement must be covered by the local school district. If residential placement is the only means by which a child receives services for educational purposes or educational benefits when there is evidence that such placement also provides noneducational benefits, the school district or the state is not relieved from its financial obligations to cover the costs related to the placement.

For example, parents of an Oregon child were awarded reimbursement for expenses incurred when they decided to place their child in a residential facility after his behavior deteriorated severely in the public school placement. Experts testified that the child could only benefit from a 24-hour, 7-day-a-week completely consistent environment. The school had a duty to place the child in the most appropriate educational placement and failed to do so.[11]

In a contrasting case, the school district decided that a child with chronic schizophrenia and disabilities could no longer attend day programs because of episodes of aggressive behavior. When the district could not identify a proper residential facility in state, it recommended one in the closest state, over the parent's objection. The court held for the parents when it was determined that the child was denied appropriate education in accordance with his current IEP by his placement in an out-of-state facility close to home. The student was awarded compensatory education for the years he had been inappropriately placed.[12]

Public school districts are required to pay private school tuition and related expenses in cases where the district fails to offer an appropriate special education program to a student with a disability. This concept was reinforced by the U.S. Supreme Court in the *Burlington* case, in which the father of a child with learning disabilities became dissatisfied with his third-grade son's lack of progress in a Massachusetts public school system.[13] A new IEP was developed for the child, which called for placement in a different public school. The father, following the advice of specialists at Massachusetts General Hospital, unilaterally withdrew his son from the school system, placing him instead at a state-approved private facility in Massachusetts. He then sought reimbursement for tuition and transportation expenses from the school committee, maintaining that the IEP was inappropriate. The state Board of Special Education Appeals (BSEA) ruled that the proposed IEP was inappropriate and that the father was justified in placing his son at a special school. The BESA ordered the school committee to reimburse the father for tuition and transportation expenses. The committee appealed to the federal courts. A U.S. district court held that the parents had violated the Education of the Handicapped Act's (EHA's) status quo provision by enrolling their child in the private school without approval. Thus, they were not entitled to reimbursement. However, the U.S. Court of Appeals, First Circuit, reversed the district court's ruling, and the committee appealed to the U.S. Supreme Court.

In affirming the court of appeals' decision, the Supreme Court ruled that parents who place a child with a disability in a private educational facility are entitled to reimbursement for the child's tuition and living expenses, if a court later determines that the school district has proposed an inappropriate individualized education program. Reimbursement could not be ordered if the school district's proposed IEP was later found to be appropriate. The Supreme Court observed that to disallow reimbursement claims under all circumstances would be contrary to the EHA, which favors proper interim placements for children with disabilities.

Private School Placement

The IDEA requires each state to provide special education and related services to all children with disabilities. Each state must ensure, to the greatest degree possible, that children with disabilities enrolled in private schools receive an appropriate education. Local school districts may provide services in a public school setting or opt to cover the cost of services in private schools. In either case, services must be comparable in quality in both settings. The statute makes a distinction between those who are placed in a private school based on their IEP versus those whose parents voluntarily place them in private schools. The child who is voluntarily placed in a private school by his or her parent has lesser entitlement than the child placed in a public school. If a free, appropriate education is provided for the child with disabilities based on the IEP and the child is placed in a private school based on the parent's desire, the district is under no obligation to cover the costs incurred in such placement. However, if the child's IEP calls for a private school placement, the district is obligated to cover all costs associated with such placement.

A rather unusual case involving harassment and private school placement of a disabled student arose when Leslie Biggs was diagnosed with epilepsy in 1995.[14] During the 1996–1997 school year, she experienced frequent seizures requiring hospitalization. By the beginning of the 1997–1998 school year, Biggs' condition had improved and she was essentially seizure-free.

In the fall of 1997, Biggs began the seventh grade. During this school year, Biggs was subjected to taunting and teasing by some classmates, apparently on the basis of her epilepsy and physical appearance. Biggs and her mother complained to the school on numerous occasions throughout the school year. In response to the complaints, the school initiated a number of steps to address the harassment. The school guidance counselor arranged a meeting with Biggs and two boys accused of teasing her to discuss the harmful effects of teasing.

Mrs. Biggs later gave the vice principal a list of the names of 11 boys whom her daughter said had teased her. In response, the vice principal scheduled meetings with each of the accused students to discuss the incidents and to explain that teasing was totally unacceptable. After speaking with each student, the vice principal sent a letter to each student's parent(s) or guardian(s) informing them of the complaints against their children and the disciplinary action that would be taken if students were found guilty of verbal harassment.

Additionally, the vice principal spoke with Biggs' teachers regarding the taunting and teasing. The vice principal informed each teacher that anyone they heard make harassing statements to Biggs should be sent to the office immediately.

While the school was taking corrective action, Biggs' parents removed her from school and home-tutored her for the remainder of the school year. In the fall of 1998, she was enrolled at Elkton Christian School and repeated the seventh grade.

On April 10, 2000, Biggs' parents filed suit against the board of education of Cecil County, Maryland. Their amended complaint sought damages in the amount of $300,000 on the grounds that Leslie was denied a free, appropriate public education and suffered damages to her education performance and opportunities by having to repeat the seventh grade, which resulted in emotional distress. The amended complaint also sought attorney's fees and costs.

The board filed a motion to dismiss all counts for summary judgment on two counts. The court denied the board's motion. The board again filed a motion to dismiss, for summary judgment. The court concluded that the state is immune from suit under Title II of the ADA and Section 504 of the Rehabilitation Act. The local school board is a state agency entitled to invoke the protections of Eleventh Amendment immunity, although there is a private right of action under Title IX for student-on-student sexual harassment. The board of education is entitled to summary judgment because there was no evidence of deliberate indifference by school officials to the taunting and teasing of Leslie Biggs.

As this case illustrates, disabled students are treated no differently than nondisabled students in harassment cases unless there is a showing that the harassing students' behavior is so severe, pervasive, and objectively offensive that it denies the victim equal access to an education. Further, they are valid when school authorities are clearly unreasonable and deliberately indifferent toward the alleged harassing conduct. There was no evidence that either of these conditions existed.

DISCIPLINING STUDENTS WITH DISABILITIES

It has long been held that children with disabilities may not be punished for conduct that is a *manifestation* of their disability. However, they may be disciplined by school authorities for any behavior that is not associated with their disability, using regular disciplinary procedures, as reflected in school policies. In situations where certain types of discipline are warranted, an effort must be made to ensure that the punishment does not *materially* and *substantially* interrupt the child's education. School expulsions, suspensions, and transfers are examples that fall into this category.

Expulsion

Expulsion represents the most serious form of punishment, because it results in permanent separation from the school district for the student. Two early cases addressed the issue of discipline and a change in placement regarding expulsion and long-term suspension of children with disabilities. The first case, *S-1 v. Turlington*,[15] involved expulsion of nine high school students in Hendry, Florida. In separate actions, these students were expelled for various acts of misconduct. One student, S-1, requested a hearing to determine whether his behavior was associated with his disability. The other eight made no such request.

School officials had determined in S-1's case that his conduct was not related to his disability, since he was not seriously disabled. S-1 brought suit, claiming that his rights had been violated under the Education for All Handicapped Children Act. The district court issued an injunction against the state, which was appealed by Turlington, the state superintendent of education.

The issue addressed during the appeal was whether a child with mild retardation could be expelled without a hearing to determine if the conduct for which the student was expelled was related to his disability. The Fifth Circuit Court ruled for S-1 by stating that a student with retardation may not be expelled without a hearing to determine whether the conduct exhibited by the child was related to his disability.

The court was not receptive to the state's claim that the other eight students requested no hearing. The court stated that those eight must be provided a hearing prior to expulsion proceedings to make the determination regarding disability-related behavior. The act places an obligation on school officials to make this determination. Even when a determination is made that the conduct exhibited by the child is unrelated to his or her disability, school officials must also be mindful that long-term suspensions or expulsion are tantamount to a change in placement, thus triggering a need for implementation of full procedural safeguards and stay-put provisions.

A leading case, *Stuart v. Nappi,* addressed this issue. Kathy Stuart was diagnosed with serious academic and emotional difficulties that stemmed from complex learning disabilities and limited intelligence. She also had a record of behavioral problems.

A meeting of the planning and placement team (PPT) was held in February 1975, at which Kathy was diagnosed as having a major learning disability. The PPT recommended that Kathy be scheduled on a trial basis in the special education program for remediating learning disabilities and that she be given a psychological evaluation. Although the PPT report specifically stated that the psychological evaluation be given "at the earliest feasible time," no such evaluation was administered.

At the beginning of the 1976–1977 school year, Kathy was scheduled to participate in a learning disability program on a part-time basis. Her attendance continued to decline throughout the first half of the school year. By late fall, she had completely stopped attending her special education classes and had begun to spend this time wandering the school corridors with her friends. Although she was encouraged to participate in the special education classes, the PPT meeting concerning Kathy's program, which had been requested at the end of the previous school year, was not conducted in the fall of 1976.

On September 14, 1977, Kathy was involved in schoolwide disturbances that erupted at Danbury High School. As a result of her involvement in these disturbances, she received a ten-day disciplinary suspension and was scheduled to appear at a disciplinary hearing on November 30, 1977. The Superintendent of Danbury Schools recommended to the Danbury Board of Education that Kathy be expelled for the remainder of the 1977–1978 school year at this hearing.

Kathy's attorney requested a hearing with the Danbury Board of Education to review Kathy's special education program, and successfully obtained a temporary restraining order that enjoined the board from conducting the hearing. Evidence revealed that Kathy's program had not been reviewed in nine months by the PPT review committee nor had the school developed a new special program for her. In ruling for Kathy, the court stated:

> The expulsion of handicapped children not only jeopardizes their right to an education in the least restrictive environment, but is inconsistent with the procedures established by the Handicapped Act for changing the placement of disruptive children. The Handicapped Act prescribes a procedure whereby disruptive children are transferred to more restrictive placements when their behavior significantly impairs the education of other children. Thus, the use of expulsion proceedings as a means of changing the placement of a disruptive handicapped child contravenes the procedures of the Handicapped Act. After considerable reflection, the Court is persuaded that any changes in plaintiff's placement must be made by a PPT after considering the range of available placement and plaintiff's particular needs.[16]

The importance of the parameters of this decision should be clearly understood. Children with disabilities are neither immune from a school's disciplinary process nor are they entitled to participate in programs when their behavior impairs the education of other children in the program. School officials may exercise at least two options in this situation. First, school authorities can take swift disciplinary measures, such as suspension, against disruptive children, disabled or not. Second, a PPT can request a change in placement to a more restrictive environment for children with disabilities who have demonstrated that their present placement is inappropriate by disrupting the education of other children. The Individuals with Disabilities Education Act thereby affords schools with both short-term and long-term methods of dealing with children with disabilities who exhibit behavioral problems.

Schools may use their normal disciplinary procedures to address behavior of such students, if that behavior is nondisability related. As emphasized earlier in the *S-1 v. Turlington* case, school authorities may not discipline a student with disabilities for behavior that is a manifestation of his or her disability.

Since certain types of disciplinary measures may involve removal of children with disabilities from their placement, care must be taken to ensure that proper procedural guidelines are followed. As established in the *Stuart v. Nappi* case, suspension of a student with disabilities is tantamount to a change in placement, thus triggering the stay-put provision of the IDEA. These decisions may involve transfers, suspensions, and expulsions. The stay-put provision of the IDEA requires that children with disabilities remain in their current placement pending the completion of the individualized educational program review process.

There has been some debate as to what constitutes a change in placement. This question has been addressed by a number of courts, resulting in several definitions. In *Concerned Parents v. New York City Board of Education,* the court ruled that a change in placement occurs when there is a change in the general education program in which the student is enrolled, as opposed to mere variations of it.[17]

In yet another case, *Tilton v. Jefferson County Board of Education,* the Sixth Circuit Court interpreted a change of placement occurring when the modified or revised program is not comparable to the program established in the original IEP. Irrespective of the precise definition, such change triggers both the procedural and stay-put provisions of the IDEA. Procedural protections are obviously designed to ensure that the required legal proceedings occur in the manner prescribed by statutes, whereas the stay-put provisions allow students to remain in their placement during the impartial hearing or subsequent appeals. When there is agreement between the parent and school authorities, the child remains in the current placement, even though it may not be deemed the most appropriate one at that time.[18]

If either the parent or the school authorities wish to temporarily change the placement before the appeals process is exhausted, a *court order* must be ascertained to affect this change. If a decision is reached that a child's placement should be changed, special education and related services cannot be discontinued. The child must receive educational support.

Suspension

School suspension is one of the most common forms of punishment used to remove disruptive students from the school environment. It is particularly useful as a disciplinary tool in cases where there is an immediate threat to health and safety of the child with disabilities or other children in the school. A temporary suspension may be justified in cases that fall into this category. There has been considerable disagreement among school authorities regarding the limits of their authority to remove, temporarily, children who are disabled in emergency situations when the health and safety of other students are threatened.

In a compelling case, *Honig v. Doe,* the U.S. Supreme Court responded to this issue. This case involved two students who were emotionally disturbed who had been suspended indefinitely for violent conduct related to their disabilities, pending the results of an expulsion hearing. Doe had a history of aggressive behavior, particularly when he was ridiculed by other students. The facts revealed that Doe choked a fellow student with sufficient force to leave visible neck abrasions. He also kicked out a window while being led to the principal's office. The other student, Smith, experienced academic and social difficulties and had a tendency to respond with verbal hostility, stealing, extorting money from classmates, and making sexual overtures to female students.

Both students filed suit, contending that the suspensions and proposed expulsions violated the stay-put provision of the IDEA. The district court ruled for the students and was later affirmed by the court of appeals. The case was reviewed by the U.S. Supreme Court. The fundamental issue confronting the high court was whether the stay-put provision of the act prohibits states from removing children from school for violent or disruptive conduct stemming from their disability. Justice Brennan, writing for the majority, reasoned that, under the act, states may not remove students with disabilities from classrooms for violent or disruptive conduct stemming from their disabilities. The language in the Individuals with Disabilities Act clearly prohibits such action while any proceedings are pending. The court cannot render an exception to this provision, as the plaintiff suggested.

Schools, however, may use their normal procedures in dealing with students who endanger themselves or others. Students who pose an immediate threat to school safety may be temporarily suspended for up to ten days without inquiring into whether the student's behavior was a manifestation of a disability. This type of suspension, consistent with an earlier case, *Goss v. Lopez,* involving nondisabled students, is considered to be a short-term suspension that allows school authorities the freedom to punish a student with disabilities by removing him or her from the classroom in anticipation of further action that might involve long-term suspension, movement to a more restrictive environment, or, as a last resort, expulsion.

The significance of this ruling is that the High Court does not interpret short-term suspension as a change in placement, and therefore does not trigger the need for elaborate procedural requirements associated with the act.[19] However, it is important to note that long-term suspensions and expulsion do constitute a change in placement and may not be used if the student's conduct is associated with a known disability. In extreme situations involving safety risks, school districts may seek a court order that permits them to initiate a temporary change of placement. In either case, educational services should be provided during the suspension.

Since the burden of proof to determine whether a student's misconduct is a manifestation of a disability rests with the school district, there must be clear and objective evidence to support the district's actions. A highly skilled and trained team of knowledgeable professionals must be charged with making this determination. Although there is some disagreement among the courts regarding whether educational services should be provided during long-term suspension of students with disabilities, the Department of Education has adopted the position of the Fifth Circuit Court by suggesting that services should be provided to those students who are serving long-term suspensions.

INDIVIDUALS WITH DISABILITIES
EDUCATION ACT OF 1997

Amendments Regarding Discipline

Under the Individuals with Disabilities Education Act Amendments of 1997, discipline with respect to suspension, manifestation, and *interim alternative educational settings (IAES)* are addressed. These amendments are designed to provide greater flexibility to school districts without violating the rights of students who are disabled. Based on these amendments, the following provisions apply

Discipline and Optional Sanctions.   When a student violates a school rule or code of conduct that is uniformly applicable to all students, the local education agency (LEA), acting through the student's IEP team, may take one of several actions:

1. It may place the student in an interim alternative educational setting or other setting for up to ten days, provided, however, that it also may use the same sanction for students who do not have disabilities (stay-put provision applies).
2. It may suspend the student for up to ten days, provided that it also may use the same sanction for students who do not have disabilities (stay-put provision applies).
3. It may place the student in an IAES for up to 45 days, provided that it also may use the same sanction for students without disabilities, if the student carries a weapon to school or to a student function or illegally uses drugs or sells or solicits the sale of a controlled substance at school or a school function (for weapons and drug discipline, stay-put rule does not apply).
4. It may ask a hearing officer to place a dangerous student into an IAES for up to 45 days (if the officer agrees, the stay-put rule does not apply).

Pre/Postsanction IEP Review, Behavior Modification Plan, and Functional Assessment.   Before it takes any disciplinary actions or within at least ten days after it does so, the LEA must convene the IEP team to take one of two actions:

1. If the LEA has not already conducted a *functional behavioral assessment* and implemented a *behavioral intervention,* then the IEP team must develop an assessment plan to address the student's behavior; or
2. If the LEA has already developed such a plan and put it into the student's IEP, then the team must review the plan and modify it, as necessary, to address the behavior for which the student was disciplined.

Premanifestation Determination Action.   Before it imposes any sanction (placement in an IAES, placement in another setting, suspension for up to ten days, or placement in an IAES for up to 45 days for weapons, drug violations, or dangerousness), the IEP team and any other qualified personnel must

1. Notify the student's parents of the decision and of the student's and parents' procedural safeguards.
2. No later than ten days after making the decision, review the relationship between the student's disability and the student's behavior.

Manifestation Determination Review.   When conducting the manifestation review, the IEP team (as supplemented by any other appropriate personnel) must determine that the behavior was *not* a manifestation of the disability if it complies with two requirements:

1. It first considers, in terms of the behavior, all relevant information, including evaluation and diagnostic results, information supplied by the parents, observations of the student, and the student's present IEP and placement.
2. After considering these matters, the team must determine that
   - The student's IEP and placement were appropriate and the LEA provided special education, related services, supplementary aids and services, and behavior intervention strategies consistent with the IEP and placement.
   - The disability did not impair the student's ability to understand the impact and consequences of the behavior.
   - The disability did not impair the student's ability to control the behavior.

If the team determines that the behavior was *not* a manifestation of the disability, then the LEA may

1. Apply to the student the same sanctions that it may apply to students without a disability, but it may not terminate altogether the student's access to free appropriate public education (FAPE) (no cessation).
2. Ensure that the student's disciplinary and educational records are transmitted for consideration by the person making the final disciplinary decision (e.g., a school principal).

Appeal from Disciplinary Action.   A parent may appeal (to an impartial hearing officer) the determination concerning "no manifestation" or any discipline-related placement decision.

1. The hearing must be expedited and must be conducted before an impartial hearing officer.
2. The hearing officer must determine whether the LEA has demonstrated that the student's behavior was not a manifestation.

During the hearing, the hearing officer may place the student in an appropriate IAES for up to 45 days, but only if

1. The officer determines that the LEA has demonstrated by substantial evidence (defined as "beyond a preponderance of the evidence") that maintaining the student's current placement is substantially likely to result in injury to the student or others (i.e., other students or staff).
2. The officer considers the appropriateness of the student's current placement.
3. The officer considers whether the LEA has made reasonable efforts to minimize the risk of harm in the student's current placement, including the use of supplementary aids and services.
4. The officer determines that the IAES allows the student to continue to participate in the general curriculum and continue to receive those services and modifications that

will enable the student to meet IEP goals as well as services and modifications that address the sanctioned behavior to ensure that it does not recur.

Placement During Appeals. The student remains in the IAES pending the decision of the hearing office, for up to 45 days, unless the parents and LEA agree otherwise.

Proposed New Placement (Following IAES). If the LEA places the student in an IAES and then proposes to change the student's placement after the IAES placement expires, and if the parents challenge this proposed change in placement, the general rule is that, during the pendency of the hearing on the parents' challenge, the student remains in the placement that existed before the interim placement. This rule, however, will not apply, and an exception to it exists, if the LEA maintains that it is dangerous for the student to be in that placement and if it also requests an expedited hearing. To determine whether the student will return to the original placement, remain in the alternative setting (converting it from an interim to a permanent placement), or be placed in another setting, the hearing officer must make the same four findings of fact and then decide on the placement.

Preemptive Strike. In order to gain the protections of IDEA's disciplinary safeguards, a student who previously was not entitled to the protections of IDEA may assert that he or she is entitled to special education and related services and to the special procedural and other safeguards of IDEA if the LEA had knowledge that the student was a student with a disability before the misconduct occurred. The LEA is deemed to have known that the student had a disability if

1. The parent expressed concern in writing to the LEA that the student is in need of services.
2. The parent has requested a nondiscriminatory evaluation.
3. The student's behavior or performance has demonstrated that he or she needs those services.
4. The student's teacher or other school personnel have a concern regarding the student's behavior or performance and have expressed that concern to the LEA's special education director or other personnel.

If, however, none of these conditions exists and the LEA has no knowledge or is not charged with knowledge that the student has a disability, then it may subject the student to the same discipline as any other student who engages in comparable behavior. If the student is evaluated during the time he or she is subjected to disciplinary measures, the LEA must expedite the evaluation.

If the LEA determines that the student is in need of special education and related services, it must provide those services in accordance with IDEA. The student, however, must remain in the educational placement determined by the school authorities pending the evaluation.

A no-manifestation case arose in Maine when parents of an eighth-grade student with a learning disability appealed a hearing officer's special education due process hearing decision issued pursuant to the IDEA and the state special education law provisions after the student was expelled for a drug violation.[20] The district court held that the pupil evaluation team (PET) was not required to conduct its review as to whether the student's behavior was a manifestation of his disability before, rather than after, its expulsion decision; the PET's delay in holding the manifestation hearing until 12 days after its expulsion decision, rather than within ten days as required under IDEA, was harmless; the PET's failure to consider, as part of its manifestation review, results of behavioral tests indicating that the student had a tendency to act impulsively, was harmless; the evidence supported the hearing officer's finding, upholding the PET's determination that the student's behavior was not a manifestation of his disability; and the PET's individualized educational program, developed for the student during his expulsion, was adequate. The school's alleged failure to give proper notice to parents before the school board voted to expel their son was not fatal to the expulsion. The PET's failure to conduct a functional behavioral assessment for use in its manifestation review was harmless. The PET's hiring of an outside consultant to compile the information necessary for functional behavioral assessment was appropriate; and the school district's failure to explicitly suspend the student under IDEA's 45-day suspension rule for drug offenders was harmless. Based on these factual findings, the court held for the school district.

Reporting Criminal Behavior and Referring to Law Enforcement and Judicial Agencies.   The LEA may report any crime committed by a student to the appropriate authorities. IDEA does not prevent those authorities from exercising any of their duties to enforce state or federal criminal law. If it files a report, the LEA must provide copies of the student's special education and disciplinary records to the authorities with which it filed the report of a crime.

Transmitting Student Information.   The state may require the LEA to include in the student's file a statement of any current or previous disciplinary action taken against the student. This information may be transmitted to educators to the same extent as such information is transmitted for students without disabilities. This statement may include a description of the student's behavior that required disciplinary action, a description of the disciplinary action taken, and any other information that is relevant to the safety of the child and others. If the state adopts a disclosure policy and the student transfers from one school to another, the student's records must include a copy of his or her original IEP and a statement of current or previous disciplinary action taken against the student.

The significance of the changes is that the IEP serves as the link between the nondiscriminatory education (NDE) and the least restrictive environment (LRE) placement. These amendments make this connection more explicit. There is also a very strong component of the LRE found in the IEP.

Discipline and Behavior Are Now Linked.   The IEP "special factors" provision requires the IEP team to include appropriate strategies, including positive behavioral interventions, strategies, and support to address (i.e., prevent and remediate) behaviors that impede the student's or others' learning. These behaviors undoubtedly include those for which the student may be disciplined. Thus, the present *harmful effects* rule (the student may not be placed in a program where there will be harmful effects to the student, other students, or staff) is not retained, but a *prevention of harmful effects* rule is substituted.

In addition, the IEP team must consist of a regular educator whose input includes determining appropriate positive interventions and strategies.[21] The 1997 amendments should provide greater flexibility for school officials without violating the personal and due process of students with disabilities, as well as their parents.

■ ■ ■ ■ ■ ▬▬▬▬▬▬▬▬▬▬▬▬▬▬▬▬▬▬▬▬▬▬▬▬▬▬▬▬▬▬▬▬▬▬▬▬▬▬▬

ADMINISTRATIVE GUIDE

STUDENT DISABILITIES

1. School districts should ensure that children with disabilities in their districts be provided equal access to a public education. Failure to provide appropriate special education may result in a court injunction as well as mandatory compensatory education.
2. A lack of funds should not be used by school districts as the basis to deny children with disabilities a public education.
3. School districts should be certain that they clearly understand the difference between medical services and related services.
4. A well-organized and coordinated staff development plan should be developed to prepare all teachers to work effectively with children who are disabled. These activities should be coherent, continuous, and well supported by the district.
5. School personnel should be aware of possible liability challenges if they fail to perform certain related services properly.
6. Parental rights must be respected and addressed in matters relating to evaluation and IEP development.
7. Children with disabilities should not be disciplined for behavior that is associated with their known disabilities.
8. Long-term suspension, if necessary, will trigger the need for change of placement requirements, but in virtually no cases should children with disabilities be without educational services. School officials should become familiar with the new IDEA amendments regarding discipline of such students and be certain that the amendments are incorporated into district policy.
9. School districts may be assessed attorney fees under the Handicapped Children's Protection Act, if a parent prevails in a suit for a violation of IDEA.
10. The burden of proof rests with the school district in determining whether misbehavior by a student with disabilities is attributed to the disability.
11. School districts should ensure that architectural barriers do not prevent or otherwise qualify individuals who are disabled from receiving services or participating in programs or activities provided by the district.
12. According to one court, school districts are expected to provide sign language interpreters at district expense to deaf parents of hearing children at school-initiated activities related to the academic or disciplinary aspects of the child's education.
13. School districts may be required to provide educational services beyond the regular school year, depending on the student's unique needs.

Attention Deficit Hyperactivity Disorder and Federal Protection

A growing number of children with attention deficit hyperactivity disorder (ADHD) are enrolled in public schools. Three federal statutes—the Individuals with Disabilities Education Act (IDEA), Section 504 of the Rehabilitation Act of 1973 (RHA), and the Americans with Disabilities Act (ADA)—cover children with attention deficit hyperactivity disorder.

Under IDEA, ADHD eligible students must possess one or more specified physical or mental impairments and must be determined to require special education and related services based on these impairments. ADHD alone is not sufficient to qualify a child for special education services unless it impairs the child's ability to benefit from education. Children with ADHD may be eligible for special education services if they are found to have a specific learning disability, be seriously emotionally disturbed, or possess other health impairments.

Section 504 provides education for children who do not fall within the disability categories covered under IDEA. This statute further requires that a free, appropriate public education be provided to each eligible child who is disabled but does not require special education and related services under IDEA. *A free, appropriate education,* as defined under Section 504, includes regular or special education and related services designed to meet the individual needs of students consistent with the provisions involving evaluation, placement, and procedural safeguards. The act stipulates:

- Parents are guaranteed the right to contest the outcome of an evaluation if a local district determines that a child is not disabled under Section 504.
- The local district is required to make an individualized determination of the child's educational needs for regular or special education or related aids and services if the child is determined to be eligible under Section 504.
- Implementation of an individualized educational program is required.
- The child's education must be provided in the regular classroom unless it is shown that the education in the regular classroom with the use of supplementary aids and services cannot be achieved satisfactorily.
- Necessary adjustments must be made in the regular classroom for children who qualify under Section 504.

The education program requirements of RHA, although not as detailed, are fairly consistent with those of IDEA. The Rehabilitation Act and Americans with Disabilities Act are similar regarding basic provisions. RHA regulates organizations that receive federal funds, whereas ADA covers virtually all public and private schools with the exception of private religious schools. Receipt of federal funds is not associated with ADA. Although there is overlap between these two laws, the requirements are essentially the same for both. Fundamental to both laws is the requirement that children with ADHD and other disabilities not be treated differently based solely on their disability.

Correctable Illnesses and ADA

The U.S. Supreme Court provided new meaning to the Americans with Disabilities Act (ADA) in three separate rulings affecting employees. The three landmark rulings held that Americans with physical impairments are not protected by ADA in instances in which their impairments are correctable. At issue were cases involving eyesight and hypertension. The High Court held that eyesight and hypertension were correctable impairments that do not receive coverage under ADA. These rulings did not affect the 43 million individuals with bona fide cases of disability. The Supreme Court held that the determination of whether a person is protected by ADA should be made with respect to measures that mitigate the individual's impairment including, in these instances, eyeglasses and contact lens. An identical ruling was made against a Kansas truck mechanic with high blood pressure that was deemed correctable with medication. The third case drew the same result in Oregon involving a truck driver who was virtually blind in one eye. The U.S. Supreme Court's decisions, while excluding over a million Americans from coverage of ADA, provided clear guidance to both employers and employees regarding the intent of ADA and its scope of coverage. These cases are summarized here.

Severely myopic twin sisters, with uncorrected visual acuity of 20/200, or worse, applied for employment as commercial airline pilots. With corrective measures, both women functioned identically to individuals without similar impairments. They applied to the defendant, a major commercial airline carrier, for employment. They were rejected because they did not meet the airline's minimum requirement of uncorrected visual acuity of 20/100 or better. They then filed suit under the Americans with Disabilities Act of 1990 (ADA), which prohibits covered employers from discriminating against individuals on the basis of their disability, which is defined as "a physical or mental impairment that substantially limits one or more . . . major life activities" or as "being regarded as having such an impairment." The district court dismissed the plaintiffs' complaint for failure to state a claim on which relief could be granted. The court held that petitioners were not actually disabled under the disability definition because they could fully correct their visual impairments. The plaintiffs had alleged only that the defendant regarded them as unable to satisfy the requirements of a particular job—global airline pilot. These allegations were insufficient to state a claim that the plaintiffs were regarded as substantially limited in the major life activity of working. The Tenth Circuit Court ruled that the petitioners did not allege that they are "disabled" within the ADA's meaning.[22]

This case was addressed by the U.S. Supreme Court in a 7–2 ruling. The high court affirmed the Tenth Circuit Court of Appeal's ruling. Justice O'Connor delivered the opinion of the Court.

> The Americans with Disabilities Act of 1990 prohibits certain employers from discriminating against individuals on the basis of their disabilities. [The plaintiffs] challenged the dismissal of their ADA action for failure to state a claim upon which relief can be granted. We conclude that the complaint was properly dismissed. In reaching that result, we hold that the determination of whether an individual is disabled should be made with reference to measures that mitigate the individual's impairment, including, in this instance, eyeglasses and contact lenses. In addition, we hold that [the] petitioners failed to allege properly that [the] respondent "regarded" them as having a disability within the meaning of the ADA.

The plaintiffs failed to state a claim on which relief could be sought under ADA. Since their illness could be corrected with appropriate measures, it did not fall under the protection of ADA.[23]

In a related case, the United Parcel Service (UPS) hired a man named Murphy as a mechanic, a position that also required him to drive commercial vehicles. To drive, he had to satisfy certain Department of Transportation (DOT) health certification requirements, including having "no current clinical diagnosis of high blood pressure that would interfere with his ability to operate a commercial vehicle safely." Despite his high blood pressure, he was erroneously granted certification and began working. After the error was discovered, the company fired him on the belief that his blood pressure greatly exceeded the DOT's requirements. Murphy brought suit under the Americans with Disabilities Act of 1990 (ADA). The district court granted UPS a summary judgment, which was affirmed by the Tenth Circuit Court. Using the Supreme Court ruling in the *Sutton v. United Airlines* case, which held that an individual claiming a disability under the ADA should be assessed with regard to any mitigating or corrective measures employed, the court of appeals held that the petitioner's hypertension is not a disability, because his doctor testified that, when medicated, the petitioner functions normally in everyday activities. The court also affirmed the district court's determination that Murphy is not "regarded as" disabled under the ADA, explaining that UPS did not terminate him on an unsubstantiated fear that he would suffer a heart attack or stroke, but because his blood pressure exceeded the DOT's requirements for commercial vehicle drivers.[24]

This case reached the Supreme Court in April 1999. In a 7–2 decision, the U.S. Supreme Court examined the Tenth Circuit Court of Appeals' ruling by deciding whether the court of appeals erred in considering Murphy's medicated state when it ruled that his impairment does not substantially limit one or more of his major life activities and whether it erred in determining that the plaintiff is not regarded as disabled. The Supreme Court concluded that the court of appeals' position of both issues was correct. This ruling clearly suggests that correctable illnesses are not deemed disabilities that trigger the application of ADA standards. The Supreme Court's ruling in these cases narrows the impact of the Americans with Disabilities Act.

Before beginning a truck driver's job with Albertson's, Inc., in 1990, Kirkingburg was examined to see whether he met the Department of Transportation's basic vision standards for commercial truck drivers, which require corrected distant visual acuity of at least 20/40 in each eye and distant binocular acuity of at least 20/40. Although Kirkingburg has amblyopia, an uncorrectable condition that leaves him with 20/200 vision in his left eye, the doctor erroneously certified that he met the DOT standards. When Kirkingburg's vision was correctly assessed at a 1992 physical, he was told that he had to get a waiver of the DOT standards under a waiver program initiated that year. Albertson's, however, fired him for failing to meet the basic DOT vision standards and refused to rehire him after he received a waiver. Kirkingburg sued Albertson's, claiming that firing him violated the Americans with Disabilities Act of 1990. In granting a summary judgment for Albertson's, the district court found that Kirkingburg was not qualified without an accommodation, because he could not meet the basic DOT standards and that the waiver program did not alter those standards. The Ninth Circuit Court reversed that decision, finding that (1) Kirkingburg had established a disability under the ADA by demonstrating that the manner in which he sees differs markedly from the manner in which most people see; (2) although the ADA allowed Albertson's to rely on government regulations in setting a job-related vision standard, Albertson's could not use compliance with the DOT regulations to justify its requirement because the waiver program was a legitimate part of the DOT's regulatory scheme; and (3) although Albertson's could set a vision standard different from the DOT's, it had to justify its independent standard and could not do so here.

The High Court observed, "An employer who requires as a job qualification that an employee meet an otherwise applicable federal safety regulation does not have to justify enforcing the regulation solely because its standard may be waived experimentally in an individual case."[25]

Albertson's job qualification was not of its own origin, but was the visual acuity standard of the Federal Motor Carrier Safety Regulations and is binding on Albertson's. The validity of these regulations is unchallenged; they have the force of law and they contain no qualifying language about individualized determinations. Were it not for the waiver program, there would be no basis for questioning Albertson's decision, and right, to follow the regulations.

The regulations establishing the waiver program did not modify the basic visual acuity standards in a way that disentitles an employer's, such as Albertson's, reliance on the basic standards. In setting the basic standards, the Federal Highway Administration, the DOT agency responsible for overseeing the motor carrier safety regulations, made a considered determination about the visual acuity level needed for safe operation of commercial motor vehicles in interstate commerce. In contrast, the regulatory record made it clear that the waiver program in question in this case was simply an experiment proposed as a means of obtaining factual data to determine if existing standards should be relaxed.

The ADA should not be read to require an employer to defend its decision not to participate in such an experiment. It is simply not credible that Congress enacted the ADA with the understanding that employers choosing to respect the government's visual acuity regulation in the face of an experimental waiver might be burdened with an obligation to defend the regulation's application according to its own terms. The U.S. Supreme Court reversed the ruling of the Ninth Circuit Court of Appeals in holding for Albertson's.

ADMINISTRATIVE GUIDE

AMERICANS WITH DISABILITIES

1. The Americans with Disabilities Act prohibits employment discrimination by employers with 15 or more employees.
2. School districts should develop nondiscriminatory policies regarding individuals with disabilities.
3. School districts should not segregate or limit job opportunities for individuals based on their disabilities.
4. School districts may not utilize and promote standards that have a discriminatory effect or perpetuate discrimination against people with disabilities.
5. Employment or employment benefits may not be denied to individuals who have a relationship with people who are disabled.
6. School authorities may not deny employment to individuals with disabilities to avoid providing reasonable accommodations.
7. Selection tests or standards may not be used that screen out individuals with disabilities unless school authorities can demonstrate that they are job related.
8. School districts must utilize standards that identify the skills of the person with disabilities rather than his or her impairments.
9. School districts should take appropriate measures to protect the confidentiality of medical records regarding individuals with disabilities.
10. School districts may be assessed compensatory and punitive damages for deliberate acts of discrimination against individuals with disabilities.
11. Correctable illnesses will not receive protection under ADA.
12. Physical and mental impairments must be bona fide and meet the full requirements of ADA to receive coverage.

STUDENT DISABILITY AND INCLUSION DECISIONS

David Sterns is a first-year principal of a middle school in an upperclass community in the eastern part of the United States. The district has an outstanding reputation for its academic programs. Sterns admittedly is not as familiar with all issues involving disabled students as a more experienced administrator might be. The parents of a moderately mentally retarded student requested that their daughter be placed in the regular classroom on a full-time basis. Sterns was only willing to place her in regular education classes for nonacademic subjects and into special education classes for academic courses. The parents are upset with his decision.

DISCUSSION QUESTIONS

1. Is Sterns justified in his decision? Why or why not?
2. Is the request by the parents a reasonable one? Why or why not?
3. What does special education law suggest with respect to inclusion?
4. How would the law apply in this case?
5. What are the administrative implications of this case?

A DISABLED STUDENT AND RELATED SERVICES

Debbie Young is a seasoned high school principal. She served as a special education teacher and an assistant principal in a progressive, affluent school district in the South. She is approached by the parents of a severely disabled tenth-grade student, Jonathan, requesting that a full-time nurse be provided under the label of "related services." Jonathan has multiple disabilities requiring constant care by a specially trained nurse. He is profoundly mentally disabled, has spastic quadriplegia, and has a seizure disorder. Young refuses the parents' request due to extraordinary expense and a view that the school is not the most appropriate placement for Jonathan.

DISCUSSION QUESTIONS

1. Is Young's decision defensible? Why or why not?
2. Is the parents' request reasonable under the law? Why or why not?
3. Is the provision of a nurse a related service if it is necessary for Jonathan to receive an appropriate education? Why or why not?
4. How do you think a court would rule in this case? Provide a rationale for your response.
5. What are the administrative implications of this case?

DISABILITY AND PARTICIPATION IN ATHLETICS

Sam Jackson, a 6-foot 5-inch tenth-grade student at Centerville High School in an athletic-oriented community, wishes to join the school's football team. Sam has excellent athletic abilities and feels that with experience in high school, he will be able to earn a scholarship to compete at the Division I collegiate level. Sam's request to participate is denied by school officials, based on the fact that he is totally blind in one eye. The school's concern is the risk of injury to Sam's other eye. Sam's parents protest, claiming denial of equal protection under the law and discrimination based on his disability.

■ ■ ■ ■ ■ ▬▬▬▬▬▬▬

DISCUSSION QUESTIONS

1. Should Sam be allowed to participate in a contact sport? Why or why not?
2. Has Sam been denied an equal opportunity to participate and earn a scholarship?
3. Would not being eligible to earn a scholarship constitute an injury to Sam?
4. Is the school justified in disallowing Sam's participation? Why or why not?
5. As principal, how would you handle Sam's request?
6. What are the administrative implications of this case?

ENDNOTES

1. *Pennsylvania Association for Retarded Children v. Commonwealth,* 334 F. Supp. 1257 (E.D. Pa. 1971), 343 F. Supp. 279 (E.D. Pa. 1972).
2. *Mills v. Board of Education of District of Columbia,* 348 F. Supp. 866 (D.D.C. 1972).
3. *Board of Education v. Rowley,* 458 U.S. 176, 102 S.Ct. 3034, 73 L. Ed. 2d 690 (1982).
4. *Timothy W. v. Rochester, New Hampshire School District,* 875 F. 2d 954 (1st Cir. 1989).
5. *Board of Education of Hendrick Hudson Central School v. Rowley,* 458 U.S. 176 (1982).
6. 20 U.S.C. § 1400 (C) (1988).
7. *Irving Independent School District v. Tatro,* 468 U.S. 883, 104 S.Ct. 3371 (1984).
8. 20 U.S.C.A. § 1412 (5) (B); 34 C.F.R. §§ 300–551.
9. *Beth B. v. Lake Bluff School District,* 211 F. Supp. 2d 1020, 168 Ed. Law Rep. 212, (N.D. Ill 2001).
10. *Alamo Heights Independent School District v. State Board of Education,* 790 F. 2d 1153 (5th Cir. 1986).
11. *Ash v. Lake Oswego School District No. 7J,* 766 F. Supp. 852 (D. Or. 1991).
12. *Todd D. by Robert D. v. Andrews,* 922 F. 2d 1576 (Eleventh Circuit), 67 Ed. Law Rptr. 1065 (1991).
13. *Burlington School Committee v. Department of Education of Massachusettts,* 471 U.S. 359, 105 S.Ct. 1996, 85 L. Ed. 2d 385 (1985).
14. *Leslie N. Biggs, et. al. v. Board of Education of Cecil County Maryland,* 229 F. Supp. 2d 437.
15. *S-1 v. Turlington,* 635 F. 2d 343 (5th Cir. Unit B Jan), cert. denied, 454 U.S. 1030 (1981).
16. *Stuart v. Nappi,* 443 F. Supp. 1235 (D. Conn. 1978).
17. *Concerned Parents v. New York City Board of Education,* 629 F. 2d 751 (2d Cir. 1980), cert. denied, 449 U.S. 1078 (1981).
18. *Tilton v. Jefferson County Board of Education,* 705 F. 2d 800, 804 (6th Cir. 1983).
19. *Honig v. Doe,* 484 U.S. 305, 108 S.Ct. 592 (1988).
20. *Farrin v. Maine School Administrative District,* 165 Ed. Law Rep. 709 (D. Maine 2001).
21. 20 U.S.C. Sec. 1415 (g) (k).
22. *Sutton v. United Airlines, Inc.,* 527 U.S. 471; 119 S.Ct. 2139; 144 L. Ed. 2d 450 (1999).
23. Ibid.
24. *Murphy v. United Parcel Service,* 527 U.S. 516; 119 S.Ct. 2133; 144 L. Ed. 2d 484 (1999).
25. *Albertson's v. Kirkingburg,* 527 U.S. 555; 119 S.Ct. 2162; 144 L. Ed. 2d 518 (1999).

CHAPTER 6

SCHOOL PERSONNEL AND SCHOOL DISTRICT LIABILITY

School districts as well as school officials and employees may incur liability for their tortious acts, when these acts result in injury to students. A *tort* is an actionable or civil wrong committed against one person by another independent of contract. If injury occurs based on the actions of school personnel, liability charges may be imminent. Liability may result from deliberate acts committed by another or acts involving negligence.

Students who are injured by school district personnel may claim monetary damages for their injury resulting from either intentional or unintentional torts. They also may, under certain conditions, seek injunctive relief to prevent the continuation of a harmful practice. Tort law further provides an opportunity for injured parties to bring charges when facts reveal that they received injury to their reputations.

In school settings, a tort may involve a class action suit affecting a number of school personnel, especially in cases involving negligent behavior. A tort may also involve actions brought against a single teacher, principal, or board member, depending on the circumstances surrounding the injury and the severity of the injury.

Educators commit a tort when they violate a legally imposed duty that results in injury to students. Before the court will allow recovery, it will determine factually where the actual fault lies and whether liability claims are justified based on the circumstances in a given situation.

THE SCHOOL AS A SAFE PLACE

Schools are presumed to be safe places where teachers teach and students learn. The prevailing view held by the courts is that prudent professional educators, acting in place of parents, are supervising students under their care and ensuring, to the greatest extent possible, that they are safe. This doctrine is designed to provide parents reasonable assurance that their children are safe while under the supervision of responsible professional adults.

This places an affirmative obligation on all certified school personnel to take necessary measures to ensure that the school environment is safe and conducive for students. Although the courts, in general, have fallen short of ruling that students have a constitutional right to be protected from harm, at least two courts have been willing to address this issue.

In the *Hosemann v. Oakland Unified School District* case, a California Superior Court judge ruled that Oakland public schools have an *affirmative duty* to alleviate crime and violence on school campuses.[1] This case involved two students, a theft, and an assault. The facts surrounding the case may not be as important as its outcome. This ruling represented the first one in which a court interpreted a state constitutional amendment that grants students and staff an "inalienable right" to attend campuses that are safe, secure, and crime free.

Subsequently, in the *Doe v. Taylor* case involving sexual abuse of a female student, the court exonerated the superintendent but not the principal, who should have known of the girl's constitutional right to be protected from sexual abuse. The court further held that a public school administrator in Texas had a duty to protect students from hazards of which he knew or should have known while students were under the school's functional custody.[2] These two cases fall short of holding school officials to a strict constitutional standard regarding safe campuses, but they do open the arena for further debate regarding the obligation school officials have in providing safe campuses, especially in light of the high incidents of crime and violence in public schools today. It would not be surprising to see courts become more stringent in their rulings involving school safety, as school violence continues to be present in the nation's public schools.

LIMITING LIABILITY FOR SCHOOL VIOLENCE

Violence continues to plague our nation's schools. During the past three years, deaths are increasingly linked with school violence. Since 1997 alone, school violence has struck U.S. schools, resulting in numerous deaths (see Table 6.1) and significant injuries.

Based on recent polls by the National Education Association, more than 5 percent of all children ages 12 through 18 enrolled in public schools in the United States fear being attacked or harmed at school. The National School Safety Center reports that during each hour of the day, 2,000 students and three to four teachers are attacked at school. Students

TABLE 6.1   School Violence and Number of Deaths Per State, 1992–1993 to 2002–2003

STATE	NUMBER OF DEATHS	STATE	NUMBER OF DEATHS	STATE	NUMBER OF DEATHS	STATE	NUMBER OF DEATHS
Alaska	2	Iowa	1	Mississippi	5	Oregon	2
Alabama	5	Illinois	10	Montana	1	Pennsylvania	14
Arkansas	6	Indiana	1	North Carolina	6	South Carolina	5
Arizona	3	Kansas	2	Nebraska	1	Tennessee	10
California	74	Kentucky	6	New Hampshire	1	Texas	23
Colorado	15	Louisiana	2	New Jersey	7	Utah	2
Connecticut	2	Massachusetts	14	New Mexico	1	Virginia	2
Washington, D.C.	7	Maryland	4	Nevada	1	Washington	12
Delaware	1	Michigan	11	New York	16	Wisconsin	1
Florida	19	Minnesota	1	Ohio	5	West Virginia	2
Georgia	17	Missouri	10	Oklahoma	1	Wyoming	1

Source: National School Safety Center's Report on School-Associated Violent Death

express a genuine fear of attending school because they do not feel safe. Parents also express concerns about safety, viewing discipline and school safety as their leading concerns. With ongoing or continuing acts of school violence and deaths, liability suits against school personnel are imminent.

Schools as Safe Places

As previously discussed, schools are presumed to be safe places by the courts. This presumption is based on the presence of licensed teachers and administrators who have been properly trained to supervise and provide for student safety during the school day. In fact, educators have been assigned three legal duties by the courts under *in loco parentis* (in place of parents)—to instruct, supervise, and provide for the safety of students. Although there is little expectation that students will never be injured, there is an expectation that school personnel exercise proper care to ensure, to the greatest extent possible, that students are protected from harm. When an unavoidable injury occurs, there is generally no liability. However, when injury is based on negligence, there are grounds for liability charges. School personnel, based on their legal duty, are expected to foresee that students may be injured under certain circumstances. Once a potential danger has been determined, reasonable steps are necessary to prevent injury. In liability cases, courts will seek to determine whether school officials knew or should have known of an impending danger and whether appropriate steps were taken to protect students. For example, when school officials receive information regarding a threat made to a student, they are expected to investigate to determine whether there is imminent danger involved. Failure to do so may bring liability charges. Simply stated, there is no defense for failure to take reasonable steps to prevent foreseeable injury to students in school. Of course, prudent action is not required in the absence of foreseeability. It would, however, be difficult for school officials to make the case that they were unaware of a potentially dangerous situation when students and teachers were aware of it.

School Violence and Negligence

In cases involving violent acts in schools, the fundamental question raised is: Could these acts have been avoided had school officials exercised the proper standard of care? Due care requires that school officials exercise the same degree of care that a person of ordinary prudence would exercise under the same or similar circumstances. This standard will vary depending on the degree of risk involved. Certainly, in cases involving threats of violence, the level of care expected of school officials would be high, particularly in instances where violent acts have occurred previously in the school. Failure to exercise the proper standard of care usually results in negligence.

Emerging Legal Issues

School personnel have a legally recognized duty and are required to adhere to a certain standard of conduct. With critical incidents of violence erupting in schools across the nation, resulting in serious injury and deaths, a host of legal questions will be raised. In fact, the first major case has surfaced in West Paducah, Kentucky, in which 45 defendants have been named, including the board of education as well as numerous teachers and administrators who allegedly failed to heed warning signals that a 14-year-old would carry out a violent act resulting in three fatalities.

In this case, plaintiffs contended that the suspect wrote violent class papers involving shooting students and detonating bombs at school, yet no action was taken by the teacher to inform school officials of the suspect's violent stories. Failure to do so, according to the plaintiffs, constitutes negligence. Given the seriousness of these charges, coupled with continuous acts of violence, school personnel are facing a serious dilemma. How far are teachers and administrators expected to go in responding to students' work that contains violent content? Are there legal consequences when they do so? What are the consequences when they fail to respond? These are perplexing questions with no simple answers.

Freedom of Expression: Prohibitions and School Violence

Students are afforded certain constitutional rights in the school setting, including freedom of expression, rights to a degree of privacy, protection against cruel and abusive treatment, and equality of treatment. They also are afforded constitutional protection against infringement of these rights, unless school officials can demonstrate that they had a legitimate need to restrict their rights, in which case the burden of proof rests with school officials. Certainly, concerns involving health and safety of students would justifiably fall in this category. For example, school officials may prevent a student from bringing a dangerous weapon to school because it obviously poses a threat to safety. Administrative action can be taken without offending the student's constitutional rights to privacy. The issue, however, that is not as clearly discernible is one involving self-expression. Under what conditions may school officials restrict a student's right to self-expression without violating his or her constitutional rights? The landmark *Tinker* case discussed in Chapter 3 provides some guidance:

> To justify a prohibition of a particular expression or opinion, school officials must be able to show that their action was caused by something more than a mere desire to avoid the discomfort and unpleasantness that always surrounds an unpopular viewpoint. There must be facts that might reasonably lead school authorities to forecast a substantial disruption or a material interference with school activities.[3]

Based on the Supreme Court's ruling in *Tinker,* to what extent can a student's right to express violent content in a class paper be restricted? Can school officials take disciplinary action against a student for writing such a paper without violating the student's rights? Probably not. Is it reasonable to prohibit student writings containing violent themes and does this prohibition necessarily prevent violence? School officials may restrict writings on violent themes if there is evidence connecting such writings with serious acts of disruption or threats to safety in school. Without a reasonable connection between the two, school officials may be hard-pressed to justify their actions as reasonable. School officials would likely be at no risk if, upon receiving information regarding a student's violent writing, they conferred with the student to determine whether there was cause for concern.

School violence will continue to plague America's schools although incidents of violence in public schools are declining. School personnel are expected to take reasonable and prudent steps to safeguard the safety of all students. They have a legal and professional duty to provide quality supervision and to be certain that they are able to reasonably foresee possible danger to students. When they do so, they are expected to act in a prudent manner to protect students under their supervision and avoid costly liability charges based on negligence. School personnel who properly execute their legal duty will succeed in minimizing acts of violence in schools and limit potential liability charges.

ADMINISTRATIVE GUIDE

SCHOOL VIOLENCE

1. Heed warning signs exhibited by disruptive students.
2. Follow up on threats made against one student by another.
3. Create an open and comfortable school climate where students can anonymously report potential problems.
4. Implement a defensible zero tolerance policy on violent behavior in school.
5. Prohibit taunting of students by others.
6. Design programs/activities to engage all students for success in school.
7. Counsel with students who are viewed as "misfits" by their peers.
8. Act swiftly but fairly to deal with disruptive or violent acts in school.
9. Hold workshops on violence and liability for school personnel.
10. Stress school safety through education and increased security.

Legal Challenges Related to School Gangs

When violent acts based on negligence by school personnel result in injury to students, liability claims are likely. These claims are made when school personnel fail to adequately foresee that students may be harmed through violent acts.

When injury occurs in a negligent situation, school personnel have breached their legal duty to protect students under their supervision. Although school personnel are not expected to guarantee that students are never harmed, they are expected to ensure that reasonable measures have been taken to prevent foreseeable injury.

Since negligence is based in part on foreseeability, gangs constitute a potential legal threat to school personnel. In schools and communities where gangs are present, it is foreseeable that violence will erupt if their activities go unchecked. In these cases, the standard of care becomes greater for school personnel. Thus, they must take extra precautions to prevent violence and foreseeable injury.

School leaders are expected to monitor gang behavior in school and respond swiftly to information that suggests that gang activity is escalating. In searching for appropriate strategies to prevent gang activity, it is helpful to learn as much as possible about gangs and their members. By keeping in touch with gang activity, school leaders may become more aware of friction between gangs and move to mediate problems before they escalate into violence. (See Chapter 4 for a more detailed discussion of gangs.)

Duty of Care and Gang Violence

Based on foreseeability, school personnel are expected to exercise the standard of care that any other reasonable professional would exercise under the same or similar circumstances. This standard of care will vary depending on the gravity of the particular situation. If school officials are aware of gang presence in their schools, there is a greater expectation for monitoring gang activity; consequently, the standard of care is higher based on prior knowledge of gang presence. In all cases, the courts expect school personnel to exhibit behavior that conforms to the standard that a reasonable, mature, and intelligent person would meet, given the gravity of the situation. Anything short of this expectation may result in liability charges.

Limiting and eliminating gang activity is a community-wide problem. Every group has a vital role to play if violence is to be controlled in schools. The school's role involves education, swift and aggressive action in response to acts of violence, defensible policies and procedures distinguishing misbehavior from criminal acts, removal of graffiti, and a close working relationship with law enforcement agencies. Parents' role involves talking with their children early and regularly about gangs, alcohol/drug use, violence, and at-risk behavior; and searching for warning signs, such as sudden changes in their child's moods, drop in grades, sudden alignment with new friends, change in dress, unaccountable sums of money, and other signs that might trigger stronger intervention. Community residents' role involves removing graffiti in their communities, reporting any suspicious gang activity to law enforcement units, and partnering with the school in addressing gang activity.

Gang violence will continue to plague public schools, as national trends show a slight decrease in gang activity. School leaders are expected to become proactive in taking appropriate steps to eliminate gang activity while providing protection for all students under their care. Simultaneously, they are also expected to create and maintain an environment where effective teaching and learning can occur. These are challenges that place school leaders in difficult and sometimes conflicting roles.

ADMINISTRATIVE GUIDE

LIABILITY AND GANG VIOLENCE

1. School leaders are responsible for recognizing gang activity in schools.
2. A mediation process should be developed to resolve conflict between rival gangs.
3. School leaders should establish and maintain close working relationships with law enforcement and social service agencies regarding gang activity.
4. Gang issues should be included in classroom discussion and lessons.
5. School leaders must follow through on threats made by gang members.
6. A schoolwide safety plan should be developed to protect students, faculty, and staff against violence.
7. Parents, community leaders, and citizens should be involved collaboratively in addressing serious incidents of violence stemming from gang activity.

LIABILITY OF SCHOOL PERSONNEL

School personnel are responsible for their own tortious acts in the school environment. Liability involving school personnel normally falls into two categories: intentional torts and unintentional. *Intentional torts*—such as assault, battery, libel, slander, defamation, false arrest, malicious prosecution, and invasion of privacy—require proof of intent or willfulness; whereas an *unintentional tort*—such as simple negligence—does not require such proof of intent or willfulness. In each case, liability charges may be sustained if the facts reveal that school personnel acted improperly or failed to act appropriately in situations involving students.

Individual Liability

In certain situations, school personnel may be held individually liable for their actions that result in injury to a student. Individual liability will not usually occur unless the plaintiff can demonstrate that a school employee's action violated a clearly established law and that the employee exhibited a reckless disregard for the rights of the plaintiff.[4]

The Supreme Court held in the *Davis* case that officials are shielded from liability for civil damages if their conduct does not violate clearly established statutory or constitutional rights of which a reasonable person would have known at the time of the incident.[5] School personnel are not liable under the Civil Rights Act of 1871, Section 1983, unless they exhibited reckless disregard for the constitutional rights of students. As discussed in Chapter 3 in the *Wood v. Strickland* case, school board members may be held individually liable for damages under Section 1983 of the Civil Rights Act of 1871 when they violate the constitutional rights of students.

The U.S. Supreme Court clarified the conditions under which recovery for damages may be awarded in *Carey v. Piphus,* where two students were suspended for 20 days.[6] One was suspended for smoking marijuana on school property during school hours and the other for wearing an earring in violation of a school rule to discourage gang activity in the school. The court ruled that both students had been suspended in violation of the Fourteenth Amendment. Furthermore, school officials were not entitled to qualified immunity from damages. It was clear that they should have known that a lengthy suspension without a hearing violated due process of law. Therefore, liability is probable when students' constitutional rights are willfully violated by school officials.

Vicarious Liability

Since school districts are deemed employers of teachers, districts also may be held vicariously liable for the negligent behavior of their employees. Under the old theory of *respondeat superior,* the master is only responsible for authorized acts of its servants or agents. As applied in vicarious liability, the board rather than the principal is held liable for the tortious acts of its teachers, even though the board is not at fault. There is a requirement, under vicarious liability, that the teacher is acting within the scope of his or her assigned duties. This concept is most prevalent in cases involving negligence where class action suits are brought not only against the teacher but also against the school district for alleged negligence by the teacher.

Foreseeability

Foreseeability is a crucial element in liability cases, especially in cases involving negligence. *Foreseeability* is defined as the teacher's or administrator's ability to predict or anticipate that a certain activity or situation may prove harmful to students. Once this determination is made, there is an expectation that prudent steps will be taken to prevent harm to students. Failure to act in a prudent manner may result in liability claims. Whether an injury is or is not foreseeable is a question of fact that is determined by a jury when deciding if liability should be imposed.

There are many instances when teachers and administrators are *expected to foresee* the potential danger associated with an activity or condition in the school. For example, if teachers or administrators observe broken glass panes in entry doors or in classrooms, it is foreseeable that a student, while entering the building or the room, might sustain an injury if contact is made with the broken glass. In this instance, school personnel have an obligation to warn students of the impending danger and to exercise caution to ensure that students are not injured by making contact with this potentially dangerous condition. The broken panes should be reported to the proper authority and repaired promptly.

Similar expectations would occur in situations involving defective playground equipment, loose stair rails, or other *nuisances* (unsafe conditions) present in the school environment. Also, if two students are observed fighting, it is foreseeable that one or both might sustain an injury. In this case, school personnel are obligated to take appropriate steps to prevent harm to students involved, without harming themselves in the process.

Nuisance

A *nuisance* is any dangerous or hazardous condition that limits free use of property by the user. The existence of such a condition may require school personnel to exercise extra care to ensure that students are protected from possible harm. The implication suggested here is that school districts have an obligation to maintain safe premises for students under their supervision. School district personnel have the responsibility to inform students of unsafe conditions and to take steps to counsel students away from dangerous situations. Reasonable measures should be taken to remove or correct hazardous conditions as soon as they become known.

In some instances, the question of attractive nuisance arises. An *attractive nuisance* is a dangerous instrument or condition that has a special attraction to a less mature child who does not appreciate the potential danger and who could be harmed. The standard of care increases in attractive nuisance cases. An attractive nuisance claim will be supported if the evidence suggests one or more of the following:

1. Those responsible for the property knew or should have known that children would be attracted to the hazardous condition.
2. The responsible party knew that the hazardous condition posed an unreasonable risk to children.
3. Children, because of their youth, were unaware of the risk.
4. The utility to the owner of maintaining the risk and the cost of eliminating it were slight, as compared to the risk to children.
5. The owner failed to exercise reasonable care in eliminating the risk.[7]

Premises liability is based on the expectation that owners and possessors of buildings and grounds have a duty to their guests to maintain the premises in a reasonably safe condition. Negligence or failure to routinely inspect buildings or grounds to ensure that they are safe could result in injury to students, and claims of liability could be brought against the district and school personnel who have supervisory responsibilities. Negligence is usually not sustained unless school personnel carelessly created a hazardous condition or allowed it to continue after being informed of the existence of such a hazard.

Negligence claims may be supported, however, if the evidence reveals that school personnel should have been aware of the hazard and were not diligent in responding to it. According to one court, it is unreasonable to expect that school personnel be required to discover or instantly correct every defect that is not of their own creation.[8] Reasonable action is required in cases involving nuisances. The courts have not required school personnel to ensure that premises are safe at all times. If reasonable measures, such as routine and periodic inspections and repairs occur, unanticipated or unexplained accidents usually will not create liability charges against school personnel.

In most states, the level of care expected of those who oversee property is related to people who enter the property. These people are divided into three groups: invitees, licensees, and trespassers.

Invitees. An *invitee* is one who is present on the premises by invitation of the owner. There is an expectation that the property is safe for invitees. They should be protected from known hazards or those that should be known by the owner. Owners have an obligation to inspect the property to ensure that it is safe for invitees.

Aside from students and employees, invitees might include those who are on school campus to conduct business (e.g., salespersons, parents, or community citizens who are invited to attend public school functions). There is no absolute duty to ensure that invitees are safe. Invitees also have a responsibility to exercise reasonable actions to care for themselves. If they observe a dangerous condition, there is an expectation that they take necessary measures to protect themselves from harm.

Obviously, the degree of care regarding students would vary with age and maturity. If the student is mature enough to appreciate the danger and commits an act that results in injury, school personnel may succeed with *contributory negligence claims* against the student. If the student is not mature enough to appreciate the danger and incurs injury, based on unsafe conditions, successful liability claims may be brought against school officials.

Licensees. A *licensee* is a person who has the *privilege* to enter school property. School officials have a duty to warn licensees of any impending dangerous conditions found on school grounds and to take reasonable steps to protect them from harm. Licensees might include salespersons or community groups using school facilities but not by invitation. School officials must be aware that licensees are on school grounds. If their presence is unknown to school officials, it would be unreasonable to expect them to meet the standards as mentioned. Licensees generally assume risks in cases where the owner is unaware of any known hazards; they take the property as they find it.

Trespassers. A *trespasser* is one who enters school property without consent. There is normally no obligation to protect trespassers who enter the property illegally. There is no duty of care owed trespassers, even in cases where dangerous conditions exist.

This would not hold true for students who return to campus after school hours to use playground equipment. School officials, in this case having knowledge that students return, must ensure that the equipment is in good repair and that known hazards on school grounds have been promptly corrected and students forewarned of their existence. In cases involving trespassers, school officials cannot *willfully or wantonly* harm the trespassers or *deliberately create* conditions to harm them. Such actions would not meet court scrutiny.

In sum, a property owner owes an invitee the duty of exercising reasonable care; owes a licensee the duty of not increasing danger; and owes a trespasser the duty of not engaging in willful or wanton conduct.

Because of their duty, teachers and administrators have a higher *standard of care* and are expected to *foresee* an accident more readily than would the average person. One of the fundamental questions raised by the courts in a case involving injury to a student is whether the teacher or principal knew or should have known of the potential for harm to students. After an examination of facts, if the judge or jury determines that either should have known of the impending danger and failed to act appropriately, liability charges will likely be imposed. On the other hand, if the facts reveal that school personnel reasonably foresaw the potential danger associated with an activity or situation and took reasonable steps to remedy the danger, no liability would likely be imposed, even if injury occurred. Factual circumstances would determine if liability claims are warranted.

The other question the court would raise involving student injury is whether the injury could have been avoided had the teacher or administrator acted prudently. School personnel may not use the defense that they were unaware of the impending danger associated with a certain activity that resulted in injury to a student in cases where they should have been aware of such a danger.

Parental Access to School Premises

There is a clear distinction between *trespass* and *parental access* to public school property. Parents have a legal right to visit schools, meet with teachers or administrators, and attend school-sponsored activities held on and off campus before and after normal school hours. Inherently, parents are afforded the privilege to do so. Unlike a trespasser who enters school property without permission, parents have the right to enter school premises. Consequently, school officials share responsibility for their safety. Unless a parent has exhibited behavior that posed a threat to the safety of administrators, teachers, students, and staff, or consistently violated school policy and procedures regarding school visitations, the privilege to visit is maintained. If the parent has been issued a court order that bars school visits, he or she may be guilty of trespassing if the parent enters school grounds without permission or privilege. School officials have no official duty of care to trespassers found on school grounds, whereas such duty is expected for those who have a right or privilege to be there. This duty ensures that the property is safe for parents and others who are authorized, and many times invited, to visit school premises.

There should be assurance that there are no unsafe conditions that may result in injury to parents since they are not obligated to take the property as they find it. If there are unsafe conditions found on school premises, visible warnings should be located in these areas, informing parents that potentially dangerous conditions exist and that caution should be exercised as they approach these areas. These steps will lessen the possibility of liability suits involving school officials and the school board.

INTENTIONAL TORTS

As mentioned earlier, torts fall into two categories: intentional and unintentional. An *intentional tort* results from a *deliberate act* committed against another person. It may or may not be accompanied by malice. When there is no intent to harm another person, but one proceeds intentionally in a manner that infringes on the rights of another, a tort has been committed. The law grants to each individual certain rights that must be respected by others. If by action or speech these rights are violated, resulting in injury, a tort has been committed.

The most common forms of intentional torts affecting school personnel include assault, battery, defamation, libel and slander, mental distress, false imprisonment, and trespassing on personal property. Each of these torts will be discussed briefly.

Assault

An *assault* is an offer to use force in a hostile manner that causes apprehension. The person being assaulted normally must feel a degree of immediacy, in the sense that the one committing the assault will execute it promptly and has the apparent capacity to do so. An assault involves a threat to inflict harm to another person's body in an offensive manner. Each of the elements identified in the definition must be present to sustain assault charges. Therefore, all elements and facts relating to an alleged assault must be examined in detail to determine whether the assault is valid.

An assault is a tort committed against a person's mind, causing fear and apprehension for his or her safety. It may be verbal or exhibited through actions. The important issue in cases involving assault is that *no physical injury is necessary.* The mere *fear* for one's personal safety is sufficient to establish an assault.

Battery

A *battery* occurs when physical contact actually takes place. In practice, a battery is a successful assault. It involves *unwelcomed and unprivileged* body contact involving another person. This contact is normally considered to be *hostile and unlawful.* The assault generally precedes the battery. It is not uncommon for these two to be combined when charges are brought against the perpetrator.

Assault and battery affect teachers, administrators, and students in the school environment. Every person is responsible for his or her actions in cases involving assault and battery. Teachers and administrators are not only responsible for their own acts of assault and battery, most notably in instances involving the administration of corporal punishment, but also may be liable if they observe a student being assaulted or battered by others and fail to exercise proper steps to prevent injury. Charges may also be brought against teachers and administrators if they fail to act when it is foreseeable that one student may injure another based on threats and no action is taken to prevent possible injury.

Typically in cases involving a battery, there must be an intent to make contact with another person. School personnel most commonly are charged with assault and battery when there is evidence that they administered corporal punishment with malice or excessive force. The type of instrument used may also be a factor, as well as considerations regarding the age, size, gender, and physical condition of the student.

Assault and Battery Involving Physical Fights.   Assaults may be associated with physical fights when the actions of the person who initiates the fight are intended to place another person in apprehension of bodily harm. Assaults usually take the form of threats to inflict bodily harm to another, which causes the person assaulted to be apprehensive and fearful of injury. If physical contact is actually made in the form of a physical fight, the person who initiated the fight may be charged with assault and battery. The injured student may file suit against school personnel for damages resulting from injuries received in a physical attack by another student when there is evidence that they had prior knowledge that the student had been threatened prior to the actual physical attack. Under these circumstances, it is foreseeable that a physical attack might result in serious injury to the student who received the threat. School personnel have an obligation to take precautions to prevent physical attacks on students.

School officials may also be liable if two students mutually engage in a physical fight when there is prior knowledge that physical contact will occur. Again, it is foreseeable that one or both students might incur serious injury when engaged in physical confrontation. Prudence requires that all preventive measures be taken by school officials to prevent assaults and physical attacks involving students. Failure to do so may prove costly if injury results from offensive contact associated with physical contact involving students.

Defamation

Defamation occurs when false statements are made about another person. These statements generally are ones that tend to harm a person's good name or reputation or subject the person to hatred, contempt, or ridicule. To succeed in sustaining defamation charges, there must be evidence to demonstrate that defamatory statements were communicated to a third party. If no third party is involved, there is no defamation. The most common forms of defamation are libel and slander, which will be discussed later.

Defamation derives from the belief that people have a right to expect their reputations to be free of false or malicious statements made by others. Teachers and administrators must be aware of liability claims that may stem from committing acts of defamation. Although school personnel enjoy what is referred to as a *qualified privilege,* this privilege does not permit them to make statements that do not meet the requirement of good faith. Certain statements are privileged if made in good faith and within the scope of the educator's duty.

Therefore, school personnel who expect to be protected by qualified privilege must not make false statements regarding students or colleagues with *malice* or the *intent to harm.* Statements made must be true and based on reasonable grounds. *Truth* as a defense against charges of defamation is only valid when there is absence of malice. School personnel do not have the right to publicize information regarding a student or colleague with the intent to maliciously injure that person, even if the statements are true.

The teacher's lounge appears to be one of the most popular places to spread rumors about students and colleagues. School personnel must understand that "off the cuff" statements about others that might injure their reputation or good standing in the school may form grounds for liability. Many times, teachers inadvertently share very sensitive information regarding a student's background, home conditions, or family history that may prove damaging to the student. Personal information regarding a student's record should be used exclusively by the teacher to assist the student in providing the best educational experiences possible and not shared with others who have no need to have access to this information. School personnel will experience difficulty making the claim that no harmful intent exists when very personal and sensitive information is shared with others who have no need to know. If the student affected is able to demonstrate that he or she has been harmed, held in low esteem by teachers, or shunned by others as a result of these comments, the student may have grounds for personal damages.

Libel and Slander

Defamation falls into two categories: libel and slander. *Slander* is considered oral defamation, whereas *libel* is considered written defamation. Both include statements or communication that result in injury to a person's reputation, good name, or standing in the school or community. As previously stated, a third party must be privileged to this communication to establish defamation. The burden of proof rests with the person who claims injury. If claims are successful, they will usually result in monetary damages. However, there are four categories of slander that are considered defamatory on their own merits. The person affected by these statements need not prove damages when statements are made regarding *criminal behavior, professional or job incompetency, possession of a contagious disease* (e.g., AIDS), and *unchastity in a woman.* The very nature of these statements may result in injury to one's good name, reputation, or esteem, or cause others to ostracize the affected person.

Mental Distress

Charges of mental distress usually arise when one exhibits conduct that exceeds the acceptable boundaries of decency. It is a form of tort liability that is construed to create mental anguish of a serious nature. Historically, it has been difficult to prove mental distress in the absence of some type of physical injury. This situation has changed in recent years, however.

School personnel may be charged with mental distress if there is evidence that their behavior or conduct was calculated to cause serious emotional distress for students. School personnel typically are charged with inflicting mental distress when they use an unreasonable and unorthodox method of discipline designed to embarrass students or cause them to be ridiculed or humiliated in the presence of their peers. Punishing students by requiring them to walk around the building with books on their heads, standing for long periods of time with one foot raised, standing and facing the corner of the room, or placing students in a locked closet are examples of actions that may cause mental distress and ones that might prove difficult to defend as reasonable actions.

As stated in Chapter 3, courts will allow school personnel to discipline students as long as the discipline is reasonable and consistent with school or district policy. There is a belief among many legal experts that actions by school personnel designed to embarrass students may be more damaging than physical harm. A student's self-esteem may be seriously damaged at a time when it should be growing and expanding. This is not intended to suggest that teachers or administrators cannot admonish a student in the classroom or hallway in front of his or her peers. This issue was clearly addressed in the *Gordon v. Oak Park School District No. 97,* which involved a verbal lashing administered to a student by the teacher. The Illinois Appellate Court held that such action by the teacher did not result in the teacher being held liable. The court recognized that within the broad delegation of parental authority, a teacher has the right to verbally chastise a student.

The teacher, however, may be held liable if the evidence reveals that there was an intentional act committed with the intent to humiliate or degrade when it is accompanied by proof of wantonness or malice.[9] The implication suggested in this case is that disciplinary methods that are deemed necessary should be carried out in a *reasonable manner,* providing the greatest degree of respect for the student.

An illustration of what a teacher might face when poor judgment is exercised is found in the *Celestine v. Lafayette Parish School Board* case. A teacher was dismissed when it was determined that poor judgment and a lack of educational purpose resulted in the teacher requiring students to write a vulgar word 1,000 times in the presence of their classmates as a disciplinary measure for having uttered the word.[10] In many cases, students will rebel when they feel embarrassed by the teacher's or principal's action in the presence of their peers.

Another troublesome incident involving poor judgment of a teacher occurred recently when a Fairfax County private school teacher was found guilty of assault charges when she taped a student's hands and mouth with masking tape as punishment for waking other students during nap time. A similar incident occurred in a Florida middle school where a teacher taped two students to a desk and a wall with masking tape. This teacher resigned after the parents filed a complaint. Mental distress is a relatively new tort, but one that should be taken seriously by school personnel.

False Imprisonment

False imprisonment occurs when a student is detained illegally by the teacher or the principal. It is considered an *intentional tort.* If a student is wrongfully detained for an unreasonable period of time for offensive behavior that does not warrant detention, a tort has occurred. If a student is confined by school personnel, there should be a reasonable basis for doing so and the confinement must be viewed as reasonable. School or district policy should serve as a guide in these situations.

Teachers and administrators may detain students and prevent their participation in playground activities, recess, and certain other extra school activities. They may detain students after school if the offense is clearly one that warrants detention and if parents are aware of the planned detention so that proper arrangements can be made to transport the student after the detention period has ended. Students should never be denied lunch breaks as a form of punishment. False imprisonment is not considered a major liability issue, but it is one that could prove difficult for school personnel, if evidence shows that detention was in violation of school or district policy and carried out with malice toward the student.

Trespassing on Personal Property

Trespassing on personal property is a tort that involves confiscating or interfering with the use of a student's personal property without proper authority. This is not an area that normally generates legal action, but one that school personnel should be mindful of since it most commonly involves teachers and administrators.

This intentional tort occurs frequently when school personnel confiscate various items from students during the school day. Many of these items may be in violation of school rules, may create disruption, or may cause harm to the student in possession of the item or to other students.

Teachers and administrators have the right to confiscate such items, but they do not have the right to keep or retain them for an unreasonable period of time. If the item(s) is considered dangerous, the student's parent or guardian should be contacted and informed of the potential danger. Arrangements should be made with the parent or guardian to ensure that the item is not returned to the student.

Nonthreatening items should be returned to the student as soon as possible, with instructions not to return them to school. If the item is not in violation of school policy, dangerous, or disrupting the educational process, school personnel have no right to confiscate the item. Even in instances where confiscation is justified, the property belongs to the student and should not be detained and discarded at the end of the year simply because the teacher or administrator failed to remember from whom it was confiscated or merely decided rather arbitrarily that the item(s) should not be returned. In no case should the student's property be damaged or destroyed by school personnel. Generally, there is no serious charge stemming from this type of tort, but it is important that school personnel project the image of respect for the personal property of others and fundamental fairness in their dealings with students in the school.

UNINTENTIONAL TORTS

An *unintentional tort* is a wrong perpetrated by someone who fails to exercise that degree of care in doing what is otherwise permissible (i.e., acts negligently). Negligence is perhaps the most prevalent source of litigation involving injury to students. Many cases regarding negligence in school settings are class action in nature, implicating teachers, principals, and boards of education. Defendants in these cases are usually released from the suit if facts reveal that they played no significant role in the injury.

Negligence is generally viewed as the failure to exercise a reasonable standard of care that results in harm or injury to another person. Most negligence cases involve civil wrongs, although there may be instances in which the accused faces both civil and criminal charges. In cases involving wanton negligence, such as injuries sustained by others based on violation of traffic laws, criminal charges may be appropriate depending on the specific circumstances relating to the injury.

For example, when charges of negligence are sought by an injured student, certain requirements must be met. The student bringing the charges must be able to prove that four elements were present. Failure to establish each of the following elements invalidates charges of liability:

> *Standard of Care:* The teacher or principal owed a legal duty to protect the student by conforming to certain standards.
> *Breach of Duty:* The teacher or principal failed to meet these standards (duty of care).
> *Proximity or Legal Cause:* The student must be able to demonstrate *proximate cause* (i.e., that a causal relationship existed between the breach of duty and the actual injury sustained by the student).
> *Injury:* The student must prove actual injury based on a breach of duty by the teacher or principal.

Standard of Care

Standard of care is an important concept in cases involving liability of school personnel. It requires that school personnel exercise the same degree of care that other professional educators holding similiar positions would exercise under the same or similar conditions. This standard of care will vary depending on particular circumstances. The level of care due students changes based on the age, maturity, experience, and mental capacity of students, as well as the nature of the learning activities in which they are involved.

For example, the standard of care for teachers of kindergarten or early primary grade students is usually higher than teachers of senior high students, due to differences in age levels, maturity, and experience. Likewise, the standard of care for a chemistry laboratory teacher or a physical education teacher is greater than that of an English teacher, based on the nature of the activities and the potential danger faced by students who are engaged during the instructional period.

As the Supreme Court of Indiana stated, the standard of care that may be adequate when dealing with adults generally will not be sufficient when dealing with students. The court observed: "The relationship of school pupils and school authorities should call into play the well-recognized duty in tort law that people entrusted with children or others whose characteristics make it likely that they may do somewhat unreasonable things, have a special responsibility recognized by the common law to supervise their charges."[11]

Courts are aware that children do not possess the same level of maturity, insight, caution, and knowledge as do adults, and therefore may not be judged by the same standard of care required by adults. This realization by the courts places a higher standard on educators to ensure that they are exercising the level of maturity and judgment that will be viewed as prudent. Standard of care becomes an important consideration in determining whether school personnel are liable in specific situations involving students under their supervision.

The courts do not expect educators to assume unreasonable personal risks to prevent all conceivable harm to students. To do so would amount to an insurer's role. However, there is an expectation that educators exhibit behavior that meets the standard that a reasonable, mature, and intelligent person would meet in the same or similar situation. Interestingly, state statutes vary regarding the standard of care prescribed for educators. Many states simply require that this standard be that of a reasonable parent. Illinois law, however, requires willful and wanton misconduct by educators—a much more liberal standard than is found in most other states. Failure to meet a prescribed duty of care resulting in injury to students may result in liability. However, liability would not exist in situations in which accidents occurred that were unavoidable or unforeseeable. The courts simply expect educators to exercise reasonable judgment in their dealings with students to ensure to the greatest degree possible that they are protected from harm. The following case illustrates what can occur when a reasonable standard of care and foreseeability are not met.

Two New York sisters were assaulted and injured by a group of students and non-students as they attempted to leave their high school after classes. Prior to the assault, one of the sisters had been threatened by one of the guilty students. This incident had been reported to a teacher, who failed to take any action. One of the sisters attempted to enter the security department to report the assault and found it closed. The sisters filed a lawsuit against the city of New York and the city board of education, alleging negligent supervision. At trial, there was evidence that no security officers were at their posts during the time of the assault. The jury returned a verdict of $750,000 for one of the sisters, and $50,000 for the other against the city and the board of education. The court granted the school board's motion to set aside the verdict and dismiss the complaint. However, the New York Supreme Court, Appellate Division, reversed this decision.

The court of appeals found that there was sufficient evidence to establish liability for negligent supervision. The evidence revealed that the teacher was aware of the assault and the school's security policy had not been enforced at the time of the assault. Schools have a duty to adequately supervise students and are *liable for foreseeable injuries related to inadequate supervision.* The court affirmed the appellate division's decision.[12] As can be seen from the *Mirand* case involving two sisters, failure to exercise due care in situations involving students can be very costly. Reasonable and prudent actions by the teacher and security office would likely have prevented harm to the assault victims.

Breach of Duty

Breach of duty is determined in part based on the nature of the activity for which the educator is held responsible. Various school activities require different levels of supervision. The question normally posed by courts regarding breach is whether the conduct of school personnel met the standard of care required in a given situation. The second issue involves a determination as to whether school personnel should have foreseen possible injury. The fact that a student is injured in a given situation does not necessarily imply that a breach of duty has occurred. School personnel are not insurers against all possible harm to students. They are, however, expected to take prudent steps, based on their duty to students, to prevent harm when it is reasonably foreseeable that students might be harmed. Failure to act in this instance would constitute a breach of duty.

Proximate Cause

Proximate cause occurs when a causal relationship existed between the breach of duty and the actual injury sustained by the student. If a student is injured and the injury is not related to the teacher or administrator's failure to exercise the proper standard of care, there is no liability involved. *There must be evidence that links the injury directly to failure of educators to act prudently in a given situation.* One issue courts would likely raise is whether the actual injury was based on the teacher or administrator's behavior. If the evidence reveals that the teacher or administrator's behavior played a direct and substantial role in the injury, proximate cause has been established.

If a teacher is absent from the classroom for a brief period of time, for instance, and an injury occurs in the teacher's absence, was the injury directly related to the teacher's absence—that is, could the injury have been avoided if the teacher had been present? If, for example, a student is accidentally stuck with a pencil when he is pushed by another student attempting to use the pencil sharpener. The teacher is not in the classroom. Might this injury have been avoided if the teacher had been present? Could she have prevented one student from pushing the other and causing his injury? Was this act reasonably foreseeable? Had there been prior pushing incidents involving students using the pencil sharpener? If the response to these questions is yes, then proximate cause has likely been established. There is no set rule for determining when an act is sufficiently connected to an injury. An analysis of facts and circumstances surrounding the injury would be factors considered by the courts.

Injury

If there is no harm or injury suffered by a student, there is no liability. There must be evidence that reveals that actual injury resulted either from acts committed by school personnel or their failure to act prudently in a given situation. The person claiming injury must demonstrate that he or she received an injury and that there are compensatory damages related to the injury. The courts will normally award compensatory damages, except in cases of wanton or willful negligence, in which case punitive damages may be considered.

DEFENSES FOR NEGLIGENCE

There are various defenses used by school personnel to reduce or eliminate the impact of liability charges. These defenses are used, even in cases where the four elements of negligence (listed previously) are present.

Contributory Negligence

If the evidence reveals that a person claiming injury exhibited conduct that fell below a reasonable standard, liability charges against school personnel may be abrogated. If, by action or decision, the student contributed to any injury received, the courts may find school personnel innocent of liability charges under many state laws.

The following examples illustrate cases where students were found to be contributorily negligent:

1. A student was found guilty of contributory negligence when he was injured by a flare-up of certain chemicals that he mixed together with the knowledge that they were dangerous.[13]
2. A high school student was injured while running in the dark after the lights went off in the school building.[14]
3. Two students were injured after knowingly mixing potassium chlorate and powdered sugar, producing an explosive charge, after convincing their chemistry teacher to allow them to acquire some potassium chlorate.[15]
4. A student was injured when he stole an oxidizing agent from the school's science lab, which resulted in a fire at his home, causing serious burns to his legs.[16]

Contributory negligence is probably the most common defense employed in charges of negligence. When a teacher or administrator is charged with negligence, neither will be assessed monetary awards when contributory negligence is proven. However, there is a common law presumption regarding the incapacity of students to be contributorily negligent. Common law precedent suggests that a child under the age of 7 cannot be charged with contributory negligence. With children between the ages of 7 and 14, there is a reasonable assumption that they are incapable of contributory negligence. A child beyond the age of 14 may be assumed to be contributorily negligent, depending on the facts surrounding the injury.

The age limits described are not absolute. They typically serve as guides in assessing whether contributory negligence did occur. The actions of school personnel, the intelligence of the student(s) involved, as well as the level of maturity are critical factors in the jury's deliberations. A question of prudence would also be relevant in contributory negligence cases. In any injury situation, did the student act as any other reasonable and prudent student of similar intelligence and maturity would have acted in the same situation? If the student did not exercise prudence and was injured based on unreasonable behavior, there would normally be no liability assessed by the courts. The following case illustrates the application of contributory negligence involving injury to a student.

A group of five students persuaded a custodian (who was very reluctant) to allow them access to play a game of basketball in the gymnasium during the Christmas holidays. Morris Albers was the leader of the group. After the custodian opened the door to the gymnasium, he proceeded with his cleaning duties. Morris assumed the responsibility for cleaning the playing surface while the other boys changed clothes. The boys then engaged in warm-up activities using two worn basketballs that they found lying in the gym, since the equipment room was locked. Morris was wearing standard basketball shoes and was a member of the high school basketball team, as was one of the other boys. After warming up, the boys divided into two teams to play a half-court game. Morris's statements indicated that the game was clean with respect to fouls and heavy body contact.

During the half-court game, a shot came off the backboard and headed toward the out-of-bounds line on the east side of the gym. Morris and an opposing player raced for the loose ball. As Morris reached to pick it up, the two collided, with Morris hitting his head against the opponent's hip. Morris fell to the floor on his back in a semi-conscious state. Upon examination, a determination was made that he had suffered a fracture in the cervical area of his spine, which necessitated corrective surgery and extended hospitalization.

Morris brought suit against the district, claiming that the district breached its duty to supervise the basketball game. The facts clearly revealed that school was not in session and there was no duty to supervise. It was further determined that the boys had no authority to be in the gym but had persuaded a reluctant custodian to allow them to enter the gym. Additionally, there was no evidence that suggested that the accident would have been avoided had there been actual supervision. Morris's injury, although accidental, was attributed to his own actions in entering the gym and engaging in playing basketball.[17]

Assumption of Risk

Assumption of risk is commonly used as a defense in situations involving various types of contact-related activities such as athletic teams, pep squads, and certain intramural activities. The theory supporting an assumption of risk is that students assume an element of risk to participate and benefit from the activity in which they wish to participate. Additionally, they have knowledge and an understanding of the potential damage involved in participating in the particular activity. Even though a student assumes an element of risk, it does not relieve school personnel in cases where they fail to meet a reasonable standard of care based on the age, maturity, risk, and nature of the risk associated with the activity. The following case illustrates how a court responds to assumption of risk claims when there was evidence of negligence by a school district.

A high school student was injured during an agility drill while at football practice. Leahy was seriously injured when his face came in contact with another player's helmet. Leahy had not been issued a helmet, which was necessary to participate in the agility drill.

The student sued the district for his injury sustained during the drill. The school district argued that Leahy assumed the risk associated in the ordinary play of football. However, the facts confirmed that Leahy was not issued a helmet because the school lacked a sufficient number of them. The Florida court rejected the assumption of risk argument presented by the district and ordered a new trial to allow a jury to hear the case.[18]

In assumption of risk cases, it must be established that the informed student knew of the risk involved and voluntarily elected to participate. Under assumption of risk, school personnel are expected to exercise prudence and to reasonably foresee that injury could result, based on either a lack of proper instruction, an absence of reasonable supervision, or improper decisions regarding the injured student.

For example, if a football coach does not properly teach sound techniques of blocking and tackling or decides to match a much larger player against a very small and fragile player, or fails to provide proper medical support for an injured player, he or she may be charged with liability, although the activity itself carried some degree of risk. Assumption of risk does not relieve school personnel of executing their duty to instruct, supervise, and provide for the safety of students under their supervision. There have been numerous cases where assumption of risk was present, but school personnel were charged because of their own negligence. The following examples are illustrations of cases in which students were injured and school personnel found negligent for failure to meet a standard of care:

1. A woodworking instructor allowed a student to operate a table saw without the use of a safeguard, which resulted in serious damage to his proximal interphalangeal joint.[19]
2. A student dislocated his shoulder during an intramural football game, when the school provided no protective equipment and improper supervision of the game.[20]
3. An 11-year-old student suffered serious head injuries from a blow to the head during a kick ball game and was without medical attention for more than an hour. The one-hour delay caused a hematoma to grow from the size of a walnut to that of an orange.[21]
4. An 8-year-old girl was seriously burned when her costume caught fire from a lighted candle on her teacher's desk.[22]
5. A 12-year-old boy was killed when he fell through a skylight at school while retrieving a ball.[23]
6. A boy was seriously injured while playing on school grounds when he fell into a hole filled with glass, trash, and other debris, due to the absence of school officials to warn him of the dangerous condition.[24]
7. A female student was in route to class when she pushed her hand through a glass panel in a smoke-colored door, causing severe and permanent damage.[25]
8. A high school student was seriously injured when he was tackled and thrown to the ground during a touch football game in gym class, based on inadequate supervision when the players began to use excessive force.[26]

Assumption of risk is a valid defense only when school personnel met the duty of care expected in a given situation.

Comparative Negligence

Comparative negligence, a relatively new concept, has grown in popularity in many states. It differs from contributory negligence in the sense that slight negligence by the plaintiff or injured party does not relieve the defendant or persons who may have greatly contributed to the injury.

Under comparative negligence, acts of those responsible are compared in the *degree of negligence* attributed in an injury situation. Juries will normally determine the degree of negligence, which may range from slight to ordinary to gross, depending on the circumstances. The jury will make a determination regarding the degree to which each party has contributed to an injury. If one party is found to have contributed more heavily to an injury than another, then that party will be assessed a greater proportion for damages. It does not prevent recovery by the injured party, but merely reduces the damages based on the fault of the injured persons. Comparative negligence may be illustrated by the following examples:

1. Two students injured each other during an off-campus fight after school.
2. Two students chased a fly ball during a softball game, causing a collision in which both received injury.
3. While one high school student was speeding in his automobile, another ran a stop sign, causing injury to both students.
4. A student was injured when he climbed a ladder that had been left leaning against the building, although he was instructed not to go near the ladder.
5. A student was injured when he ran, at an excessive rate of speed, through a glass panel at the end of the gymnasium floor.
6. A student lost two teeth in a gymnasium fall when he slipped, as a result of not using gym shoes. He had been told that he could participate in gym activities if he wished to do so.

If the jury determines that both parties, through their individual acts, contributed equally to the injury, then neither party is assessed damages. Comparative negligence will increasingly become popular in school settings based on the growing tendency of state legislatures to adopt it as a legal concept. It is considered by many legal experts to be the fairest method of assessing liability because it places proportional responsibility on both or all parties and apportions responsibility based on the degree of fault exhibited by each party involved in the injury. The following case illustrates the application of comparative negligence.

A 14-year-old Arkansas student exited his school bus and proceeded to walk to his family's mailbox. The bus driver turned off the bus safety devices and proceeded down the highway. As the boy attempted to cross the street, he was struck by a logging truck. The student's estate brought a wrongful death action against the school district. The jury determined that there was negligence by both the school district and the student. The jury assessed responsibility to the school district at 90 percent and the student at 10 percent.

The school district appealed to the Supreme Court of Arkansas. The district contended that the truck driver's operation of the logging truck was the primary cause of the student's death, and that any negligence by the school district did not cause the student's death. The facts revealed that the Arkansas Department of Education school bus driver's handbook stated explicitly that the bus should not move until the student had safely crossed the road. The court noted that this policy was not followed. Therefore, the truck driver's operation was not independent of the bus driver's negligent acts. The court affirmed the decision of the lower court.[27]

Immunity

Immunity as a legal concept has diminished in terms of impact. It is based on the old common law of sovereign immunity, "The King can do no wrong," meaning that the state or federal government is protected from suit and cannot be held liable for injuries that resulted in the proper execution of governmental functions. This doctrine was extended to school districts, since they are involved in state action and are agents of the state.

Some states have abrogated school board immunity, while others recognize the concept based on whether an activity is classified as *governmental* or *proprietary*. For example, if the activity is considered proprietary, liability may be imposed based on the facts involving negligence. Proprietary activities are normally those in which admission fees are charged.

One court defined proprietary in this manner: "In general . . . it has been said that if a given activity is one which a local government unit is not statutorily required to perform, or if it may also be carried out by private enterprise, or it is used as a means of raising revenue, the function is proprietary."[28]

Other states use the terminology *ministerial* and *discretionary* in determining whether liability may be imposed on school boards. Ministerial (governmental) acts are those required by state mandate or local school board policy and ones for which school personnel do not exercise choice. Examples of *ministerial acts* may include the following:

1. Providing school-sponsored transportation for certain students
2. Holding public and open board of education meetings
3. Taking and reporting attendance
4. Reporting suspected cases of child abuse
5. Developing a school calendar

In these examples, local school districts or schools are obligated to perform these duties, some of which may not be delegated.

On the other hand, discretionary acts are ones for which school personnel may exercise judgment. Examples of *discretionary acts* may include the following:

1. Deciding to hold field day activities
2. Deciding whether to allow outside groups to use school facilities before or after school
3. Deciding on the nature of field trip experiences for students
4. Determining what extracurricular organizations should be sponsored by the school

These activities involve planning, assessment, and the exercise of judgment. Difficulties often arise based on the manner in which states classify these functions. Some states consider all school district activities to be governmental, whereas others do not. This sometimes creates confusion and difficulty in addressing immunity issues.

While immunity exists to a limited degree in some states, teachers and administrators are not covered by this concept. They are considered employees of the board and are thus responsible for their individual tortious acts. They cannot rely on immunity as a defense to their individual acts that result in injury to students.

Immunity Costs. School personnel are well advised to affiliate with their state and national educational associations, since membership carries liability protection for its members during the execution of their professional duties. This obviously should not be the primary motivation for becoming affiliated, but should be considered as an important aspect of membership.

DUTIES OF SUPERVISION

All teachers and administrators are expected to provide reasonable supervision of students under their charge. The degree of supervision will vary with each situation. The less mature the students, the greater the need for supervision. The greater the potential for injury to students engaging in certain activities, the greater the need for supervision.

Whether school personnel have adequately fulfilled their duty of supervision is a question of fact for a jury to decide. Each case rests on its merits. Reasonable supervision is established when a jury decides it is based on facts presented. Since standards of care vary depending on each unique situation, adequate supervision in one situation may be totally inadequate in a different situation. Courts will consider such factors as the nature of the activity involved, the age and number of students engaged in the activity, and the quality of supervision.

Supervision Before School

School personnel have a responsibility to provide some form of supervision for students who arrive on campus before the normal school day begins. The amount of supervision would depend on the circumstances involving early arriving students. For example, foreseeability is established when a group of students arrives early on campus without some form of supervision. Teachers and administrators are expected to foresee that students might be harmed if no form of supervision is provided. The same principle would apply for students who are retained on campus after school, waiting for their parents to arrive. Once foreseeability has been established, it is necessary to ensure that reasonable and prudent measures be taken.

There is no expectation that teachers and administrators guarantee that students will never be injured in either case. Certainly, this would be impossible to achieve. What must be demonstrated, however, is that reasonable measures are taken, based on foreseeable harm to students. For example, there would be no expectation that teachers and administrators arrive on campus during unreasonable hours to provide supervision. Although the courts have not addressed the time frame issue, per se, it would be a factor in deciding if teachers or administrators failed to meet a reasonable standard of supervision.

Certainly, parents should be informed in writing that school personnel are not available during the very early morning hours to supervise students. Parents should be discouraged from bringing their children to campus during these early hours. Although these steps should be taken, they do not in themselves totally relieve teachers and administrators of supervisory responsibilities. The courts will usually reason that students' presence on campus is not based on their own choices. They are there because of parents' decisions.

Administrators have the responsibility for assuring that the campus is safe for early arriving students. Students and their parents should be informed of the behavior that is expected of students when arriving before or remaining after school. Once students are informed, some type of periodic supervision should occur to ensure that students are exhibiting proper conduct and are not engaged in potentially harmful activities. The key point that should be emphasized is that adequate supervision must be provided for a reasonable period of time while students congregate on campus as they wait for the school day to begin. Again, this does not imply that there be constant around-the-clock supervision, but rather prudence in ensuring that students are behaving properly and not engaged in potentially dangerous or harmful activities such as contact games, throwing dangerous objects, wrestling or playing pranks that might result in injury, leaving the campus after early arrival, and/or crossing busy or dangerous thoroughfares. Involvement in these activities without proper warning or periodic supervision by school personnel may result in liability charges based on specific facts related to each case.

Liability involving school personnel for injury sustained before the school day begins would be based on a number of factors such as the age and maturity of the students congregating on campus and the propensity for them to engage in prohibited activities. If the students are relatively mature and are inclined to follow directives from school administrators and teachers regarding appropriate behavior, then the standard of care would not be as high as would be the case if these students were younger, less mature, and more inclined to be involved in pranks or prohibited activities. If the school has experienced previous problems regarding accidents and injury to students before the school day begins, obviously the need for more intense supervision becomes paramount. Conversely, if there is a record of early morning student assaults committed by fellow students or people who do not attend school, intense supervision must be provided. If the school is located in an area that is surrounded by heavily traveled thoroughfares and busy intersections, it is conceivable that young children, while engaged in various activities, might wander into the path of an automobile. All of these factors would be assessed by the courts in determining whether liability charges are appropriate in a given situation.

It is conceivable that students may contribute to their own injury by engaging in prohibited activities or failing to follow directives by administrators and teachers. In these cases, students must be sufficiently mature enough to understand and appreciate the potential danger associated with their actions. If not, school personnel may be held liable in the absence of quality supervision. In states that have adopted *comparative liability* as a legal concept, a determination would be made regarding the degree of fault by the student and school personnel. Liability would be assessed based on the extent to which each party contributed to the injured party.

Titus v. Lindberg is a classic case involving on-campus supervision of students before the school day begins. Nine-year-old Robert Titus arrived at Fairview School campus at approximately 8:05 A.M. and headed toward the bicycle rack to park his bike. As he turned the corner of the building, he was struck in the eye by a paper clip shot by Lindberg, a 13-year-old who was not a student at Fairview at that time but was awaiting a bus to transport him to his school. The facts revealed that Lindberg had shot another student with a paper clip just 5 minutes earlier. Since Fairview classes did not begin until 8:15 A.M., the principal, Smith, provided supervision for all students who were early arrivals. On the morning of the incident, Lindberg arrived early and played around with an elastic band before he struck another student in the back and subsequently injured Titus.

Titus filed a suit, alleging that his personal injury was caused by Lindberg's negligent shooting of the paper clip and by Smith's negligence in providing proper supervision.

The record shows that Lindberg had attended Fairview up to two years before and was described as a "bully."

Smith admitted that he had known of previous pranks involving Lindberg, but was unaware of the incident leading to the injury of Robert Titus. Although the school day did not begin until 8:30 A.M., it was not uncommon for students to arrive on campus on or before 8:00 A.M. Smith typically would supervise milk truck deliveries as he supervised students. He sometimes walked outside the building as he moved from one part of the campus to the other, while on other occasions he walked inside. On the day Titus was injured, Smith was walking inside.

The trial court ruled for Titus and awarded him $44,000 for damages, holding Lindberg and Smith responsible for his injury. Smith sought a reversal of the trial court's ruling by the State Appellate Court and subsequently the State Supreme Court. Both courts affirmed the ruling of the trial court in holding Smith and Lindberg responsible for Robert's injury.

The State Supreme Court stated that school personnel are liable for injuries received by students under their supervision, when such personnel fail to exercise reasonable supervision. The fact that students arrived early did not relieve Smith of an obligation to provide reasonable supervision, since he was aware of their presence on campus. Further, Smith had not announced any rules governing student behavior before classes began, nor had he assigned other teachers supervisory responsibilities before classes began. The decision of the court of appeals was affirmed.[29]

This case illustrates what can happen when there is absence of quality supervision. There were large numbers of students congregating on campus, many of whom were engaged in various types of activities. It seems prudent that the principal would have foreseen possible injury to students and taken other measures such as involving other teachers or school personnel in campus supervision.

Supervision During School

It is obvious that school personnel have a duty to supervise students during the normal school day. Since certified personnel operate *in loco parentis,* they assume the responsibility to provide reasonable supervision during the period of time in which they are assigned students. Students are viewed as agents of teachers and administrators, and thus are accountable to them for their behavior and academic performance. Since the school is considered a safe place by the courts, there is the presumption that school personnel are exercising prudence in supervising students. Supervision, in this instance, covers the full range of school-related activities involving students.

Certainly, teachers have the leading responsibility to provide reasonable supervision for students to whom they have been assigned. However, they also have a responsibility to caution or warn other students attending the school if they observe these students engaged in activities that may be potentially dangerous or harmful. That students are not directly assigned to a particular teacher, during a specified time frame, does not relieve that teacher of responsibility.

Supervision After School

Because common law and statutory requirements vary among states regarding standards of care, it is difficult to form any generalized conclusions in tort liability cases involving the duty to supervise students after the school day ends. School personnel, in the absence of statutory or board requirements, assume no duty to supervise students who are en route to school or departing for home, unless school-sponsored transportation is involved. Courts generally do not expect school personnel to provide supervision after the school day has ended, unless students are engaged in a school-sponsored activity. However, if there is common knowledge and awareness that students are left on campus after school, certain precautions should be taken by school personnel.

First and foremost, parents should be informed that the school does not provide supervision after the normal school day ends. They should be further encouraged to make proper arrangements to arrive promptly at the end of the school day to transport their child home. This information should be included in the student handbook and reflected by school policy. Parents should verify by their signature that these policies have been read and understood.

These steps, while appropriate, do not completely absolve the school of any responsibility for supervision, should it be determined that unsupervised students are engaged in potentially dangerous activities on school grounds after the school day has ended. More importantly, a duty of care may also be established if the school has written policies and procedures for after-school supervision, especially if these are communicated to parents. Generally speaking, there is no duty to provide extensive supervision beyond reasonable measures after the school day ends. While no duty exists beyond reasonable measures, there would be an expectation of a teacher or administrator who observed students engaged in potentially harmful activities en route home after school to warn them of the impending danger and to instruct them to discontinue the potentially harmful activity. The teacher or administrator does not have the right to ignore students en route home when they observe potentially dangerous situations involving students. They must foresee that students may be harmed, even though the students involved may not be under the direct supervision of the teacher or administrator.

So long as the student is enrolled in the school, teachers and administrators must take reasonable steps to protect them from harm. In some instances, the standard of care might be higher for students left on campus after the school day ends, particularly if there is evidence that unauthorized individuals are attracted to campus after hours. Particular caution should be exercised if there have been instances in which unauthorized people have attempted to abduct or assault younger students by offering them money, candy, or other inducements. Another particularly hazardous condition may exist if students are left on campus in the late afternoon. It is foreseeable that students might be assaulted more frequently if they are left unsupervised after darkness. Every effort should be made to convey the potential danger to parents who have their children remain late on campus after the school day ends. As a last resort, school district security or local police officers should be engaged if parents fail to arrive in a timely fashion to transport children home after the school day ends. The school district should have well-developed policies addressing responsibilities of all parties, parents, students, and school personnel in these potentially dangerous situations.

The courts have denied recovery to parents in a number of cases where damages were sought regarding after-school injuries involving voluntary and unorganized student activities. For example, a school district was held not liable for the wrongful death of a 12-year-old student who entered the playground after school hours, either through an unlocked gate or a hole in the fence, and suffered fatal injuries in a skateboard game. The court held that even if the school officials knew that the playground was used for such games, alleged defects in the fence or gate merely allowed access to the area and thus related to the district's duty of supervision and control over its property. The parents failed to establish that their son was a student enrolled at the school and on school grounds during the normal school day in connection with a school function. Rather, he was there for his own amusement. The court held that there was no duty on the part of the school district to supervise and control activities on school grounds at all times.[30]

In a different case, a teacher was not held liable for an injury sustained by a third-grade student that occurred while unsupervised students cleaned a classroom after school. While cleaning the room, one student rummaged through the teacher's desk and discovered a knife that subsequently resulted in injury. The facts revealed that the students had been forbidden to go near the teacher's desk. The court held for the teacher, due to the student's disobedience. The teacher did not place the knife in the student's hand. The injury occurred based on the student's actions.[31]

Field Trips

School-sponsored field trips are considered to be mere extensions of normal school activities, and therefore require a reasonable standard of supervision by school personnel. In many instances, special supervision is required, due to the fact that students visit unfamiliar places and have a greater need for supervision. These activities normally provide valuable learning experiences for students. Since schools are moving toward connecting classroom learning to real-life situations, school-sponsored field trips will likely increase in popularity and instructional value.

School personnel are expected to exercise reasonable standards of supervision during field trip experiences. Students should be informed prior to the actual activities of the circumstances surrounding the activity. If there are special instructions or concerns, they should be properly conveyed by the teacher who has responsibility for supervising the field trip activity. Students, as well as parents, particularly those whose children are enrolled in the lower grades should be informed of rules and expected behavior during the activity.

The *standard of care* involving field trips will vary depending on the age and maturity of students and the nature of the field experience. Teachers who organize field trips and administrators who approve them should be certain that there is adequate supervision in terms of *quality* and *quantity*. For example, it is foreseeable that if one teacher attempts to supervise 50 young, immature students during a trip to the zoo, some student might be harmed if an insufficient number of chaperones is not available to assist with supervisory duties.

It is an acceptable practice to request that parents serve as chaperones during these excursions, in which case parents should be fully informed of the nature of the activities involved, the type of students who will be supervised, and specific instructions regarding their supervisory duties. Students who are extremely active or have a history of misbehavior should be closely supervised by the classroom teacher, as it is foreseeable that they may be injured under certain conditions.

If field trips are well organized and supervised, they will meet the standard of care expected of school personnel as well as provide a valuable learning experience for students. The following case illustrates the court's willingness to examine factual details involving liability charges against school personnel during field trips.

An eighth-grade class consisting of 110 students took a field trip to Nashville, Tennessee. This trip included lunch at a restaurant directly across the street from the park. Teachers supervised all students as they crossed the street en route to the restaurant. Three students finished their meals early and requested permission to return to the park. The teachers granted permission, advising the three to be careful. One student reached the curb, stopped and looked in both directions before stepping into the street, and was subsequently struck by a car. The student's parents brought action against the teachers who coordinated the field trip, claiming that the teachers were negligent for not escorting the students back across the street to the park. The lower court held for the parents, finding the teachers negligent.

Upon review, the Tennessee Court of Appeals noted that the injured student was 13 years of age, experienced no hearing or vision problems, and was regarded as very mature for his age. The court further noted that the street was not considered unreasonably dangerous to cross. The appellate court reversed the lower court findings by concluding that the teachers had taken reasonable measures and were not required to escort the students across the street.[32]

Parental Consent and Written Waivers

It is a common practice for school districts to require parents to sign permission slips allowing their children to participate in certain school-sponsored activities away from the school. This practice has obvious value, as parents are involved in the decision-making process regarding these activities.

In some cases, these consent forms also will contain a waiver or disclosure statement that relieves the school of any legal responsibility in the event a student is injured during a field-based, school-sponsored activity. Psychologically, this practice might discourage a parent who has endorsed such a form from raising a legal challenge in the event of an injury to his or her child, but it does not in any way relieve school personnel of their duty to provide reasonable supervision. *Such forms have very limited, if any, legal basis in law.* If a parent grants permission for the child to engage in an activity and also signs a waiver, legal action may still be brought against school personnel if negligence occurs or a lack of proper supervision is established. School personnel should be aware that permission forms, although valuable, do not abrogate their legal duty to supervise and provide for the safety of students during these excursions. Depending on the statute of limitations, it also is probable that a student may later bring suit against the district when he or she reaches majority age, even if the parent elects not to do so during the time in which the student actually received an injury.

LIABILITY INVOLVING CIVIL RIGHTS STATUTES

The *Wood v. Strickland* case, involving student expulsion (discussed in Chapter 3), briefly addressed the issue of liability of school board members in relation to civil rights violations of students. The Civil Rights Act of 1871, 42 U.S.C. § 1983, prohibits denial of constitutional and statutory rights by public officials. It states

> Every person who, under color of any statute, ordinance, regulation, custom, or usage of any state or territory, subjects or causes to be subjected, any citizen of the United States or

other person with the jurisdiction thereof to the deprivation of any rights, privileges, or immunities secured by the Constitution and laws shall be liable to the party injured in an action at law, suit in equity, or other proper proceeding for redress.[33]

The significance of section 1983 was recognized by the U.S. Supreme Court in 1972: Section 1983 opened the federal courts to private citizens, offering a uniquely federal remedy against the incursion of their civil rights under the claimed authority of state law.[34]

In the school setting, this federal statute allows students to seek monetary damages from state officials for acts that violated their constitutional rights. The courts have been fairly consistent in holding public school officials and board members responsible for acts that violated students' constitutional rights. Students are successful in their suits if there is evidence that school officials or board members acted in bad faith in violating their constitutional rights. School officials will not succeed in claiming that they were unaware of the violation. The question raised by the courts is whether school officials should have been aware, as any other reasonable person in their position, that a student's rights were violated. (See the *Woods v. Strickland* case discussed in Chapter 3 and *Doe v. Taylor* discussed previously in this chapter.)

■ ■ ■ ■ ■ ▬▬▬▬▬▬▬▬▬▬▬▬▬▬▬▬▬▬▬▬▬▬▬▬▬▬▬▬▬▬
ADMINISTRATIVE GUIDE

SCHOOL LIABILITY

1. School district personnel must be aware of the standard of care that must be met as they instruct and supervise students in various activities to which they have been assigned.
2. Every teacher or administrator has a responsibility to ensure to the fullest extent possible that school buildings and grounds are safe for student use.
3. The absence of foreseeability by school personnel will not be upheld by the courts when the facts reveal that school personnel were expected to foresee the potential danger of a situation resulting in injury to a student.
4. School personnel have a legal duty to instruct, supervise, and provide a safe environment for students.
5. Reasonable and prudent decisions regarding student safety will withstand court scrutiny.
6. A higher standard of care may be expected during field trips and excursions involving students, especially in cases where students are viewed as licensees.
7. School grounds should be accessible and considered safe for authorized visitors.
8. School personnel must refrain from any actions that may fall under the categories of assault and battery, especially in cases involving physical punishment.
9. Personal information regarding students should be kept confidential. Only those who have a vested interest in working with a student should have access to such personal information.
10. School personnel should be mindful that qualified privilege is limited when information is shared concerning a student. They must operate in good faith with no intent to harm a student's reputation.
11. Students should not be coerced to use equipment or perform a physical activity for which they express serious apprehension. Coercion of this type could result in injury to the student and liability charges against school personnel.

(continued)

■ ■ ■ ■ ■ ▬▬▬▬▬▬▬▬▬▬▬▬▬▬▬▬▬▬▬▬▬▬▬▬▬▬▬▬▬▬▬▬▬▬

ADMINISTRATIVE GUIDE (*continued*)

12. Teachers and administrators should be reminded that the infliction of mental distress involving students may result in personal liability charges.
13. The conduct of school personnel should not be calculated to cause emotional harm to students.
14. Unorthodox and indefensible practices aimed at disciplining students should be avoided.
15. Unacceptable behavior by teachers and administrators that exceeds the boundaries of professional conduct should be clearly stated in school or district policy, with the consequences for violations spelled out.
16. Schools should develop a culture and a set of values that place a high premium on respect for the dignity of every individual involved in the school community.
17. When possible, interactions involving students that might tend to embarrass them or create mental distress should occur in private, and not in the presence of their peers.
18. Board of education members may be held liable for their individual acts that result in the violation of a student's rights.
19. Students should not be detained after school for unreasonable periods of time for behavior that does not warrant detention.
20. Items retrieved from students, if not illegal, should be returned to students or their parents within a reasonable time frame and not retained permanently by school personnel.
21. Illegal items, with the administrators' consent, should be presented to law enforcement officials upon notification of parents.
22. A higher standard of care is necessary in laboratories, physical education classes, and contact sports.
23. School officials should provide some form of supervision for students before the school day begins or after the school day ends.
24. Well-planned liability workshops/seminars should be offered periodically to ensure that school personnel are aware of the limits of liability.

LIABILITY AND THE ASSUMPTION OF RISK

Brent Thomas, principal of Homewood High School, located in a very affluent community, recommended and received approval to hire George Banks as his new physical education teacher. George organized the first hockey program for the school. Students who wanted to participate were required to undergo a physical examination and submit a written permission slip from their parents. One day during practice, Ricky Watts, a 14-year-old student, sustained serious injuries to his mouth and jaw when he used an improper technique to block the hockey puck. His parents were upset and filed liability charges against the principal and coach.

■ ■ ■ ■ ■ ▬▬▬▬▬▬▬▬▬▬▬▬▬▬▬▬▬▬▬▬▬▬▬▬▬▬▬▬▬▬▬▬▬▬

DISCUSSION QUESTIONS

1. What factors would determine whether the principal may be liable?
2. What factors would determine whether George Banks is liable?
3. Can either Thomas or Banks successfully use the defense of assumption of risk to avoid liability charges? Why or why not?

DISCUSSION QUESTIONS (*continued*)

4. Develop a set of defensible guidelines governing supervision of competitive athletic activities.
5. What factors would determine whether assumption of risk may be used as a legitimate defense?
6. Discuss the administrative implications of this case.

LIABILITY AND THE SUBSTITUTE TEACHER

Linda Collins was employed as a substitute teacher for Walnut Grove High School in a mid-size industrial city. She generally substitutes 15 to 20 days per month at various schools in the district. On the day she substituted in a shop class, one student was sexually assaulted by another student behind a portable chalkboard. Parents of the assaulted child filed a suit against the school district.

DISCUSSION QUESTIONS

1. Is a substitute teacher held to the same standard as a regular teacher? Why or why not?
2. Does sexual assault of a student by another automatically result in liability? Why or why not?
3. What factors would determine whether liability claims are valid?
4. How would the court likely view this case, based on factors you identified in question 4?
5. Defend your response regarding the court's position in this case.

LIABILITY AND PLAYGROUND SUPERVISION

Three elementary teachers are assigned to supervise their children who are playing on the playground. There are approximately a hundred children engaged in a number of playground activities. Since these teachers do not have much opportunity to chat with each other during the school day, all of them decide to bring chairs to the playground and engage in conversation while observing their children. During this time, one child sustains a serious injury when he is struck by a rock thrown by another student.

DISCUSSION QUESTIONS

1. What is the legal issue in this situation?
2. Who is responsible for this incident?
3. Can all three teachers be held liable? Why or why not?
4. How do you think the court will rule in this case? Give a rationale for your response.
5. Develop a set of guidelines regarding playground supervision.

LIABILITY AND SCHOOL SUSPENSION

Ray Knight, a middle school student, was suspended for three days due to unexcused absences. Although school district procedures required telephone notification and a prompt written notice by mail to his parents, the school only sent a notice by the student, who threw it away. Thus, Ray's parents were unaware of his suspension. During his first day of suspension, Ray was accidentally shot while visiting a friend's house.

DISCUSSION QUESTIONS

1. Where should fault reside in this case?
2. Do Ray's parents have defensible grounds to pursue liability charges against school officials? Why or why not?
3. How would failure to follow required district procedures factor into this case?
4. What factors would determine whether Ray's parents are successful in their suit?
5. How do you feel the court would rule in this case? Give a rationale for your response.

TORT LIABILITY

Jack Bellingham, a school principal, has a growing tendency to call teachers to his office for various reasons.

DISCUSSION QUESTIONS

When he does so,

1. What risks if any does Bellingham incur?
2. If a student were injured during the teacher's absence, who would be liable—the teacher, the principal, or both?
3. What factors would the courts consider in this situation if a student were injured during the teacher's absence?
4. What are the principal's obligations in this situation?
5. What guidelines would you suggest in this situation?
6. What are the administrative implications?

ENDNOTES

1. *Hosemann v. Oakland Unified Sch. Dist.,* No. SD11025, Supreme Court of California, 1989 Cal. LEXIS 4187, August 17, 1989.
2. *Doe v. Taylor I.S.D., et al.,* 15 F. 3d 443 (5th Cir., 1994).
3. *Tinker v. Des Moines Independent Community School District,* 393 U.S. 503, at 511, 89 S.Ct. 733, 21 L. Ed. 2d 731 (1969).
4. *Mitchell v. Forsyth,* 472 U.S. 511, 105 S.Ct. 2806 (1985).
5. *Davis v. Scherer,* 468 U.S. 183, 104 S.Ct. 3012 (1984).
6. *Carey v. Piphus,* 435 U.S. 247, 98 S.Ct. 1042, 55 L. Ed. 2d 252 (1978).
7. Restatement of Torts, Second § 339.
8. *Jackson v. Cartwright School District,* 607 P. 2d 975 (Ariz. 1980).
9. *Gordon v. Oak Park School District No. 97,* 24 Ill. App. 3d 131, 320 N.E. 2d 389 (1974).
10. *Celestine v. Lafayette Parish School Board,* 284 So. 2d 650 (La. 1973).
11. *Miller v. Griesel,* 308 N.E. 2d 701 (1974).
12. *Mirand v. City of New York,* 84 N.Y. 2d 44; 614 N.Y.S. 2d 372, 637 N.E. 2d 263 (1994).
13. *Wilhelm v. Board of Education of City of New York,* 227 N.Y.S. 2d 791 (1962).
14. *Tannenbaum v. Board of Education,* 255 N.Y.S. 2d 522 (1969).
15. *Hutchinson v. Toews,* Dept. 2, 4 Or. App. 19, 476 P. 2d 811 Court of Appeals of Oregon (1970).
16. *Brazell v. Board of Education of Niskayuna Public Schools,* 161 A.D. 2d 1086 557 N.Y.S. 2d 645 Supreme Court (1990).
17. *Albers v. Independent School District No. 302 of Lewis City 94,* 342 487 P. 2d (Supreme Court of Idaho 1971).
18. *Leahy v. School Board of Hernando County,* 450 So. 2d 883 (Fla. App. 5th Dist. 1984).
19. *Barbin v. State,* 506 So. 2d 888 (1st Cir. 1987).
20. *Locilento v. John A. Coleman Catholic High School,* 523 N.Y.S. 2d 198 (A.D. 3d Dept. 1987).
21. *Barth v. Board of Education,* 490 N.E. 2d 77 (Ill. App. 186 Dist. 1986).
22. *Smith v. Archbishop of St. Louis,* 632 S.W. 2d 516 (Mo. App. 1982).
23. *Stahl v. Cocalico School District,* 534 A. 2d 1141 (Pa. Cmwlth. 1987).
24. *Dean v. Board of Education,* 523 A. 2d 1059 (Md. App. 1987).
25. *Bielaska v. Town of Waterford,* 491 A. 2d 1071 (Conn. 1985).
26. *Hyman v. Green,* 403 N.W. 2d 597 (Mich. App. 1987).
27. *State Farm Mutual Auto. Ins. Co. v. Pharr,* 808 S.W. 2d 769 (Ark. 1991).
28. *Morris v. State District of Mt. Lebanon,* 144 A. 2d 737 (Pa. 1958).
29. *Titus v. Lindberg,* 49 N.J. 66, 228 A. 2d 65 (1967).
30. *Bartell v. Palos Verdes Penninsula School District,* 83 Cal. App. 3d 492 147 Cal. Rptr. 898 (1978).
31. *Richard v. St. Landry Parish School Board,* 344 So. 2d 1116 (La. Ct. App. 1977).
32. *King v. Kartenson,* 720 S.W. 2d 65 (Tenn. App. 1986).
33. U.S.C. § 1983 (1988).
34. *Mitchum v. Foster,* 407 U.S. 225 (1972).

CHAPTER 7

LIABILITY AND
STUDENT RECORDS

The primary purpose of maintaining educational records should be to aid school personnel in developing the best educational program for each student enrolled in the school. An effective student file contains information used for counseling, program development, individualized instruction, grade placement, college admissions, and a variety of other purposes. In addition to certain types of directory information, student files typically include family background information, health records, progress reports, achievement test results, psychological data, disciplinary records, and other confidential material.

Public Law 93-380, the Family Educational Rights and Privacy Act (FERPA), protects confidentiality of student records. This act, commonly referred to as the Buckley Amendment, was enacted by the Congress in 1974 to guarantee parents and students a certain degree of *confidentiality* and *fundamental fairness* with respect to the maintenance and use of student records. The law is designed to ensure that certain types of personally identifiable information regarding students will not be released without parental consent. *If a student is 18 years of age or attends a postsecondary institution, parental consent is not required.* In that event, the student has the authority to provide consent. If the student is a dependent, for tax purposes, parents retain a coextensive access right with students over 18 years old. Since P.L. 93-380 is a federal statute, it applies to school districts and schools that receive federal funds. Schools should develop policies and procedures, including a listing of the types and locations of educational records and persons who are responsible for maintaining these records. Copies of these policies and procedures should be made available to parents or students on request.

SANCTIONS FOR VIOLATING FAMILY
PRIVACY RIGHTS

An excerpt of the Family Educational Rights and Privacy Act states the following:

> No funds shall be available under any program to any educational agency or institution which has a policy of denying access or which effectively prevents the parents of students who are or have been in attendance at a school of such agency, the right to inspect and review the educational records of their children. If any material or document in the educational record of a student includes information on more than one student, the parents of one

of such student shall have the right to inspect and review only such part of such material or document as related to such student or be informed of the specific information contained in such part of such material.[1]

At a minimum, the school district should provide, on an annual basis, information to parents, guardians, and eligible students regarding the content of the law and inform them of their right to file complaints with the Rights and Privacy Act Office of the Department of Education. If non-English-speaking parents are affected, the district has a responsibility to notify them in their native language.[2] Annual notification must include the following information:

1. Right to inspect and review educational records
2. Right to seek amendment of records believed to be inaccurate, misleading, or in violation of student's privacy act
3. Consent to disclose personally identifiable information contained in student's records except where act authorizes disclosure without consent
4. Right to file with the department a complaint under §§ 99.63 and 99.64 concerning alleged failures by the educational agency or institution to comply with requirements of the act
5. Notice must include the following:
   a. Procedures for exercising the right to inspect and review educational records
   b. Procedures for requesting amendment of records
   c. Specification of criteria for determining who constitutes a school official and what constitutes a legitimate educational interest
6. An educational agency or institution shall effectively notify parents or eligible students who are disabled
7. An educational agency or institution of elementary and secondary education shall effectively notify parents who have a primary or home language other than English

Additionally, parents, guardians, or eligible students should be provided information regarding procedures for accessing educational records, if they desire to do so. The content of education records is shown in Table 7.1.

The school district may release directory information regarding students, provided that such information is published yearly in a public newspaper. Directory information normally includes:

1. Name
2. Address
3. Telephone number
4. Date and place of birth
5. Participation in extracurricular activities
6. Weight, height, and membership on athletic teams
7. Dates of attendance
8. Diploma and awards received

If any parents or guardians object to the release of directory information on their child, their objection should be noted in the record and honored by the school district. School

TABLE 7.1   Content of Educational Records

EDUCATIONAL RECORDS INCLUDE	EDUCATIONAL RECORDS DO NOT INCLUDE
Records	Instructional records
Files	Supervisory records
Documents	Records maintained by law enforcement units for law enforcement purposes
Other materials which 1. contain information directly related to a student 2. are maintained by an educational agency, institution, or person acting for agency of institution	Records on an 18-year-old student attending a postsecondary institution that are maintained by a physician, psychiatrist, psychologist, or other recognized professional or paraprofessional involved in the treatment of the student

Source: P.L. 93-380.

policy should define what items are considered directory information and the conditions under which this information should be released.

Except for directory information, all personally identifiable records directly related to the student shall be kept confidential, unless the parent or guardian signs a consent form releasing certain such information.

RIGHTS OF PARENTS

Parents or legal guardians have the right to inspect their child's record. A school official should be present to assist a parent or guardian in interpreting information contained in the files and to respond to questions that may be raised during the examination process. Parents or legal guardians may challenge the accuracy of any information found in the files regarding their child. The school should schedule a conference, within a reasonable period of time (ten days or less although the act calls for no more than 45 days) with appropriate personnel to discuss the information that may be deemed inaccurate, inappropriate, or misleading. If agreement is reached to the satisfaction of the parent, no further action is necessary. Appropriate deletions or corrections are executed, recorded in the student file and communicated to parents or guardians in written form.

If the conference does not result in changes to the satisfaction of parents, they may request a hearing with the Director of Pupil Personnel or a designee to appeal the decision reached during the conference. The hearing should be scheduled within ten days or less. The parent or guardian may be represented by legal counsel. A final decision should be rendered within ten days subsequent to the hearing. If the school official hearing the case decides that the information is accurate and correct, the parent should be informed of such and provided an opportunity to place statements of disagreement in the file with reasons for the disagreement. This explanation must become a permanent part of the record and must be disclosed when the records are released. The parent or guardian may also seek relief in civil court. If student records are subpoenaed by the courts, the parent, guardian, or eligible student should be contacted prior to the release of records.

When consent is necessary to release student records, it must be provided in written form, signed and dated by the consenting person. The consent form should include a specification of the records to be released, reason for the release, and the names of the individuals to whom the records will be released. Once records are received by the requesting party, it should be emphasized that this information is not to be divulged to others without the expressed permission of the parents, guardians, or eligible students. *Parents, guardians, or eligible students must be notified before a school or district complies with a judicial order requesting educational records.* School officials in another school district in which a student plans to enroll may access that student's records, provided parents or guardians are notified in advance that the records are being transferred to the new district.

RIGHTS OF NONCUSTODIAL PARENTS

Occasionally, controversy arises regarding the rights of a noncustodial biological parent to access his or her child's educational records. School officials often find themselves caught between a custodial parent's request that the noncustodial parent not be permitted to access the child's educational records. School or district policy should provide guidance in these situations. One such case arose in New York when the mother of a child requested that the school not allow the child's father to see their son's educational records. The father challenged the school's refusal to allow him access to the child's records. The district court ruled that neither parent could be denied access to the child's records under the Family Educational Rights and Privacy Act. The court held that schools should make educational records accessible to both parents of each child fortunate enough to have both parents interested in the child's welfare.[3]

RIGHTS OF ELIGIBLE STUDENTS

As previously mentioned, the student may exercise the same rights afforded parents or guardians, if he or she has reached the age of 18 or is enrolled in a postsecondary institution. The student may inspect confidential records and challenge the accuracy of information contained in the file. Additionally, the student may determine whether anyone other than authorized individuals may have access to personal files. Students also have a right to receive a copy of their personal file, if they choose to have one. Eligible students are afforded the same due process provisions as parents are offered, if they choose to challenge the accuracy of information contained in their file. They may also, under certain conditions, bring liability charges for defamation against school personnel (discussed later in this chapter).

RIGHTS OF SCHOOL PERSONNEL

Teachers, counselors, and administrators who have a legitimate educational interest in viewing records may do so. A written form, which must be maintained permanently with the file, should indicate specifically what files were reviewed by school personnel and the date in which files were reviewed. Each person desiring access to the file is required to sign this written form. These forms should be available for parents, guardians, or eligible students, since they remain permanently with the file. If challenged, school personnel must demonstrate a legitimate interest in having reviewed the student's file.

In 1994, FERPA was amended to emphasize that institutions are not prevented from maintaining records related to a disciplinary action taken against a student for behavior that posed a significant risk to the student or others. Likewise, institutions are not prevented from disclosing such information to school officials who have been determined to have a legitimate educational interest in the behavior of the student. School districts also are permitted to disclose information regarding disciplinary action to school officials in other schools that have a legitimate educational interest in the behavior of students.

Table 7.2 summarizes the rights of all parties affected by FERPA.

ENFORCEMENT OF STATE OR FEDERAL STATUTES

Federal and state officials may inspect files without parental consent in order to enforce federal or state laws or to audit or evaluate federal education programs. In these cases, personally identifiable information may not be associated with any student unless Congress, by law, specifically authorizes federal officials to gather personally identifiable data. Information may also be released without consent in connection with applications for student financial aid. Authorized representatives who may access records include (1) the Comptroller General of the United States, (2) the Secretary of State (3) an administrative head of an educational agency, and (4) state and educational authorities. School district policies should address these issues so that parents, guardians, and eligible students are informed of these exceptions.

FAMILY EDUCATION RIGHTS AND PRIVACY ACT

Recent U.S. Supreme Court Rulings

On February 19, 2002, the U.S. Supreme Court ruled in *Owasso ISD v. Falvo*[4] that peer grading does not violate FERPA. The Department is currently reviewing the Court's ruling and may issue additional guidance or regulations to further clarify the scope of the term "education records."

On June 20, 2002, the U.S. Supreme Court ruled in *Gonzaga University v. John Doe.*[5] In the Gonzaga case, a student brought litigation against the university for disclosing personally identifiable information, without his consent, in violation of FERPA. The Supreme Court ruled that students and parents may *not* sue for damages under 42 U.S.C. § 1983 to enforce provisions of the Family Educational Rights and Privacy Act (FERPA).

U.S. Court of Appeals for the Sixth Circuit Ruling

On June 27, 2002, the Sixth Circuit Court of Appeals unanimously affirmed a lower court's ruling that university disciplinary records are "education records" under FERPA and that disclosing such records without students' consent constitutes a violation of FERPA. In

TABLE 7.2   Rights Under FERPA

RIGHTS OF STUDENTS WHO ARE 18 YEARS OLD OR ATTEND A POSTSECONDARY INSTITUTION	RIGHTS OF PARENTS	RIGHTS OF SCHOOL PERSONNEL
Have knowledge of types of records and location of records and inspect confidential records	Inspect child's record if under age of 18 years old	Access to confidential information for legitimate educational purposes
Challenge the accuracy of information contained on records	Challenge the accuracy of information contained on records	Maintain personal notes on students for personal use
Have appropriate deletions or corrections executed	Have appropriate deletions or corrections executed	Disclose educational records to comply with judicial orders for state and various federal agencies
Request hearing to contest information on records thought to be inaccurate	Request hearing to contest information on the records thought to be inaccurate	Disclosure of disciplinary proceedings conducted against perpetrators of a crime
Consent to disclosure of personally identifiable information contained in files	Place statement of disagreement regarding contested information remaining on the records	Disclosure of directory information on students
Determine what type of confidential information is released and to whom other than those authorized to access confidential information	Determine what type of confidential information is released, to whom it is released other than authorized personnel, and reasons to be released	Privilege against lawsuits when making truthful statements in good faith within the scope of professional duties
Place statement of disagreement regarding any contested information remaining on the records	Receive annual notice of rights under the act	Record truthful negative information on education records that should remain a part of the permanent record
Receive a copy of personal records	Receive prior notice of any records subpoenaed by the courts	Receive training on handling sensitive and confidential information on students with disabilities
Receive a copy of released record upon request	File complaints with the U.S. Department of Education concerning alleged violations	Receive protection when factual references of students are provided on request
Under certain conditions, bring charges of defamation against school personnel and other appropriate parties	Seek relief in civil court if necessary	Destroy records when no longer needed after student graduates

Source: P.L. 93-380.

1998, the Department asked a federal district court in Ohio to enjoin Miami University and the Ohio State University from disclosing records containing the names of student victims and accused students as prohibited under FERPA.[6] On March 20, 2000, the U.S. District Court for the Southern District of Ohio permanently enjoined the two Ohio universities from disclosing their on-campus disciplinary records to the public under the state's open-records law.

In affirming the ruling, the circuit court concluded that continued release of student disciplinary records "will irreparably harm the United States" and the Department of Education. This is important for three reasons:

1. The court agreed with the lower court that the Student Right-to-Know and Campus Security Act provides parents and students with statistical information about the type and amount of crimes on campus.
2. The court reaffirmed the department's broad reading of the term "education records" and stated that Congress, in amending FERPA in 1998 to allow postsecondary institutions to disclose the final results of disciplinary proceedings, must have intended that disciplinary records be education records or this amendment would be "superfluous."
3. The court held that the Department of Education was within its rights in seeking an injunctive relief in this case because none of the administrative remedies authorized by FERPA would have stopped the violations. In effect, the court held that the department can take preemptive actions in enforcing FERPA, rather than only after violations occur.

NO CHILD LEFT BEHIND ACT OF 2001

Annual Notification Requirements

The Secretary of Education is now required to annually inform each State Education Agency (SEA) and each Local Education Agency (LEA) of their obligations under both FERPA and Protection of Pupil Rights Amendment. This provision is found in § 1061(c)(5)(C), which are the amendments to PPRA, discussed below. The Family Policy Compliance Office (FPCO) is in the process of finalizing the notices to be provided to SEAs and LEAs.

Transfer of School Disciplinary Records

FERPA currently permits schools to transfer any and all education records, including disciplinary records, on a student who is transferring to another school. See § 99.31(a)(2) and § 99.34 of the FERPA regulations. This new provision requires states that receive funds under the Elementary and Secondary Education Act (ESEA), within two years, to provide an assurance to the Secretary of Education that the state "has a procedure in place to facilitate the transfer of disciplinary records, with respect to a suspension or expulsion, by local educational agencies to any private or public elementary school or secondary school for any student who is enrolled or seeks, intends, or is instructed to enroll, on a full- or part-time basis, in the school."

Armed Forces Recruiter Access

FERPA currently allows schools to designate and disclose without consent certain items of information as "directory information." The FERPA regulations define "directory information" under § 99.3 of the regulations and set forth the requirements for implementing a "directory information" policy under § 99.37 of FERPA. Generally, "directory information" may be disclosed by a school to any party, provided the requirements of FERPA are followed.

Congress passed a provision in the No Child Left Behind Act that addresses the disclosure of directory-type information (students' names, addresses, and telephone listings) to military recruiters. Congress also included similar language in the National Defense Authorization Act for Fiscal Year 2002. Both laws, with some exceptions, require schools to provide directory-type information to military recruiters who request it. Typically, recruiters request names, addresses, and telephone listings on junior and senior high school students that will be used for recruiting purposes and college scholarships offered by the military.

Student Privacy and Physical Exams

The No Child Left Behind Act contains a major amendment to PPRA that gives parents more rights with regard to the surveying of minor students, the collection of information from students for marketing purposes, and certain nonemergency medical examinations. PPRA has been referred to as the Hatch Amendment and the Grassley Amendment, after the authors of amendments to the law. School officials may also hear the law referred to as the Tiahrt Amendment, after Congressman Todd Tiahrt, who introduced the changes regarding surveys to the PPRA. The statute is found in 20 U.S.C. § 1232h and the regulations are found in 34 CFR Part 98.

U.S. Department of Education Surveys

Subsection (a) of the legislation was not changed. Subsection (b) added an additional category and made minor changes to the existing seven categories. This provision applies to surveys funded in whole or part by any program administered by the U.S. Department of Education (ED). PPRA provides the following:

- That schools and contractors make instructional materials available for inspection by parents if those materials will be used in connection with an ED-funded survey, analysis, or evaluation in which their children participate
- That schools and contractors obtain prior written parental consent before minor students are required to participate in any ED-funded survey, analysis, or evaluation that reveals information concerning
  1. Political affiliations or beliefs of the student or the student's parent
  2. Mental and psychological problems of the student or the student's family
  3. Sexual behavior or attitudes
  4. Illegal, antisocial, self-incriminating, or demeaning behavior
  5. Critical appraisals of other individuals with whom respondents have close family relationships

6. Legally recognized privileged or analogous relationships, such as those of lawyers, physicians, and ministers
7. Religious practices, affiliations, or beliefs of the student or student's parent
8. Income (other than that required by law to determine eligibility for participation in a program or for receiving financial assistance under such program)

Subsections (a) and (b) of PPRA generally apply when a survey is funded, at least in part, by any program administered by the Secretary of Education.

Surveys Funded by Other Sources

The new provisions, contained in subsection (c), apply (as does FERPA) to educational agencies or institutions that receive funds from any program of the Department of Education. Thus, public elementary and secondary schools are subject to the new provisions of PPRA. The new requirements are listed below:

- Schools are required to develop and adopt policies, in conjunction with parents, regarding the following:
  1. The right of parents to inspect, on request, a survey created by a third party before the survey is administered or distributed by a school to students
  2. Arrangements to protect student privacy in the event of the administration of a survey to students, including the right of parents to inspect, on request, the survey, if the survey contains one or more of the same eight items of information noted above
  3. The right of parents to inspect, on request, any instructional material used as part of the educational curriculum for students
  4. The administration of physical examinations or screenings that the school may administer to students
  5. The collection, disclosure, or use of personal information collected from students for the purpose of marketing or selling, or otherwise providing the information to others for that purpose
  6. The right of parents to inspect, on request, any instrument used in the collection of information, as described in number 5
- LEAs must "directly" notify parents of these policies and, at a minimum, provide the notice at least annually, at the beginning of the school year. The LEA must also notify parents within a reasonable period of time if any substantive change is made to the policies.
- In the notification, the LEA shall offer an opportunity for parents to opt out of (remove their child) from participation in the following activities:
  1. Activities involving the collection, disclosure, or use of personal information collected from students for the purpose of marketing or for selling that information, or otherwise providing that information to others for that purpose
  2. The administration of any third-party (non-Department of Education-funded) survey containing one or more of the above described eight items of information
  3. Any nonemergency, invasive physical examination or screening that is (1) required as a condition of attendance; (2) administered by the school and scheduled by the school in advance; and (3) not necessary to protect the immediate health and safety of the student or of other students.

- In the notification, the LEA shall notify parents the specific or approximate dates during the school year when these activities are scheduled.
- An LEA is not required to develop and adopt new policies if the SEA or LEA has in place, on the date of enactment of the No Child Left Behind Act of 2001, policies covering the requirements set forth in this law.
- The requirements concerning activities involving the collection and disclosure of personal information from students for marketing purposes do not apply to the collection, disclosure, or use of personal information collected from students for the exclusive purpose of developing, evaluating, or providing educational products or services for, or to, students or educational institutions, such as the following:
  1. College or other postsecondary education recruitment, or military recruitment
  2. Book clubs, magazines, and programs providing access to low-cost literacy products
  3. Curriculum and instructional materials used by elementary schools and secondary schools
  4. Tests and assessments used by elementary schools and secondary schools to provide cognitive, evaluative, diagnostic, clinical, aptitude, or achievement information about students
  5. The sale by students of products or services to raise funds for school-related or education-related activities
  6. Student recognition programs
- This law is not intended to preempt applicable provisions of state law that require parental notification.
- This law does not apply to any physical examination or screening that is permitted or required by state law, including such examinations or screenings permitted without parental notification.
- The requirements of PPRA do not apply to a survey administered to a student in accordance with the Individuals with Disabilities Education Act (IDEA).
- These requirements do not supersede any of the requirements of FERPA.
- The rights provided to parents under PPRA transfer from the parent to the student when the student turns 18 years old or is an emancipated minor under applicable state law. The law applies to LEAs, but does not apply to postsecondary institutions.
- An SEA or LEA may use funds provided under part A of title V of the ESEA to enhance parental involvement in areas affecting the in-school privacy of students.

Source: U.S. Department of Education, October 28, 2002

DEFAMATION INVOLVING SCHOOL PERSONNEL

Defamation, discussed in Chapter 6, regarding liability applies to student records. When school personnel communicate personal and sensitive information to another unauthorized person that results in injury to the student's reputation or standing in the school or that diminishes the respect and esteem to which the student is held, they may face charges of *libel* or *slander,* depending on the manner and intent in which such information was communicated. *Defamation* is a tort or civil wrong committed against another in which recovery is appropriate with a showing that the offended party received injury based on the deliberate or malicious action of others.

Slander

Slander is oral defamation, which occurs when school personnel inadvertently communicate sensitive and damaging information contained in student files to others who have no need to be informed. Libel and slander involve communication to a third party. Information contained in student files is there for the exclusive use of the teacher, principal, or counselor who has a legitimate interest in accessing this information as each works with the student. Information should not be accessed without meeting this requirement.

Once the information is ascertained, it should be used only in providing and improving educational opportunities for the student. By no means should confidential information be discussed in a canny and joking manner. Under no circumstances should the student be ridiculed. The law is very specific in indicating that personally identifiable information should not be communicated to third parties without proper consent. When this is done, not only has the law been violated, but the educator has run the risk of defaming the student. Off-the-cuff remarks and sharing sensitive information regarding a student is absolutely prohibited and may result in liability damages to those who are guilty of committing this act.

School personnel are well advised to maintain strict confidentiality in all cases involving students' personal files. In cases involving claim of personal injury, the burden of proof rests with the student in demonstrating that actual harm occurred based on deliberate communication to a third party.

Libel

Libel, unlike slander, is written defamation. Teachers, counselors, and principals should refrain from including damaging information in the student's record for which there is no basis. Any information recorded should be factual and specific with respect to serious infractions committed by the student—for example, time and place in which infractions occurred and possible witnesses who might verify, if needed, that the incident described is an accurate account of what actually occurred.

Another consideration involves a determination as to whether certain types of information should be included in the student's permanent file. Some legal experts feel that information that is subject to change and minor disciplinary infractions should be maintained in a separate file and destroyed after the student leaves school. For example, if there is no evidence of serious and recurring behavior problems, one might question the wisdom of including a single occurrence on the student's permanent records. On the other hand, if there is a strong belief that the behavior is sufficiently serious that it needs to be passed on to those who will be working with the student in the future, it might be appropriate, under the circumstances, to do so. Sound and rational judgment is required in these cases. These decisions must be carefully drawn, due to the serious implications involved. When it becomes necessary to record a serious disciplinary infraction on the student's record, it should be executed in the presence of the student, who should be provided a copy of the document.

Schools should refrain from statements that are based on opinion, particularly those involving questions of *morality, contagious diseases, family marital conditions,* and *mental or emotional issues.* These statements are damaging, based on their content, and, if communicated to others, may result in injury to the student's reputation, self-esteem, or standing in the school. Categorical statements or stereotypical statements should be avoided. If educators adhere to confidentiality and respect for the privacy rights of students, they will avoid liability claims involving injury to students. Professionalism and ethics dictate that these practices be followed.

Privilege

On many occasions, school personnel are requested to provide either oral or written information regarding a student, some of which might be contained in the student's file. When such requests are made and school personnel respond in a truthful and reasonable manner in accordance with their prescribed duties, they are protected by *qualified privilege*. When school personnel and the recipient of the information both have a common interest, they also are protected by a qualified privilege when the communication is reasonable to achieve their objective. Those who have common interest would likely include counselors, subject matter teachers, administrators, and parents. Interestingly, this privilege is lost if the communication is transmitted to another who does not share this common interest and consequently has no need to be apprised of the information.

Good Faith

Qualified privilege is based on the premise that the educator is operating in *good faith*. When damaging or sensitive information is communicated to others who have no need to know, good faith has been violated. Good faith requires that a legitimate purpose be served by communicating the information. Common interest in the student's well-being would constitute a legitimate purpose. Good faith efforts dictate that as information is shared with other eligible parties, it is communicated for legitimate purposes and without any intent or desire to damage the student. An absence of good faith may result in personal damages against those who do not operate in a reasonable and prudent manner.

An unusual case arose in Maryland when a special education student was sexually abused by her grandfather, who was charged with child abuse. Prior to his trial, he attempted to subpoena his granddaughter's school records. The child was enrolled in a special education program for emotionally disturbed children. The school district refused to furnish the records and filed a motion for a protective order. The defense attorney argued that the records were relevant in that they could reveal mental deficiencies that affected the child's ability to control her actions. The judge examined the records privately and determined that there was nothing contained in them that would serve to impeach the child's testimony. The grandfather was convicted and then appealed his conviction, contending that his rights were violated when the judge refused to allow him access to his granddaughter's records.

Maryland requires parental consent or a court order before a student's record can be disclosed. The Sixth Amendment to the Constitution requires that a criminal defendant be allowed to confront and cross-examine his accusers. The defendant in this case (*Zall v. State*) argued that the information contained in personal records was needed in order to cross-examine the student. The court ruled that the defendant's right to cross-examine was not violated, since it had been established by the lower court that the files contained no material evidence pertinent to the case. The Sixth Amendment only requires that the defendant receive material evidence. It is the court's role, not the defendant's, to determine material evidence. The defendant's appeal was denied.[7]

Finally, a case involving libel arose in Wisconsin, when a speech therapist in the Cudahy School System brought charges against his former superintendent. Hett, the plaintiff, alleged that his professional reputation had been damaged based on libeled responses made by the superintendent while responding to an inquiry from a prospective employer.

Hett had been employed as a traveling therapist who served six schools to teach students who were in need of his skill. He was not recommended for renewal of his contract by the six principals in the schools in which he worked. Ploetz, the superintendent, informed Hett that his contract would not be renewed and allowed him to resign so that his record would not reflect his nonrenewal.

Hett applied for another position in an adjoining district, citing a lack of advancement in the previous district as his reason for leaving. He also used Ploetz, his former superintendent, as a reference and granted permission to the employing district to contact Ploetz. Hett claimed that he was libeled by the defendant's response to an inquiry from the prospective employer.

The court addressed two issues in this case—whether any privilege insulated Ploetz's letter and whether his response was motivated by malice. The court held for Ploetz, stating that his letter was entitled to a conditional privilege. As such, he was entitled to provide a critical appraisal of Hett to allow the prospective employer to evaluate Hett's qualifications. Further, there was no evidence of malicious intent. Therefore, the plaintiff's charges were without merit.[8]

Acts of Malice

Malice exists when there is intent to harm or injure another. Intent is an important element regarding malicious behavior. When statements are communicated about a student, either written or oral, with the intent to injure his or her reputation, a tortious act has occurred, especially if these statements are false. *Truth* is a defense for liability, if no malicious intent is present. School personnel should exercise care in ensuring that statements communicated to others are free of malice, based on defensible evidence, and communicated in a professional, nonbiased, and truthful manner. When evidence reveals that school personnel acted in *bad faith* with the *intent* to injure a student's reputation and standing in the school or community, liability charges may be justified, even if statements are true. Students are entitled to a *liberty right* with respect to the expectation that their reputation be protected against unwarranted attacks.

There are essentially two types of malice. In *implied malice,* the offender has no defense for conveying harmful information. Such statements normally fall in the category of unsolicited or derogatory statements aimed at another person. In *actual malice,* the offended person must demonstrate that the person making the offensive comment had a motive for doing so and that this motive was calculated to generate ill will against the offended person. Both types may create serious legal problems for school personnel.

Since the passage of FERPA, numerous forms of litigation have surfaced, covering a full range of legal issues. The following cases summarize a number of issues faced by the courts related to the enforcement of FERPA:

1. A New York court ruled that a public school was required to release names of bilingual students with English deficiencies, because complainants had demonstrated a genuine need for the information that outweighed the privacy rights of students.[9]

2. Another New York court ruled that a father's request to release third-grade test scores of other students so that they could be compared to his child's score could be honored if the test results were not identified by student names.[10]
3. A Missouri court upheld a school board member against charges of defamation who commented during a board meeting that marijuana cigarettes had been found in a student's car. His statement was held to be privileged.[11]
4. A federal court in New York ruled against a student who withheld his records from a grand jury, when he could not show that they bore any relevance to the subject under investigation.[12]

In other developments, a case emerged in Illinois when a group of parents requested their school district to disclose standardized achievement scores for students for certain years, grades, and schools within the district, along with a listing of educational programs available in those schools. The district, using FERPA as its defense, refused to comply with their request. Suit was filed by parents, seeking disclosure under the Freedom of Information Act. The district court dismissed the case, which was then appealed to the Illinois Court of Appeals. The appeals court reversed the district's court decision and remanded, finding that the district had an obligation to release and mask all released information regarding students. The school district then appealed, contending that releasing masked information was in conflict with the Freedom of Information Act and would not protect the privacy rights of students. The Supreme Court held that the act was designed to open governmental records to public scrutiny. The act did not prohibit disclosure of masked student records. Since no students were identified, there is no invasion of privacy and the records must be released.[13]

A recent case arose in Kentucky concerning disclosure without consent involving a verbal statement made between the principal and the basketball coach that was challenged as violating the student's confidentiality rights.[14]

John Doe, diagnosed with hemophilia at an early age, suffered from hepatitis. Despite John's illness, he had participated in athletics throughout his life without problems. As a freshman at Woodford County High School, he became a member of the school's ninth-grade junior varsity basketball team. The school had a "no-cut" policy for ninth-graders wishing to play on the team. Any ninth-grader wishing to play on the junior varsity team was automatically selected to be a member of the team. On the basis of this policy, John began practicing with the team.

A few days after the team began practicing, defendant Roy Chapman, principal of Woodford County Middle School, noticed John in the gym practicing with the team. Chapman, who was aware of John's medical condition, approached Bobby Gibson, the team's coach, and suggested to Gibson that he check John's medical records on file with the school to see if it was prudent for him to play. According to John, he overheard this conversation between Chapman and Gibson and alleges other players heard the conversation as well. This allegation serves as grounds for the plaintiff's Family Education Rights and Privacy Act violation. The school board filed for summary judgment, which was granted by the district court. The case was appealed to the Sixth Circuit Court by the plaintiff. After weighing the evidence, the Sixth Circuit Court upheld the decision by the district and stated:

> Plaintiff argues the fact that John and other basketball players heard Chapman's disclosure of information effectively rules out any argument that the conversation is covered by any

exceptions. We find, based on the record, that plaintiff fails to provide anything more than paucity evidence to support the claim that other players overheard the conversation. In reviewing grants of summary, "the mere existence of scarcity of evidence" in support of the plaintiff's position is insufficient to overturn a grant of summary judgment. There must be evidence on which a jury could reasonably find for the plaintiff.[15]

Another issue pertinent to this case is that there are exceptions that allow disclosure of confidential information to certain individuals, including other school officials who have a legitimate educational interest in the child. In this case, that interest involved the health and safety of John Doe.

In yet another case, involving the disclosure of student grades in the classroom, parents brought suit, challenging the practice of teachers in Oklahoma's Owasso Independent School District of allowing students to grade each other's papers and to call out their grades in class.[16] The issue involves whether this practice violates either the Fourteenth Amendment to the Constitution or the Family Educational Rights and Privacy Act. The district granted summary judgment in favor of all defendants.

The case reached the district court after Kristja J. Falvo, the mother of three children enrolled in the district, learned that a number of her children's teachers would sometimes have their students grade one another's work assignments and tests and then have the students call out their own grades to the teacher. During the 1997–1998 and 1998–1999 school years, Falvo complained about this grading practice to school counselors and to the superintendent, claiming it severely embarrassed her children by allowing other students to learn their grades. Falvo was told that her children always had the option of confidentially reporting their grades to the teacher, and the school district refused to disallow the grading practice.

On appeal to the circuit court, Falvo contended that the right to privacy under the Fourteenth Amendment prohibits public disclosure of students' grades. She also argued that the district court erred in dismissing her Fourteenth Amendment claim because the grading practice employed by her children's teachers impermissibly infringes on that constitutional privacy right. Although this court acknowledges the existence of a Fourteenth Amendment right to prevent disclosure of certain types of personal information, the school work and test grades of presecondary school students do not rise to the level of this constitutionally protected category of information.

With respect to the FERPA claim, the court of appeals found that the grading practice did violate FERPA, and therefore reversed the district court's grant of summary judgment in favor of the school district. The appellate court remanded the case for further proceedings consistent with its opinion. Although the district's practice was not supported by the appellate court, the Appellate court will be liable only if the plantiff can demonstrate that the illegal actions of teachers were based on official school or district policy custom or were executed by a school official who has final policy-making authority regarding the challenged practice.

Based on the finding of the appellate court, any practice involving disclosure of student grades to unauthorized individuals violates FERPA and should not be executed by the school or district.

DEFENSES AGAINST DEFAMATION

The most common defenses cited against defamation are privilege, good faith, and truth.

Privilege

Because education is of great public interest, courts have generally recognized the importance of statements made by school personnel in executing their official duty. They enjoy some degree of freedom so long as they have an interest in the information and act in good faith. It is important to remember that qualified privilege is not without limits. Certain statements must be made within the scope of the educators' duty. One court stated that qualified privilege is established where there is no evidence that statements were made based solely on personal spite, ill will, or culpable recklessness or negligence.[17] In this instance, there is no recovery. When educators operate within these parameters, they will generally be supported by the courts. However, if they act unreasonably, with indefensible motives, there is no protection and they are open to legal challenges.

Good Faith

Good faith is essential in establishing a qualified privilege. Educators only enjoy qualified privilege when there is evidence that they acted in good faith and without an intent to harm others. As cited earlier, statements should also be made within the scope of their official duties. Again, these statements should be based on reasonable grounds and not motivated by ill will or spite. Since educators occupy professional positions that influence the lives of children, there is an expectation that their actions are guided by good faith. There should always be a reasonable regard for protecting the interest of all parties involved.

Since the passing of the Freedom of Information Act, statements made by public school officials while serving in their official capacities are subject to disclosure. Students are not required to waive their rights to examine statements made about them by school personnel. In fact, they have the option to examine these statements, if they so choose. Qualified privilege will be supported if statements are reasonable and made without malice in one's official professional capacity.

Truth

Truth is generally considered a defense to charges involving defamation. In other words, if the person making the statement is doing so based on information believed to be accurate and reasonable, courts will generally recognize these statements as being nondefamatory in nature. However, statements that are true will not be supported as a defense, if there is evidence that malice was involved. For example, educators are frequently called on to provide references for students as well as colleagues. There may be inquiries regarding personal traits, personality, and overall fitness.

Educators should be very careful not to invoke opinions about students or colleagues that might be damaging without having the qualifications to make such statements. Any statements regarding another's mental, psychological, or emotional status are very risky. These types of statements should be avoided. Educators should only provide reasonable information based on good faith for which they are qualified to make. Even though truth is a defense against defamation claims, it is not absolute. If statements are made about another that will automatically result in injury to that person's reputation, truth will not be a reasonable defense. As cited in Chapter 3, statements involving marital status, sexual preference, or contagious diseases—even if they are true—may result in defamation charges, if individuals against whom these statements are made can prove that they were damaged.

ADMINISTRATIVE GUIDE

LIABILITY AND STUDENT RECORDS

1. School districts and schools should have legally defensible policies and procedures consistent with the requirements of FERPA. Students, parents, and legal guardians should be informed of their rights under this act.
2. Accurate records should be maintained in the student's file, indicating the name, title, date, description of educational interest, specific records examined, and the place of examination of student records for those who have access.
3. Any corrections or adjustments to student records should be dated and initialed by the person responsible, with the knowledge and approval of school officials.
4. School personnel should avoid labeling children.
5. When it becomes necessary to place disciplinary infraction information on student records, the information should be specific regarding the infraction committed—time, place, and witnesses, as appropriate. The student should be present when such information is recorded.
6. School personnel should refrain from aimless chatter involving third parties regarding confidential information found on student records. Gossip or careless talk among school personnel calculated to harm a student is not protected by qualified privilege.
7. Student records should be maintained in a safe and secure place and should not be removed from school premises by school personnel unless proper authorization is secured.
8. Unless prohibited by court order, the noncustodial parent should be afforded the same right to access student records as the custodial parent.
9. To avoid allegations of malicious intent, transmit only the information that is requested by a prospective employer.
10. Refrain from releasing information over the telephone, unless identity of the other party has been firmly established.
11. Where conflict or difficulty arises regarding interpretation of FERPA, consultation with the school district's attorney would be appropriate.
12. Public disclosures of students' grades will not likely be supported by the courts. Such practices violate the intent of FERPA and should not be supported by school officials.

STUDENT RECORDS FAMILY EDUCATIONAL RIGHTS AND PRIVACY ACT

Bernice Evans, mother of a 12-year-old daughter, sued the board of education for releasing information regarding her daughter's medical condition to a local newspaper reporter. The newspaper article referred to a 12-year-old female hermaphrodite with severe emotional and behavioral problems. School board members asserted that they were simply attempting to explain why the district needed to expand emergency funds to meet the needs of students with special problems. They further argued that the information did not personally identify the student because no name was revealed to the reporter.

DISCUSSION QUESTIONS

1. Did the school board err in releasing this information? Why or why not?
2. Does Mrs. Evans have a valid claim? Why or why not?
3. Does the school board have a defensible basis for revealing the information? Why or why not?
4. How does the Family Educational Rights and Privacy Act apply in this case?
5. How do you think the court would rule in this case?
6. Provide a rationale for your response.
7. What are the administrative implications of this case?

STUDENT RECORDS AND BREACH OF CONFIDENTIALITY

Joe Price, a teacher in an affluent high school, reviewed the educational records of one of his students and discovered some very confidential information which he shared with another teacher during their break in the teacher's lounge. Because the other teacher had not personally accessed the information, she felt comfortable sharing this information with another colleague.

DISCUSSION QUESTIONS

1. Is there a risk in sharing confidential student information with a colleague? Why or why not?
2. What legal options might the student exercise in this situation, and under what circumstances might these options be pursued?
3. What is Price's defense if challenges about his divulging this information arise?
4. How might the courts rule in this case if a legal challenge arises?
5. What factors might influence this ruling?
6. What advice would you provide for teachers regarding sharing confidential information to a second or third party?

DEFAMATION AND STUDENT RECORDS

A high school principal and a tenured teacher investigated a situation regarding suspected drug involvement of students. They also provided counseling for students and their parents. When they revealed their findings to the local law enforcement agency that drug involvement was present among specified groups of students, the parents sued, alleging defamation.

DISCUSSION QUESTIONS

1. Do these parents have a valid claim? Why or why not?
2. Did releasing information on a specified group of students constitute defamation? Why or why not?
3. What defense might the principal and teacher use to justify revealing the information?
4. How would a court likely rule in this situation?
5. What criteria would the court use in reaching a decision?
6. What are the administrative implications in this case?

RELEASE OF DIRECTORY INFORMATION WITHOUT PARENTS' KNOWLEDGE

A Western school district of 6,000 students customarily releases directory information regarding its students. In doing so, it has been challenged by several parents who objected to the release of this information on their children. Unfortunately, the district had not informed parents, on an annual basis, that it would release directory information on its students.

DISCUSSION QUESTIONS

1. How vulnerable is the district in this situation?
2. How valid are the parents' concerns regarding the release of directory information without their knowledge?
3. Can the district be held liable in this situation? Why or why not?
4. Is this an issue that the court would likely entertain if a legal challenge is brought by the parents? Why or why not?
5. If you were superintendent of this district, how would you respond to the parents' charges?
6. What are the administrative implications of this situation?

ENDNOTES

1. 20 USC S. 1232 g.
2. C.F.R. § 99.6.
3. *Page v. Rotterdam-Mohonasen Central School District,* 441 N.Y.S. 2d 323 (Sup. Ct. 1981).
4. *Owasso Independent School District No. I-011 v. Falvo,* 534 U.S. 426; 122 S.Ct. 934; 151 L. Ed. 2d 896 (2002).
5. *Doe v. Gonzaga,* 143 Wash. 2d 687, 24 P. 3d 390 (2001).
6. *United States of America v. Miami University,* 294 F. 3d 797 (6th Cir. 2002).
7. *Zall v. State,* 584 A. 2d 119 (Md. App. 1991).
8. *Hett v. Cudahy School System,* 20 Wis. 2d 55, 121 N.W. 2d 270 (Sum. Ct. of Wis. 1963).
9. *Rios v. Read,* 73 F. Rd. 589 (1977).
10. *Kryston v. Board of Education, East Rampano,* 77 A.D. 2d 896 (1980).
11. *Springfield R-12,* 447 S.W. 2d 256 (MO 1969).
12. *Frascas v. Andrews,* 463 F. Supp. 1043 (1979).
13. *Bowie v. Evanston Community Consolidated School District,* 538 N.E. 2d 557 (Ill. 1989).
14. *Doe v. Woodford County Board of Education,* Lexis 11752, 213 F. 3d 921 (U.S. App. 2000; Fed. App. 2000).
15. Ibid.
16. *Falvo v. Owasso Independent School District,* Lexis 18316, Colo J.C.A.R. 4563 (U.S. App. 2000).
17. *Kilcoin v. Wolansky,* 428 N.Y.S. 2d 272 (1980).

CHAPTER 8

TEACHER FREEDOMS

Public school teachers do not relinquish their rights as a condition of accepting an employment position in the public schools. Although teachers are expected to be sensitive to the professional nature of their positions and have a regard for the integrity of the profession, they do enjoy certain constitutional freedoms that must be respected by school authorities. Since teachers enter the profession with constitutional rights and freedoms, boards of education must establish a compelling reason to restrict these freedoms. In these instances, the burden rests with school authorities to demonstrate that their actions are not arbitrary, capricious, or motivated by personal and political objectives.

The courts, in addressing conflicts involving constitutional freedoms of teachers, attempt to balance the public interest of the school district against the personal rights of each individual employee. Thus, teachers are subject to reasonable restraints only if a legitimate, defensible rationale is established by the school district.

SUBSTANTIVE AND PROCEDURAL CONSIDERATIONS

As stated in Chapter 4, there are two types of due process, both of which apply to teachers: substantive and procedural. *Procedural due process* means that the state may not deprive any person of life, liberty, or property, without due process of law. Therefore, a teacher must be given proper notice that he or she is to be deprived of his or her personal rights. The teacher must be provided an opportunity to be heard and the hearing must be conducted in a fair manner. Failure to follow procedural requirements will result in a violation of the teacher's constitutional rights. *Substantive due process* means that the state must have a valid objective when it intends to deprive a teacher of life, liberty, or property, and the means used must be reasonably calculated to achieve its objective. Most importantly, both procedural and substantive requirements must be met in teacher dismissal proceedings. Many administrative decisions that were correct in substance have been overturned on appeal based simply on the grounds that procedural requirements were not met. Conversely, procedural requirements may be met by school officials when the evidence reveals that a valid reason did not exist that warranted depriving a teacher of his or her rights. The administrative decision in this case would be overturned as well.

FREEDOM OF EXPRESSION

By virtue of the First Amendment to the Constitution, teachers are afforded rights to freedom of expression. Within limits, they enjoy the same rights and privileges regarding speech and expression as other citizens. Free speech by teachers, however, is limited to the requirement that such speech does not create *material disruption* to the educational interest of the school district. Material disruption, for an example, may involve an interference with the rights of others or may involve speech that creates a negative impact on proper school discipline and decorum. The level of protection provided teachers is generally lower in cases where the teacher speaks on matters that are personal in nature, as opposed to those that are of interest to the community.

In either case, school officials may not justifiably prohibit or penalize the teacher in any manner for exercising a constitutionally protected right without showing that a legitimate state interest is affected by the teacher's speech or expression. As usual, in cases where the teacher's speech is restricted, the burden of proof justifying such restriction rests with school authorities. Districts have succeeded in their actions to restrict speech and to discipline teachers when there was evidence that the teacher's personal speech undermined authority and adversely affected working relationships. In the absence of such showing, the teacher's speech is protected.

In fact, the Supreme Court addressed the application of the First Amendment in employment situations by emphasizing in the *Connick v. Myers* case the distinction between speech involving public concern and grievances regarding internal personnel matters. Expressions regarding public concerns, according to the High Court, receive First Amendment protections, whereas ordinary employee grievances are to be handled by the appropriate administrative body without involvement of the court.[1] In this case, the issue involved a petition, circulated within an office, that was related to the proper functioning of the office. This type of personal speech did not receive First Amendment protection.

Another example involved a sarcastic, unprofessional, and insulting memorandum written by a teacher to various school officials. The teacher found that expressing his private disagreement with school policies and procedures, which he refused to follow, was unprotected speech not related to a matter of public concern. Further, he was not speaking as a private citizen but rather as an employee of the district. Another court stated that "to hold for the teacher in private expressions would be to transform every personal grievance into protected speech when complaints are raised about classroom materials, teacher aids, laboratory equipment and other related issues."[2]

Speech Outside the School Environment

Teachers are afforded First Amendment rights outside the school environment. They may speak on issues that interest them and the community, even though their speech may not be deemed acceptable by school district officials. This, of course, has not always been the case.

In the past, there was a commonly held belief that public employees, including teachers, had only a limited right to freedom of expression. This restrictive posture stemmed from the commonly held view that public employment was a privilege. While the courts have failed to support this view, many teachers in the past were restricted in their rights to freedom of expression.

Freedom of speech outside the school environment is well established; however, when exercising such speech, *a teacher should preface his or her comments by indicating that he or she is speaking as a private citizen rather than an employee of the board.* This public disclosure is significant in establishing that the teacher's speech is not the official position of the school district. This disclosure further reinforces the notion that a teacher possesses the same First Amendment privileges as regular citizens. Although teachers enjoy First Amendment rights, those rights are not without reasonable restrictions, based on the nature of the position held and the positive image teachers are expected to project. In all cases, the teacher's speech should be professional in nature and not designed to harm or injure another's reputation or render the teacher unfit, based on the content of the speech itself. These standards apply whether the speech is verbal or written.

A leading Supreme Court decision in the *Pickering* case[3] established the limits on freedom of expression rights by school personnel. This case arose in Will County, Illinois, when Marvin Pickering, a teacher in the district, was dismissed from his position by the board of education in connection with sending to the local newspaper an editorial that was critical of the school's administration and the allocation of tax funds raised by the school. Excerpts extracted from the Pickering letter are as follows:

> The superintendent told the teachers, and I quote, "any teacher that opposes the referendum should be prepared for the consequences." I think this gets at the reason we have problems passing bond issues. Threats take something away; these are insults to voters in a free society. We should try to sell a program on its merits, if it has any.
> . . . to sod football fields on borrowed money and then not be able to pay teachers' salaries is getting the cart before the horse.
> If these things aren't enough for you, look at East High. No doors on many of the classrooms, a plant room without any sunlight, no water in a first aid treatment room are just a few of many things. The taxpayers were really taken to the cleaners. A part of the sidewalk in the building has already collapsed. Maybe Mr. Hess would be interested to know that we need blinds in that building also.
> As I see it, the bond issue is a fight between the Board of Education that is trying to push tax-supported athletics down our throats with education, and a public that has mixed emotions about both of these items because they feel they are already paying enough taxes, and simply don't know whom to trust with any more tax money.
> I must sign this letter as a citizen, taxpayer, and voter, not as a teacher, since that freedom has been taken from the teachers by the administration. Do you really know what goes on behind those stone walls at the high school?
>
> Respectfully,
> Marvin L. Pickering

Pickering's dismissal resulted from a determination by the board, after a full hearing, that the publication was detrimental to the efficient operation and administration of the school. Hence, under relevant Illinois statutes, in the "interest of the school," dismissal was required. Pickering's claim that his speech was protected by the First and Fourteenth Amendments was rejected. He appealed the board's ruling to the circuit court of Will County, which supported his dismissal on the grounds established by the school board. On appeal, the Supreme Court of Illinois affirmed the judgment of the circuit court.

Pickering's letter criticized the school board's handling of the 1961 bond issue proposals and the subsequent allocation of financial resources between the school's educational and athletic programs. The board dismissed Pickering for writing his editorial, charging that numerous statements contained in the letter were false and that the letter unjustifiably impugned the motives, honesty, integrity, truthfulness, responsibility, and competence of the board and school's administration. The board further claimed that the false statements damaged the professional reputation of its members and the administration.

The U.S. Supreme Court reversed the Illinois State Supreme Court's decision and held for Pickering. The High Court concluded, "The extent to which the State Supreme Court's opinion may be read to suggest that teachers may constitutionally be compelled to relinquish First Amendment rights they would otherwise enjoy as citizens to comment on matters of public interest in connection with the operation of the public school in which they work, it proceeds on the premise that has been unequivocally rejected in numerous prior decisions of this court."

Although some of Pickering's statements proved to be untrue, the High Court held that teachers are afforded First Amendment rights, which Pickering had been denied. In responding to several incorrect statements contained in Pickering's letter, the Supreme Court stated, "Absent proof of false statements knowingly or recklessly made by him, a teacher's exercise of his rights to speak on issues of public importance may not furnish the basis for his dismissal from public employment."[4]

The *Pickering* ruling represented a significant victory for public school teachers. Prior to this ruling, it would not have been uncommon to find teachers seeking new employment if they publicly criticized their school district's practices. *Pickering* also was significant in generating guidelines regarding freedom of expression issues involving teachers. If the teacher's speech disrupted superior-subordinate relationships or resulted in a breach of loyalty or confidentiality, the teacher may be disciplined. Further, if the teacher's speech created disruption of a material and substantial nature, affected the efficient operation of the school, or rendered the teacher unfit based on the content of the speech, appropriate action also may be taken against the teacher.

In addition to the *Pickering* guidelines, a Connecticut court generated the following guidelines involving freedom of expression issues regarding the operation of the public schools:

1. The impact on harmony, personal loyalty and confidence among coworkers
2. The degree of falsity of statements
3. The place where speech or distribution of material occurred
4. The impact on the staff and students, and
5. The degree to which the teacher's conduct lacked professionalism.[5]

This case illustrates the level of protection afforded public school teachers by the court during the exercise of their First Amendment rights. The case arose in Mississippi when an art teacher, with 21 years of experience, criticized the superintendent for eliminating the art program at a historically African American junior high school while retaining the program at a historically white junior high school. The superintendent justified his action by stating that no instructors could be located for the African American school. The teacher subsequently located viable candidates for the position and joined in ongoing criticism of the superintendent by community supporters.

The teacher wrote an editorial in the local newspaper, spoke out during public forums, and sent a letter of no confidence to the superintendent. The superintendent then arranged for a demotion of the teacher to the African American junior high school. The teacher filed a suit against the superintendent and the board of education. The superintendent requested summary judgment, which was denied by the district court. The superintendent appealed to the Fifth Circuit Court of Appeals.

The appeals court, in holding for the teacher, noted that the teacher had joined in public criticism of the superintendent and was not merely expressing a personal grievance regarding his demotion. His actions were regarded as protected public speech and the district court's ruling denying summary judgment was appropriate. Because the superintendent's actions in demoting the teacher may have been motivated by personal reasons, the teacher's First Amendment right was properly retained. The superintendent's appeal was dismissed.[6]

In a slightly different case, a teacher did not prevail based solely on First Amendment protection. In the *Mt. Healthy* case, a nontenured teacher who previously had been involved in several altercations with other teachers, employees, and students—including an incident in which he made obscene gestures to female students—phoned into a radio station the contents of the principal's memorandum to faculty regarding the dress code for teachers.[7] The radio station announced the adoption of the dress code. The board, on the recommendation of the superintendent, informed the teacher that he would not be rehired based on a lack of tact in handling professional matters and specifically referenced the obscene gesture and radio station incident. The teacher challenged the validity of the termination. The court held that in order to prevail in a First Amendment case, an employee must show that his expression is protected and that it was the motivating factor in the board's action. Also, the board must fail to show that it would have taken the same action in the absence of the employee's conduct.

Since the teacher's conduct did not disrupt the orderly operation of the school, it was constitutionally protected and could not serve as the basis for employment termination. However, by engaging in constitutionally protected conduct, a teacher should not be able to prevent an employer from assessing his or her entire performance record and reaching a decision not to rehire on the basis of the record.

As one can see, the teacher's freedom of expression rights are protected. They are, however, subject to reasonable considerations regarding order, loyalty, professionalism, and overall impact on the operation of the school. If prudence is exercised by the teacher in expressing views of public interest, he or she should not be subject to disciplinary measures by the school district. However, if his or her overall performance record does not meet the school's expectation, dismissal may occur in spite of Fifth Amendment privileges.

Academic Freedom

Public school teachers are afforded a judicially recognized academic interest in their classrooms, based on the teacher's right to teach and the students' right to learn. Academic freedom, as a concept, originated in the German universities during the nineteenth century with the expressed purpose of allowing professors to teach any subject they deemed educationally appropriate.

Public school teachers, of course, are not provided the same broad latitude extended to professors in higher education. *Academic freedom is a very limited concept in public schools.* It supports the belief that the classroom should be a marketplace of ideas and that teachers should be provided freedom of inquiry, research, and discussion of various ideas and issues. Since public school teachers teach children of tender years who are impressionable, their freedom of expression in the classroom is limited by factors such as grade level, age, experience, and readiness of students to handle the content under discussion.

The teacher should also be certain that the subject matter introduced into classroom discussion is within the scope of students' intellectual and social maturity levels. Public school teachers are further restrained by the requirement that *content introduced into classroom discussion be related to and consistent with the teacher's certification and teaching assignment.* Controversial material unrelated to the subject taught and inappropriate, based on content, will not be supported by the courts.

The point was clearly illustrated in the *Fowler* case, which arose when a tenured teacher was discharged for insubordination and conduct unbecoming of a teacher.[8] The basis for her dismissal was that she had a R-rated movie, Pink Floyd's *The Wall,* shown to a high school class on the last day of school. A group of students requested that Fowler allow the movie to be shown while she completed grade reports. Fowler was not familiar with the movie and asked students whether the movie was appropriate for viewing at school. One student who had seen the movie indicated that it had one bad spot in it. She instructed the student who had seen the movie to edit out any parts that were not suitable for viewing by the class. He attempted to do so by covering a 25-inch screen with an $8^1/_2$-inch by 11-inch letter-sized folder. The facts revealed that there was nudity and a good bit of violence contained in the movie. Fowler testified that in spite of the fact she had not seen the movie and left the classroom several times during its viewing, it had significant value. Furthermore, she would show an edited version again if given an opportunity. The board viewed the edited version of the movie during an executive session and voted unanimously in an open session to terminate Fowler for insubordination and conduct unbecoming of a teacher. The court recognized that Fowler was entitled to First Amendment protection under certain circumstances and that a motion picture is a form of expression that may be entitled to First Amendment protection. However, it ruled that Fowler's conduct in having the movie shown under the circumstances presented did not constitute expression protected by the First Amendment. The board was upheld in the discharge of Fowler.

Much of what is taught in public schools is influenced by state and local board curriculum policies and guidelines, as well as statutory provisions. Public school teachers must always be mindful of these considerations. *Teachers may not use their classrooms to promote a personal or political agenda.* The classroom may not be used to indoctrinate or to encourage students to accept beliefs, attend meetings, or disregard parent wishes regarding involvement with religious groups.[9]

In light of certain restrictions, the concept of the classroom as a marketplace of ideas does apply to elementary and secondary schools. This point was well expressed in a ruling by a district court:

> Most writings on academic freedom have dealt with the universities where the courts supported the essentiality of freedom in the community of American universities. Yet, the effects of procedures which smother grade school teachers cannot be ignored. An environment of free inquiry is necessary for the majority of students who do not go on to college; even those who go on to higher education will have acquired most of their working and thinking habits in grade school and high school. Moreover, much of what was formerly taught in many colleges in the first year or so of undergraduate studies is now covered in upper grades of good high schools. . . .
>
> The considerations which militate in favor of academic freedom—our historical commitment to free speech for all, the peculiar importance of academic inquiry to the

progress of society in an atmosphere of open inquiry, feeling always free to challenge and improve established ideas—are relevant to elementary and secondary schools, as well as to institutions of higher learning.[10]

This passage adequately summarizes the importance of the recognized academic interests of elementary and secondary teachers. These privileges may not be abridged without evidence by the district that a legitimate state interest is threatened by the teacher's actions in the classroom.

The following summaries of cases reflect the court's position on various issues regarding academic freedom in public schools. One case dealt with the question of whether a teacher could, for educational purposes, assign and discuss in class an article containing a term for an incestuous son that was offensive to many. The article was written by a highly respected psychiatrist and appeared in a high-quality publication. Any student who felt the assignment to be personally offensive was permitted to choose an alternative one. The teacher would not agree, based on the district's demand, never to use the word again in the classroom. The court found the district's rule to be unenforceable. It observed that the word in question appeared in at least five books in the library, but the court did not rest its decision on this ground.[11]

In another case, the teacher had discussed the meaning of "taboo" words by using another word, deemed highly offensive to many, for sexual intercourse. The First Circuit Court affirmed the teacher's right, but did indicate that teachers do not have a license to say or write whatever they choose in the classroom. The court was not in total agreement as to whether the First Amendment protected the teacher's actions, but it held for the teacher on the grounds of due process, because school officials had enforced a vague rule after the incident had occurred.[12]

In yet another case, a New York teacher assigned students to write essays expressing their views regarding the firing of a local television sports commentator. The teacher provided background material to her students, including her own reaction to his firing. The district's superintendent felt that the distribution of the teacher's personal view was inappropriate. He requested that the teacher rescind the assignment and submit her lesson plans and grade book. The teacher refused to comply. A disciplinary hearing was held in which the teacher claimed that the superintendent's actions infringed on her academic freedom in her classroom. The hearing panel refused to consider her defense and found her guilty on one of three specifications for her refusal to rescind the assignment and on all three specifications regarding her refusal to turn over lesson plans and grade book. Her actions resulted in a one-semester suspension without pay.

The school district then appealed to the state commissioner of education, seeking to increase the penalty from suspension to dismissal. The commissioner also concluded that the directives concerning rescinding the assignment infringed on the teacher's rights to academic freedom, but failure to hand over the lesson book did not. Her penalty was reduced to a three-month suspension without pay. A New York trial court affirmed the commissioner's decision. The district and the teacher appealed to the New York Supreme Court, Appellate Division.

The appellate court stated that the school board had broad discretion in the operation and management of the district, but their discretion is limited by the requirements of the First Amendment. The district had no legal basis to require the teacher to rescind the assignment. However, requesting that the teacher turn over her grade book did not violate the teacher's right to academic freedom. The commissioner's decision was appropriate and its ruling was confirmed.[13]

A freedom of expression case arose in New York when a substitute teacher challenged her termination.[14] In her complaint, which arose under 42 U.S.C. § 1983 and state law, Rosario alleged that the defendants-appellees violated her due process, equal protection, and First Amendment free exercise and free speech rights by terminating her employment as a substitute teacher at Hunts Point Middle School in the Bronx. Rosario also brought claims for wrongful termination and intentional infliction of emotional distress, *inter alia.*

Rosario was dismissed for using the classroom to espouse her religious views. On the morning of June 8, 1998, an announcement was made over the school intercom that a Hunts Point student had died. The school was asked to observe a moment of silence. After the announcement, Rosario's sixth-grade students began to cry and hold each other. In an attempt to comfort her students, Rosario spoke for several minutes about her religious views. She stated that according to the Bible, "Jesus was the son of God" and that "one must come through Jesus to get to God." Rosario also approached each student, placing her hand on each child's forehead, and asked God to protect the child and his or her family. Prior to beginning her discussion, Rosario told the students that they need not participate but could instead go to their computers or open their books. Rosario also specifically asked a student whether she wanted her to pray for her, because Rosario knew that the student was a Jehovah's witness and that her mother had requested that the girl not participate in the Pledge of Allegiance.

The following day, the child's mother lodged a complaint. Rosario testified that for the next three days, she was not permitted to teach her class and was told to remain in a storage room during school hours. She also testified that the principal of the school forced her to write a statement about the incident without allowing sufficient time for preparation. A hearing was heard by the Presiding Judge of Chancery Court. Rosario testified and was assisted by two union representatives. At the conclusion of the hearing, Rosario was informed that she had been terminated from her position and that her license had been revoked.

After Rosario rested her case, the school board moved for summary judgment on all of Rosario's claims. At that time, Rosario withdrew her free exercise claim. The district court granted the school board's motion and entered a directed verdict in its favor on all claims except Rosario's equal protection claim for wrongful dismissal based on religion or national origin and her claim against the principal for intentional infliction of emotional distress. The jury ruled against Rosario on those claims.

The district court found that Rosario's due process claim for wrongful termination failed because, as a nontenured substitute teacher, she did not "enjoy a property right in . . . continued employment." The court dismissed Rosario's state law claims for wrongful termination and violation of the state's education laws on the grounds that she was an at-will employee and that her collective bargaining agreement, which afforded her limited protections, did not provide for dismissal only "for cause." The court also held that Rosario's free exercise and free speech claims failed as a matter of law because her actions on June 8, 1998 sufficiently introduced religious matter into the classroom and placed defendants at risk of violating principles animated by the establishment clause.

FREEDOM OF ASSOCIATION

The First Amendment guarantees citizens the right to peacefully assemble. Freedom of association is included within this right of assembly, since teachers, as citizens, are entitled to the same rights and privileges provided other citizens. *Freedom of association* grants people the right to associate with other individuals of their choice without threat of punishment. Although teachers enjoy these rights, they should exercise them in light of the nature and importance of their positions as public employees. Further, they should be concerned with the "role-model image" they project and the impact of their actions on impressionable young children. The Supreme Court stated, "A teacher serves as a role model for his students, exerting a subtle but important influence over their perceptions and values."[15]

The High Court's view was further expressed in a case in which two unsuccessful applicants for teaching certification in New York filed suit enjoining the enforcement of a state statute that forbids aliens from obtaining public school teacher certification. Both teachers were married to U.S. citizens, had been in the country for more than ten years, and had earned degrees at U.S. colleges. The New York statute allowed the commissioner of education to determine a special need for the person's skills and competencies. The Court held for the state of New York, ruling that a statute that generally prohibits, with some exceptions, aliens from obtaining teacher certification is constitutional. The court further stated that a citizenship requirement for teaching bears a rational relationship to the legitimate state interest in public education, because the people of New York, through their lawmakers, have determined that people who are citizens are better qualified than those who have rejected the open invitation extended to qualify for eligibility to teach by applying for citizenship in this country.[16]

Freedom of association has not always been recognized as a constitutional freedom by school districts, as there were countless restrictions placed on teachers by their districts. In the early to mid-1900s, African American and white teachers were forbidden to socialize with one another. In some districts, membership in the NAACP or the Ku Klux Klan was fatal to the teacher if there was public awareness of such affiliation.

In some instances, school personnel who had been involved in organized labor organizations or educational associations received questionable treatment by their school districts. This treatment was oftentimes reflected in the form of demotions, unwarranted transfers, nonrenewals, and even terminations. An example of such treatment is illustrated by the following case. A Missouri school board voted not to renew the contracts of three probationary teachers. These three teachers had publicly advocated higher teacher salaries and affiliation with the Missouri National Education Association. They alleged that their contracts were not renewed in retaliation for these activities in violation of their First Amendment rights to free speech and association. The court held for the teachers by awarding $7,500 in damages and reinstatement to their teaching positions. The district appealed. On appeal, the U.S. Court of Appeals for the Eighth Circuit agreed that despite the probationary or nontenured status of these teachers, the school board could not constitutionally refuse to renew their contracts in retaliation for the exercise of their First Amendment rights. The court remanded the issue of damages to the lower court regarding the awarding of back pay and attorney fees.[17] As illustrated by this case, school districts will not succeed when they retaliate against school personnel for the proper exercise of their rights regarding their involvement in union-related activities. They may not be legally penalized for such involvement.

Since the late 1960s, there has been a discernible trend by the court toward providing teachers more freedom regarding their personal lives than was true in the past. Courts now hold that teachers, including administrators, are free to join their professional organizations, assume a leadership role, campaign for membership, and negotiate with the school board on behalf of the organization without fear of reprisal. School personnel must ensure that their participation in external organizations does not, in any manner, reduce their effectiveness as district employees or create material or substantial disruption to the operation of the district.

School personnel may also engage in various types of political activities. They may become a candidate for public office or campaign for their favorite candidate. However, school personnel may be requested to take personal leave when they run for public office. These are permissible activities, as long as these occur after school hours and do not interfere with job effectiveness.

Membership in Subversive Organizations

There has been controversy in the past regarding membership in subversive organizations by school personnel that resulted in threats of dismissal. The Supreme Court has held that *mere membership in subversive organizations is not sufficient within itself to justify dismissal.* The teacher must have demonstrated that he or she actually participated in an unlawful activity or intended to achieve an unlawful objective before punishment may be meted.

In a leading case, the Supreme Court in *Elfbrandt v. Russel* indicated, "Those who join an organization but do not share its unlawful purposes and who do not participate in its unlawful activities surely pose no threat, either as a citizen or as a public employee."[18]

This case involved an Arizona act that required an oath by employees of the state. A teacher challenged the act, refusing to take the oath based on good conscience. She further claimed that the oath was unclear in its meaning, and she was unable to secure a hearing to have the meaning clarified. The oath read as follows: "I do solemnly swear . . . that I will support the Constitution of the United States and . . . of the State of Arizona; that I will bear true faith and allegiance to the same and defend them against all enemies, foreign and domestic, and that I will faithfully and impartially discharge the duties of the office (name of office)."

Anyone taking the oath was subject to prosecution for perjury and discharge from office if he or she knowingly or willfully became or remained a member of the Communist Party or any other organization that advocated an overthrow of the government.

The High Court ruled that a loyalty oath statute that carries sanction to membership without requiring specific intent to further the illegal objectives of the organizations is unconstitutional. The court stated further that the due process provision of the Fourteenth Amendment requires that a statute that infringes on protected constitutional rights, in this case freedom of association, "be narrowly drawn to define and punish specific conduct as constituting a clear and present danger to a substantial interest of the state."[19]

Another significant Supreme Court decision was rendered in the *Keyishian v. Board of Regents of University of State of N.Y.*[20] This case emerged, based on a complex set of laws in New York, calling for the discharge of employees of the state education system who utter treasonable or seditious words, perform the same acts, advocate or distribute material supporting an overthrow of the government, or belong to subversive organizations. Keyishian and a number of faculty and staff at the University of New York who refused to certify that they were not and had not been members of subversive organizations were faced with dismissal from their jobs. They sought declaratory relief from the statute and sought to have it declared unconstitutional. The High Court held for the plaintiffs, stating that loyalty oaths that make membership in an organization sufficient for termination of employment are constitutionally impermissible. To be valid, a loyalty statute must be confined to knowing active members who aid in pursuing the illegal goals of the organization.

Without exception, public school employees are protected from arbitrary loyalty oaths and undue intrusion with respect to their rights of association. There must be defensible evidence of the employee's actual participation or planned participation in unlawful activities to mete any form of discipline. Mere association without an unlawful intent is not sufficient cause to penalize employees and is in violation of their First and Fourteenth Amendment rights.

Political Rights

Based on the State Interest Test, state laws prohibiting public employees from participating in all types of political activities have been deemed unconstitutional. Public school teachers have the same political rights and freedoms enjoyed by all citizens. These include, but are not limited to, running for public office, campaigning for themselves or others, developing and expounding political ideologies, and engaging in political debate. These rights, however, should be exercised with a degree of restraint inasmuch as they are not unlimited. There has to be at all times an awareness on the teacher's part of the effect of his or her actions on others, especially children. Teachers should also ensure that engaging in political activities does not have an adverse effect on classroom performance. Teachers must limit their political activity to acts away from the classroom and outside of the normal school day. They must further ensure that their political activity in no way interferes or infringes on their duties and responsibilities in the classroom.

Right to Hold Office

State laws vary regarding the extent to which school personnel may legally participate in political activities and hold public office. Generally speaking, any public official (which may include a teacher) is prohibited from using his or her office or position for personal gain. The board of education may require a teacher to take a leave of absence when he or she becomes a candidate for public office. Generally, this requirement has been upheld by a number of courts. In no case, however, should a teacher's contract be canceled because he or she becomes a candidate for public office. This would be arbitrarily unjust and an indefensible act by a school board.

In recent years, however, courts tend to be somewhat divided on the teacher's right to run for political office. As stated previously, some courts support the requirement that the teacher should resign before actively campaigning for public office. Other courts view the prohibition against running for a political office as a violation of the teacher's constitutional right. For example, in the *Minielly v. State* case in Oregon, the district court held to be invalid a state law that prohibited public employees from running for political office. The court ruled that the state had no authority to limit the First Amendment rights of teachers.[21]

In an interesting ruling, a Kentucky court held that a requirement calling for mandatory leaves for all teachers who pursued a part-time public office violated the teacher's right to equal protection, since no such requirements applied to teachers who were engaged in other types of time-consuming activities.[22] However, there seems to be a trend toward greater political freedom for teachers by the courts, so long as the teacher exhibits prudent professional behavior, does not neglect his or her professional duties, and does not use the classroom as a political forum. School boards do have the capacity to ensure that political activity does not create material or substantial disruption to the educational process, which would constitute a legitimate state interest.

Participation in Political Campaigns

The right to campaign is afforded teachers and other employees. However, they should understand that their professional role transcends their roles as citizens. Teachers and other employees must understand the time commitment required and be certain that it does not present any conflict of interest regarding job responsibilities. Additionally, school district facilities, equipment, or supplies should not be used for campaign purposes. Districts normally adopt policies and procedures pertaining to employees who wish to run for public office. These policies generally will establish the terms and conditions that the employee must meet with respect to employment status regarding leave or continuing employment.

The teacher's or employee's employment status should not be impaired by the exercise of his or her political rights. Teachers' political rights should not be exercised in the school or district's name. It should be very clearly established that the teacher or employee is exercising political rights as a citizen and not as a representative of the school district. The school district may not prevent, threaten, harass, or discriminate against any employee who elects to run for public office. Additionally, the district should grant a leave of absence if requested by the employee based on the individual merits of each case presented for its consideration.

DRESS AND GROOMING

Numerous cases regarding personal appearance issues involving teachers have been litigated by the courts. School authorities generally contend that proper dress and decorum create a professional image of teachers that has a positive impact on students. Teachers, on the other hand, contend that dress code regulations governing their appearance invade their rights to free expression. Teachers further believe that they should enjoy freedom without undue restrictions on their personal appearance.

The courts generally have not been in disagreement regarding the authority of school officials to regulate teacher appearance that may disrupt the educational process. What has not been settled, however, is the *degree* of constitutional protection teachers are entitled to receive in disputes regarding dress and the type of evidence needed to invalidate restrictions on dress. To further complicate the issue, community standards and mores are also factors considered in dress and grooming rulings. School districts have traditionally restricted dress that is contrary to acceptable community norms.

Litigation involving dress and grooming issues reached its peak in the late 1960s and early to mid-1970s, as numerous challenges were raised by teachers and students regarding these issues. The courts established the position that school dress codes must be reasonably related to a legitimate educational purpose, which must be justified by standards of reasonableness.

Rules that restrict dress based on health, safety, material and substantial disruption, or community values have been generally supported by the courts. Rules that extend beyond these areas generally have not been supported. It seems evident that the courts recognize that teachers should be free of unreasonable restrictions governing their appearance. However, the difficulty comes with variations in standards by different communities, as well as changing societal norms. Community standards, values, and expectations play an important role in determining the legality of local school dress code regulations when considered in conjunction with these other factors.

The courts will not support restrictive dress and grooming codes that are unrelated to the state's interest. When challenged, the district must demonstrate that the code is related to a legitimate educational purpose, and not designed to place undue and unnecessary restrictions on teachers' dress. The burden of proof rests with the school district.

On the other hand, courts have assumed the posture that dress is a generalized liberty interest and is only entitled to minimal constitutional protection. One example of the court's posture is illustrated in *East Hartford Education Association v. Board of Education of Town of East Hartford.*[23] In this case, Richard Brimley, a public school teacher, was reprimanded for failure to wear a necktie while teaching his English class. With the support of the teacher's union, he filed suit against the board of education, claiming that the reprimand deprived him of his rights of free speech and privacy. Brimley further claimed that his refusal to wear a tie made a statement on current affairs, which aids him in his teaching by presenting himself as one who is not tied to the establishment, thus enabling him to establish greater rapport with his students. Brimley concluded by claiming that his refusal to wear a tie is symbolic speech and is protected by the First Amendment.

Brimley had appealed earlier to the principal and was told that he must wear the tie while teaching English but could dress more casually during film-making classes. He later appealed to the superintendent and the board without success.

The appeals court was faced with the issue of balancing the alleged interest in free expression against the goals of the school board in requiring its teachers to dress somewhat more formally than they might wish. The court, in balancing the two issues, indicated that the school board's position must prevail. The court concluded that balancing against the teacher's claim of free expression is the school board's interest in promoting respect for authority and traditional values, as well as discipline in the classroom by requiring teachers to dress in an appropriate and professional manner.[24]

The appellate court did not discern in this case that basic constitutional rights were violated by the dress code, and consequently did not weigh the matter heavily on the constitutional scale. The court presumed that the dress code was constitutional and within the scope of local authorities to decide.

In a later case, the Louisiana School Board extended its dress code to forbid school personnel from wearing beards. The board's policy was unsuccessfully challenged. The Fifth Circuit Court of Appeals, while recognizing the liberty interest of the individual in deciding how to wear his hair, held for the board. The court stated that the board had made a prudent decision in establishing the rule as a reasonable means of achieving the school board's undeniable interest in teaching hygiene, instilling discipline, and requiring uniformity in application of policy.[25]

The following case demonstrates the negative effects that result from a teacher's failure to comply with district dress code policy. McGlothin, a high school teacher, began wearing berets and African-style head wraps to school. The principal warned her on each occasion in which these items were worn, indicating that head wraps were inappropriate for the classroom. McGlothin continued to wear occasional head wraps for roughly three years, which resulted again in warnings by the principal. The district subsequently adopted a multicultural policy, which McGlothin claimed justified her head wraps. After a memorandum and lengthy discussion, McGlothin's employment was terminated. She followed the district's grievance procedure, claiming for the very first time that her head covering was in conformity with her religious beliefs. The school district did not support her grievance. She then appealed to the U.S. District Court.

The court found that McGlothin had sincere religious beliefs; however, she did not convey those to the school administration at any earlier time, but instead in the final stage of her grievance. Since she failed to convey her religious beliefs to the district in a timely fashion, the district was under no obligation to accommodate her beliefs under the First Amendment or Title VII of the Civil Rights Act. The facts revealed that the district had offered McGlothin an opportunity for reemployment following denial of her grievance, if she would agree to remove her head wraps. McGlothin refused to accept the district's offer. On the basis of those facts, the court held for the district by granting a motion to dismiss the lawsuit.[26]

Community Norms and Expectations

Courts are sensitive to community norms and expectations with respect to standards involving dress. Dress code standards that conform to community sentiments generally are more likely to be supported by the courts. While it is recognized that these standards and expectations vary from community to community, courts have been lenient in allowing school districts to develop such policies. Many communities have established norms, shared values, and expectations regarding behaviors they expect of teachers. These norms, values, and expectations may be most prevalent in smaller and more conservative communities, but can affect both the nature and substance of school board policies.

Since public school boards consist of lay citizens who represent, in large part, the will and sentiment of their constituents within their communities, they will often consult community citizens as school district policies are drafted. Most often, community representatives are included in district policy development committees where they are provided opportunities to participate in drafting policies. As community groups participate in formulating and recommending policies, they have an opportunity to rely on community norms and values as policies are drafted for the board's consideration.

In determining the defensibility of school board policies affecting constitutional freedoms such as dress and grooming, courts often place high value on the process by which these policies were developed, and specifically those who participated in the process. If evidence reveals that policies affecting dress and grooming reflect community sentiment through community involvement in the policy development process, the courts are less likely to challenge the validity of such policies. Additionally, school districts may build a stronger case for such policies when there is evidence that dress codes were developed that promote the educational mission of the district.

Community norms and the district's educational mission are important factors in the court's assessment of the feasibility of dress codes. As illustrated in the *East Hartford*

Education Association v. Board of Education of Town of East Hartford case involving teacher dress, the Second Circuit Court of Appeals held the view that it was not the role of the courts to override the decisions of school officials based on the court's view as an absence of wisdom on their part. The court stated further that the system of public education relies heavily on the discretion and judgment of school officials. The courts will not intervene in the administration of schools unless there is evidence of specific constitutional violations. In this case, the teacher's clash with school officials failed to demonstrate the implication of basic constitutional values. The court thereby refused to set aside the policies established by the school board. Although this case involved teacher dress, the courts take a similar view on matters involving dress in general, particularly when community involvement is an important aspect of the policy development process.

One effective means of demonstrating community support for student dress codes is to include parents, citizens, and students in the formulation of such policies, if there is sentiment to have them. This process ensures a broad-based participation and opportunities to entertain perspectives from those affected by the administration and enforcement of these policies.

Unwed Pregnant Teachers

Courts tend to vary in rulings regarding unwed pregnant teachers. During the early 1960s and 1970s, courts were more inclined to rule against single teachers who were dismissed by school boards when they reported their pregnancy. However, during the mid-1970s and early 1980s, with increased attention focused on individual rights of teachers, courts became less inclined to rule against unwed pregnant teachers without carefully weighing all aspects of each case. In doing so, the courts considered the teacher's overall performance record, the impact of the teacher's actions on students, and, more importantly, the extent to which the teacher's actions adversely affects her effectiveness as a teacher. Courts may also consider community standards and the degree to which the teacher's conduct violates the ethics of the community and renders the teacher unfit to teach. The following summary of cases shows the variance among courts in addressing pregnancy among unwed teachers:

1. In 1975, a federal appeals court ruled against a school board policy in Mississippi that automatically disqualified school employees who were parents of illegitimate children on the grounds that unwed parents do not necessarily represent improper models for students.[27]
2. In 1976, a district court upheld Omaha, Nebraska, officials in dismissing an unwed junior high school teacher because of her pregnancy on the grounds that permitting the teacher to remain in the classroom would be viewed by students as condoning pregnancy out of wedlock.[28]
3. In 1982, the Fifth Circuit Court of Appeals ruled against officials in Homewood, Alabama, for dismissal of a pregnant unwed teacher on the basis that her discharge was in violation of the Fourteenth Amendment. The school board could not demonstrate that the teacher's failure to report her pregnancy in a timely fashion would have resulted in dismissal had she been married.[29]
4. In 1986, a district court in Illinois upheld a teacher who was dismissed for being a pregnant unwed mother on the grounds that the teacher had a substantive due process

right to conceive and raise her child out of wedlock without undue intrusion by the school board.[30]

5. In 1979, a federal appeals court struck down a school board practice of not renewing teachers' contracts where a foreseeable period of absence could be predicted for the next school year.[31]

RIGHT TO PRIVACY

It is commonly held that teachers enjoy a measure of privacy in their personal lives. These rights should be respected to the extent that they do not violate the *integrity* of the community or render the teacher ineffective in performing professional duties. Within the context of privacy rights, teachers are afforded an opportunity to exercise personal choices, which may range from living with a person of the opposite sex, giving birth to a child out of wedlock, or other lifestyle choices. In many instances, school boards cite privacy issues involving teachers as the basis to dismiss them from their employment positions or recommend revocation of the teaching certificate. While there does not appear to be a clear distinction drawn between protected and unprotected lifestyle choices, the burden of proof resides with school officials to demonstrate that lifestyle choice adversely affects the integrity of the district or that the teacher's conduct has a detrimental affect on his or her relations with students.

Teachers, in exercising lifestyle choices, must also be reminded of the professional nature of their position and the impact that their behavior has on children, who often view them as role models. For example, when a teacher engages in a private adulterous activity, it does not necessarily follow that this act, within itself, forms grounds for action to be taken against the teacher. Teachers are entitled to rights to privacy, as are other citizens, and these rights must be respected. Whether a school district is successful in penalizing a teacher for private conduct would again be based on a district's capacity to demonstrate that the teacher's effectiveness is impaired by his or her conduct. The burden of proof clearly resides with school officials.

When a teacher has demonstrated a strong record of teaching, has been effective in relationships with students, and is respected in the community by his or her peers, it is unlikely that school officials will succeed in bringing serious actions against the teacher, such as removal from an employment position or revocation of certificate. On the other hand, if private conduct becomes highly publicized to the point that the teacher's reputation and relationships with parents and students have been impaired, rendering the teacher ineffective in executing his or her duties, appropriate actions may be taken by school officials and supported by the courts.

A leading case involving private, adulterous activity arose in Iowa involving Erb, a native Iowan and a high school fine arts teacher. He was married with two children. A complaint against Erb was filed by Robert M. Johnson, a farmer whose wife, Margaret, taught home economics at another school in the district. Johnson's goal was to have Erb removed from the school but not to revoke his certificate. Johnson read an extensive statement in which he detailed observations regarding an adulterous relationship between Erb and his wife, Margaret, which began and ended in the spring of 1970.

Johnson became suspicious of his wife's frequent, late-night absences from home. He suspected that Erb and Margaret were meeting secretly and engaging in an illicit activity in Margaret's automobile. One night in May, Johnson hid in the trunk of the car. Margaret drove the car to school, worked there for a while, and later drove to a secluded area in the country where she met Erb. They had sexual intercourse in the back seat of the car, while Johnson remained hidden in the trunk.

When Johnson consulted his lawyer with a view toward divorcing Margaret, he was advised that his interest in a divorce would be better served if he had other witnesses to his wife's conduct. After several days of fruitless efforts, he finally located them in a compromising situation. He and his raiding party surrounded the car and took pictures of Margaret and Erb, who were partially disrobed in the back seat. Erb and Margaret terminated their affair, and Erb offered his resignation, but the local school board unanimously decided not to accept it. The board president testified that Erb's teaching was highly rated by his principal and superintendent. He had been forgiven by his wife and the student body, and he had maintained the respect of the community. Witnesses before the board included Erb, past and present principals, his minister, parents of children in the school, and a substitute teacher.

The state board voted 5–4 to revoke Erb's teaching certificate, and without making any findings of fact or conclusions of law, ordered it revoked. Revocation was stayed by the trial court. The trial court held that Erb's admitted adultery was sufficient basis for revocation of his certificate. Erb appealed the trial court's ruling, charging that the board acted illegally in revoking his certificate without substantial evidence. This case reached the state supreme court, which ruled for Erb. The court, in ruling for Erb, stated that the private conduct of a man, who is also a teacher, is a proper concern to those who employ him only to the extent it mars him as a teacher. When his professional achievement is unaffected, when the school community is placed in no jeopardy, his private acts are his own business and may not be the basis of discipline. The court further concluded by stating, "Surely incidents of extramarital heterosexual conduct against a background of years of satisfactory teaching would not constitute immoral conduct sufficient to justify revocation of a life diploma without any showing of an adverse effect on fitness to teach."[32]

The outcome of the *Erb* case should not be interpreted to convey that adulterous acts may not result in dismissal by school boards. One such case involving dismissal occurred in Delaware when a highly successful school district administrator developed an amorous affair with another person who was married. The administrator also was married. Their relationship grew in intensity, involving school time. The administrator took nude pictures of his lover and used them to threaten her husband by suggesting that he would disclose them to the husband's employer if the husband did not consent to allow the relationship to continue. The school district, on being informed of the situation and gathering the facts, dismissed the administrator. The administrator alleged that his acts were private and bore no relationship to his effectiveness as an administrator. He further alleged that he was not forewarned that his private conduct would lead to dismissal.

A U.S. District Court rejected the administrator's claims based on the evidence that his affair resulted in gross neglect of duty. The district court held that it should have been obvious that his behavior would lead to dismissal due to the public impact of such conduct on the profession and finally that such conduct does not receive the protection of the right to privacy.

As can be seen from two contrasting cases, the courts will not support teacher conduct that has an adverse impact on one's effectiveness or performance and will support dismissal if professional conduct and community standards are violated. The fact that school time was abused during the affair in this case and that unprofessional and illegal tactics were used to coerce the husband into support the adulterous affair were also pivotal in the court's ruling.[33] Private adulterous acts that become public and create serious community and professional concerns will not likely be supported by the courts.

In a rather unusual ruling regarding rights to privacy, the District Court of Appeals of Florida reversed the findings of the state's Education Practice Commission (EPC) when it supported a 48-year-old assistant principal who married a 16-year-old former student. The EPC disciplined the administrator by suspending his teaching license for two years and denied him employment as an administrator. The assistant principal appealed the commission's ruling. The court of appeals did not challenge the EPC's power to take disciplinary action, but disagreed with the findings of the hearing officer in the case.

Based on the court's assessment, there was no clear or convincing evidence of an inappropriate personal relationship between the two prior to marriage. Although both had been seen together by other individuals, it only gave rise to suspicion, which could not form the basis for disciplinary action. There was no credible evidence of sexual engagement prior to marriage or any other inappropriate activity. The EPC had taken action without the benefit of firsthand knowledge and based its ruling on conclusive evidence alone.[34]

Although there is a certain aura of protection afforded school personnel regarding their private lives, involvement with a former student who has not reached majority age is, at best, very risky and not advisable. Privacy acts that do not involve former students will likely receive greater support by the courts than acts in which former students are implicated. In all cases, the privacy rights of teachers must be balanced against the district's need to maintain professional integrity of its employees and the moral values of the community.

ADMINISTRATIVE GUIDE

TEACHER FREEDOMS

1. Teachers and administrators do not lose their constitutional rights when they enter the educational profession. Within limits, they possess the same constitutional rights as do other citizens.
2. School personnel should avoid personal attacks or libelous or slanderous statements when exercising freedom of expression rights or expressing concerns of interest to the community.
3. School personnel should not knowingly report false information, when criticizing a district's decision or actions.
4. School officials may not penalize or otherwise discriminate against teachers for the proper execution of their First Amendment rights, especially regarding issues of public concern.
5. Academic freedom is not a right. It is a judicially recognized academic interest for elementary and secondary teachers. Teachers should introduce appropriate material in the classroom that is related to their assigned subject matter. The classroom should never be used as a forum to advance the teacher's political or religious views.

■ ■ ■ ■ ■ ▬▬▬▬▬▬▬▬▬▬▬▬▬▬▬▬▬▬▬▬▬▬▬▬▬▬▬▬▬▬▬▬▬▬

ADMINISTRATIVE GUIDE (*continued*)

6. Teachers and administrators may associate with whomever they wish, as long as their association does not involve illegal activity or their behavior does not render them unfit to perform their job functions effectively.
7. Dress, grooming, and appearance may be regulated by school boards, if a compelling educational interest is demonstrated or if such codes are supported by community standards.
8. Teachers and administrators are entitled to rights of privacy and cannot be legally penalized for private noncriminal acts.
9. Pregnant unwed teachers may not be automatically dismissed unless there is a definite reason for doing so.

RELIGIOUS FREEDOMS

The First Amendment guarantees religious freedom to all citizens. Title VII of the Civil Rights Act of 1964 further prohibits any forms of discrimination based on religion. Therefore, it is unlawful for a school district to deny employment, dismiss, or fail to renew a teacher's contract based on religious grounds. Teachers, like all citizens, possess religious rights that must be respected. As with all rights, religious rights are not without limits. Since teachers are public employees and schools must remain neutral in all matters regarding religion, there are reasonable restraints that affect the exercise of religious rights in the school setting. However, teachers are completely free to fully exercise their religious rights outside of normal school activities.

For example, teachers may not refuse to teach certain aspects of the state-approved curriculum based on religious objections or beliefs. Although the courts recognize the existence of the teacher's religious rights, they also recognize the compelling state interest in educating all children. One court held that education "cannot be left to individual teachers to teach the way they please." Teachers have no constitutional right to require others to submit to their views and to forego a portion of their education they would otherwise be entitled to enjoy.[35] In short, teachers cannot subject others, particularly students, to their religious beliefs or ideologies. They, too, must remain neutral in their relationship with students.

Religious Rights of Teachers in the School Environment

Based on the free exercise of religion, teachers should be afforded the right to meet with other teachers for religious speech, including prayer or Bible study, at times when teachers are allowed to meet with their colleagues for other forms of expression. These should be activities protected by the free speech clause so long as they occur in a private area where students cannot observe them or participate in such activities. Such activities should ideally occur before or after school. It is difficult to determine precisely how the courts would view these activities, since this issue has very rarely been presented to the courts.

In one of the rare cases involving the use of school facilities by teachers for religious meetings, a teacher brought suit against the school board, its members, and the superintendent, seeking an injunction against banning religious meetings by teachers on school property. The U.S. District Court for the Southern District of Indiana granted the school district a motion for summary judgment. The teacher appealed. The court of appeals held that teachers had no right under the First Amendment free speech clause to hold prayer meetings on school property before the school day began and students arrived. The court observed further that school officials had consistently applied a policy prohibiting the use of school facilities for religious activity. The teacher contended that the school was an open forum in that it was used for meetings on other subjects. The court found her claim to be clearly erroneous.[36] Teachers generally should have a right to express themselves to other teachers while on school property during noninstructional times so long as students are not involved and the expression only involves willing teachers. Teachers should be cautious that their speech is not construed as harassment of another teacher who does not wish to be involved in these discussions. Therefore, willing parties would be important in this instance. As previously stated, this issue has not been decided by courts; however, it appears that the First Amendment should provide some degree of protection to teachers regarding their right to express personal views on religion in conversation with their peers, just as they would on other topics. Until these issues are addressed by the courts, it is difficult to determine precisely how the courts might rule.

This view is based in part on "Guidelines on Religious Exercise and Religious Expression in the Federal Workplace," which was generated by the U.S. Department of Health and Human Services.

These guidelines principally address employees' rights to religious exercise and religious expression when the employees are acting in their personal capacity in the federal workplace and the public does not have regular exposure to the workplace. These guidelines do not comprehensively address whether and when the government and its employees may engage in religious speech directed at the public. They also do not address religious exercise and religious expression by uniformed military personnel, or the conduct of business by chaplains employed by the federal government. Nor do the guidelines define the rights and responsibilities of nongovernmental employers—including religious employers—and their employees. Although the following guidelines address the most frequently encountered issues in the federal workplace, actual cases sometimes will be complicated by additional facts and circumstances that may require a different result from the one the guidelines indicate.

Section 1. Guidelines for Religious Exercise and Religious Expression in the Federal Workplace. Executive departments and agencies ("agencies") shall permit personal religious expression by federal employees to the greatest extent possible, consistent with requirements of the law and interests in workplace efficiency as described in this set of guidelines. Agencies shall not discriminate against employees on the basis of religion, require religious participation or nonparticipation as a condition of employment, or permit religious harassment. And agencies shall accommodate employees' exercise of their religion in the circumstances specified in these guidelines. These requirements are but applications of the general principle that agencies shall treat all employees with the same respect and consideration, regardless of their religion (or lack thereof).

Religious Expression. As a matter of law, agencies shall not restrict personal religious expression by employees in the federal workplace except where the employee's interest in the expression is outweighed by the government's interest in the efficient provision of public services or where the expression intrudes on the legitimate rights of other employees or creates the appearance, to a reasonable observer, of an official endorsement of religion.

As a general rule, agencies may not regulate employees' personal religious expression on the basis of its content or viewpoint. In other words, agencies generally may not suppress employees' private religious speech in the workplace while leaving unregulated other private employee speech that has a comparable effect on the efficiency of the workplace—including ideological speech on politics and other topics—because to do so would result in presumptively unlawful content or viewpoint discrimination. Agencies, however, may, in their discretion, reasonably regulate the time, place, and manner of all employee speech, provided such regulations do not discriminate on the basis of content or viewpoint.

The federal government generally has the authority to regulate an employee's private speech, including religious speech, where the employee's interest in that speech is outweighed by the government's interest in promoting the efficiency of the public services it performs. Agencies should exercise this authority evenhandedly and with restraint, and with regard for the fact that Americans are accustomed to expressions of disagreement on controversial subjects, including religious ones. Agencies are not required, however, to permit employees to use work time to pursue religious or ideological agendas. Federal employees are paid to perform official work, not to engage in personal religious or ideological campaigns during work hours.

Expression in Private Work Areas. Employees should be permitted to engage in private religious expression in personal work areas not regularly open to the public to the same extent that they may engage in nonreligious private expression, subject to reasonable content- and viewpoint-neutral standards and restrictions: Such religious expression must be permitted so long as it does not interfere with the agency's carrying out of its official responsibilities.

Examples An employee may keep a Bible or Koran on her private desk and read it during breaks.

An agency may restrict all posters, or posters of a certain size, in private work areas, or require that such posters be displayed facing the employee, and not on common walls; but the employer typically cannot single out religious or antireligious posters for harsher or preferential treatment.

Expression Among Fellow Employees. Employees should be permitted to engage in religious expression with fellow employees, to the same extent that they may engage in comparable nonreligious private expression, subject to reasonable and content-neutral standards and restrictions: Such expression should not be restricted so long as it does not interfere with workplace efficiency. Though agencies are entitled to regulate such employee speech based on reasonable predictions of disruption, they should not restrict speech based on merely hypothetical concerns, having little basis in fact, that the speech will have a deleterious effect on workplace efficiency.

Examples In informal settings, such as cafeterias and hallways, employees are entitled to discuss their religious views with one another, subject only to the same rules of order that apply to other employee expression. If an agency permits unrestricted nonreligious expression of a controversial nature, it must likewise permit equally controversial religious expression.

Expression Directed at Fellow Employees.   Employees are permitted to engage in religious expression directed at fellow employees, and may even attempt to persuade fellow employees of the correctness of their religious views, to the same extent as those employees may engage in comparable speech not involving religion. Some religions encourage adherents to spread the faith at every opportunity, a duty that can encompass the adherent's workplace. As a general matter, proselytizing is as entitled to constitutional protection as any other form of speech—as long as a reasonable observer would not interpret the expression as government endorsement of religion. Employees may urge a colleague to participate or not to participate in religious activities to the same extent that, consistent with concerns of workplace efficiency, they may urge their colleagues to engage in or refrain from other personal endeavors. But employees must refrain from such expression when a fellow employee asks that it stop or otherwise demonstrates that it is unwelcome.

Expression in Areas Accessible to the Public.   Where the public has access to the federal workplace, all federal employers must be sensitive to the establishment clause's requirement that expression not create the reasonable impression that the government is sponsoring, endorsing, or inhibiting religion generally, or favoring or disfavoring a particular religion. This is particularly important in agencies with adjudicatory functions.[*]

These guidelines only apply to federal employees. They may or may not be generalized to public school settings. Religious issues involving public school employees will likely receive clarity in the future as challenges arise through the courts. The law regarding teachers' religious expression is, at best, unsettled.

Use of Religious Garb by School Personnel

The wearing of religious garb by public school teachers has created legal questions regarding freedom of expression rights versus religious violations based on dress. It has been well established that public school districts may not legally deny employment opportunities to teachers based on their religious beliefs or affiliation. However, the wearing of religious garb by public school teachers raises the issue as to whether such dress creates a sectarian influence in the classroom. Many state statutes prohibit public teachers from wearing religious garb in the classroom. Some legal experts believe that the mere presence of religious dress serves as a constant reminder of the teacher's religious orientation and could have a proselytizing affect on children, since they are impressionable, particularly those in the lower grades.

Conversely, public school teachers advance the argument that religious dress is a protected right regarding freedom of expression. The courts, however, have clearly established the position that the exercise of one person's rights may not infringe on the rights of others and that public interest supersedes individual interests. Further, prohibiting a teacher from wearing religious dress does not adversely affect the teacher's belief. It merely means that teachers cannot exercise their beliefs through dress during the period of

[*]*Source:* Executive Guidelines on Religious Exercise and Religious Expression in the Federal Workplace (August 14, 1997).

the day in which they are employed. There is no interference outside of the school day. Thus, a teacher is free to exercise full religious rights and freedoms outside normal hours of employment. The courts have not reached total consensus on this issue, as can be discerned through the following analysis.

In a significant case, the Supreme Court of Pennsylvania supported the authority of a local board of education to employ nuns as teachers and to permit them to dress in the custom of their order.[37] Subsequent to the Pennsylvania decision, the legislature enacted a statute prohibiting the wearing of any religious dress as insignia by public school teachers representing any religious order. The constitutional validity of this statute was upheld by the Pennsylvania Supreme Court, noting that the law was not passed against belief but rather against acts as teachers in performing their duties.[38]

Another court disqualified all nuns from teaching in public schools on the grounds that their lives were dedicated to teaching religion.[39] Recent court interpretations seem to suggest that religious dress which creates a reverent atmosphere and may have the potential to proselytize, thereby creating a sufficient sectarian influence, to violate the First Amendment neutrality clause.

TITLE VII: RELIGIOUS DISCRIMINATION

Title VII addresses any forms of religious discrimination regarding employment. *Religion* is defined under Title VII to include "all aspects of religious observances, practices and beliefs."[40] This section also requires that an employer, including a school board, make reasonable accommodations to the employee's religion, unless the employer can demonstrate the inability to do so based on undue hardship. Consequently, school officials must respect and, where possible, make allowances for teachers' religious observances if such observances do not create substantial disruption to the educational process. Accommodations may include personal leave to attend a religious convention or to observe a religious holiday. Unless there is a showing of undue hardship, reasonable accommodation must be provided. If such requests are deemed excessive, resulting in considerable disruption to children's education, a denial would be appropriate.

In a recent case, a teacher was absent for approximately six school days per year because his religion, the Worldwide Church of God, required him to miss employment during designated holidays. Under the collective bargaining agreement between the school board and the teacher's union, teachers were permitted to use three days' leave each year for observance of religious holidays, but they were not permitted to use any accumulated sick leave or personal leave for religious holidays. The teacher requested that the school board adopt a policy allowing the use of three personal leave days for religious observance or to allow the teacher to pay the cost of a substitute and receive full pay for the holidays he was absent. The board rejected both proposals.

The teacher filed suit, alleging that the board had violated his rights under Title VII's prohibition against religious discrimination. The court held that the school board must make a reasonable accommodation for an employee's religious beliefs, as long as an undue hardship is not present. However, the board is not required to provide the employee preferred alternatives when more than one reasonable accommodation is possible. The alternative of unpaid leave is a reasonable accommodation, if personal or other paid leave is provided without discrimination against religious purposes.[41]

In a slightly different case, a Chicago public school teacher filed suit against the superintendent, board of education, and other school officials in the U.S. District Court, claiming that a 1941 Illinois statute designating Good Friday as a school holiday violated the First Amendment to the U.S. Constitution. The district filed a motion for summary judgment. The court, in its review of the case, noted that Christians observed Good Friday as one of their holiest days. However, members of other religions were required to request accommodations for special treatment on their holy days. Unlike Christmas and Thanksgiving, which have both secular and religious aspects, Good Friday has no secular aspect and is associated only with Christianity. The recognition of Good Friday was more than a mere accommodation to Christian religion. Recognition of the holiday conveyed an impermissible message that Christianity was a favored religion in the state. The court held for the teacher by ruling that the holiday designation violated the Constitution.[42]

In cases where school officials deny excessive leaves for religious purposes, the burden of proof rests with the teacher to show that the officials' decision involved the denial of certain religious freedoms. If the teacher is able to demonstrate discriminatory intent, then the burden shifts to school officials to show a legitimate state interest, such as a disruption of educational services to children. The Equal Education Opportunity Commission (EEOC) or a court would be hard-pressed to challenge a legitimate state interest involving the proper education of children. (See Chapter 2 for a more comprehensive discussion of religion involving teachers in public schools.)

ADMINISTRATIVE GUIDE

RELIGIOUS DISCRIMINATION

1. Wearing of religious garb by teachers may be disallowed if their dress creates a reverent atmosphere or has a proselytizing impact on students.
2. The religious rights of teachers must be respected, so long as they do not violate the Establishment Clause of the First Amendment by creating excessive entanglement in the school.
3. School officials must make reasonable accommodations for teachers regarding observance of special religious holidays, so long as such accommodations are not deemed excessive or disruptive to the educational process.
4. Teachers should not be coerced to participate in nonacademic ceremonies or activities that violate their religious beliefs or convictions.
5. In cases involving the performance of their nonacademic duties, teachers may be requested to present documentable evidence that a religious belief or right is violated.
6. No form of religious discrimination may be used to influence decisions regarding employment, promotion, salary increments, transfers, demotions, or dismissals.

TEACHER RIGHTS—UNWED TEACHERS LIVING TOGETHER

Tom Davis is a newly appointed principal in a small conservative community. He has just been assigned Mark Scott, a dynamic, energetic seventh-grade math teacher. Davis later learns that Scott and his girlfriend are living together. The principal is informed of this by a group of parents who are outraged that Scott is setting a poor example for young children. They are upset and are calling for action. Davis talks with Scott, who does not deny that he and his girlfriend are living together. He further informs Scott in a very professional manner that what he does in his private life is his business.

DISCUSSION QUESTIONS

1. Is Tom justified in approaching Mark on personal and private matter? Why or why not?
2. How does Davis handle this situation with Scott?
3. Does the principal have a right to infringe on a teacher's private life? Why or why not?
4. Outline a plan to resolve this situation.
5. Would the courts likely support your plan of resolution?

TEACHER'S FREEDOM OF SPEECH—RACIAL CONTENT

Freddie Watts, principal, and Jimmy Brothers, assistant principal, are African-American administrators assigned to administer a predominantly black high school. Ann Griffin, a white tenured teacher, during a heated conversation with the two administrators stated that she "hated all black folks." When word leaked on her statement, it caused negative reactions among colleagues both black and white. The principal recommended dismissal based on concerns regarding her ability to treat students fairly and her judgment and competency as a teacher.

DISCUSSION QUESTIONS

1. Is Watts justified in his recommending Ann's dismissal? Why or why not?
2. Is the principal overreacting to Ann's statement? Why or why not?
3. Does Ann's statement establish a basis for dismissal? Why or why not?
4. Can Ann make the case that her statement was a private statement that does not give rise to serious disciplinary action? Why or why not?
5. As principal, would you have made a similar recommendation for dismissal? Why or why not?
6. How do you feel the court would rule in this case? Provide a rationale for your response.

FLAG SALUTE—A NONCONFORMING TEACHER

As principal of Rockville Elementary, Steve Jones finds that his community is extremely patriotic and the school has had a long-standing practice of reciting the Pledge of Allegiance and saluting the flag every morning. He is informed by students and other teachers that Sarah Allen does not recite the pledge with her class or salute the flag. Steve Jones is obviously upset because he feels that Mrs. Allen is setting a poor example for students and not conforming to community sentiments. He calls her into his office.

■ ■ ■ ■ ■
DISCUSSION QUESTIONS

1. Does Steve have a justifiable reason to challenge Sarah's failure to recite the pledge? Why or why not?
2. Does Sarah Allen have a right not to participate in the morning ritual? Why or why not?
3. Are there legitimate grounds on which she may refuse to participate? If so, identify them.
4. If she fails to participate at the principal's request, could her refusal amount to insubordination? Why or why not?
5. As principal, how would you handle this situation?
6. How would the court likely rule in this case?
7. What are the administrative implications?

ENDNOTES

1. *Connick v. Myers,* 461 U.S. 138 (1983).
2. *Daniels v. Quinn,* 801 F. 2d 687 (4th Cir. 1986).
3. *Pickering v. Board of Education,* 391 U.S. 563 (1968).
4. Ibid.
5. *Gilbertson v. McAlister,* 403 F. Supp. 1 (D. Conn. 1975).
6. *Tomkins v. Vickers,* 26 F. 3d 603 (5th Cir. 1994).
7. *Mt. Healthy City School District Board of Education v. Doyle,* 429 U.S. 274, 97 S.Ct. 568 (1977).
8. *Fowler v. Board of Education of Lincoln County, Kentucky,* U.S. Court of Appeals, 6th Cir. 817 F. 2d 657 (1987).
9. *LaRocca v. Board of Education of Rye City School District,* 63 A.D. 2d 1019, 406 N.Y.S. 2d 348 (1978).
10. *Albaum v. Carey,* 283 F. Supp. 3, 10-11 (U.S. District Ct. N.Y. 1968).
11. *Keefe v. Geanakos,* 418 F. 2d 359 (1st Cir. 1969).
12. *Mailloux v. Kiley,* 448 F. 2d 1242 (1st Cir. 1971)
13. *Malverne School District v. Sobol,* 586 N.Y.S. 2d 673 (A.D. 3d Dept. 1992).
14. *Rosario v. Board of Education of the City of New York,* 36 F. Appx. 25, U.S. App. (Dist. Court N.Y 2002).
15. *Ambach v. Norwick,* 441 U.S. 68, 99 S.Ct. 1589, 60 L. Ed. 2d 49 (1979).
16. Ibid.
17. *Greminger v. Seaborne,* 584 F. 2d (8th Cir. 1978).
18. *Elfbrandt v. Russel,* 384 U.S. 11, 17 (1966).
19. Ibid., 18.
20. *Keyishian v. Board of Regents of University of State of N.Y.,* 385 U.S. 589, 87 S.Ct. 675 (1967).
21. *Minielly v. State,* 411 P. 2d 69 (Or. 1966).
22. *Allen v. Board of Education,* 584 S.W. 2d 408 (Ky. Ct. App. 1979).
23. *East Hartford Education Association v. Board of Education of Town of East Hartford,* 562 F. 2d 838, 2nd Cir. Ct. of Appeals (1977).
24. U.S. Court of Appeals, Second Circuit, 562 F. 2d 856 (1977).
25. *Domico v. Rapides Parish School Board,* 675 F. 2d 100 (5th Cir. 1982).
26. *McGlothin v. Jackson Municipal Separate School District,* 829 F. Supp. 853 (S.D. Miss. 1993).
27. *Andrews v. Drew Municipal Separate School District,* 507 F. 2d 611 (5th Cir. 1975).
28. *Brown v. Bathke,* 416 F. Supp. 1194 (D Neb. 1976), rev'd 566 F. 2d 588 (8th Cir. 1977).
29. *Avery v. Homewood City Board of Education,* 674 F. 2d 337 (5th Cir. 1982).
30. *Eckmann v. Board of Education of Hawthorn School District,* 636 F. Supp. 1214 (N.D. Ill.1986).
31. *Mitchell v. Board of Trustees of Pickens County School District,* A. 599 F. 2d 582 (4th Cir. 1979).
32. *Erb v. Iowa State Board of Public Instruction,* 216 N.W. 2d 339 (Sup. Ct. Iowa 1974).
33. *Sedule v. The Capitol School District,* 425 F. Supp. 552 (U.S. Dist. Delaware 1976).
34. *Tenbroeck v. Castor,* 640 So. 2d 164 (Fla. App. 1st Dist. 1994).
35. *Palmer v. Board of Education of the City of Chicago,* 603 F. 2d 1271, 1274 (7th Cir. 1979), cert. denied, 444 U.S. 1026, 100 S.Ct. 689 (1980).

36. *May v. Evansville,* 787 F. 2d 1105 (97th Cir. 1986).

37. *Hysong v. Gallitzin Borough School District,* 164 Pa. 629, 30 A. 482 (1894).

38. *Commonwealth v. Herr,* 229 Pa. 132 78 A. 68 (1915).

39. *Harfst v. Hoegen,* 349 Mo. 808, 163 S.W. 3d 609.

40. 42 U.S.C. § 2000e(2).

41. *Ansonia Board of Ed. v. Philbrook,* 107 S.Ct. 367 (1986).

42. *Metzl v. Leiniger,* 850 F. Supp. 740 (N.D. Ill. 1994).

DISCRIMINATION IN EMPLOYMENT

Constitutional, federal, and state statutes prohibit discriminatory practices in employment on the basis of sex, race, age, color, or religion. A significant number of federal statutes has been enacted specifically to address discrimination in employment. The social and political movements during the early 1960s focused major attention on inequalities of employment opportunities and past discriminatory practices. Many important pieces of federal legislation were enacted during the 1960s and 1970s, one of the most significant being Title VII of the Civil Rights Act of 1964, which prohibited employment discrimination based on race, color, religion, sex, or national origin.

The equal protection clause of the Fourteenth Amendment provides protection against group discrimination and unfair treatment. It is used as a vehicle for individuals who seek relief from various forms of discrimination. A significant number of personnel practices in public schools pertaining to race, gender, age, and religion have been challenged, based on allegations of discrimination. Many school districts have responded to these challenges by noting that many of their current practices have been based on custom rather than a deliberate intent to discriminate. Nonetheless, courts have responded to challenges brought by school personnel in cases regarding alleged discrimination in employment practices based on issues involving gender, race, age, and pregnancy.

TITLE VII: DISCRIMINATION

One of the most extensive federal employment laws, the Civil Rights Act of 1964 Title VII, provides, in part, that

    (a) It shall be an unlawful employment practice for any employer

        (1) to fail or refuse to hire or to discharge any individual or otherwise to discriminate against any individual with respect to his compensation, terms and conditions or privileges of employment, because of such individual's race, color, religion, sex or national origin;

        (2) to limit, segregate or classify his employees or applicants for employment in any way which would deprive or tend to deprive any individual of employment opportunities or otherwise adversely affect his status as an employee, because of such individual's race, color, religion, sex or national origin.

(b) It shall be an unlawful employment practice for an employment agency to fail or refuse to refer for employment, or otherwise to discriminate against any individual, because of his race, color, religion, sex or national origin, or to classify or refer for employment any individual on the basis of his race, color, religion, sex or national origin.[1]

The original statute, enacted in 1964, covered employers and labor unions, and did not apply to discriminatory employment practices in educational institutions until 1972, when the law was amended. Since its amendment, it has been employed by educators to challenge questionable discriminatory practices in public schools. As stipulated in Title VII and Title IX, discrimination in employment based on gender is prohibited. Title VII protects males and females from gender-based discrimination.

Title VII was amended by the Civil Rights Act of 1991 (Public Law 102-166). This act provides for compensatory, punitive damages, and jury trial in cases involving intentional discrimination. An individual claiming discrimination under Title VII must file a complaint with the Equal Employment Opportunity Commission (EEOC) within 180 days following the alleged unlawful employment practice or within 300 days if the individual has filed a claim with a local or state civil rights agency. Failure to meet these time limits results in a loss of legal standing to challenge the alleged act. Remedies available under Title VII include compensatory damages, punitive damages, back pay, and reinstatement (for disparate treatment discrimination), which will be discussed later in this chapter.

To succeed under Title VII, a plaintiff must demonstrate that the employer's reasons for the challenged employment decision is false and that the actual reason is discrimination. This burden is oftentimes difficult to prove because there are very few instances in which plaintiffs have objective evidence or proof of discrimination. Many, however, have succeeded with indirect proof of discrimination in which the pretext for discrimination is established and the defendant is unable to convince the court that the reasons for his or her actions are worthy of belief.

Under the law of discrimination, for example, a teacher or administrator must demonstrate that he or she has made application for a position, is qualified for the position, and was not given fair consideration for the position. If the teacher or administrator is able to demonstrate a bona fide case of discrimination, then the burden shifts to the school district to demonstrate that its employment decision was not based on discriminatory practices.

In two leading noneducational cases, *McDonnell Douglas Corp. v. Green*[2] and *Furnco Construction Corp. v. Waters,*[3] the Supreme Court developed a three-step procedure for Title VII challenges:

1. The plaintiff carries the initial burden of establishing a prima facie case of employment discrimination.
2. The burden shifts to the defendant to refute the prima facie case by demonstrating that a legitimate nondiscriminatory purpose forms the basis for its actions.
3. If the defendant is successful in its contention, then the burden shifts back to the plaintiff to show that the defendant's actions were a mere pretext for discrimination. If, of course, the defendant can demonstrate the absence of a discriminatory motive, there is no need for step three.[4]

Although these are noneducational cases, the same procedures apply in all cases involving alleged discrimination including those in public schools.

These procedures were applied to *Marshall v. Kirkland,*[5] in a gender-based discrimination case that arose in the Eighth Circuit when a group of female teachers in Barton-Lexa school district challenged the assignment or promotion to one of three "specialty" positions—positions to which extra duties are attached and extra compensation is awarded. These administrative positions included an elementary principalship, a high school principalship, and a superintendency position. The plaintiffs contended that promotion to these positions was influenced by the sex of the applicant and statistically favored men. The plaintiffs challenged this practice under the equal protection provision of Title VII. The district court held for the district, ruling that plaintiffs failed to demonstrate that discrimination based on sex was present within a three-year period from the initiation of this litigation. The plaintiffs appealed to the Eighth Circuit Court of Appeals.

The court of appeals found the district court's finding erroneous and contrary to articulated constitutional principles respecting the assignment of specialty personnel and promotion of teachers to administrative positions. The evidence, according to the appellate court, raised the question of whether the district violated the rights of female teachers, administrators, and applicants to equal protection of the law under the Civil Rights Act, § 1983.

The record indicated that, during the relevant years, there were 10 to 11 administrative and specialty positions. The 7 or 8 specialty positions carried supplemental pay, which included positions in physical education, coaching, counseling, agriculture, and home economics. The practice in the district was to promote within the ranks for the three administrative positions. The only specialty positions occupied by women were the positions in home economics and physical education. All remaining positions were held by men. Further evidence revealed that the women specialty teachers received less pay than the men. The superintendent testified that football, track, and basketball coaches had traditionally been men and should continue to be. He also testified that men had previously taught girls' physical education and would be capable of coaching girls' basketball, stating that he felt that men would do a better job of handling a group of men than would women.

With respect to administration, evidence revealed that women were virtually disqualified from holding the position of high school principal or superintendent. Mrs. Todd, the elementary principal during the relevant years, was the lowest paid of the three administrators. In 1973, David Bagley, a high school teacher, was promoted to the high school principal's position to replace Mr. Kirkland, who assumed the duties of the superintendency. Mrs. Todd was concededly better qualified than Bagley, but was not considered for the job. On viewing the evidence, the appellate court stated, "A clear pattern of disproportionate gender representation in administrative and specialty positions was evident and that the sex of the teacher was an important part of assignment and promotion decisions." At the very least, appellants made a *prima facie,* showing that decision makers in the district sought to maintain women teachers in a "stereotypic and predefined place" within the district. The appellate court concluded by reversing the district court's ruling to dismiss the case and remanded the case to the district court for further proceedings.

This case illustrates that *prima facie* evidence of discrimination is a key factor in sex discrimination cases. The defendant school district must then prove that no discriminatory intent was present. In light of the overwhelming evidence in this case, this burden was not met by the district.

Significant litigation has surfaced since the enactment of Title VII. The following summary describes the nature of significant rulings regarding sexual discrimination:

1. One court ruled that when a district passes over a female who has equal or more impressive credentials than a male for promotion to administrative positions, the district has violated Title VII.[6]
2. When a school board was able to defend its decision not to promote an African American female teacher on subjective but observable factors, such as the lack of interpersonal skills and an abrasive personality, the court held these reasons to constitute a legitimate nondiscriminatory decision.[7]
3. When a female teacher presented clear evidence of discrimination, the board's defense in showing that she would not have been promoted had she been a man was sufficient to counter the teacher's charges.[8]

In summation, the courts simply require gender-neutral decision making when employment opportunities are available.

Sexual Discrimination

Discrimination based on sex is also covered under Title IX of the Education Amendments Act of 1972, 20 U.S.C. § 1681 et seq., which prohibits sexual discrimination by public and private educational institutions receiving federal funds. The basic provision of the act states, "No person in the United States shall on the basis of sex, be excluded from participation in, be denied the benefits of, or be subjected to discrimination under any educational program or activity receiving federal financial assistance."[9]

Title IX is administered by the Office for Civil Rights (OCR) of the Department of Education. The provisions of this act are similar to the provisions in EEOC's guidelines found in Title VII. Title IX, also like Title VII, makes a provision for sexual distinctions in employment where sex is a bona fide occupational qualification.[10] There were numerous challenges raised during the mid-1970s by educational institutions questioning the applicability of Title IX to discrimination in employment issues. After a series of highly debated cases, the U.S. Supreme Court ruled in the *Northhaven Board of Education v. Bell* that Title IX does apply to and prohibit sexual discrimination in employment.[11]

Following the enactment of Title IX, two local school boards in Connecticut challenged the act, contending that Title IX was not intended to address practices of school districts. The Supreme Court addressed two questions in this case: (1) whether Title IX statute applies to employment practices of educational institutions and (2) if so, whether the scope and coverage of Title IX employment regulations were consistent with Title IX statutes.

The court reasoned that since Title IX neither expressly nor by implication excludes employees from its reach, it should be interpreted as covering and protecting employees, as well as students. The court based its decision on the wording of the statute, the legislative history, and the statute's postenactment history in Congress and at the Department of Health, Education and Welfare.

Another highly debated issue regarding the interpretation of Title IX centered on the precise definition of *education programs and activities* with respect to sanctions. Since documented Title IX violations may result in a loss of federal funds, at issue was whether an entire educational institution is subject to a loss of funds or only the specific programs or activity affected.

This question was addressed initially in the *Grove City College v. Bell* case.[12] Grove City, a private coeducational liberal arts college, intentionally sought to preserve its autonomy as a private institution by failing to accept state and federal financial assistance. The facts revealed that a number of students attending the college received Basic Educational Opportunity Grants (BEOGs) from the government. Based on its findings, the U.S. Department of Education concluded that the college was a recipient of federal financial assistance and would have to comply with Title IX regulations.

The college refused to execute the assurance of compliance as stipulated by the regulations, which resulted in the Department of Education initiating procedures to declare the college and its students ineligible for the BEOG funds. The college and four students filed suit to enjoin the Department of Education from enforcing the policy as interpreted.

The court held for the college and its students by stating that Title IX applies only to specific programs that receive the federal assistance and not the entire institution. This decision was considered landmark during the mid-1980s; however, the Civil Rights Restoration Act of 1988 reversed this decision. The act now affects the entire institution or school district, even if only certain programs or activities receive state or federal financial assistance. Federal law now makes it clear that Title IX applies to everything involving the school, even if only one activity or program receives federal funds.

THE REHABILITATION ACT OF 1973 AND
THE AMERICANS WITH DISABILITIES ACT OF 1990

The *Americans with Disabilities Act (ADA),* in conjunction with the IDEA, protects individuals with disabilities against discrimination and assures equal access and opportunity. Section 504 of the *Rehabilitation Act of 1973* prohibits discrimination against any otherwise qualified person who has a disability with respect to employment, training, compensation, promotion, fringe benefits, and terms and conditions of employment. The act states that "no otherwise qualified individual with handicaps . . . shall solely by reason of his or her handicap be excluded from the participation in, be denied the benefits of, or be subjected to discrimination under any program or activity receiving federal financial assistance."[13] The ADA is similar to Section 504 and protects not only students with disabilities but any person who has a physical or mental impairment that substantially limits one or more major life activities, has a record of such impairment, or is regarded by others as having such an impairment.[14]

Major life activities, as interpreted by the act, may include such tasks as caring for oneself, performing manual tasks, hearing, seeing, speaking, breathing, walking, learning, and working.[15] Section 504 extends beyond the school environment and covers all people who are disabled in any program receiving federal financial assistance. Contrary to popular belief, the Rehabilitation Act does not require affirmative action on behalf of people with disabilities. It simply requires the absence of discrimination against such individuals.

Regulations interpreting the Rehabilitation Act's prohibitions against disability discrimination by federal contractors have been revised to conform to ADA provisions found in 34 C.F.R. § 104.11 and 29 C.F.R. § 1641. The regulations include explicit prohibitions regarding employee selection procedures and preemployment questioning. As a general rule, the fund recipient cannot make any preemployment inquiry or require a preemployment medical examination to determine whether an applicant is disabled or to determine the nature or severity of a disability.[16] Nor can a recipient use any employment criterion, such as a test, that has the effect of eliminating qualified applicants with disabilities, unless the criterion is job related and there is no alternative job-related criterion that does not have the same effect.[17] These prohibitions are also found in the ADA and its regulations.

The Americans with Disabilities Act prohibits the use of any standard criteria or administrative method that has the effect of discriminating or perpetuating discrimination based on a disability. Section 12132 of this act includes a similar provision to Section 504. It states that no qualified person with a disability shall, by reason of such disability, be excluded from participation in or be denied the benefits of services, programs, or activities of a public nature or be subject to discrimination by any such public agency. School districts must make reasonable accommodations for people with known disabilities, including job applicants and/or employees. See Figure 9.1 for trends involving discrimination charges based on disability.

Qualifications for Employment

Any individual with a disability is qualified under the Americans with Disabilities Act, if with or without reasonable accommodations, he or she can perform the core functions of the employment position held or desired to be held. Core job functions are not those that are considered marginal, but rather those that are essential to successfully execute designated tasks. The act prohibits any individual with a disability to be denied a job on the basis of not being able to meet physical or mental tasks that are not essential to perform the desired job tasks.

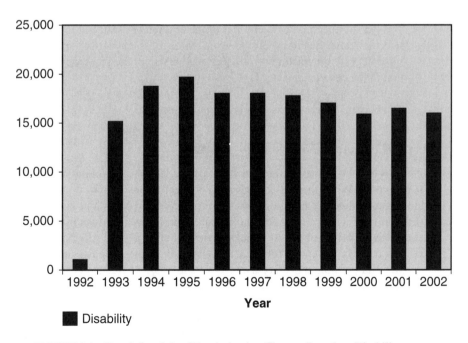

FIGURE 9.1   Trends Involving Discrimination Charges Based on Disability

Source: U.S. Equal Employment Opportunity Commission

Employers, therefore, must make reasonable accommodations to any known physical or mental impairment of an otherwise qualified individual who has disabilities. Based on the law, reasonable accommodations include the following:

1. Existing facilities used by employees must be readily accessible to and usable by individuals with disabilities.
2. Job restructuring, part-time or modified work schedules, reassignment to a vacant position, acquisition or modification of equipment or devices, appropriate adjustment or modifications of examinations, training materials or policies, the provision of qualified readers or interpreters, and other similar accommodations for individuals with disabilities.[18] An employer may be exempt if it can be demonstrated that an undue hardship is involved in making a reasonable accommodation.

The term *undue hardship* means an action requiring significant difficulty or expense, when considered in light of the following factors:

1. The nature and cost of the accommodation needed under this act
2. The overall financial resources of the facility or facilities involved in the provision of the reasonable accommodation; the number of persons employed at such facility; the effect on expenses and resources, or the impact otherwise of such accommodation upon the operation of the facility
3. The overall financial resources of the covered entity; and the overall size of the business of a covered entity with respect to the number of its employees and the number, type, and location of its facilities
4. The type of operation or operations of the covered entity, including the composition, structure, and functions of the work force of such entity; and the geographic separateness, administrative, or fiscal relationship of the facility or facilities in question to the covered entity.[19]

The burden of proof rests clearly with the employer.

Scope of Protection: Section 504 and ADA

Both ADA and the Rehabilitation Act affect public schools by prohibiting *disability-based discrimination.* When there is an allegation brought against school districts claiming discrimination, individuals bringing these charges may file a complaint with the Department of Education. If a violation is found, the Education Department can mandate that federal funds be terminated, subject to judicial review of such action. Affected individuals also may seek relief in the courts for such violations. Available remedies may include injunctive relief and possible monetary damages when there is evidence of malicious intent or bad faith in discriminating against individuals with disabilities.

Teachers, staff, and students with disabilities are protected in public school under both acts. For example, school employees, staff, or students with AIDS would be considered disabled under both statutes. Such persons would be considered a protected class, as long as they have a physical impairment that substantially limits one or more major life activities, has a record of such an impairment, or is regarded by others as having such an impairment.

In a leading case, *School Board of Nassau County, Florida v. Arline,* the Supreme Court addressed the issue of whether a person with a contagious disease is considered to be "handicapped" for purposes of Section 504 of the Rehabilitation Act. Arline was an elementary teacher who was hospitalized for tuberculosis. The disease went into remission for roughly 20 years, during which time she continued to teach elementary children. She experienced a recurrence of the disease in 1977 and 1978. Responding to her condition, the board of education suspended her for the remainder of the school term and subsequently terminated her based on a recurrence of the disease.

Arline filed suit, alleging that her discharge was in violation of Section 504 of the Rehabilitation Act. The district court held for the school board, holding that the act did not apply to Arline, since she was not considered a handicapped person for the purposes of the act. However, the court of appeals reversed, and the U.S. Supreme Court agreed to hear the case.

The Supreme Court upheld the court of appeals ruling by stating that a person with a contagious disease may be considered handicapped under Section 504 of the statute. The act defines handicapped individuals as any person who has a physical impairment that substantially limits one or more major life activities, has a record of such an impairment, or is regarded as having such an impairment. The fact that Arline was hospitalized 20 years ago for tuberculosis which then and now substantially limits her capacity to work clearly places her within the provisions of Section 504. Because the disease is contagious does not effectively remove her from coverage of the act. The Court was unable to determine whether Arline was otherwise qualified, due to the district's failure to properly inquire into the nature of the risk, the duration of the risk, the severity of the risk, and the probability that the disease may be transmitted and cause harm to others. The High Court affirmed the court of appeal's decision and remanded.[20]

As demonstrated by the Court's ruling in the Arline case, the term *handicap* carries a broad definition, as interpreted under Section 504. As long as the person with the handicap meets the definition enumerated in the act, he or she is covered under the act and is entitled to reasonable accommodations. Failure to provide reasonable accommodations violates the spirit of the act as well as the constitutional rights of individuals with disabilities.

A similar conclusion was reached by the Ninth Circuit Court of Appeals in *Chalk v. U.S. District Court, Central District of California,* when the court ruled that a person with AIDS is considered "otherwise qualified" under Section 504 of the Rehabilitation Act and therefore afforded full protection under the provisions of the act.[21] Although individuals with a contagious disease are covered under Section 504, the courts will allow school districts to balance the rights of employees with contagious diseases against the risk that their presence might create health hazards for others who must come in contact with them. The ultimate test would rest squarely on expert medical advice, rather than unfounded fear or apprehension. Through expert medical advice regarding possible heath risks to others, the rights of all parties are preserved.

Gender Discrimination

In an interesting case, the U.S. Supreme Court held that an employer's conduct need not be independently egregious to satisfy requirements for punitive damages in an employment discrimination case. In the *Kostad v. American Dental Association* case,[22] the plaintiff (Kolstad) sued the defendant under Title VII of the Civil Rights Act of 1964 (Title VII), asserting that defendant's decision to promote a male employee over her was a proscribed

CHAPTER 9

act of gender discrimination. Kolstad alleged, and introduced testimony to prove, that, among other things, the entire selection process was a sham, that the stated reasons of the company's executive director for selecting a male were pretext, and that he had been chosen before the formal selection process began. The district court denied Kolstad's request for a jury instruction on punitive damages, which is authorized by the Civil Rights Act of 1991 for Title VII cases in which the employee demonstrates that the employer has engaged in intentional discrimination and did so "with malice or with reckless indifference to the employee's federally protected rights." In affirming that denial, the court of appeals concluded that, before the jury can be instructed on punitive damages, the evidence must demonstrate that the defendant has engaged in some "egregious" misconduct, and that the plaintiff had failed to make the requisite showing in this case, which was heard by the Supreme Court. The U.S. Supreme Court held that "an employer's conduct need not be independently 'egregious' to satisfy requirements for a punitive damages award, although evidence of egregious behavior may provide a valuable means by which an employee can show the 'malice' or 'reckless indifference' needed to qualify for such an award."[23]

The 1991 act provided for compensatory and punitive damages in addition to the back pay and other equitable relief to which prevailing Title VII plaintiffs had previously been limited. The High Court vacated the court of appeal's ruling and held that the case be remanded for further proceedings consistent with its opinion. Based on this important ruling, egregious conduct by an employer is not required to pursue compensatory and punitive damages under the Civil Rights Act of 1991.

Racial Discrimination

Court-ordered desegregation since the landmark *Brown v. Board of Education*[24] case has resulted in numerous challenges of racial discrimination, as schools that were predominantly African American were closed and teachers and administrators reassigned to other schools. In many instances, African Americans who held significant administrative positions prior to court-ordered desegregation found themselves in lesser positions or in nonadministrative positions during the aftermath of the desegregation movement. Even though the courts, in their ruling, attempted to achieve some degree of equity in assignment of African Americans to predominantly white schools, their efforts fell short of achieving this objective.

The equal protection clause of the Fourteenth Amendment was relied on by African Americans to eradicate patterns of racial discrimination in public schools. The equal protection standards prohibited discrimination that can be linked with a racially motivated objective.[25] Unlike Title VII, no remedial action was attached to the equal protection clause, unless there was clear evidence that segregation was caused by *de jure* (official and deliberate laws or policies to promote segregation).

Perhaps one of the most compelling cases involving social discrimination, *Griggs v. Duke Power Company,*[26] did not occur in a public school setting. While it was not public school-based, it had a profound affect on discriminatory practices in public schools. Duke Power Company had openly discriminated on the basis of race in hiring and assigning employees in one of its plants. These practices were well established before the passage of Title VII. In 1955, the company implemented a policy requiring employees to hold a high school diploma for initial assignment to any but the lowest paid, traditionally African American departments and for transfer to the higher paying white departments. In 1965, the company began the practice of requiring that transferees to higher paying white departments obtain satisfactory scores on professionally prepared general aptitude tests. Evidence revealed, however, that whites who met neither of these criteria had been adequately performing jobs in the higher paid departments for years.

African-American employees challenged these testing requirements, which showed a disproportional impact on African Americans. The evidence revealed that a disproportionate number of African Americans did not meet the company's eligibility requirements for employment and transfer.

The Supreme Court held that a diploma requirement and generalized aptitude test may not be used when they result in the disqualification of a disproportionate number of minority group members, unless the employer can show a direct relationship between the skills tested and adequate on-the-job performance. This ruling was profound in that it set the stage for many challenges in public school districts where various types of entry examinations were used that also showed a disproportionate affect on groups of African Americans.

Duke Power Company's practices were in direct conflict with the provisions of Title VII, which prohibited employers from using tests and diploma requirements that worked to disqualify a disproportionate number of African Americans. These practices are deemed impermissable unless there is evidence that the requirements were job and performance related or were justified as a business necessity.

After the *Griggs* decision, a number of courts invalidated the use of the National Teachers' Examination and the Graduate Record Examination using the *Griggs criteria* of job relatedness. The burden was passed to the districts to demonstrate job relatedness in their use of these examinations.

One state succeeded in demonstrating job relatedness through its use of test scores for both certification purposes and as a salary factor. In the *United States of America v. State of South Carolina,* the state was charged with violations of the Fourteenth Amendment and Title VII of the Civil Rights Act of 1964 through the use of minimum score requirements on the National Teachers' Examinations (NTE) to certify and determine pay levels of teachers within the state. The policy had been practiced for more than 30 years as local school districts used scores on the NTE for selection and compensation of teachers. The initial minimum score was set at 975. After an exhaustive validation study by Educational Testing Services (ETS) and a critical review and assessment of this study by the Board of Education, the state established new certification standards requiring different minimum scores in various areas of teaching specialization ranging from 940 to 1198.

Plaintiffs challenged the use of the NTE for both purposes. They claimed that more African Americans than whites historically have failed to achieve the required minimum score, resulting in a racial classification in violation of the Fourteenth Amendment and Title VII of the Civil Rights of 1964.

One of the burdens faced by the plaintiffs was to prove that the state intended to create and use a racial classification. Evidence revealed that the tests could be taken an unlimited number of times. There was some evidence that the test had a disproportional impact on African Americans. Furthermore, ETS recommended that the minimum score requirement not be used as a sole determinant of certification where other appropriate information or criteria are available. However, plaintiffs did not produce any other appropriate or reasonable criteria on which decisions could be made, nor was there a showing that the NTE examinations themselves discriminated on the basis of race.

The court held for the defendant by stating, "We are unable to find a discriminatory intent from the facts and that there was no discriminatory intent, without independent proof, in linking the certification and salary systems."[27] The court supported the conclusion that the NTE is professionally prepared to measure the critical mass of knowledge in academic subject matters. Also, the court concluded that the state's use of the NTE for both certifications met a "rational relationship" standard and thus found the plaintiffs unable to establish a right to relief sought in their respective complaint.

In the absence of proof of a discriminatory intent, teachers will not succeed in their claims of discrimination if the state is able to establish a reasonable relationship between the examination requirement and minimal skills needed to teach. *Prima facie* evidence of discrimination rests with plaintiff. As viewed in this case, plaintiffs failed to meet this burden of proof.

Title VII involves two basic types of claims: disparate treatment and disparate impact. The Supreme Court addressed these two important issues in a later case involving discrimination on disparate treatment and disparate impact. *Disparate treatment* simply means that an employer treats some people more unfavorably than others regarding employment, job promotion, or employment conditions based on race, color, religion, sex, or national origin. *Disparate impact* is merely a showing that numbers of people of a similar class are affected adversely by a particular employment practice that appears neutral, such as a requirement that all employees pass a test (as illustrated in the previously discussed *Griggs* case). The protected class categories usually involve race, gender, religion, and national origin. Disparate impact suits differ from disparate treatment in that they do not allege overt discriminatory action.

The Supreme Court in *International Brotherhood of Teamsters v. United States* stated that disparate treatment may be distinguished from disparate impact. "Impact involves employment practices that are facially neutral in their treatment of different groups but do, in fact, fall more heavily on one group than another and cannot be justified by business necessity . . . proof of discriminatory motive, we have held it not required under a disparate impact theory."[28]

Thus, the Supreme Court, through its rulings, has identified two avenues for plaintiffs to seek relief under Title VII: impact and treatment. Many cases regarding racial discrimination have been addressed by the courts. The following represents a brief summary of the court's responses to challenges of racial discrimination involving allegations of disparate treatment.

A white social worker challenged her layoff by a Colorado school district. She, along with all terminated social workers, requested hearings. After the hearings, the officer found that the board should give special consideration to the African American social worker since he was the only African American administrator in the district. The board rescinded his termination. The board subsequently rehired a Hispanic social worker with less seniority than the white social worker.

After exhausting administrative appeals, the white social worker filed a discrimination suit in federal district court. The court found that the district's actions constituted intentional racial discrimination and were not justified by legitimate nondiscriminatory reason. The social worker was awarded back pay and attorney fees. The district appealed to the U.S. Court of Appeals, claiming that its actions were appropriate, based on the district's affirmative action plan. The court noted that the purpose of such a plan was to remedy past discrimination against a particular group. Since there was no evidence of past discrimination, the court held that the affirmative action plan discriminated against the white social worker. The court affirmed the trial court's decision.[29]

In another case, an African American college senior filed an application with a Virginia school district for a teaching position. When she became certified to teach, she notified the district to update her file. The district failed to do so and did not notify her of job openings on three different occasions. For one position, the district hired a less qualified white applicant who was the spouse of a teacher currently employed in the district. The student filed a discrimination suit under Title VII, claiming racial discrimination. She requested monetary damages and an injunction to prevent the district from continuing its discriminatory practices. The district claimed that a clerical error resulted in the applicant being overlooked. The trial court held for the district. The appeals court was bound by the trial court's finding of no intent to discriminate. The court, however, did find a poor record of past hiring practices regarding African Americans. The court, based on its findings, remanded the case and instructed the trial court to issue an injunction requiring the district to advertise future openings and fill them in a nondiscriminatory manner.[30]

Finally, an African American Tennessee junior high school band director attended a band contest in another school district. There, he caught two boys in the restroom with marijuana, which he confiscated. On his way home, he was stopped by police officers, who discovered the marijuana. The school board informed the band director that he would be dismissed from his position, even though he was charged with only a misdemeanor and fined $25. Two other white teachers had committed misdemeanors of shoplifting and driving while intoxicated, for which there was no penalty by the district.

The African American teacher sued in federal district court for civil rights violations, alleging discrimination. The court stated that the African American teacher was treated differently from white teachers under similar circumstances. This disparate treatment was not adequately justified or explained by the board. Although there was no discernible pattern of racial discrimination found, the court concluded that a discriminatory reason likely motivated the board's decision. The teacher was reinstated with back pay and attorney fees.[31]

The implications of the court's decisions in these cases suggest that school districts will not be supported when their rules and policies are discriminatory based on race, whether they are intentional or unintentional. Once challenged and *prima facie* evidence of discrimination is shown, school districts must bear the burden of proof to demonstrate a nondiscriminatory purpose. In cases where there is a preponderance of evidence of discriminatory intent, this becomes an insurmountable task for school districts. See Figure 9.2 for trends involving discrimination based on race.

Religious Discrimination

The First Amendment and Title VII provide protection to employees against religious discrimination. *Religion* is defined by Title VII to include all aspects of religious observances, practices, and beliefs. Under this act, employers are expected to make reasonable accommodations to an employee's religious observance unless a hardship can be demonstrated. The burden of proof rests with the employee to demonstrate undue hardship. Most states have enacted legislation that requires employers to make accommodations for employees' religious practices. Thus, caution must be exercised by employers to ensure that the religious rights of employees are not violated. Employers must also make sure that the *Establishment Clause* of the First Amendment is not violated.

For example, in the *Estate of Thornton v. Caldor, Inc.,* the court ruled that state statutes imposing an absolute duty on employers to fashion their business practices to

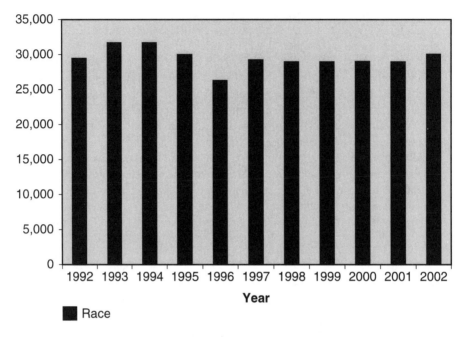

FIGURE 9.2   Trends Involving Discrimination Charges Based on Race

Source: U.S. Equal Employment Opportunity Commission

accommodate the religious practices of their employees was in conflict with the First Amendment. The court held further that these statutes provided no flexibility for employers and amounted to an advancement of religion in violation of the establishment clause.[32]

In a related case, *Transworld Airlines Inc. v. Hardison,* an employee challenged the company's policy that prevented him from observing Saturdays as a religious holiday. The court held for the company and stated that Title VII did not require the company to set aside special exemptions to accommodate the employee's belief. To require the airline to make special exemption for the employee—Saturdays off—is an undue hardship.[33]

The issues relating to religious discrimination involve fairness and balance. For example, an employer cannot legally require an employee to choose between his or her job and religion. Such a requirement would represent religious discrimination. Additionally, employees cannot be penalized by a placement that would require that employee to ignore a religious tenet of his or her faith to preserve a job. See Figure 9.3 for trends involving discrimination based on religion.

AFFIRMATIVE ACTION:
CALIFORNIA AND PROPOSITION 209

Controversial Proposition 209 emerged in California as a means of eliminating affirmative action programs supported by governmental agencies within the state. At issue were state and local programs that granted preferential treatment to any group or individuals on the

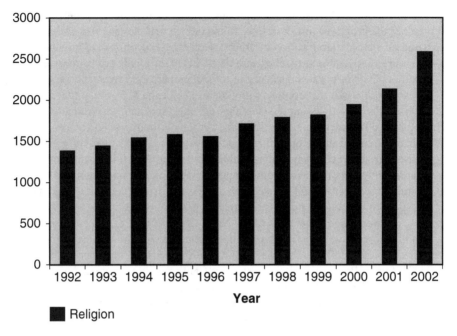

FIGURE 9.3 Trends Involving Discrimination Charges Based on Religion

Source: U.S. Equal Employment Opportunity Commission

basis of race, sex, ethnicity, color, or national origin. Proposition 209 does not affect any voluntary affirmative action programs in the private sector but rather focuses on those embraced by governmental agencies.

Proposition 209, described as one of the most divisive issues within the state, passed by a 55–45 percent vote. In effect, it prohibits discrimination and preferential treatment on the basis of the factors listed in the previous paragraph. Proponents of this measure hailed it as a victory against discrimination by the government. The intent of governmentally administered programs regarding affirmative action is to ensure that women as well as racial and ethnic minorities are provided increased opportunities to participate and benefit from such programs. For example, many states identify goals and specific timetables for participation of minority-owned businesses involving work associated with state contracts. In many instances, numerical percentages are written into these laws to ensure that minority-owned businesses succeed in acquiring state contracts. Some state laws mandate that departments reject bids from companies that have not shown good faith in meeting affirmative action goals.

Proposition 209 affects a whole variety of affirmative action programs and initiatives throughout the state. For example, public college and university admission policies, scholarships, tutorial and outreach initiatives aimed at minorities are affected in cases where preferential treatment is based on race, sex, ethnicity, color, or national origin. Also, goals and time lines designed to encourage minority hiring by state government are affected, as well as state and local programs required by the federal government as a condition for receipt of federal funds.

Proposition 209 eliminated state and local governmental affirmative action programs in all of the programs just described, to the degree that they involve preferential treatment based on special classification of groups. However, exceptions are provided, if necessary, to ensure that state and local governments maintain eligibility to receive federal funds. Additionally, court orders currently in force are unaffected by Proposition 209, as well as any state initiatives that comply with federal law or the U.S. Constitution. The California Civil Rights Initiative simply states that the state shall not discriminate against or grant preferential treatment to any individual or group on the basis of race, sex, color, ethnicity, or national origin in the operation of public education and contracting. The intent of this measure is to prevent any program that attempts to provide advantages for women or minorities where similar programs do not exist for men or nonminorities. It does not have an impact on other special groups such as veterans or people over age 65, as these groups are still allowed to seek preferential treatment.

A three-judge panel of the U.S. Ninth Circuit Court of Appeals lifted an injunction against Proposition 209. This development, coupled with the U.S. Supreme Court's failure to hear the case, left standing the Ninth Circuit's decision, thus upholding Proposition 209 in California. Proposition 209 affects only California, but the impact of this Ninth Circuit Court's decision may have significant implications for affirmative action programs in other states. It will not be surprising to see other states adopt similar measures in the foreseeable future. Proposition 209 and other similar measures initiated by other states will continue to be highly controversial until the U.S. Supreme Court finally makes a ruling on this issue.

In a recent development, the U.S. Supreme Court refused to address the issue of whether university regents were justified in using race and ethnicity in the admissions process of a University of California at Los Angeles Laboratory School. The High Court let stand a decision by the U.S. Court of Appeals for the Ninth Circuit, which held that the use of racial and ethnic criteria in the admissions policy was narrowly tailored to serve a compelling state interest. UCLA withstood a constitutional challenge by the parent of a student whose application was not accepted for admission.[34]

Landmark U.S. Supreme Court Rulings

The U.S. Supreme Court agreed to address the legality of race-based admissions in higher education in December, 2002. A landmark decision rendered on June 23, 2003, has set the stage for the implementation of affirmative action policies that will have a far-reaching impact on college and university admissions as well as diversity in higher education for decades to come. This recent decision is the most significant in almost two and a half decades and certainly the most important decision by the Supreme Court during the twenty-first century regarding affirmative action. The Supreme Court accepted two appeals involving admissions policies at the University of Michigan in Ann Arbor. The first, *Grutter v. Bollinger*, involved policies in Michigan's law school program designed to boost enrollment of underrepresented minority groups, namely African Americans, Hispanics, and Native Americans.[35]

The second case, *Gratz v. Bollinger*, pertained to admission at the university's undergraduate program in the College of Literature, Science and Arts.[36] The University of Michigan employed a point system for admissions that was altered after a lawsuit was filed. The point system was executed in the following manner: The University of Michigan's undergraduate policy includes a 150-point "selection index" that assigns a numerical value to each of several factors. That score was sometimes, but not always, the basis for final admissions decisions. Also, race alone did not admit a student to the undergraduate point system used by the university:

- Membership in an underrepresented minority group, socioeconomic disadvantage, attendance at a predominantly minority high school, athletics or the provost's discretion (20 points)
- Michigan residency (10 points)
- Residency in a Michigan county underrepresented at the university (six points)
- Residency in an underrepresented state (two points)
- Alumni relationships (one to four points)
- Personal essay (up to three points)
- Activities, work experience, and awards (up to five points)
- Personal achievement (five points)

The university's law school did not use a point system but attempted to ensure that minorities made up 10 to 12 percent of each class. Its admissions policy included a requirement that a "reasonable proportion" of each class contained underrepresented groups.

The university did not consider Asian students or Arabic students as underrepresented groups or victims of discrimination. Michigan's former president, Lee Bollinger, and the current president, Mary Sue Coleman, based their defense on the grounds that policies designed to promote racial diversity on campus met the highest legal standards for evaluating race conscious government action. The university presented empirical data in the trials regarding the two admission policies demonstrating that both had educational benefits. The university received support from labor unions, civil rights organizations, General Motors, and 84 major corporations and educational groups. The fundamental issue raised by those who supported the plaintiffs is whether the Fourteenth Amendment's equal protection clause and nondiscrimination have the same meaning for all races. Jennifer Gratz and Patrick Hamacher challenged the undergraduate admission policies. Gratz applied during the fall of 1995 at the Ann Arbor campus with a high school grade-point average (GPA) of 3.8 and an ACT score of 25 out of a possible 36. She was initially placed on the waiting list but later rejected. She graduated in 1979 from the University of Michigan at Dearborn. Hamacher applied during the fall of 1997 at the Ann Arbor campus with a 3.32 GPA and a 28 on the ACT. He was also rejected and later admitted to Michigan State University from which he graduated in 2002. Separate federal district cases heard the undergraduate case and the law school case.

Surprisingly, in 2000, a district judge upheld the consideration of race in the undergraduate case while opposing it in the law school case.

The full U.S. Circuit Court of Appeals for the Sixth Circuit in Cincinnati heard arguments in both cases in December 2002. In May 2003, it ruled 5–4 in the law school case, supporting the university. The majority suggested that Justice Lewis F. Powell, Jr.'s concurring opinion in *Bakke* established diversity as a legitimate governmental interest that justified the use of racial preferences. However, without explanation, the Sixth Circuit Court failed to rule on the undergraduate case. The Center for Individual Rights appealed the law school ruling to the U.S. Supreme Court and filed a brief requesting that the High Court bypass the Sixth Circuit and accept the undergraduate case, so as to enable the court to fully discern race conscious admissions practices.

Finally, the much-anticipated decision was reached by the U.S. Supreme Court in both cases at the University of Michigan on June 23, 2003. The High Court held that schools can consider race in admission decisions but that quota systems are illegal. The Court's rulings marked its first intervention into the issue of affirmative action in university admissions since its 1978 decision in *Regents of the University of California v Bakke.* The Court's resolution of *Bakke* foreshadowed Monday's decision in Michigan as Justice Lewis Powell wrote for a divided court in *Bakke* holding that admissions policies can consider race as one of many qualifications but could not set a quota reserving a specific number or percentage of seats for minorities.

Justice O'Connor wrote the majority opinion in the law school case. Joining O'Connor's opinion were Justices John Paul Stevens, David Souter, Ruth Bader Ginsburg, and Stephen Breyer. Dissenting were Chief Justice William Rehnquist and Justices Antonin Scalia, Anthony Kennedy, and Clarence Thomas. Thomas wrote perhaps the most stinging dissent. The Court's only black justice equated the university's admissions policy to nineteenth-century black Civil Rights leader Frederick Douglass's call for abolitionists not to perform special favors for black people that are demeaning. "Like Douglass, I believe blacks can achieve in every avenue of American life without the meddling of university administrators."

In the case involving undergraduate admissions, the Supreme Court in a 6–3 ruling held unconstitutional a separate point system used by the University of Michigan that showed minority preference in undergraduate admissions. In effect, the Court supported diversity but disallowed quotas, which is essentially the position the Court has taken during the past 25 years. Justice Sandra O'Connor stated that "effective participation by members of all racial and ethnic groups in the civic life of our nation is essential if the dream of one nation, indivisible, is to be realized." O'Connor also wrote on behalf of the five-justice majority that affirmative action at universities "must be limited in time," noting that the Constitution forbids permanent racial classifications. She urged universities to prepare to move beyond such admissions policies.

In a large sense, the Supreme Court's decisions represent a victory for parties in both cases. It allows race to be considered as a factor in admission decisions to foster diversity. But it disallowed a point or quota system as a component of the admission process. Thus, both groups have claimed victory. Perhaps the greatest victory may rest with a higher education system that values diversity, which happens to be one of America's greatest strengths.

Age Discrimination

Age discrimination in public schools primarily affects teachers. In past years, many districts forced teachers to retire when they reached a specified age. These policies and practices were challenged by teachers under equal protection guarantees. Many of these challenges received mixed reviews by the courts. For example, the U.S. Supreme Court supported mandatory retirement for police officers, based on the rigorous physical demands associated with their positions. Conversely, the Seventh Circuit Court of Appeals rejected a practice of forced retirement for teachers at age 65, noting no justification to presume that teachers at age 65 lacked the academic skill, intellect, or physical rigor to teach.[37]

All challenges and uncertainties became insignificant with the passage of the Age Discrimination in Employment Act of 1967 (ADEA) as amended in 1978. These acts effectively prohibited forced retirement of employees by protecting people above age 40 from discrimination on the basis of age with respect to hiring, dismissal, and other terms and conditions of employment. Prior to the act's amendment in 1978, the maximum age limit was set at 65 years. The 1978 amendment raised the limit to age 70. Amendments added in 1986 removed the limit completely, except for people in certain public safety positions (e.g., police officers and firefighters). The act covers teachers and other public employees. However, there is no prohibition against failure to renew a teacher contract, so long as nonrenewal is not based on age.

Litigation under this act is similar to that involving race or gender. If a district is charged with age discrimination, it must be able to demonstrate that other legitimate factors affected its action other than age. Since teachers enjoy the same constitutional rights as other citizens, the burden of proof rests with the district to demonstrate the equal protection guarantees and that the requirements of the law are respected.

Many districts, as well as universities, have instituted early retirement incentive plans. These are generally held acceptable by the courts, if they are strictly voluntary in nature. There can be no evidence that suggests that any force or coercion is used to enforce such plans. Currently, mandatory retirement plans for public schools, colleges, and universities are prohibited, as universities were exempt until 1993. They must now comply with the law.

Since the passage of ADEA, a number of cases have still made their way into the legal arena. One such case arose in Florida when a tenured public teacher turned 70 during the school year. School officials informed him that he would subsequently be employed on a year-to-year basis under the terms of a state statute that provides that no person shall be entitled to continued employment as a public school teacher at the end of the school year following his or her seventieth birthday.

When the district failed to employ him for the next year, he filed suit, claiming discrimination based on age. The Florida Supreme Court ruled that no person over age 70 shall be entitled to continued employment with respect to tenure rights, but termination could not be made solely on the basis of age. The court held for the teacher and awarded back pay, benefits, and reevaluation of his reemployment request without reference to age.[38]

A similar case arose in Oklahoma when a public school teacher, who was soon to be 70, received notice that her contract would not be renewed for the following year. The letter stated that the sole reason for nonrenewal was the mandatory retirement policy and that she was otherwise qualified to teach. At a hearing, the officer determined that the board had authority to set mandatory age limits. She then filed suit in the trial court, which affirmed the hearing officer's decision. An appeal was filed with the Court of Appeals of Oklahoma. The court noted that the board may exercise those powers that are expressed and granted in writing. The teacher charged that no such powers existed. The evidence revealed that the legislature excluded a reference to mandatory retirement age for teachers in its laws. In the absence of such law, the district is without authority to adopt a policy based on age. The court reversed the trial court's decision.[39]

In a final case in Kentucky, a teacher was employed as an English instructor from 1959 to 1972. From 1972 to 1983, she worked for a private business. In 1983, she interviewed with the school district for several positions for which younger people were hired. She was subsequently hired as a permanent part-time librarian. She filed suit in 1988, alleging discrimination based on age in violation of ADEA, when the district hired younger people for permanent positions. She further challenged the board's salary policy, which limits the credit a teacher receives for experience that is more than ten years, as a violation of ADEA, because it adversely affects people over 40 years of age. The trial court entered summary judgment for the board. The teacher appealed to the U.S. Court of Appeals in the Sixth District.

The facts revealed that the teacher had proven a *prima facie* case of age discrimination. The board responded with a legitimate nondiscrimination reason for failure to hire, which was the teacher's experience level. The board's policy limiting credit for teachers' experience to less than ten years suggests common sense in that the policy treats teachers whose experience is greater than ten years old differently from those whose experience is more recent. The teacher failed to produce any statistical evidence demonstrating that the policy had any adverse impact on any individuals. The board's intent was to give more recent experience greater value. On the basis of those findings, the circuit upheld the trial court and granted summary judgment to the board.[40]

The evidence is quite clear that the burden of proof rests with plaintiffs to establish a *prima facie* case of age discrimination. Once established, the district must demonstrate a legitimate state interest on which to base its action. In the absence of a legitimate state interest, school districts may not discriminate on the basis of age. Stated differently, *age cannot be the sole criterion that motivates a board decision to discriminate against school personnel.* There must be other defensible nondiscriminatory objectives established by the district. The ADEA is very clear in its intent. School officials would be well served to adhere to the provisions of the law and avoid unnecessary litigation. See Figure 9.4 for trends involving discrimination based on age.

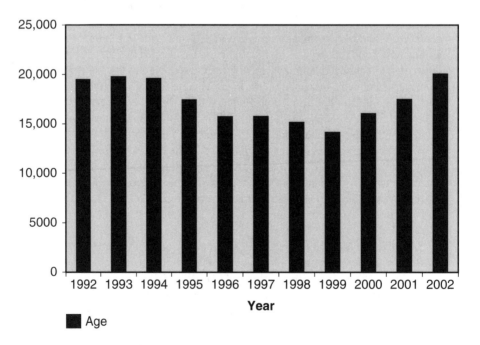

FIGURE 9.4   Trends Involving Discrimination Charges Based on Age

Source: U.S. Equal Employment Opportunity Commission

PREGNANCY AND PUBLIC SCHOOL EMPLOYMENT

Teachers in public schools are protected by the Pregnancy Discrimination Act of 1978 (P.L. 95-555). This law is an amendment to Title VII, which extends protection to pregnant employees against any forms of discrimination based on pregnancy. The courts have been fairly consistent in their rulings regarding issues related to pregnancy. Prior to the enactment of this law, it was not uncommon for districts to enforce policy cut-off dates in which females were required to leave their positions due to their pregnant status. In a significant case, *Cleveland Board of Education v. LaFleur*,[41] the court held that mandatory maternity termination specifying the number of months before anticipated childbirth violated the equal protection clause of the Fourteenth Amendment, noting that arbitrary cut-off dates served no legitimate state interest in maintaining a continuous and orderly instructional program.

Districts may not assume that every pregnant teacher is physically unable to perform her teaching duties and responsibilities effectively because she is at a specific point in her pregnancy. Courts have also not been supportive of district policies that bar a female teacher, after giving birth, from returning to the district until the next regular semester or year. There have also been numerous challenges brought by female teachers regarding disability benefits, sick leave, and adequate insurance coverage.

Many of these challenges led to the enactment of the Pregnancy Discrimination Act of 1978. The basic intent of the act is to ensure that pregnant employees are treated in the same manner as other employees with respect to the ability to perform their duties. The act covers pregnancy, childbirth, and related medical conditions. Under the Pregnancy Discrimination Act, no longer can a woman be dismissed, denied a job, or denied promotion due to pregnancy. Women must be able to take sick leave as other employees do for medical reasons and return to work when they are released by their physicians. Pregnancy must be treated as a temporary disability, thus entitling female employees to the same provisions of disability benefits, sick leave, and insurance coverage as any other employee who has a temporary disability. There has not been as much litigation since the passage of the act, due in large part to the consistency in which the courts have ruled on matters involving the rights of pregnant employees.

However, one interesting case arose in 1991 regarding the interpretation and intent of the Pregnancy Act regarding the use of sick leave. In 1981, a teacher employed by Leyden Community High School became pregnant. She requested, by letter to the superintendent, that she be allowed to use the sick leave she had accumulated during her employment for the period of disability relating to her pregnancy. She further informed the superintendent that following this period of disability, she would begin a maternity leave that would extend over the remainder of the 1981–1982 school year.

The superintendent responded by indicating that the collective negotiation agreement between Leyden and the teachers' union barred teachers from taking maternity leave immediately following a period of disability for which they used sick leave. After obtaining a right-to-sue letter from the EEOC, she brought action against Leyden, alleging that the leave policy had the impact of preventing female teachers from using their accumulated sick leave to cover pregnancy-related disabilities, and consequently violated Title VII as amended by the Pregnancy Discrimination Act.

The teacher further argued that the policy had the statistical effect of forcing females to accumulate more sick days than males, which, at retirement, were compensated at a lower rate than the teacher's per diem pay. The district court found in its ruling that the district policy did not have a disparate impact on women based on pregnancy. The teacher appealed to the Seventh Circuit Court, which was faced with determining whether the district's policy forced teachers to choose between sick leave or taking maternity leave, creating a disparate impact on women, in violation of Title VIII.

The court ruled that the scope of the Pregnancy Act was limited to policies that have an impact on or treat medical conditions relating to pregnancy and childbirth less favorably than other disabilities. Further, the court added that the statistical evidence focusing on the absolute number of sick days accumulated by female teachers over their career was insufficient, standing alone, to establish that the district's policy had a requisite impact on females. Therefore, the district court's ruling was affirmed.[42]

■ ■ ■ ■ ■ ▬▬▬▬▬▬▬▬▬▬▬▬▬▬▬▬▬▬▬▬▬▬▬▬▬▬▬▬▬▬▬▬▬▬▬▬▬▬▬

ADMINISTRATIVE GUIDE

DISCRIMINATION

1. School districts will not be supported by the courts when there is evidence that districts discriminated against employees on the basis of race, color, religion, gender, or national origin.
2. Once *prima facie* evidence is presented by the employee affected, school officials must demonstrate that a compelling educational interest motivated their decisions.
3. School districts may not discriminate against employees because employees opposed practices made unlawful under discrimination laws or participated in an investigation regarding employment discrimination.
4. School officials may be held liable in any cases involving discrimination or harassment when it is determined that they were aware of these actions.
5. No employee may be coerced to retire from employment based on age, nor may the employee be denied rights and privileges afforded other employees based on age, such as promotion and other benefits.
6. Race discrimination affects all employees, not merely minority employees.
7. Punitive damages may be awarded in employment discrimination cases if the employer's conduct is not viewed as egregious.
8. Differential employment criteria may not be used that have an adverse affect on a special group of employees, even though the criteria appear to be neutral.
9. Employment examinations, if used, must bear a rational relationship to performance requirements for the position sought by the prospective employee.
10. Racial or statistical quotas are legally indefensible in rendering decisions regarding reduction on teaching staffs, unless mandated by court orders.

Sexual Harassment

Sexual harassment is prohibited by Title VII and Title IX. In spite of these prohibitions, incidents of sexual harassment persist. Cases involving charges of sexual harassment have remained fairly constant over the past several years (see Figure 9.5). Based on statistics filed with the Equal Employment Opportunity Commission, sexual harassment charges increased significantly from 1992 to 1995. Since 1995 there has been a gradual decrease

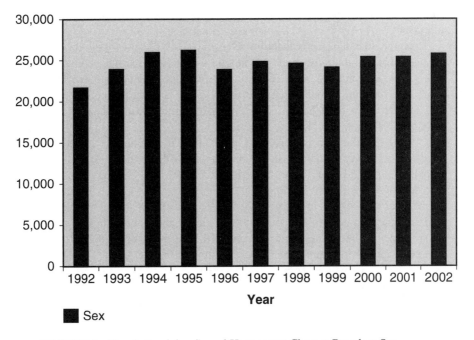

FIGURE 9.5   Trends Involving Sexual Harassment Charges Based on Sex

Source: U.S. Equal Employment Opportunity Commission

in the number of cases involving sexual harassment. Sexual harassment charges filed with EEOC declined by only 2 percent over this same period. These trends suggest that education and awareness training are critical factors in combating harassment in the workplace.

Interestingly, sexual harassment was not included in Title VII of the Civil Rights Act of 1964 until 1980. Its primary intent is to protect employees from harassment in their work environments. Harassment is considered to be a form of sex discrimination. It can manifest itself in many forms, from verbal statements and gestures, to overt behavior. The victim, as well as the harasser, may be male or female, not necessarily of the opposite sex. The victim may not be the person harassed but may be anyone affected by the offensive conduct. Economic injury is not necessary to bring a successful case of harassment against a supervisor.

There are various levels of *verbal harassment behavior,* including, but not limited to, making personal inquiries of a sexual nature, offering sexual comments regarding a person's anatomy or clothing, and repeatedly requesting dates and refusing to accept "no" as an answer. *Nonverbal harassment* may include prolonged staring at another person, presenting personal gifts without cause, throwing kisses or licking one's lips, making various sexual gestures with one's hand, or posting sexually suggestive cartoons or pictures.

More serious levels may involve sexual coercion or unwanted physical relations. This type of behavior *quid pro quo* is commonly associated with superior-subordinate relationships in which the victim, for fear of reprisal, unwillingly participates. This relationship is best described as a power relationship. The supervisor, in this case, has the capacity to refuse to hire, promote, grant, or deny certain privileges, based on his or her position.

In many instances, the promise of some job-related benefit is offered in exchange for sexual favors.

Another level of harassment involves *unwanted touching of another's hair, clothing, or body.* Undesirable acts involving hugging, kissing, stroking, patting, and massaging one's neck or shoulders are examples of physical harassment that contributes to a hostile work environment. Verbal harassment may include off-the-cuff comments such as referring to a female as babe, honey, or sweetheart, or turning work discussions into sexual discussions, including sexual jokes or stories.

Each of these levels represents a serious form of sexual discrimination for which the victim may recover for damages. The burden rests with the victim to establish that the various levels of harassment are unwanted. Once established, the harasser has an obligation to discontinue such behavior immediately. Failure to do so usually creates a hostile work environment and results in charges of sexual harassment by the victim. Sexual harassment claims are sometimes difficult to pursue in court for the victim. In many instances, embarrassing and graphic details must be revealed, which are often denied by the person(s) against whom charges are made. Many victims of various forms of discrimination have been awarded monetary damages. The dollar amounts have increased significantly in recent years (see Figure 9.6).

The definition of *harassment,* under the act, is sufficiently broad to allow coverage of most forms of unacceptable behavior. Any type of sexual behavior or advance that is *unwanted* or *unwelcomed* is considered covered under the act. As indicated earlier, the person affected by such behavior has an obligation to inform the party that his or her behavior is unwelcomed or unwanted. If this does not occur, it is difficult to claim harassment,

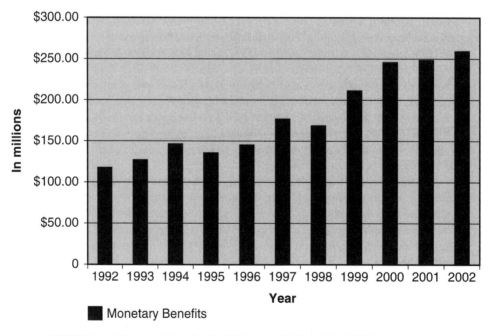

FIGURE 9.6   Monetary Benefits for All Statutes Enforced by EEOC

because the accused party is unaware that his or her behavior is unwelcomed. The regulation implementing sexual harassment is very broad, on the one hand, but yet fairly prescriptive with respect to coverage. It defines sexual harassment in the following manner:

> Unwelcome sexual advances, requests for sexual favors and other verbal or physical contact of a sexual nature constitute sexual harassment when (1) submission to such conduct is made either explicitly or implicitly as a term or condition of an individual's employment (2) submission to or rejection of such conduct by an individual is used as the basis for employment decisions affecting such individuals or (3) such conduct has the purpose or effect of unreasonably interfering with an individual's work performance or creating an intimidating, hostile or offensive working environment.[43]

Legally, employees may not be denied promotions or other benefits to which they are entitled on the basis of their unwillingness to accept sexual misconduct by their superiors, nor may they be subjected to hostile, unfriendly environments by superiors or peers if they refuse to accept sexual misconduct. Under the Civil Rights Act, every person is entitled to an environment free of unwelcomed sexual conduct and one that allows the person to perform his or her duties without intimidation or fear of reprisal.

EEOC guidelines cover two types of sexual harassment: *quid pro quo* and *non-quid pro quo*. In *quid pro quo* harassment, an employee exchanges sexual favors for job benefits, promotion, or continued employment. In *non-quid pro quo* or hostile environment, the employee is subjected to a sexually hostile and intimidating work environment that psychologically affects the employee's well-being and has an adverse affect on job performance.

A landmark case involving sexual harassment occurred in the private sector in which a female bank employee filed action against the bank and her supervisor. The employee alleged that she had been subjected to sexual harassment by her supervisor during her employment, in violation of Title VII. The supervisor's contention was that the sexual relationship was consensual and had no bearing on the employee's continued employment. The bank indicated that it had no knowledge or notice of the allegation and therefore could not be held liable.

The Supreme Court, in a landmark ruling on the case, *Meritor Savings Bank v. Vinson*,[44] held that unwelcomed sexual advances that create an offensive or hostile work environment violate Title VII. It further held that, while employers are not automatically liable for sexual harassment committed by their supervisors, absence of notice does not automatically insulate the employers from liability in such cases.

The significance of the ruling set the stage for subsequent sexual harassment cases by providing the definition of specific acts that fall within the category of harassment. The High Court suggested that Title VII guidelines are not limited to economic or tangible injuries. Harassment that leads to noneconomic injury may also violate Title VII. The Court considered the claim that sexual activity was voluntary to be without merit. The test, according to the Court, was whether such advances were unwelcomed.

The implications suggested from this case are that employers may be held liable for sexual harassment acts involving employees when the employer knew or should have known of the undesirable conduct. If the employer knew of the conduct, there is an expectation that immediate and corrective actions be taken. Failure to take decisive action generally results in liability charges against the employer. Based on a Supreme Court decision in the *Gebser* case,[45] students who are sexually abused by teachers cannot recover monetary damages from school officials unless officials knew of the harassment, were in a position to act, and failed to do so.

In another rather unusual case, a tenured teacher in New Jersey claimed that she was fired because she refused unwelcomed sexual advances from her supervisor. She further claimed that her supervisor and another lesbian teacher sought to embarrass and discredit her for rejecting the unwelcomed sexual advances. The school district initiated dismissal proceedings against her. The teacher filed an unsuccessful challenge against the termination action in the state court. She subsequently filed a Title VII discrimination complaint against the school principal and school board in the U.S. District Court of New Jersey. The court granted summary judgment for the board.

The teacher appealed to the U.S. Circuit Court of Appeals for the Third Circuit. The appeals court determined that Title VII is generally inapplicable after the cessation of the employment relationship, but the act was written broadly to cover discrimination actions following the termination of an employment relationship. Because postemployment black-listing could prove more damaging than on-the-job discrimination, the district improperly granted summary judgment. The court reasoned that the board's continued inquiries into the revocation of the teacher's certificate were retaliatory in nature and violative of Title VII.[46]

Finally, in a significant case regarding sexual harassment and abuse involving a student, the U.S. Supreme Court in *Franklin v. Gwinnett County Public Schools* illustrates the type of risk school districts and employees face under federal statutes, as well as common law. The court unanimously held that when a teacher is alleged to have harassed and abused a student by coercive sexual intercourse, unwelcomed kissing on the mouth, and placing calls to the student's home requesting social meetings, damages could be available to the student under Title IX for virtually all forms of sexual misconduct. More importantly, these damages may be levied against the district and its supervisors, as well as the accused teacher.[47]

Based on the significant ruling in the *Gwinett* case, plaintiffs may very well be more inclined to pursue claims under Title IX, as opposed to Title VII, given the caps on damages associated with Title VII. Additionally, Title IX does not require the exhaustive administrative remedies found with Title VII and generally has a statute of limitations based on state laws, thus providing a longer period of time to bring legal claims.

Sexual harassment is prevalent in the United States and will likely continue to present legal challenges. This issue continues to evolve in the courts, where they are defining the legal limits of acceptable sex-related behavior in the workplace.

ISSUES INVOLVING NATIONAL ORIGIN: PROPOSITION 187

Proposition 187 was enacted in 1994 and supported by the voters of California in an effort to force undocumented aliens out of the state and, furthermore, to deter their entry by ending educational, medical, and other public services. Proposition 187 denies public social services to people who are unable to establish their status as U.S. citizens, lawful permanent residents, or aliens lawfully admitted for a certain period of time (except for cases involving emergency medical care). This measure also limits public school attendance to

U.S. citizens and aliens lawfully admitted to the United States as permanent residents. Under this act, school districts must verify the status of students and their parents' legal status. If there is reasonable suspicion that a violation has occurred, school authorities must notify the Immigration and Naturalization Service. This requirement alone will prove to be enormously expensive and time consuming for schools, which are already overburdened with budget restrictions.

Proposition 187 also raises two interesting legal questions: (1) does the undocumented status of aliens within itself form sufficient grounds for denying governmental services or benefits and (2) is a state's action in this situation in conflict with federal program objectives, particularly with respect to preventing students from receiving the benefits of an education? In fact, one such issue arose in the *Plyler v. Doe* case, where the Supreme Court invalidated a Texas finance law that totally excluded illegal alien children from obtaining a free public education. Although illegal aliens do not represent a protected class, the High Court held that total denial of educational services to any child in the state's service area violated the equal protection clause of the Fourteenth Amendment.[48]

Should innocent students, in fact, be denied an educational opportunity in a situation over which they have no control? These are crucial issues surrounding Proposition 187 that must be addressed in determining the legality of the measure. Opponents of this measure assert that its procedures violate the Fourteenth Amendment's due process clause by threatening to deprive valuable rights without a hearing, which is mandatory before a deportation order may be entertained. Constitutional violations may occur if essential health care is terminated or if a child is dismissed from school and asked to leave the country without some form of due process or assessment of individual rights. Of course, these issues may be of no significance if aliens cannot document their legal status.

Proposition 187 has been and will likely continue to be a controversial issue. U.S. District Judge Mariana Pfaelzer, who ruled in November 1997 that much of Proposition 187 was unconstitutional, has held that the rest of this controversial measure is illegal. The U.S. District Court pointed out that California is powerless to enact its own legislative scheme to regulate access to public benefits. Judge Pfaelzer ruled that the state was permanently enjoined from implementing and enforcing the measure. In all likelihood, this decision will be appealed to the Ninth Circuit based on the overwhelming support among citizens of the state to pass this measure and the commitment from the governor's office to challenge the decision of the district court.

DISCRIMINATION AND THE INTERPRETER
FOR DEAF STUDENTS

Ruby Tyler, a member of the United Pentecostal Church, was employed by a school district as an interpreter and tutor for deaf students. In this capacity, she worked at an elementary school for one year and at a middle school for two years. During her interpreting, Tyler modified language she found objectionable or informed students that the speaker had used undesirable language. The school district developed new guidelines mandating that interpreters convey all information verbatim. In addition to word-for-word interpretation to hearing impaired students the district assigned her to work at the high school. Tyler refused to work at the high school under the new guidelines and was terminated by the district. She sued, claiming discrimination.

DISCUSSION QUESTIONS

1. Does Tyler have a valid claim of discrimination? Why or why not?
2. Was the district's action arbitrary, capricious, or in violation of Tyler's religious beliefs?
3. How would you assess Tyler's refusal to interpret personally objectionable material versus a deaf student's right to know what is communicated by speakers?
4. Is Tyler justified in her actions? Why or why not?
5. Is the district justified in its action? Why or why not?
6. How would the court likely rule in this case?
7. What are the administrative implications based on your assessment of this case?

DISCRIMINATION—DRIVING UNDER THE INFLUENCE

Mary Martin, a female, tenured teacher in a rural district, was stopped by the local police and charged with driving under the influence. She explained to the police that she had just left a Christmas party given by her principal and that she only consumed a few glasses of wine. She was also aware that some of her male colleagues were stopped in the past but not charged. Nevertheless, she was still charged. As her arrest becomes public, there is pressure from the school board for her to resign.

DISCUSSION QUESTIONS

1. Can the board force Martin to resign? Why or why not?
2. Is the infraction serious enough to warrant dismissal? Why or why not?
3. What about male colleagues who were not charged for similar offenses?
4. What rights does Martin have as a teacher in this situation?
5. What factors would the court consider in ruling on her case?
6. What conclusion do you think the court would reach in this situation? Provide a rationale for your response.

DISCRIMINATION AND A RECOGNIZED ACADEMIC INTEREST IN TEACHING

Martie Lyons, a seventh-grade teacher in an industrial city taught a course in life science using a school board-approved textbook. The course included a six-week section on human growth and sexuality. After instructing her students to get signed parental permission slips, Lyons showed two films on human reproduction and sexual development. Both films were provided by the county health department. The films were shown with boys and girls in separate rooms. When rumors spread that the films were explicit, some parents demanded that the teacher be fired. The board suspended Lyons without pay. Lyons subsequently filed a § 1983 lawsuit alleging a violation of her constitutional rights.

DISCUSSION QUESTIONS

1. Was the board's action justified? Why or why not?
2. Does Lyons have a legitimate claim? Why or why not?
3. Is the challenge by parents an invasion of Lyons' academic interest in teaching her subject matter? Why or why not?
4. Is there evidence of discrimination against Lyons? If so, when did it occur? If not, why not?
5. How do you think a court would rule in this case? Provide a rationale for your response.
6. What are the administrative implications of this case?

AGE DISCRIMINATION AND TEACHER EMPLOYMENT

Beth Stuart, a 55-year-old teacher, applied for a position in an upper-middle-class community in the eastern part of the United States. She had recently relocated and had accumulated over 25 years of teaching experience in another state. In fact, she had served as a substitute teacher in the district in which she applied for six months. She was interviewed for a permanent position to fill a sudden vacancy. The superintendent asked her to be prepared to begin teaching on August 28. Meanwhile, the superintendent continued to interview candidates for the vacant position. Stuart had decorated her classroom and was prepared to begin teaching when, three days before school opened, she was informed that another teacher had been hired instead. Stuart learned that the new hire was 25 years old.

DISCUSSION QUESTIONS

1. Did Stuart err in decorating her room in the absence of a contract? Why or why not?
2. Does Stuart have legal recourse? Why or why not?
3. Did the superintendent breach a verbal contract with Stuart?
4. Does Stuart have defensible grounds to file suit based on age discrimination? Why or why not?
5. How do you think a court would rule in this case?
6. What are the administrative implications of this case?

ENDNOTES

1. 42 U.S.C. § 2000e et seq.
2. *McDonnell Douglas Corp. v. Green,* 411 U.S. 792 (1973).
3. *Furnco Construction Corp. v. Waters,* 438 U.S. 567 (1978).
4. Ibid. 411 U.S. 792 (1973).
5. *Marshall v. Kirkland,* 602 F. 2d 1282 (8th Cir. 1979).
6. *Spears v. Board of Education of Pike County, Kentucky* 843 F. 2d 822 (6th Cir. 1988).
7. *Patterson v. Masem,* 774 F. 2d 751 (8th Cir. 1985).
8. *McCarthney v. Griffin, Spalding County Board of Education,* 791 F. 2d 1549 (11th Cir. 1986).
9. 20 U.S.C. § 1681 et seq. (1972).
10. 34 C.F.R. § 106.61.

11. *Northaven Board of Education v. Bell,* 456 U.S. 512 (1982).
12. *Grove City v. Bell,* 465 U.S. 555 (1984).
13. 29 U.S.C. § 794 (A) (1988).
14. 29 U.S.C. § 706 (8) (B) (1988).
15. 34 C.F.R. § 104. 3 (i) (2) (ii) (1991).
16. Ibid., 104.14 (a)
17. Ibid., 104.13 (a)
18. 42 U.S.C. § 12111(9).
19. Ibid.. (10).
20. *School Board of Nassau County Florida v. Arline,* 480 U.S. 273, 107 S.Ct. 1123 (1987).
21. *Chalk v. U.S. District Court, Central District of California,* U.S. Court of Appeals, 840 F. 2d 901 (1988).
22. *Kolstad v. American Dental Association,* 527 U.S. 526; 119 S.Ct. 2118; 144 L. Ed. 2d 494 (1999).
23. Ibid.
24. *Brown v. Board of Education,* 347 U.S. 483, 74 S.Ct. 686 (1954).
25. *Keyes v. School District No. 1,* 413 U.S. 189, 93 S.Ct. 2686 (1973).
26. *Griggs v. Duke Power Company,* 401 U.S. 424, 91 S.Ct. 849 (1971).
27. *United States of America v. South Carolina,* 445 F. Supp 1094, affirmed 434 U.S. 1026, 98 S.Ct. 756 (1978).
28. *International Brotherhood of Teamsters v. United States,* 431 U.S. 324, 97 S.Ct. 1843 (1977).
29. *Cunico v. Pueblo School Dist. No. 60,* 917 F. 2d 431 (10th Cir. 1990).
30. *Thomas v. Washington County School Board,* 915 F. 2d 922 (4th Cir. 1990).
31. *Daniels v. City of Alcoa,* 732 F. Supp. 1467 (E.D. Tenn. 1989).
32. *Estate of Thornton v. Caldor, Inc.,* 472 U.S. 703 (1985).
33. *Transworld Airlines Inc. v. Hardison,* 432 U.S. 63, 97 S.Ct. 2264 (1977).
34. *Hunter v. Regents of the University of California,* 190 F. 3d 1061 (9th Cir. 1999).
35. *Grutter v. Bollinger,* 123 S.Ct. 2325 U.S., 2003.
36. *Gratz v. Bollinger,* 123 S.Ct. 2411 U.S., 2003.
37. *Massachusetts Board of Regents v. Murgia,* 427 U.S. 307 (1976).
38. *Morrow v. Duval County School Board,* 514 So. 2d 1086 (Fla. 1987).
39. *Carlyle v. Independent School District,* 811 P. 2d 618 (Okl. App. 1991).
40. *Wooden v. Board of Education of Jefferson County,* 931 F. 2d 376 (6th Cir. 1991).
41. *Cleveland Board of Education v. LaFleur,* 414 U.S. 632 (1974).
42. *Maganuco v. Leyden Community High School Dist. 212,* 939 F. 2d 440 (7th Cir. 1991).
43. 29 C.F.R. § 1604.11(a) (1991).
44. *Meritor Savings Bank v. Vinson,* 106 S.Ct. 2399 (1986).
45. *Gebser v. Lago Vista Indep. Sch. Dist.,* 524 U.S. 274; 118 S.Ct. 1989; 141 L. Ed. 2d 277.
46. *Charlton v. Paramus Board of Education,* 25 F. 3d 194 (3rd Cir. 1994).
47. *Franklin v. Gwinnett County Public Schools,* 112 S.Ct. 1028 (1992).
48. *Plyler v. Doe,* 457 U.S. 202 (1982).

CHAPTER 10

RECRUITMENT, TENURE, DISMISSAL, AND DUE PROCESS

RECRUITMENT OF PERSONNEL

School officials should recognize and value the need for a diverse workforce within their districts. Therefore, efforts should be made to recruit and retain the mose diverse pool of qualified candidates the district can afford to compensate. With the critical shortage of teachers across the country, especially minorities, the recruitment and retention process becomes increasingly competitive. Many districts have created incentives to attract the brightest and best personnel through low-interest mortgages, forgivable college loans, and discounts on certain purchases, as well as signing bonuses.

However, one important dimension of the recruitment/retention process is the image that the district projects through the recruitment process. A district that projects a professional image and has well-defined processes to support its mission is generally more appealing to prospective candidates. Therefore, it is important to make a positive impression on candidates as school officials assess them and they assess the district. A well-organized and legally defensible interview process contributes significantly to the candidates' overall impression of the district and further protects the district from allegations of unfair treatment.

The Employment Interview

An important component of the recruitment process is the employment interview. The interview process is most effective when each candidate is assessed by a select panel of interviewers. The panel should resist judging candidates until the interview has been completed. Time should be allocated between interviews for all interviewers to conduct an evaluation of each candidate. A scoring system, particularly one that is linked to competencies, may enhance the process enormously. Those conducting interviews should be trained to avoid racial and other biases. Written guidelines should be developed for all persons conducting interviews. Checklists are also valuable tools to ensure that all relevant areas are covered.

Questions raised during the interview should relate to the position each candidate is pursuing. Any questions needed to determine whether the candidate meets the job requirements with respect to hours, overtime, and mobility should be raised equally of men and women. The assessment of candidates, wherever possible, should be based on factual evidence of past performance, behavior, and achievements. Open-ended questions should be raised by using such words and phrases as *who, what, tell us more*, and *describe* to encourage candidates to express themselves as much as possible. Questions regarding marital status, credit rating, number of children, spouse employment, and arrest record are potentially discriminatory questions and should be avoided. Questions dealing with pregnancy, plans for a family, or intent to marry should be avoided. Questions regarding religious beliefs or affiliation are illegal and should be avoided. Inquiries regarding the type of military discharge a candidate received may be potentially discriminatory, as well as questions about organizations with which a candidate is affiliated. Employment applications typically should not include requests for the following:

- Race
- Age
- Birthdate
- Birthplace
- National origin
- Marital status
- Number of children
- Gender
- Height
- Weight (unless demonstrably necessary as requirements for certain jobs)
- Home ownership
- Religious affiliation
- Type of military discharge
- Photograph

A record should be maintained regarding why each candidate was or was not recommended. This type of documentation may prove useful in the event that a candidate files a legal challenge if he or she was not recommended for an employment position.

When an applicant is under serious consideration for employment, a thorough reference check is appropriate and should be expected. A background check regarding criminal convictions is also appropriate and should be initiated to ensure that students are not exposed to undesirable personnel.

Hiring Discrimination

School districts that develop a well-defined and focused process that is legally defensible tend to have a greater opportunity to attract and retain quality personnel while minimizing legal challenges. Legal challenges do arise during the employment process as illustrated.

One such case involving religious discrimination arose in California when two Jehovah's Witnesses applied for positions with the California community college district.[1] In accordance with state-mandated preemployment procedures, the district required applicants to sign an oath swearing allegiance to the U.S. and California constitutions. The applicants refused to take the oath because it conflicted with their religious beliefs. The district rejected their applications. They then filed suit against the district under the Religious Freedom Restoration Act (RFRA) in the U.S. District Court for the District of

California, challenging the validity of the loyalty oath. The district moved for summary judgment. The court held that requiring applicants to take a loyalty oath placed an undue burden on their right to free exercise of religion. Although employee loyalty was a compelling state interest, the evidence failed to establish that a loyalty oath was an effective way to achieve this goal. An alternative oath directed to an applicant's actions rather than his or her beliefs would be equally effective and less restrictive. Because the loyalty oath could not be justified under the compelling interest test articulated in the RFRA, the court enjoined the district from administering the oath.

Another case involving employment discrimination arose when a black Florida man applied for a full-time teaching position with a county school district.[2] He was not hired. He then filed a complaint with the Florida Commission of Human Relations, alleging that he had been denied employment because of his sex and race. A formal hearing was conducted. The hearing officer determined that the teacher had presented a *prima facie* case of discrimination and that the school board had failed to present a legitimate, nondiscriminatory reason for not hiring the teacher. The commission then ordered the school board to cease discriminating on the basis of race and sex, to offer the teacher the next available full-time position for which he was qualified, and to pay the teacher back pay. The school board appealed to the District Court of Appeal of Florida.

The appellate court first noted that the evidence supported the commission's determination that the teacher had been discriminated against. However, it stated that the teacher had presented no evidence that he had been economically damaged by the discriminatory actions of the board. Therefore, the commission did not have the authority to permit an award of back pay to the teacher. The court affirmed that part of the commission's decision which ordered that the teacher be hired to the next available full-time teaching position, but reversed the commission's authorization of back pay.

TENURE

Tenure in public schools is prescribed by state statute. Although there are variations among states, most tenure laws are designed to protect teachers. The *tenure contract* is designed primarily to provide a measure of security for teachers and to ensure that they are protected from arbitrary and capricious treatment by school authorities. Tenure also is viewed as a means of providing a degree of permanency in the teaching force from which students ultimately benefit. Any teacher who earns tenure or continuing service status also acquires a property right or a legitimate claim to the teaching position. Once a property right is acquired, the teacher may be dismissed only for cause. Tenure does not guarantee continued employment, but it does ensure that certified school personnel may not be arbitrarily removed from their employment positions without due process of law. The intended purpose of tenure laws has been described by the courts. One court described it in this manner:

> While tenure provisions . . . protect teachers in their positions from political or arbitrary interference, they are not intended to preclude dismissal where the conduct is detrimental to the efficient operation and administration of the schools of the district. . . . Its objective is to improve the school system by assuring teachers of experience and ability a continuous service based upon merit, and by protecting them against dismissal for reasons that are political, partisan or capricious.[3]

Through this protection, teachers are insulated from special-interest groups and political factions, thereby enabling them to perform their professional duties without undue interference. When this occurs, the educational system is improved and students derive the benefits of quality education.

Acquisition of Tenure

In a number of states, tenure may be attained only after the teacher has successfully completed three successive years (the probationary period) and receives an offer for reemployment for the succeeding year. The *probationary period* is one in which the nontenured teacher is seeking tenure. School boards are provided broad latitude in determining whether tenure should be granted. During the probationary period, a teacher may be nonrenewed at the end of the contract year without cause or dismissed during the year with cause. In the case of the latter, the teacher must be afforded full due process rights. There is no requirement for due process provisions in cases involving nonrenewal, unless the teacher is able to demonstrate that nonrenewal was based purely on personal or political motives or motivated by arbitrary and capricious actions involving infringement on constitutional rights. This is usually a difficult burden of proof to meet, but the ultimate burden rests with the probationary teacher.

Since state laws prescribe that certain substantive and procedural requirements be met regarding tenure, it is essential that school districts adhere to these requirements (see Chapter 8). Generally, state statutes identify a specific date in which a probationary teacher must be informed that employment opportunities will no longer be available for the succeeding year. This notice informing the teacher of nonrenewal is normally forwarded to the teacher by certified or registered mail to the latest known address on or before a specified date. If the district fails to meet this requirement, the teacher may have gained employment for the following year. When a teacher has completed three consecutive years in the same district and does not receive timely notice of nonrenewal, the teacher may have acquired tenure by *default*. It is essential that school officials meet statutory requirements in matters involving proper notification.

An interesting case arose in New Jersey regarding the interpretation of requirements for attaining tenure. The case involved a New Jersey learning disabilities teacher who was later classified as a school psychologist. She had worked as a psychologist for over two years, until a work-related injury forced her to take an involuntary leave of absence. Her employment was terminated by the board six months after her leave was approved. The psychologist alleged that she was wrongly terminated and had, in fact, accumulated the necessary 30 months to attain tenure, even though she had worked for only 28 months at the time of her injury. She filed an appeal with the state board of education, which agreed that the termination violated her tenure rights.

The New Jersey Superior Court, Appellate Division, affirmed the state board's decision. The school district then appealed to the Supreme Court of New Jersey. The court held that employees who took sick leave remained school district employees for the duration of their leave.[4] Therefore, the psychologist was not prohibited from completing her probationary period while on leave. The use of the leave did not prevent the psychologist from attaining tenure.

In reviewing this case, it is apparent that an official and sanctioned sick leave may not prevent a teacher from accumulating time toward statutory tenure. Boards of education must be aware of the specific provisions of their state's tenure law to avoid costly and unnecessary litigation.

A rather intriguing case arose in New York involving a recommendation for tenure based on a clerical error.[5] The plaintiff, Shaffer, began working as a part-time special education teacher for the district in November 1994 and was appointed the following year to a probationary, tenure-track position for the three-year term from September 1, 1995, through September 1, 1998. In early 1998, she was recommended for tenure by her principal and immediate faculty supervisor. However, on March 30, 1998, the district superintendent wrote to Shaffer advising her that he would be recommending to the school board that her services be discontinued as of June 30, 1998. The superintendent's decision was based on Shaffer's record of excessive absenteeism. Shaffer's absences did not exceed those permitted in the collective bargaining agreement, and she maintained that she was never warned that such contractually permissible absences could jeopardize her tenure eligibility.

After receiving the superintendent's letter, Shaffer began a campaign to convince the board and superintendent to grant her tenure. The teachers' union, various colleagues, Shaffer's supervisor, and a former board member contacted board officials on Shaffer's behalf.

On May 29, 1998, the superintendent submitted a recommendation containing a list of tenure appointments to the school board for their approval. Shaffer's name was on the list with an effective tenure date of September 1, 1998. Officials contended that Shaffer's name was included as the result of a clerical error in the superintendent's office. Shaffer brought § 1983 suit claiming that the defendants had illegally revoked her tenure and dismissed her after listing her among teachers to whom tenure had been awarded. School defendants moved to dismiss her claim on grounds that grant of tenure had been a clerical error that was promptly rescinded. The U.S. District Court for the Northern District of New York issued an injunction granting tenure to Shaffer and ordering her reinstated with back pay. The school board appealed. The court of appeals held that certification was appropriate because of the undecided questions involving whether the board's action gave the teacher protections accorded tenured teachers and whether the board could lawfully revoke tenure thereafter by its action.

The disposition of Shaffer's federal claims depended on questions of state law as to whether Shaffer was granted tenure and, if so, whether the board's subsequent revocation of that tenure was lawful. Under New York law, a "tenured teacher has a protected property interest in her position and a right to retain it subject to being discharged for cause in accordance with the provisions of education law." As outlined in N.Y. Educ. Law § 3012, the causes for which a tenured teacher may be dismissed do not appear to encompass contractually permissible absences—the reason given in this case. However, the services of a probationary teacher may be discontinued at any time during the probationary period, on the recommendation of the superintendent of schools, by a majority vote of the board of education. Thus, the grounds for Shaffer's dismissal may well have been an improper basis for the denial of tenure to a probationary teacher. Tenured teachers, unlike probationary teachers, may be dismissed only pursuant to procedures outlined in the education law, which include, *inter alia*, formal filing of charges and a hearing before an impartial labor arbitrator—procedures that were not followed in Shaffer's case. Certification to New York Court of Appeals was appropriate for determining whether the school board's action in granting tenure to persons on the superintendent's list gave the teacher protections accorded tenured teachers even if her name was included by mistake and whether board actions thereafter could lawfully revoke tenure, as these issues involved unanswered questions about New York law. The court of appeals certified the ruling of the lower court, holding for the teacher.

School officials are well advised to avoid clerical errors, conflicting information that is communicated to nontenured teachers, and undocumented concerns that are introduced without the teacher's prior knowledge in cases involving an award of tenure.

In most states, no reasons need be given for nonrenewal of a probationary teacher's contract. These laws have been consistently challenged. One such challenge arose in New York when nontenured teachers were notified before the statutory deadline that they would not be reemployed for the succeeding year. The teachers challenged on the grounds that reasons were not given and due process was not provided. The court ruled that because they had not completed three years of teaching when notified of nonrenewal, they were neither entitled to due process nor the showing of cause for nonrenewal upon receiving the notice.[6] In sum, nontenured status involves

- No expectation for employment beyond the contracted year
- No right to be provided reasons for nonrenewal
- No right to due process
- No hearing

These conditions are valid unless the nontenured teacher produces evidence that a liberty or property right exists, in which case due process must be provided. A *liberty right* exists when damaging statements are communicated that may limit the teacher's range of future employment opportunities.

In a leading case, the U.S. Supreme Court addressed contract nonrenewal with respect to the legal dimensions impacting the process. In the *Roth* case, a nontenured teacher was hired by a state university for a fixed term of one year. He was later notified that he would not be rehired for the following year. State statute, university policy, and the teacher's contract did not provide for a pretermination hearing or require that reasons be given for nonrenewal. The teacher challenged the constitutionality of the university's action in dismissing him without notice of the reasons for its decisions and without the benefit of a hearing. The Supreme Court held that the state may opt not to renew a nontenured teacher's contract at the end of the fixed period of employment without providing reasons for the decision or without a pretermination hearing if he has not been deprived of liberty or property. In this case, no liberty or property interest was impaired; consequently, no due process or Fourteenth Amendment right is violated.[7]

Nonrenewal

The primary reason due process does not apply to probationary status centers around a limited property interest. During the probationary period, the teacher typically is offered a one-year contract, which is renewable each year, if the school board elects to do so. The probationary teacher, then, only has a property right for the duration of the one-year contract. When the contract period ends each year, the teacher loses the inherent property right because both the teacher and the district have met contractual obligations to each other. Due process and cause are necessary only if there is a showing that a property interest continues to exist. A property interest does not exist if there is no legal contract in force. As stated previously, if a district decides to dismiss a probationary teacher during the contract period, then full due process provisions are required, including notice, cause, and a formal hearing, because the teacher has a property right for the contract year.

Two interesting cases have arisen, in New York and Michigan, regarding nonrenewal of a teacher's contract. In the first case, a teacher who was denied tenure brought § 1983 action challenging the school board's refusal to allow her attorney to raise tenure issues during a public session.[8] On the school district's motion to dismiss, and the teacher's motion for partial summary judgment, the district court held that the teacher had no First Amendment right to appear through her agent at regularly scheduled, nonadversarial board meetings at which no action was going to be taken with respect to her property rights.

In that case the teacher, Prestopnik, was employed with the Greater Johnstown School District from September 1, 1999 through June 30, 2002. The district superintendent did not recommend her for tenure, and the board of education affirmed the superintendent's recommendation. Prestopnik then hired an attorney to represent her in connection with her denial of tenure and termination of employment. Her attorney attended a public board meeting and attempted to request that the board reconsider the tenure decision concerning his client. The district attorney informed him that he would not be permitted to raise the issue of Prestopnik's tenure during the public session of the meeting. He was invited to address the board in writing on behalf of the plaintiff.

In the Michigan case, Flaskamp was a physical education teacher at Fordson High School from 1997 until 2001.[9] Teachers employed in the Dearborn public school system are eligible to receive tenure after a four-year probationary period. The board voted to deny Flaskamp tenure at the end of her four years because of an alleged sexual relationship with a former student that the board found to be inappropriate and the principal's statement that he could no longer trust her. Flaskamp brought § 1983 action against the school district and school board based on the board's denial of tenure due to her alleged intimate relationship with a high school student. On the parties' cross-motions for summary judgment, the district court held that (1) Flaskamp had qualified immunity from the right to privacy claim, (2) a constitutional right to intimate association did not extend to teacher-student relationships, and (3) her substantive due process rights were not violated. The district court granted the school board's motion. Under Michigan law, a teacher in probationary period that is denied tenure is not entitled to a hearing.

■ ■ ■ ■ ■ ▬▬▬▬▬▬▬▬▬▬▬▬▬▬▬▬▬▬▬▬▬▬▬▬▬

ADMINISTRATIVE GUIDE

TENURE

1. Teachers are entitled to fundamental fairness, irrespective of tenure status.
2. Tenure is not designed to protect teachers who are inept or ineffective.
3. Tenure should protect competent and effective teachers.
4. Teachers may be dismissed only for specified reasons that are based on objective and documentable evidence.
5. Due process procedural safeguards, as established by state statutes, should be followed to ensure that dismissal decisions are legally defensible.
6. Nonrenewal of a nontenured teacher's contract does not generally require due process or reasons, unless there is an alleged constitutional violation involved.

Tenure for Principals

Some states provide tenure protection for principals based on principals meeting certain statutory requirements. Most requirements for principal tenure are similar to those required of teachers—that is, three successive years of employment in the same district with an offer of reemployment at the end of the third year. There has been considerable debate regarding the merits of tenure protection for principals. Advocates of tenure contend that school administrators need protection against arbitrary and capricious actions of school boards. They also cite tenure as providing incentives to attract prospective candidates into administrative positions. Opponents argue that school administrators who are performing their jobs effectively need not be concerned with job security and that tenure tends to protect principals who are not effective as school leaders. Nationwide, only 13 states provide some type of tenure for principals:[*]

Alabama	New York
Hawaii	North Dakota
Iowa	Pennsylvania
Minnesota	Utah
Montana	Washington
Nebraska	West Virginia
New Hampshire	

In 38 states, principals have the option to return to a teaching position if terminated as a principal:[†]

Alabama	Georgia	Maryland	North Carolina	Utah
Alaska	Hawaii	Michigan	North Dakota	Vermont
Arizona	Idaho	Minnesota	Ohio	Virginia
California	Illinois	Missouri	Oklahoma	Washington
Colorado	Indiana	Montana	Pennsylvania	West Virginia
Connecticut	Iowa	Nebraska	Rhode Island	Wyoming
Delaware	Kentucky	New Hampshire	Tennessee	
Florida	Louisiana	New Jersey	Texas	

Principals are provided certain due process safeguards in 33 states:

Alabama	Kentucky	North Carolina
Alaska	Louisiana	Ohio
Arizona	Maine	Oklahoma
Arkansas	Maryland	Pennsylvania
Colorado	Michigan	Rhode Island
Connecticut	Minnesota	South Dakota
Georgia	Mississippi	Texas
Hawaii	Montana	Utah

Illinois	Nebraska	Vermont
Indiana	New Hampshire	Washington
Iowa	New York	West Virginia

Fixed-term contracts for principals appear to be growing in popularity among legislatures across the country. These contracts generally offer some degree of protection with respect to procedural safeguards if dismissal is recommended by school boards. While these fixed contracts vary in length from one to five years, the most common term appears to be three-year renewable contracts. There are 36 states that offer fixed-term contracts for principals.

Trends across the nation tend to support fixed-term contracts that are renewed based on performance. The intent of fixed-term contracts centers on creating increased accountability among principals based on the quality and effectiveness of their performance. Tenure as a concept for principals appears to be rapidly disappearing.

ADMINISTRATIVE GUIDE

PRINCIPAL TENURE

1. Principals on fixed-term contracts are entitled to due process hearings if their contract is cancelled prior to the contract expiration date.
2. If a principal is nonrenewed with timely notice at the end of the contract period, reasons need not be provided for the nonrenewal.
3. Principals may challenge nonrenewal if they believe such action was based on arbitrary or capricious action by the school board.
4. The burden of proof rests with principals who challenge nonrenewals to demonstrate arbitrary and capricious action by school boards.

DISMISSAL FOR CAUSE

Dismissing a teacher for cause is a serious matter, since the teacher has an inherent property right to hold the employment position. State statutes prescribe permissible grounds on which dismissal is based. In these cases, the burden of proof resides with the board of education to show cause based on a preponderance of evidence. The obvious benefit of tenure is that dismissal cannot occur without a formal hearing and the presentation of sufficient evidence to meet statutory requirements. This assures the teacher that procedural and substantive due process requirements are met.

Tenure laws include grounds for dismissal in virtually all states. While there are variations among states, these grounds normally include incompetency, insubordination, immorality, justifiable decrease in the number of teaching positions, or financial exigency, and a statement indicating "other good and just cause." This latter phrase provides the board with broader latitude to address other grounds that may not be specified in statute. A board of education may dismiss a teacher for almost any reason, so long as the reason is valid and meets the substantive and procedural due process requirements.

Incompetency

One of the more frequently used grounds for dismissal involves charges of incompetency. *Incompetency* is a vague term in many respects. In some states, incompetency is the sole grounds for dismissal, using almost any reason to comprise this category. Most commonly, *incompetency* refers to inefficiency, a lack of skill, inadequate knowledge of subject matter, inability or unwillingness to teach the curricula, failure to work effectively with colleagues and parents, failure to maintain discipline, mismanagement of the classroom, and attitudinal deficiencies. Since the court views the teaching certificate as *prima facie* proof of competency, the burden of proof challenging a teacher's competency rests with the school board. The competent teacher is generally viewed as a person who has the knowledge, skills, and intelligence of the average or ordinary teacher.

Courts often view incompetency as a term characterized by a lack of knowledge, skill, intelligence, and, in some instances, professionalism. These characterizations may impede the teacher's effectiveness in the classroom, his or her teaching methods and strategies, as well as the teacher's overall ability to create a proper learning environment for students. It is very difficult to sustain charges of incompetency in the absence of a systematic and continuous evaluation process with feedback designed to assist the teacher in improving performance.

Fundamental fairness dictates that an evaluation process be employed. For example, a case involving charges of incompetency arose in Missouri when an elementary administrator determined that a teacher had numerous communication problems. After giving her warnings, the administrator created a professional development plan, requiring her to attend teaching workshops and read materials on communication and instruction. After a number of evaluations, the principal determined that the teacher's performance was still unsatisfactory. There also was evidence of classroom management problems. After further meetings and warnings, the administrator issued a letter to the teacher, in compliance with the state tenure act, informing her that formal charges would be forthcoming unless she showed improvement within 120 days.

The administrator videotaped classes held by the teacher and followed with discussion meetings with the teacher. Although the teacher's deadline was extended, the administrator eventually recommended termination. The board approved the dismissal, which was affirmed by the Missouri Court of Appeals. The appellate court recognized that the tenure act mandated reasons and procedures for removing teachers—incompetency, insubordination, or inefficiency—and further, that a written warning specifying grounds for actions was initiated by the administrator consistent with the law. The court held for the district and against the teacher, stating that the board did act in good faith in contradiction to the teacher's argument. The evidence revealed that the administrator had made many efforts to assist the teacher in improving her performance and had provided additional time beyond what was legally required to comply with the development plan. The court affirmed the board's decision.[10]

It is clear from this case that proper evaluation, documentation, assistance rendered, and timely notice were crucial to the district's efforts to remove an ineffective teacher. Furthermore, all conditions of the tenure act were met. This case challenges the misconception that a tenured teacher cannot be dismissed. Tenured teachers can, in fact, be dismissed on incompetency charges when proper evaluation, defensible documentation, and procedural guidelines are followed consistent with the state's tenure laws.

If charges of incompetency are brought against a teacher, these charges should be preceded by systematic evaluations and documentation of performance as well as a thoroughly developed teacher improvement plan. Proper documentation and a reasonable time frame designed to allow the teacher to meet expected performance standards are critical to sustain charges of incompetence should it become necessary to do so.

There are many excellent examples of professional improvement plans, but any plan should minimally include the following components (see Figure 10.1):

- Teacher's name
- Teacher's position
- Evaluator's name
- Date of evaluation
- Competencies/Skills to be addressed
- Professional development goals related to each competency/skill
- Specific objectives to be met under each goal for a specific competency/skill
- Recommended activities to meet professional goals/objectives
- Time frame in which goals/objectives are to be met
- Types of support systems provided by school/district to assist the teacher in improving performance
- Performance assessment methodology and documentation that the teacher improvement plan was agreed upon by the teacher and the evaluator
- Documentation that the teacher and the evaluator discussed assessment results/improvements based on clearly defined goals/objectives

When these components are present in the absence of an unfair or arbitrary teacher performance assessment, school officials will likely succeed in sustaining charges of incompetency against a teacher who has consistently failed to meet required performance standards.

Insubordination

Insubordination is generally viewed as the willful failure or inability to obey a reasonable and valid administrative directive. In most cases, there is a discernible pattern in the teacher's behavior that reveals that the teacher has been insubordinate. However, there are other instances in which one serious violation may form the basis for charges of insubordination. Most cases involving insubordination are those in which the teacher has been given distinct warning regarding the undesirable conduct and has failed to heed the warning. In such cases, charges of insubordination are usually sustained.

To succeed with insubordination charges, administrators must have documented evidence of the alleged misconduct with further evidence that the administrative order or directive was valid. Insubordination charges are more likely to succeed when they are linked with teaching performance or related academic issues. If the evidence reveals that the directive or administrative order was biased against the teacher or unreasonable, insubordination charges will be difficult to defend. Also, there should be no evidence that the order or rules violated the teacher's personal rights.

An interesting case involving insubordination arose in Alabama when a school board reorganized the district, combining its high school and vocational school into a single

School _____ School District _____ Evaluator _____ Date _____

Teacher _____ Grade Level(s) _____

Competency/Skill Area(s)	Professional Development Goals/Objectives	Proposed/Planned Activities	Designated Time Frame	Support Services Provided by the School District	Assessment Methods	Progress Checkpoints (Dates) 1 2 3

Summary of Assessment Results/Improvements

Evaluator's Responses	Recommendations for Continued Growth and Development	Teacher's Comments

Agreement on plan as developed   Teacher _____ Date _____ Evaluator _____ Date _____

Confirmation of discussion regarding assessment results/improvements   Teacher _____ Date _____ Evaluator _____ Date _____

FIGURE 10.1 Sample Teacher Improvement Plan

facility. The board notified all affected teachers of its intent to transfer them prior to the beginning of the new year. The new facility had not been completed when the new year commenced, so teachers and students continued to report to the old facility. When the new facility was completed, teachers and students reported. The auto mechanics teacher was ordered to report to the new facility. The teacher claimed that the new facility was not secure enough to protect his tools and equipment, and he refused to comply. A meeting was held in which the teacher was provided an opportunity to voice his concerns. Following the meeting, the teacher stated that he would report to the new facility. When he failed to do so, the school board voted to terminate his contract. The state tenure commission affirmed the dismissal. The teacher appealed to the Court of Civil Appeals of Alabama.

The court of appeals held that the teacher's termination for insubordination and neglect of duty was justified under the state tenure law. *Insubordination* was defined by state law as the willful refusal of a teacher to obey an order that a superior is entitled to have obeyed so long as such order is reasonably related to the duties of the teacher. Because the order to report to the new school was reasonable, the teacher's refusal to do so, after receiving two reprimands, constituted insubordination. The dismissal was affirmed.[11]

In this case, insubordination was sustained based on failure to follow a reasonable order from superiors. Unlike many cases of insubordination, no discernible pattern was evident, although two reprimands were issued to the teacher. Those two reprimands, coupled with the teacher's refusal to comply, formed the basis for charges of insubordination. In many ways, insubordination is easier to document and prove than most other grounds for dismissal.

Immorality

Immorality is cited in relevant state statutes as grounds for dismissal and involves conduct that violates the ethics of a particular community. Some state laws refer to *immorality* as "unfitness to teach" or behavior that sets a poor example for students and violates moral integrity. One court has held that the conduct in question must not only be immoral under the particular community standards test but must also be found to impair the teacher's ability to teach.[12] This latter statement seems to reflect the consensus of court decisions regarding issues of immorality in that there must be a showing that the conduct in question impairs the teacher's effectiveness in the classroom.

Other acts that have fallen under the category of immorality include homosexual conduct, unprofessional conduct, criminal activity involving moral turpitude, and sexual activities involving students. Any act or behavior that substantially interferes with the education of children and has a direct impact on the teacher's fitness to teach usually forms the basis for immorality charges. One fundamental issue courts seek to address is a determination of whether the teacher's alleged conduct adversely affects teaching performance and effectiveness. The response to this issue, in many cases, will determine whether a teacher should be dismissed.

Homosexuality and Employment

State statutes, in many instances, cite unprofessional conduct as grounds for teacher dismissal. Since homosexual lifestyles may call into question concerns regarding professional conduct, courts have been consulted, with increasing frequency, to adjudicate issues regarding homosexual behavior involving public school teachers. The courts have not been altogether consistent in their rulings regarding employment rights of homosexual public school teachers. A few state laws, however, have become more liberal by not regarding homosexual relationships among consenting adults as a violation.

There seems to be a growing trend toward liberalizing state statutes based on the national recognition of gay rights and greater acceptance of lifestyle issues across the country. In fact, eight states and more than 100 municipalities prohibit discrimination based on sexual orientation. Even though there is a disparity among the courts in ruling on homosexuality, one pivotal issue seems to involve *private acts versus public acts.* If the act is private and does not involve students, there is a greater tendency to be supported by the courts. However, if the act becomes public knowledge or if it is committed in public, there is a greater likelihood that the courts will uphold dismissal on grounds of immorality. The following examples illustrate the disparity among the courts on the issue of homosexuality:

1. The U.S. Sixth Circuit Court of Appeals held that the Constitution permitted dismissal of a teacher who divulged to her colleagues that she was homosexual and in love with another woman.[13]
2. A teacher admitted, when asked, that she was homosexual. She was promptly dismissed on grounds of immorality when it became known to the public, who became very agitated. The teacher filed suit, alleging wrongful dismissal. The court ruled that immorality as a ground for dismissal was unconstitutionally vague. Strangely, the teacher was awarded monetary damages but not reinstatement to her teaching position.[14]
3. A district court held that a teacher's private homosexuality would not be permissible grounds for dismissing him from his teaching position. On appeal, the Fourth Circuit Court ruled that even when the teacher made public comments on television regarding his homosexuality, such statements were protected by First Amendment freedoms.[15]

However, the Supreme Court has recently ruled on the constitutionality of private consenting homosexual acts. While this case did not involve teachers, it has implications for teachers who enjoy most of the personal rights of average citizens.

A recent landmark 7–2 U.S. Supreme Court ruling grew out of a case in Texas when John Geddes Lawrence and Tyron Garner were arrested by police officers who entered Lawrence's apartment and observed Lawrence and Garner engaging in intimate sexual conduct.[16] The two men were arrested, held in custody overnight, charged, and convicted before a justice of the peace. The arresting officers were responding to an anonymous call regarding an alleged weapons disturbance in a private residence. Texas maintained a statute making it a crime for two persons of the same sex to engage in certain intimate sexual conduct. In this case, the statute applied to adult males who had engaged in a consensual act of sodomy in the privacy of home.

One similar Georgia statute was upheld in a previous U.S. Supreme Court case *Bowers v. Hardwick* in 1986 when the High Court held that school boards may validly dismiss teachers for homosexual activity. Justice Stevens dissented by concluding that (1) the fact that a state's governing majority has traditionally viewed a particular practice as immoral is not sufficient reason for upholding a law prohibiting the practice, and (2) individual decisions concerning the intimacies of physical relationships, even when not intended to produce offspring, are a form of liberty protected by due process.

The two petitioners in Texas argued that they had equal protection under both the equal protection and due process clauses of the Fourteenth Amendment. The U.S. Supreme Court heard this case and held that the Texas statute making it a crime for two persons of the same sex to engage in certain intimate sexual conduct violates the due process clause. Prior to the U.S. Supreme Court's ruling, the Court of Appeals for the Texas Fourteenth District considered the petitioners' federal constitutional arguments. After hearing the case *en banc*, the court, in a divided decision, rejected the petitioners' constitutional arguments and affirmed the convictions, which called for a $200 fine for each petitioner in addition to court costs.

The question facing the U.S. Supreme Court involved a determination as to whether the petitioners were free as adults to engage in private conduct in the exercise of their liberty under the due process clause of the Fourteenth Amendment. The High Court noted that laws prohibiting sodomy do not seem to have been enforced against consenting adults acting in private. A substantial number of sodomy prosecutions and convictions involve predatory acts against those who could not or did not consent, as in the case of a minor, the victim of an assault.

The Supreme Court, in handing down its ruling, stated that

> The present case does not involve minors. It does not involve persons who might be injured or coerced or who are situated in relationships where consent might not easily be refused. It does not involve public conduct or prostitution. It does not involve whether the government must give formal recognition to any relationship that homosexual persons seek to enter. This case does involve two adults who, with full and mutual consent from each other, engaged in sexual practices common to homosexual lifestyle. The petitioners are entitled to respect for their private lives. The state cannot demean their existence or control their destiny by making their private sexual conduct a crime. Their right to liberty under the Due Process Clause gives them full right to engage in their conduct without intervention of the government. It is a promise of the Constitution that there is a realm of personal liberty which the government may not enter. The Texas statute furthers no legitimate state interest which can justify its intrusion into personal and private life of the individual. The judgment of the Court of Appeals for the Texas District is reversed and the case is remanded for further proceedings not inconsistent with this opinion.[17]

Although this case did not involve public school employees, it does have serious ramifications for school districts. Private sexual relations between consenting adults are now viewed as a liberty right that receives Fourteenth Amendment protection. Therefore, punishment for these acts violates the equal protection and due process rights of those involved. Based on this recent ruling by the U.S. Supreme Court, school officials will not be able to approach this issue under the guise of immoral or illegal conduct, as was the case in *Bowers v. Hardwick*. School officials will increasingly need to focus on verifiable knowledge of the act and whether the act rendered the employee, particularly a teacher, ineffective in meeting his or her teaching responsibilities. School officials can no longer validly dismiss teachers for private homosexual activity. Thus, the nexus between private, homosexual activity and teaching effectiveness becomes increasingly pivotal in cases when school officials bring dismissal charges against consenting adults who engaged in sexual relations with persons of the same gender. The burden of proof will likely rise to a higher standard and rest squarely on the shoulders of school officials.

As early as 1969, California's Supreme Court held that a teacher who had engaged in a limited noncriminal homosexual relationship could not have his teaching certificate revoked unless there was a showing that he was *unfit* as a teacher. The court indicated that the board may consider the likelihood that the teacher's conduct may have adversely affected students or fellow teachers. The degree of the adversity anticipated, the remoteness in time of such conduct, and the extent that the board's action may adversely affect the constitutional rights of the teacher or other teachers involved in similar conduct are relevant considerations.[18] The courts generally recognize the state's authority to consider moral conduct of public school teachers and allow them by statute to determine if just cause warrants dismissal proceedings based on issues involving moral conduct. As stated previously, the weight centers around the teacher's acts and whether they render the teacher ineffective or unfit in performing his or her duties and responsibilities as a professional.

An historical case that addressed the question of fitness to teach arose in the state of Washington, where James Gaylord was discharged from his employment as a high school teacher by the school district. Gaylord had engaged in homosexual relationships for more than 20 years. He actively sought homosexual company and participated in homosexual acts. He was aware that his status as a teacher would be jeopardized, his reputation damaged, and his parents hurt if his homosexual lifestyle were revealed.

Gaylord's school superiors first became aware of his sexual status on October 24, 1972, when a former Wilson High School student informed the vice principal that he thought Gaylord was a homosexual. The vice principal confronted Gaylord at his home the same day with a written copy of the student's statement. Gaylord admitted he was a homosexual and attempted, unsuccessfully, to have the vice principal drop the matter.

On November 21, 1972, Gaylord was notified by the board of directors of the Tacoma School Board that it had found probable cause for his discharge, due to his status as a publicly known homosexual. His status was contrary to a school district policy that provided for discharge of school employees for immorality. After a hearing, the board of directors discharged Gaylord, effective December 21, 1972.

The court ruled against Gaylord, finding that an admission of homosexuality connotes illegal, as well as immoral acts, because sexual gratification with a member of one's own sex is implicit in the term *homosexual*. After Gaylord's homosexual status became publicly known, it would and did impair his teaching efficiency. A teacher's efficiency is determined by his relationship with students, their parents, the school administration, and fellow teachers. If Gaylord had not been discharged after he became known as a homosexual, the result would be fear, confusion, suspicion, parental concern, and pressure on the administration by students, parents, and other teachers.

The court concluded: "Appellant was properly discharged by respondent school district upon a charge of immorality based on his admission and disclosure that he was a homosexual" and that relief sought should be denied.[19] Even though there is a discernible trend toward national acceptance of gay rights, no court has yet held that homosexuals must be allowed to teach in public schools.

As previously mentioned, there is a lack of consistency in court rulings involving homosexual behavior, and the basic standard centers on *fitness to teach*. The overriding issues in recent years seems to evolve on the question of whether a homosexual lifestyle prevents the teacher from effectively executing his or her teaching duties. Courts have shown a reluctance to support or prohibit certain types of questionable conduct, based solely on conformity. Instead, they have required that there be a nexus between the questionable conduct and teaching effectiveness.

An unusual case involving homosexual behavior arose in the Tenth Circuit Court of Appeals of Oklahoma. The court addressed the question of whether a state may constitutionally mandate the firing of a public school teacher who engages in public homosexual conduct that poses a substantial risk of coming to the attention of school children or employees. An Oklahoma statute provided that its public schools could dismiss teachers for engaging in *public homosexual conduct,* which was defined as indiscreet same-sex relations not practiced in private. Public homosexuality was considered to involve advocating, soliciting, or promoting public or private homosexual activity in a manner that created substantial risk that the conduct would come to the attention of schoolchildren or employees.

The Gay Rights Task Force, a national organization promoting homosexual rights, some of whose members included teachers in the Oklahoma City Public School District, challenged the statute on constitutional grounds, claiming that the statute violated its members' rights of free speech, privacy, and equal protection. The district court held for the district, although indicating that the statute did restrict protected speech, it was constitutionally valid, given the Supreme Court requirement in the *Tinker v. Des Moines* ruling. The National Gay Rights Task Force appealed.

The Tenth Circuit Court also held for the district, stating that a state may constitutionally require the discharge of a public school teacher who engages in public homosexual activity, such as public acts of oral or anal intercourse, that poses a substantial risk of coming to the attention of school children or employees. The court further stipulated that the equal protection clause does not, at this time, view homosexuals as a suspect classification warranting strict scrutiny of laws that treat homosexuals differently from other groups. However, the Oklahoma statute does penalize free speech concerning homosexuality, without limiting the firing sanction to advocacy or inciting imminent breaking of the law. The First Amendment does not permit a person to be punished for advocating illegal conduct at some indefinite future time. Consequently, the part of the statute requiring dismissal or suspension for speech alone is severed as unconstitutional, while the remainder is permitted to stand. The decision was reversed.[20]

This case supported the state's right to constitutionally mandate the dismissal of a public school teacher who engages in public homosexual conduct, but disallowed the state to do so on the basis of speech in which one may advocate illegal conduct at some time in the unforeseeable future. A penalty cannot be imposed prior to the actual engagement in illicit behavior.

Conduct Involving Morality

Public school teachers serve in highly visible and significant positions. In many instances, they exert important influence on the views of students and the formation of their values. Based on their roles, there is an expectation that a teacher's character and personal conduct be elevated above the conduct of the average citizen who does not interact with children on a daily basis.

Questions involving teacher morality often involve personal behavior and lifestyle issues, as communities have developed expectations that teachers serve as positive role models for their students, particularly in such areas as dress, grooming, and moral and social behavior.

The recent U.S. Supreme Court sodomy ruling in Texas supports greater acceptance of diverse lifestyles. However In a significant number of cases, community norms, standards, and expectations are pivotal considerations in determining acceptable professional conduct. Due to variations among communities, court rulings have been fairly inconsistent. Although there is inconsistency in court rulings, it has been determined that teachers need not be viewed as *exemplary* in certain areas regarding their personal conduct. In fact, there appears to be a noticeable trend toward providing teachers more freedom in their private lives than has been provided in the past.

As previously mentioned, eight states currently prohibit discrimination on the basis of sexual orientation: California, Connecticut, Hawaii, Massachusetts, Minnesota, New Jersey, Vermont, and Washington recognize the rights of individuals to determine their particular lifestyles. Conceivably, other states may assume a similar posture regarding lifestyle issues. It will be interesting to determine the precise impact of sexual orientation on employment decisions rendered by school districts in the future. As emphasized earlier in this chapter, there has to be a nexus between an act committed by the teacher and his or her efficiency and effectiveness in the classroom to succeed in dismissal proceedings. Other examples of teacher morality may involve issues such as dishonesty, pregnant and unmarried teachers, unmarried teachers of the opposite sex living together, homosexuality, adulterous conduct, sex change operations, sexual advances toward students, and other related behaviors.

One of the most quoted definitions of the term *immorality* was established by the Supreme Court of Pennsylvania in 1939. It was defined as "a course of conduct as offends the morals of the community and is a bad example to the youth whose ideals of a teacher is supposed to be fostered and elevated."[21]

This course of conduct is sometimes referred to as *immorality* or *unfitness*, depending on state statutes. The courts have taken the position that immorality is not considered unconstitutionally vague in most jurisdictions. Although a high degree of vagueness is involved, courts have supported charges of immorality when it is related to fitness to teach.

The following summary illustrates the inconsistent nature of court decisions in the area of unprofessional conduct:

1. The Court of Appeals of California upheld the dismissal of a teacher who had executed an affidavit recounting her long and beneficial use of marijuana, which attracted national publicity.[22]
2. The Fifth Circuit held that being an unwed mother does not, per se, constitute immorality. The court invalidated a rule prescribing the employment or retention of unwed mothers.[23]
3. Lying was considered immoral when a tenured teacher was denied permission to attend a conference but did so anyway, and upon her return submitted a request for excused absences due to illness.[24]
4. A female teacher was not dismissed for writing letters to a former student. The mother of the male student discovered the letters and turned them over to the police and subsequently to a newspaper, which printed the letters. According to the court, the letters contained language that many adults would find gross, vulgar, and offensive. The court noted the teacher's excellent record and also noted that the letters did not adversely affect the welfare of the school community until public disclosure, which was not the result of any misconduct by the teacher.[25]

5. The Eighth Circuit Court of Appeals held for a teacher who was charged with unbecoming conduct for having allowed men not related to her to stay overnight in her apartment. The guests were friends of her sons.[26]
6. A court upheld the dismissal of a male teacher who underwent sex change surgery to alter his external anatomy to that of a female.[27]

These cases clearly illustrate the difficult task courts face in ruling on issues involving proper conduct of teachers. Again, given the changing dynamics of society and a general acceptance of various lifestyles in the United States, it is anticipated that the courts will face greater difficulty in the future as they attempt to balance the rights of the teacher with the interest of the state.

Criminal Activity

Charges of criminal activity committed by public school teachers will normally result in dismissal, based on general unfitness, immorality, and unprofessional conduct. Depending on the severity and specifics of the criminal act, revocation of the teaching certificate also may be appropriate, especially in cases where a conviction occurs. In a number of states, conviction of a felony or crime of moral turpitude will form defensible grounds for the revocation of the teacher's certificate. In other instances, a series of convictions for misdemeanors may also prove sufficient to remove a teacher from an employment position by revocation of the teaching certificate.

It is well established that dismissal for unfitness may not necessarily be dependent on criminal conviction. The fact that a teacher is charged with a criminal activity and is not subsequently convicted does not imply that the teacher cannot be dismissed from an employment position. The school district may address the teacher's behavior from the standpoint of fitness to teach, irrespective of whether a conviction is sustained through the courts, simply because the standard of proof is higher to sustain a conviction than it is to dismiss a teacher.

In a leading case, a school board dismissed a teacher for immorality and unfitness when he was charged with a criminal act involving oral copulation with another man. Even though he was acquitted of criminal charges, the school district dismissed him for immorality and unfitness. State statute permitted the board to dismiss teachers for sex offenses. The court held for the board, indicating that it was the board's purview to determine overall fitness of its employees, even in cases where the teacher has been acquitted of criminal charges.[28]

In another case, a tenured teacher was arrested and charged with disturbing the peace while under the influence of alcohol. He was also charged with attempting to fight and displaying a gun. The board dismissed the teacher for "other good and just cause." The board's decision was supported by the court as reasonable, based on the evidence.[29]

Drug possession convictions have also resulted in dismissals by school boards. Most state statutes make no specific reference to drugs as grounds for dismissal, but "other good and just cause" found in most statutes is sufficient to cover issues involving drug possession, use, and convictions. For example, a case arose in Georgia in which a tenured teacher was arrested for possession of cocaine and marijuana. The teacher pleaded guilty to violating the state's Controlled Substances Act. The evidence revealed that this was the teacher's first offense, and the court was lenient in placing her on probation. Due to the publicity surrounding the case, the district transferred her to two other teaching positions during the remainder of the school term. The board later brought charges against the teacher, resulting in her dismissal for immorality and other good and just cause based on her plea of guilty for possession of controlled substances. The court held for the board, stating that there were proven facts supporting drug possession charges by the teacher that were sufficient to support charges of immorality, even in the absence of criminal purpose or intent.[30]

It is important to note that when criminal activity involving teachers does not result in a conviction, school boards may still bring charges against the teacher strictly for school-related purposes. If the behavior associated with the criminal act is such that it meets the standards for *unprofessional conduct or unfitness*, the teacher may be dismissed.

Sexual Advances Toward Students

Courts have left little doubt that they will deal judiciously with matters involving improper sexual conduct toward students. The courts support the general view that teaching is an exemplary professional activity, and those who teach should exhibit behavior that is above reproach in their dealings with students. Many state statutes include provisions that require teachers to impress upon the minds of their students principles of truth, morality, temperance, and humanity. These are very high standards that teachers are expected to meet in their professional roles. Given the position of the courts and the provisions in many state laws governing teacher conduct, it is not surprising to find that courts consistently uphold school districts when they produce evidence that a teacher has engaged in unlawful sexual involvement with students.

One of the most flagrant cases, *Doe v. Taylor* (see Chapter 6), involving improper sexual conduct with a student arose in Texas. This case involved a Texas teacher who sexually abused a 15-year-old female student. Over a two-year period, the teacher cultivated a relationship with the student through overt favoritism and assigning grades she did not earn. He sent her love letters and cards and encouraged a friendly relationship with his daughter. The relationship with his daughter led to the student spending time at his home. He attempted to convince her to engage in sexual intercourse after kissing and caressing her over a period of time. After continuous efforts, she finally submitted to his advances, feeling that he was becoming angry and upset with her.

The principal received complaints from students and parents, as it became common knowledge that the teacher and student were having an affair. When news of the teacher's misconduct reached the superintendent, he instructed the principal to speak to the teacher. The superintendent was unable to substantiate the rumors, until an incident occurred six months later in which the teacher danced with the student in the presence of his wife at a school-sponsored activity and took her to a field and engaged in sexual intercourse.

When the victim's parents reported the abuse to the superintendent, the teacher was immediately suspended. The teacher subsequently resigned, after pleading guilty to criminal activity. The court held that school officials should have known that the student's constitutional right was violated. The superintendent was granted immunity but the principal was denied immunity by the Fifth Circuit Court.[31]

Courts in other jurisdictions have taken strong positions in ruling against teachers for sexual misconduct, as illustrated by the following rulings:

1. A teacher was dismissed for immoral conduct when he placed his hands inside the jeans of a student in the area of her buttocks and on other occasions squeezed the breast of a female student. The court determined the teacher's conduct to be grossly inappropriate.[32]
2. A male teacher was dismissed for professional misconduct when he tickled and touched female students on various parts of their bodies while engaged in a field trip experience. He also touched them between the legs. He was found lying on a bed, watching television with one of the female students. The court determined that his activities were sufficient to sustain charges of unfitness to teach.[33]
3. A tenured art teacher was dismissed for immoral conduct when he placed his hands on female students by giving back rubs which resulted in further sexual contact. Evidence was also presented that he had engaged in sexual intercourse with two students at various places in the building.[34]

Another interesting case arose involving undisclosed immoral conduct by a teacher. This case reached the court when a former student of a teacher, now employed in Alaska, informed the district that she was impregnated by the teacher when she was a 15-year-old student. The facts revealed that prior to the birth of the child, the teacher, then employed in Idaho, signed a confidential written agreement with the student's father under which the teacher was required to resign his position prior to the beginning of the new semester. He then pursued a teaching position with an Alaska school district and was subsequently employed. Ten years later, the district received notice from the student of the prior relationship.

On investigation and verification of facts, the district terminated the teacher's employment on grounds that his prior conduct constituted immorality. The teacher argued that his conduct prior to being hired by the district could not be used to constitute immorality. The teacher appealed to the trial court, which granted the district summary judgment. The teacher then appealed to the Supreme Court of Alaska. The state supreme court refused to accept the teacher's argument that prior conduct should not constitute immorality and grounds for dismissal. The court ruled for the board and stated that a practice would insulate from punishment any teacher who engaged in prior illegal or immoral acts and successfully concealed it. The teacher's prior immoral conduct and failure to disclose his criminal behavior provided more than sufficient evidence that the teacher's employment had been properly terminated.[35]

There are two important administrative implications regarding this case: (1) prior incidents involving immoral conduct may be used to form grounds for immorality charges and (2) districts should avoid the tendency to allow a teacher who has committed a serious act of professional misconduct to resign under special circumstances. The district has a professional obligation to dismiss the teacher and allow the record to reveal the basis for dismissal. Under no circumstances should the teacher be allowed to resign. Further, the teacher should not be supported for another teaching position in some other school district. To do so creates serious concerns regarding professional ethics. The courts have allowed no tolerance for acts of sexual misconduct by teachers involving students. This issue, perhaps more than any other, has received the most consistent rulings by the courts. There is no evidence suggesting that the court's posture is likely to change. Teachers are well advised to refrain from any improper advances or activities involving students.

A tenure dismissal case emerged in Oklahoma when a teacher made a threat to physically assault the school superintendent and another teacher on school grounds.[36] The question facing the court was whether such an act constituted moral turpitude justifying dismissal. Ballard, a teacher, was employed by the Colbert School District from 1984 until his termination on September 28, 1998. According to Ballard's complaint, from 1984 until 1991 he was employed as both a teacher and a baseball coach. In June 1991, Ballard protested a reduction in the baseball budget to the school board. Shortly thereafter, he was notified that the school board had decided not to renew his coaching contract. Another baseball coach was hired. In June 1992, the school board eliminated Ballard's teaching position as part of a limited reduction in force. After Ballard brought suit in state court, the parties settled. He was reinstated as a teacher and baseball coach in 1994. In July 1997, defendant Jarvis Dobbs was hired as school superintendent. Ballard alleged that school board members influenced the new superintendent to form a negative opinion of him. In May 1998, on the superintendent's recommendation, Ballard's contract was terminated. On August 3, 1998, the state court again ordered him reinstated.

The complaint alleged a series of interactions between Ballard and the school district preceding the event that formed the basis for Ballard's termination. Although the district court held that these events were irrelevant to the moral turpitude question, the allegations were included to permit the fullest consideration of whether Ballard's conduct constituted moral turpitude as a matter of Oklahoma law.

For the 1998–1999 school year, Ballard was assigned to teach physical education at the elementary school. On the morning of August 14, 1998, the school superintendent observed him in the copy room of the adjacent middle school. When the bell for first period rang, the superintendent instructed Ballard and another teacher to report to their assigned areas. After the other teacher left the copy room, Ballard informed the superintendent that he was already in his assigned area. When the superintendent threatened to write him up for not reporting to his assigned area, Ballard stated in a threatening tone, "If you do, I'll beat the shit out of you." When the superintendent asked if Ballard was threatening him, he replied "no, I'm telling you like it is—I'll do it right here."

The superintendent left the copy room to get a witness to the exchange, and returned with the assistant principal. When the superintendent again asked whether Ballard was threatening him, he replied, "What I said before still stands. I'll do it right here." After Ballard refused to leave the copy room, the superintendent left. Ballard told the assistant principal that he was going to hit the superintendent. Some of Ballard's threats were also heard by a teacher from the hallway outside the copy room.

Ballard then caught up with the superintendent and stated they needed to talk to straighten things out. The superintendent replied that they no longer had anything to talk about. At this point the two men were joined by the school principal. Ballard stated that he was tired of people talking about his wife, and that if it did not stop he would take matters into his own hands. In particular, he complained about comments made by the new baseball coach and stated in a threatening manner that "if the coach makes any further comment, he would pick something up and knock his head off."

On August 17, 1998, the superintendent and principal notified Ballard that he was suspended for his comments. After a hearing, the school board voted to terminate Ballard for moral turpitude pursuant to Oklahoma statute. Moral turpitude was the sole ground on which Ballard was terminated. Ballard brought a civil rights action in the federal district court and included a state law claim for a *de novo* hearing on his dismissal. After conducting a hearing and making the above findings of fact, the district court affirmed the board's conclusion that Ballard's conduct constituted moral turpitude justifying termination. On Ballard's motion, the court then dismissed the remaining claims.

ADMINISTRATIVE GUIDE

DISMISSAL

1. The teacher must be informed if an evaluation is conducted for any purpose other than the improvement of performance.
2. School authorities should avoid any actions regarding evaluation for dismissal that may be viewed as harassment or intimidation by the affected teacher.
3. School officials should be knowledgeable of their state's statutory definition of insubordination and ensure that cases involving insubordination are well documented. Professional disagreements between superiors and subordinates do not normally constitute insubordination.
4. Community norms and expectations regarding professional conduct of teachers are important considerations in cases involving alleged immoral conduct and dismissal.
5. Private acts of homosexuality and adultery may not form grounds for dismissal, unless there is evidence that such acts rendered the teacher ineffective in performing assigned duties.
6. There must be a showing that lifestyle choices adversely affect the teacher's fitness to teach and his or her effectiveness to perform assigned duties before disciplinary action can be taken by the school district.
7. Conviction of a felony or a series of misdemeanors may form grounds for dismissal and revocation of the teaching certificate.
8. Sexual misconduct involving students by school personnel will almost always result in dismissal.

Financial Exigency (Abolition of Positions)

Financial exigency occurs when the district faces a bona fide reduction in its budget that results in abolishing certain employment positions. Positions may also be abolished when the district encounters reductions in student enrollment. The courts will generally support districts that demonstrate the need to reduce their teaching force, commonly called *reduction in force (RIF)*, when there is evidence that a legitimate financial problem exists. Obviously, districts should implement RIF policies and procedures that ensure that substantive and procedural due process requirements involving school personnel are met. Generally, these due process expectations are not as stringent, since dismissal decisions are based on financial concerns as opposed to personal or performance issues. The courts, in supporting financial exigency, usually require school districts to demonstrate the following:

1. A bona fide financial crisis exists.
2. There is a rational relationship between the benefits derived from dismissal and the alleviation of the financial crisis.
3. A fair and uniform set of due process procedures is followed in dismissal decisions.

School districts attempt to use objective criteria in building their reduction in force policies. Districts will generally use the following criteria in making RIF decisions:

1. Subject matter needs
2. Teacher's length of experience (seniority) in the district
3. Teacher's length of experience in the teaching profession
4. Highest degree or certificate earned
5. Length of time in which the degree or certificate has been held
6. Subject matter qualifications
7. Teaching performance

School districts should also attempt to achieve staff reduction through voluntary retirements, resignations, leaves of absence, and transfers. These areas should normally be addressed before action is taken to implement a RIF plan.

In implementing a RIF policy, the name of an employee who has been terminated is usually placed on a recall list and remains on such list for a minimum of one year. Any teacher desiring to be placed on the recall list for an additional year may apply in writing, by registered mail, for retention of his or her name on such list on or before a specified date as determined by the district's RIF policy.

No new employee may be hired to fill a position for which an employee on the recall list is qualified and certified or immediately certifiable. In cases where more than one employee on the recall list is qualified, certified, or immediately certifiable for a particular position to be filled, employees with tenure must be given preference.

Any teacher on the recall list should receive, by registered letter, a written offer of reappointment, at a reasonable period of time prior to the date of reemployment. The teacher may accept or reject the appointment in writing, by registered letter, within a required period after receipt of the offer, or the offer is deemed rejected. A teacher may refuse to accept an offered assignment and remain on the recall list.

An employee who is reappointed should be entitled to reinstatement of any benefits earned or accrued at the time of layoff, and further accrual of salary increments and fringe benefits should resume at the point where they ceased. No years of layoff will normally be credited as years of service for compensation or retirement purposes. It should be understood that a layoff is a termination of employment subject to administrative and judicial review in the manner set forth in the relevant state statutes.

The courts view RIF policies favorably that include seniority as one of the major criteria in rendering termination decisions. School districts would be hard-pressed to defend dismissal of a seasoned teacher with a longer record of seniority in favor of one with considerably less seniority, when both are teaching in the same teaching area or the senior teacher is qualified to teach in an area in which the younger teacher is assigned.

A case of this nature arose in Oklahoma. This case involved a tenured teacher who had completed nine years as a classroom teacher in the same district. After a few parents complained about her teaching style, the district reassigned her to the position of elementary librarian. During the following school year, after the district's enrollment dropped, the superintendent recommended to the board that a reduction in force plan be implemented for the school term and that the elementary librarian position be eliminated. Further, the special education program had to be decreased by one staff member. The board voted to implement the policies, which resulted in nonrenewal of 15 teachers. When the board met to consider nonrenewal, the tenured teacher was provided an opportunity to state her case. The board voted not to renew her as librarian in accordance with its RIF policy. During the same meeting, however, the board voted to reemploy 15 nontenured teachers.

The tenured teacher filed suit in district court, seeking reinstatement. The Oklahoma Supreme Court held that the state's tenure law gives tenured teachers priority over nontenured teachers during RIF in those instances where the teacher is qualified to teach the subject for which the nontenured teacher is retained. Further, the board's RIF program violated the statutory tenure system. The court specifically found that even though the teacher had been reassigned to an elementary librarian's position, she had tenure at the time but because of RIF procedures, she was locked into a nonteaching classification. This classification prevented her from priority consideration for employment over nontenured teachers with less seniority.

The court stated that when a school board's RIF plan gives tenure-like priority to nontenured teachers, the board, in effect, has elevated its nontenured personnel to the status of tenured teachers. Whether taken in good faith or not, the court cannot support a school board's action that manipulates job assignments in a manner that defeats the rights of tenured teachers with seniority and circumvents the purpose and spirit of the state's tenure law.[37] RIF policies should make allowances for teachers with longer lengths of service who might hold certification in other areas to be considered for those positions held by teachers with less seniority. When a district is able to demonstrate that objective and verifiable criteria were used in its decisions and all persons affected were provided full due process rights consistent with state statutes, they should encounter few problems with the courts.

In a more recent case, a school district that created several new positions was required to rehire most of the employees it laid off rather than filling the positions with similarly qualified candidates.[38] The district laid off a number of employees due to a decrease in student enrollment. A high school that experienced severe disciplinary problems temporarily closed and four new positions were created to address student discipline when the school reopened. The district failed to rehire the laid-off employees into any of the new positions. The laid-off employees sued the district in a state trial court for violation of the Pennsylvania School Code. The court held that at the time the positions were filled, one or more of the laid-off employees had seniority for each of them. It ordered the district to hire the most senior laid-off employee for each position, retroactive to the position hire date. The district and affected employees appealed to the Pennsylvania Commonwealth Court, contending that the laid-off employees were required to pursue available administrative and collective bargaining remedies before filing a lawsuit.

The commonwealth court held that the trial court maintained the discretion to hear the case, since the labor union had not filed a grievance on behalf of any of the employees and it had concurrent jurisdiction to hear the case. It also rejected the district's assertion that the replacement employees were more qualified for the new positions than the laid-off employees. Although the educational needs of a school district may outweigh seniority as an employment consideration, the district in this case had failed to demonstrate that the new positions required any special certification or other criteria that justified the appointment of less-experienced employees. Since three of the laid-off employees demonstrated the proper certification for one of the new positions and had greater seniority than the selected replacement employees, the court affirmed the judgment in their cases. The fourth position required special certification and the district obtained an experienced, qualified employee to fill it. With the exception of this case, the court affirmed the judgment for the laid-off employees.

■ ■ ■ ■ ■

ADMINISTRATIVE GUIDE

FINANCIAL EXIGENCY

1. All employees affected by a reduction in force must be afforded full due process provisions.
2. The burden of demonstrating bona fide financial exigency rests with the board of education.
3. School districts may not use financial exigency as a means to remove an employee who has exercised a constitutionally protected right.
4. Seniority and job performance should receive priority in RIF decisions.
5. School district policy and/or state statutes should be followed judiciously in implementing RIF policies.

Good or Just Cause

Just cause is designed to provide the district broader latitude in dismissing teachers for causes not specifically identified in state statutes. It is not designed to allow the district to dismiss a teacher for personal, political, arbitrary, or capricious reasons. The same due process provisions must be met under this category as would be met under the more specific causes for dismissal. So long as the board can justify its actions as being fair and reasonably related to a legitimate state interest, there should be no challenge by the courts. Just cause is not a category used frequently by school districts; most tend to rely on the more specific causes previously identified.

Occasionally, a case involving other just cause is addressed by the courts. Such a case was decided by a Colorado Court when a fourth-grade teacher encouraged boys to come to his home for homework assistance and game play. Over a period of time, the teacher developed a close relationship with a 10-year-old student, who gradually began to spend most of his time at the teacher's home, with his mother's consent. Within the year, a father-son relationship had developed between the teacher and the child wherein the teacher engaged in a custody battle with the student's illiterate Spanish-speaking mother. The custody became widely publicized, appearing in the local newspaper. Dependency and child neglect charges were filed against both the teacher and the mother, after which six sets of parents requested that their children be reassigned to a different teacher.

The school superintendent, after having assessed the situation very carefully, recommended dismissal of the teacher. The school board supported the recommendation of the superintendent. Upon investigating the situation, a hearing officer also determined that there was adequate grounds for dismissal. After an unfavorable ruling at the district court level, the teacher filed an appeal with the Colorado Court of Appeals. The appeals court affirmed the decision of the district court, upholding the hearing officer's findings.

The court observed that the student had experienced no academic or behavioral problems prior to his close relationship with the teacher. Further, the teacher had taken advantage of his position to foster a relationship with the child. "Good cause" for dismissal was found under Colorado statute. Because the teacher's actions were reasonably related to his overall fitness to execute his duties and they had adversely affected his performance as a teacher, the court supported termination. The trial court decision was affirmed.[39]

Good cause may be used to bring dismissal charges against a teacher, particularly when there is a showing that performance and effectiveness are impaired and a question of fitness to teach arises as a major concern. Since this category is covered by many state statutes, school districts may use it so long as due process provisions are met. As with all charges, the burden of proof rests with school officials. In this particular case, the district met this burden.

ADMINISTRATIVE GUIDE

GOOD OR JUST CAUSE

1. Good cause provisions should not be used to arbitrarily dismiss a teacher from an employment position.
2. Good cause should never be motivated by actions that affect the constitutional protection rights of teachers, such as free speech and association.
3. The burden of proof should always reside with school officials to demonstrate that just cause is valid.
4. There should be evidence that the teacher's performance and effectiveness are adversely impaired based on his or her conduct.

COLLECTIVE BARGAINING

Collective bargaining has grown in popularity and appeal in public education. Although it has always provoked controversy, many educators view collective bargaining as a mechanism to achieve a greater role in management and operation of public schools. Since many of the issues involving collective bargaining focus on the rights of employees as well as terms and conditions of employment, its very nature sometimes evokes conflict and adversarial relationships between school boards and union representatives.

It is well recognized that collective bargaining has not always enjoyed the popularity it does today. In fact, it did not gain legal protection until the early 1930s in the private sector. The evolution of this concept in the public sector developed very slowly, due primarily to the belief and acceptance of governmental sovereignty. Public schools, as agents of the state, exerted almost complete control of school operations as well as terms and conditions of employment consistent with their state's statutory mandates and local district policy. There was a prevailing view among state lawmakers that this sovereign power should not be abrogated.

Collective bargaining gradually emerged in the public sector in the late 1940s, when Wisconsin became one of the first states to enact legislation allowing bargaining to occur. However, it was not until the 1960s that teachers launched a major effort to gain a greater level of involvement in the administration and operation of their schools. Most states currently permit some form of bargaining between teachers and school boards. These agreements may vary from required bargaining to some form of *meet and confer provision.*

Irrespective of these variations, the basic intent is to create teacher empowerment and shared power between teachers and school boards. Obviously, some states are more liberal than others in deciding on items that are negotiable. For example, arbitration is mandated in some states yet prohibited in others. In any case, the primary objective is to create conditions where school employees are afforded the opportunity to affiliate with a union without fear of reprisal for their participation. One common element found in most state statutes is a *good faith* requirement imposed on employers, which implies that they must bargain with the recognized bargaining unit with the sincere intent to reach a reasonable agreement. In fact, this good faith provision affects both parties during the bargaining process.

Private Sector versus Public Sector Bargaining

There are obvious differences between private sector and public sector bargaining. One of the most notable differences is that private sector employees do not enjoy constitutional protections, as do public sector employees. Public sector employees are afforded equal protection rights under due process as well as certain rights enacted by state statutes for their protection.

Private sector rights were severely restructured in 1947 with an amendment to the National Labor Relations Act (NLRA), which had passed in 1935 to support collective bargaining as an effort to improve management and labor relations. The National Labor Relations Board was formed during this time to remedy unfair labor practices. With the amendments to the NLRA, limitations were imposed on various union practices after widespread evidence of union corruption surfaced. The amended version resulted in the Labor Management Relations Act, commonly called the Taft-Hartley Act. This act was subsequently amended in 1959 with the Labor Management Reporting and Disclosure Act (LMRDA), which provided protection to private sector employees who faced various forms of union abuse. It also invoked penalties for misappropriation of union funds.

Another significant difference is that, in many instances, public school teachers are not permitted to strike. Proponents of public sector negotiations view this restriction as a real limitation in the sense that bargaining strength is weakened regarding the capacity to reject the terms and conditions offered during the negotiation process. In the private sector, rejection of an offer is most often followed by a strike when an impasse occurs. In states where strikes are not permitted by law, penalties are imposed on teachers and union officials, which may range from loss of salary to dismissal for teachers and stiff fines for union officials. When an impasse occurs, public sector bargaining is also affected by state and local budget restraints. Since funding is determined by state legislatures and dependent on tax projections and revenue, regulations regarding salary issues are limited by state appropriations to education, irrespective of bargaining agreements.

State Involvement

A number of states have passed permissive legislation to aid recognized union organizations. Some states support an *agency shop* measure, which stipulates that teachers must be a member in good standing with the union through dues payment or some form of service charge, if the teachers are not affiliated with the recognized bargaining unit. A few state laws make union affiliation mandatory for teachers as a condition to continuing their employment. This agreement is commonly referred to as *union shop*. Other states require teachers to affiliate with the recognized bargaining unit when they make application for a teaching position. This arrangement is commonly referred to as *closed shop*. Still other states have enacted legislation that protects employees from harassment by other employees and union officials because they elect not to affiliate with the bargaining unit. When a bargaining unit is granted the exclusive right to represent employees, it must do so on a fair and equitable basis, irrespective of whether the employee is a member or not. State law in most cases will require the union to do so.

Scope of Collective Bargaining

State laws vary regarding issues that are deemed negotiable. These issues normally fall under the categories of mandatory, permissive, and illegal. Issues involving conditions of employment—such as length of workday, school, teaching workload, extra-duty assignments, leaves of absences, and other fringe benefits—are almost always considered mandatory, which means that there must be bargaining issues involving both parties. Permissive subjects are generally based on common agreement between both parties and would not constitute a breach of duty to bargain in good faith. Issues involving personnel recruitment, selection, and induction are considered administrative prerogatives not subject to mandatory negotiations. Since these areas vary among states, there is an obvious lack of a clear distinction among these areas.

In areas involving mandatory bargaining, school boards are required to operate in good faith bargaining. As previously indicated, state statutes establish the framework regarding the scope of collective negotiations in public schools. Several basic issues emerge in relation to negotiation agreements. These normally cover areas that a school board can negotiate as well as those in which it cannot negotiate. Also covered are issues that must be negotiated until agreement is reached by both parties. There are issues that are not mandatory or permissive in some states. They are a function of negotiations between the teacher's union and the school board. They have included areas such as teacher's planning periods, changes in the length of class periods, nonteaching assignments, sick leave banks, academic policies, and many other issues.

By way of illustration, a case arose in Pennsylvania in which the local education association challenged the school board on an honor roll policy change. The association contended that such change required bargaining between the board and the association. The controversy arose when the school board raised the requirements for achieving honor roll status by one-quarter grade point as a part of a statewide effort by the state department to improve statewide education quality and accountability. A grievance was filed by the association against the board under the collective bargaining agreement. The arbitration held that its board violated the collective bargaining agreement by not involving the association in the policy amendment decision. The trial court, however, supported the district in holding that the new policy was the school board's inherent managerial prerogative. The association appealed to the commonwealth court, which held that the district was not required to bargain away matters of inherent managerial policy, particularly those dealing with academic standards, personnel matters, organizational structure, budgeting, and technology. The decision clearly established the prerogatives that the school board has that are not subject to negotiations. Although there are variations among the states regarding negotiable items, there is a great deal of consistency with respect to managerial prerogatives that must remain under the purview of the school boards.[40]

Impasse and Bargaining

On numerous occasions, the parties involved in negotiations fail to reach an agreement, and it becomes obvious that no further progress is possible toward resolution. When this occurs, an *impasse* has emerged. Some state laws include provisions that require both parties to continue to bargain beyond the termination date of the previous contractual agreement when an impasse is reached, which means that certain commitments must be honored by the school board before the expiration of the previous contract.

The regular negotiation process calls for a series of options designed to resolve the dispute. These options are as follows:

1. *Mediation* occurs when a neutral party is engaged to assist both parties in reaching objective solutions to the dispute at hand. The mediation is normally chosen by common agreement between parties. If mediation fails, another option is to engage a fact-finder.
2. A *fact-finder* is a third party who attempts to analyze facts and determine where compromise might occur. The fact-finder offers solutions that are not binding on either party. If the fact-finding process fails to resolve the dispute, the final step involves arbitration.
3. *Arbitration* occurs when a third party performs similar functions to those performed by the fact-finder. If the arbitration is *binding*, then what is recommended as a resolution to the dispute is binding on both parties.

Legal Issues

Numerous legal challenges have had an impact on collective bargaining in public schools. These challenges cover a broad range of issues, such as the right to strike, preferential treatment regarding the exclusive bargaining agency, preferential layoffs, free speech rights of teachers not affiliated with the union, good faith issues involving school boards, and many others. The courts have found it necessary to intervene in an attempt to settle disputes involving teachers, school boards, and union officials.

An interesting case arose in Wisconsin during negotiations toward a collective bargaining agreement when the union demanded that a provision be enacted to require all teachers within the bargaining unit to pay dues irrespective of their affiliation decision. During the discussion of this issue in an open meeting, one teacher, who was not a union affiliate, spoke briefly, urging that a decision be delayed pending further study. The state had passed a law prohibiting school boards from negotiating with individual teachers once an exclusive agent had been chosen. Thus, the state employment relations committee charged the district with violating state law by allowing the teacher to speak and further ordered that the board disallow this practice in the future. This ruling was challenged by the school board.

The court, in ruling against the board, indicated that an order that prohibits teachers who are not union representatives from speaking during public meetings is unconstitutional. Further, teachers enjoy First Amendment rights to express their views during public meetings when speaking on issues of common interest and such speech by the teacher was not an attempt to negotiate with the board but rather to express public concern.[41]

A case involving preferential treatment reached the Supreme Court when a layoff policy was challenged as discriminatory based on an agreement between the board of education and the teacher's union. The bargaining agreement between the board and the union included a clause that provided protection to members of certain minority groups against layoffs. The board did not comply with this provision until it was challenged to do so. When layoffs occurred, minority teachers were maintained, whereas nonminority teachers were not. This policy was challenged by the nonminorities, alleging discrimination.

The Court held that this action amounted to reverse racial discrimination, which must be justified by a compelling state interest. The board responded by suggesting the importance of maintaining a diverse work force and providing minority role models for students. The High Court ruled that the board's rationale did not constitute a compelling interest and could not be justified. The district's policy was held unconstitutional.[42]

In a final case involving a strike by public school teachers, the Supreme Court of Pennsylvania held that such strike presented a threat to the health and safety of the public welfare. This case arose when teachers voted to strike after only four days of instruction. The Jersey Shore Area School District filed for an injunction, requesting that teachers return to work. After a successful hearing for the district, the Court of Common Pleas issued an injunction, ordering teachers to return to work. The Jersey Shore Association subsequently filed for reconsideration and an additional hearing on the matter. When the Chancellor of the Court of Pleas refused to lift the injunction, the association appealed to the Supreme Court of Pennsylvania.

The state supreme court held for the district upon a preponderance of evidence, which revealed that senior high school students were placed at a competitive disadvantage with respect to instruction that would assist them in preparing for national tests for college admissions. Furthermore, many faced deadlines with respect to filing for scholarship aid with no direction provided by the counseling and guidance services. Other students at lower grades also were placed at competitive disadvantages with respect to state-mandated tests to determine whether remediation was needed. Finally, with only four days of instruction, students would be forced into remedial courses that they otherwise would not have needed. These findings, coupled with the threat of the district losing roughly $27,000 per day in state subsidies for each day it fell short of the mandated 180 days of school, resulted in the court's conclusion that such a strike created a threat to the health, safety, and welfare of the public. The court therefore upheld the commonwealth's order that teachers return to work.[43]

Workers' Compensation

Teachers are protected by workers' compensation in most states when they are injured during the course of performing their professional duties. The theory supporting workers' compensation is that the employing agency should assume responsibility for injury suffered by employees during the conduct of the agency's business. Workers' compensation does not normally apply in situations where an employee is willfully or wrongfully injured by the employer or a colleague. The injured employee does not need to prove that any injury resulted from a certain incident.

In recent years, increased flexibility and latitude have been provided in allowing compensation for a job-related injury that developed over a period of time. For example, a teacher might incur an injury over a period of time for lifting heavy equipment or performing routine tasks, such as rearranging furniture in the classroom. In some instances, an employee is covered by workers' compensation if he or she aggravates a preexisting condition. In all cases, there must be supportive evidence that the injury grew out of the executing of professional duties and responsibilities. It is very difficult, in most instances, to receive coverage for psychological or mental illness unless the employee can adequately demonstrate that he or she was involved in an unusually and unavoidable stressful work environment. An employee will not normally succeed in cases of self-induced stress that grows out of his or her ineffectiveness in performing expected job duties and responsibilities. Most states have explicit processes and procedures that employees must follow to receive workers' compensation, including a specified time in which injury must be reported, in injury situations covered by state statutes. Virtually every state has an agency that administers the program. As a last resort, employees may resort to the courts in cases where they are denied workers' compensation benefits once the state's procedures have been exhausted.

ADMINISTRATIVE GUIDE

COLLECTIVE BARGAINING

1. The collective negotiations process should always be guided by a good faith effort involving both parties—school boards and union officials.
2. School boards should not negotiate items for which they have no legal authority to negotiate (e.g., setting salaries and employing personnel) unless there is expressed statutory authority to do so.
3. Any sustained action taken by striking teachers that may disrupt educational opportunities for students will not likely receive court support.
4. Constitutionally protected rights and freedoms of teachers should not be impaired by collective bargaining agreements.

DISMISSAL OF TENURED TEACHERS

As the Principal you have recommended that two of your tenured teachers be terminated for cause. (You may determine cause.)

DISCUSSION QUESTIONS

1. Outline the procedure that must be followed in this situation.
2. Write a legally defensible letter to both teachers informing them of possible termination.
3. Cite relevant court rulings to document your written response.

NONTENURED TEACHER AND LIBERTY
INTEREST CLAIM

Mary Glendale was a ninth-grade social studies teacher. She completed her second year with Millsdale High School, which is located in a moderate-size middle class community.

She received notice from the superintendent and school board that her contract would not be renewed for the following year. Glendale later learned from reliable sources, that she had been described by her principal as antiestablishment and did able to relate well to colleagues. Mary filed charges claiming that her liberty interest was affected by her principal's comments.

DISCUSSION QUESTIONS

1. What does liberty interest involve?
2. Based on the definition, has a liberty interest been affected in this case? Why or why not?
3. If so, what steps should be followed to address liberty interest?
4. If not, does the district have any obligation to Mary Glendale?
5. How would the court rule in this case?
6. What are the administrative implications of this case?

INCOMPETENCY AND QUESTIONABLE PERFORMANCE

Gloria Williams, a well-respected tenth-grade social studies teacher, has taught at Johnson High School for over 15 years. Her formal evaluations were quite good under the previous administration. She was informally evaluated each year during her 15-year tenure. The new principal, Bob Mason, who has held his position for only two years, recommended dismissal for incompetency based on two informal assessments of William's performance.

DISCUSSION QUESTIONS

1. What are the chances that Williams may be dismissed for incompetency?
2. Is there sufficient evidence to sustain such a charge? Why or why not?
3. Ideally, what process should be used to successfully remove a teacher for incompetence? Outline the process.
4. Based on information provided in this case, has Gloria Williams been treated fairly? Why or why not?
5. How would the court likely rule in this case? Provide a rationale for your response.
6. What are the administrative implications of this case?

INSUBORDINATION—FAILURE TO CHANGE A STUDENT'S GRADE

Alice Hill, an eleventh-grade English teacher at Fairview High School, located in a fairly progressive school district, assigned the grade of F to a star basketball player, Tom Benson, who had failed to turn in assigned work. Hill encountered considerable criticism from coaches and other colleagues at school. A request was made by the principal, Jim Martin, for Hill to return to school and change the grade. Due to stress associated with this event, Hill was unable to do so and arranged for a substitute to cover her classes for two days. The principal recommended dismissal based on charges of insubordination for failure to return to change the grade.

■ ■ ■ ■ ■

DISCUSSION QUESTIONS

1. Was Alice Hill justified in not returning to change the grade? Why or why not?
2. Does the principal have sufficient grounds to recommend insubordination? Why or why not?
3. Did Alice Hill's failure to return constitute insubordination? Why or why not?
4. As principal, would you have taken the position the principal took in this situation? Why or why not?
5. How would the court likely rule in this case? Provide a rationale for your response.

UNPROFESSIONAL CONDUCT—SEXUAL ACTIVITY

Paula Gibson, an elementary school teacher in an upscale progressive city, was arrested by an undercover policeman for openly engaging in sexual activity with two men at a singles' club party. She was recommended for dismissal by her principal, Hank Doss, based on this conduct. Her defense was that these acts took place at a private party and should have no impact on her capacity to teach.

■ ■ ■ ■ ■

DISCUSSION QUESTIONS

1. Is the principal justified in recommending dismissal? Why or why not?
2. Should acts that occur in private be held against teachers? Why or why not?
3. Does Paula have a justifiable defense in this situation? Why or why not?
4. What standards would the court use in ruling in this case?
5. What do you feel the court's ruling would be? Provide a rationale for your response.
6. What are the implications for teachers and administrators in this case?

EXTRA DUTY ASSIGNMENT—CLUB SUPERVISION

Jack Smith is a nontenured teacher in a fairly progressive district. Because he expects to be married soon, he takes a part-time evening job to supplement his salary. Jack's principal, Carol Martin, has requested that he supervise a student club that meets twice a week after school. This will obviously conflict with Jack's part-time job. Jack does not want to cause trouble, but he really needs the part-time job.

■ ■ ■ ■ ■

DISCUSSION QUESTIONS

1. What is Smith's obligation to supervise a student club that meets twice a week after school?
2. Does the principal have the right to infringe on Smith's personal time?
3. Does Smith have a right to refuse to supervise the club?
4. How should Smith respond to Martin?
5. Can action be taken against Smith if he refuses? Why or why not?
6. How would the courts view this issue if the principal were to recommend nonrenewal based on Smith's unwillingness to supervise the student club? Provide a rationale to support your response.

ENDNOTES

1. *Bessard v. California Comm. Colleges*, 867 F. Supp. 1451 (#. D. Cal. 1994).
2. *School Board of Leon County v. Weaver*, 556 So. 2d 443 (Fla. App. 1st Dist. 1990).
3. *Pickering v. Board of Education*, 225 N.E. 2d 16 (Ill. 1967).
4. *Kletzkin v. Board of Education of the Borough of Spotswood*, 136 N.J. 275, 642 A. 2d 993 (1994).
5. *Shaffer v. Schenectady City School District*, 245 F. 3d 41 (Sec. Cir. 2001).
6. *Merhige v. Copiague School District*, 429 N.Y.S. 2d 456 (1980).
7. *Board of Regents of State College v. Roth*, 408 U.S. 564, 92 S.Ct. 2701 (1972).
8. *Prestopnik v. Johnstown School District*, 2003 WL 1678580 (N.D.N.Y. 2003).
9. *Flaskamp v. Dearborn Schools*, 232 F. Supp. 2d 230, 687, 172 Ed. Law Rep. 651 (E.D. Mich. 2002).
10. *Johnson v. Francis Howell R-3 Board of Education*, 868 S.W. 2d 191 (Mo. App. E.D. 1994).
11. *Stephens v. Alabama State Tenure Commission*, 634 So. 2d 549 (Ala. Civ. App. 1993).
12. *Thompson v. Southwest School District*, 483 F. Supp. 1170 (Mo. 1980).
13. *Rowland v. Mad River Local School District, Montgomery County*, 730 F. 2d 444 (6th Cir. 1984), cert. denied, 470 U.S. 1009 (1985).
14. *Burton v. Cascade School District Union High School No. 5*, 353 F. Supp. 254 (U.S. District Court, Oregon 1973), cert. denied, 423 U.S. 879 (1977).
15. *Acanfora v. Board of Education of Montgomery County*, 359 F. Supp. 843 (D. Md. 1973).
16. *Lawrence v. Texas*, 123 S.Ct. 2472, (2003).
17. *Bowers v. Hardwick*, 478 U.S. 186, 106 S.Ct. 2841, 92 L. Ed. 2d 140 (1986).
18. *Morrison v. State Board of Education*, 461 P. 2d 375, 386-387 (Cal. 1969).
19. *Gaylord v. Tacoma Sch. Dist. No. 10*, 88 Wash. 2d 286, 559 P. 2d 1340 (1977).
20. *National Gay Task Force v. Board of Education of Oklahoma City*, 729 F. 2d 1270 (10th Cir. 1984).
21. *Horosko v. Mt. Pleasant School District*, 335 Pa. 369 6 A. 2d 866 (1939), cert. denied, 308 U.S. 553 (1939).
22. *Governing Board of Nicasio School District of Marin County v. Brennan*, 18 Cal. App. 3d 396, 95 Cal. Rptr. 712 (1971).
23. *Andrews v. Drew Municipal Separate School District*, 507 F. 2d 611 (5th Cir. 1975).
24. *Bethel Park School District v. Krall*, 67 Pa. Cmwlth. 143, 445 A. 2d 1377 (1982).
25. *Darvella v. Willoughly by East Lake City School Dist. Board of Education*, 12 Ohio Misc. 288, 233 N.E. 2d 143 (1967).
26. *Fisher v. Synder*, 476 F. 2d 375 (8th Cir. 1973).
27. *In re Grossman*, 127 N.J. Super. 13, 316 A. 2d 39 (1974).
28. *Board of Education v. Calderon*, 35 Cal. App. 3d 490, 110 Cal. Rptr. 916 (1973), cert. denied, and appeal dismissed, 414 U.S. 807, 95 S.Ct. 19 (1974).
29. *Williams v. School District No. 40 of Gila County*, 4 Ariz. App. 5, 417 P. 2d 376 (1966).
30. *Dominy v. Mays*, 150 Ga. App. 187, 257 S.E. 2d 317 (1979).
31. *Doe v. Taylor Independent School District*, 15 F. 3d 443 (5th Cir. 1994).
32. *Fadler v. Illinois State Board of Education*, 153 Ill. App. 3d 1024, 106 Ill. 840, 506 N.E. 2d 640 (5 Dist. 1987).
33. *Weissman v. Board of Education of Jefferson County School District No. R-1*, 190 Colo. 414, 547 P. 2d 1267 (1976).
34. *Johnson v. Beaverhead City High School District*, 236 Mont. 532, 771 P. 2d 137 (1989).

35. *Toney v. Fairbanks North Star Borough School District Board of Education*, 881 P. 2d 1112 (Alaska 1994).

36. *Ballard v. Independent School District No. 4 of Byran County, Oklahoma*, 320 F. 3d 1119; U.S. App. (Okla. 2003).

37. *Babb v. Independent School Dist. No. 1–5*, 829 P. 2d 973, 74 Ed. Law Rptr 977.

38. *Davis v. Chester Upland School District,* No. 2701 C.D. 1999, 2000 Pa. Commw. Lexis 349 (Pa. Commw. Ct. 2000).

39. *Kerin v. Board of Ed Laman School Dist No. Re-2 Prowers County*, 860 P. 2d 574 (Colo. App. 1993).

40. *Rochester Area School District v. Rochester Education Association*, No. 2915 C.D. 1999 (Pa. Commw. Ct. 2000).

41. *Madison v. Wisconsin Employment Relations Commission*, 429 U.S. 167, 97 S.Ct. 421 (1976).

42. *Wygant v. Jackson Board of Education,* 476 U.S. 267, 106 S.Ct. 1842 (1986).

43. *Jersey Shore Area School District v. Jersey Shore Education Association*, 519 Pa. 398, 438 A. 2d 1202 (1988).

CHAPTER 11

THE INSTRUCTIONAL PROGRAM

CONTROL OF PUBLIC SCHOOLS

It is well established that citizens of the United States have no federal constitutional right to public education. In fact, the U.S. Constitution makes no reference to education. By virtue of the Tenth Amendment to the U.S. Constitution, the powers not delegated to the United States by the Constitution, nor prohibited by it to the states, are reserved to the states respectively, or to the people. The Tenth Amendment essentially places the responsibility on each state to provide free public schools. Thus, each state constitution places the responsibility on its legislature to provide schooling for all children within the state at public expense.

The legal authority for defining the curriculum of public schools resides with the state legislature. Based on constitutional provisions in a few states, this duty is shared between the legislature and the state board of education. The legislature may, at its discretion, prescribe the basic course of study, testing, and graduation requirements. In most cases, state legislatures delegate curriculum matters to state boards of education and to local school districts. Many local school districts in turn have the latitude to establish local school-based management councils that are empowered to make decisions in matters regarding curriculum and instructional practices, and selection of textbooks and other instructional materials.

The state's responsibility for public education was clearly established in *State v. Harworth,* as early as 1890, when the court enunciated the following:

> Essentially and intrinsically, the schools . . . are matters of state, and not local jurisdiction. In such matters, the state is the unit and the legislature the source of power. The authority over schools and school affairs is not necessarily a distributive one to be experienced by local instrumentalities; but on the contrary, it is a central power residing in the legislature of the state. It is for the law-making power to determine whether the authority shall be exercised by a state board of education, or distributed to county, township, or city organization throughout the state.[1]

An example of legislative control is further demonstrated by the court in the following case:

The legislature has entire control over the schools of the state . . . the division of the territory of the state into districts, the conduct of the school, the qualifications of teachers, the subjects to be taught therein, and all within its control . . .[2]

Children who enroll in public schools are subject to state laws and local regulations governing the operation of public schools. The state has police powers, which allow it to exercise rules and regulations designed to protect the health, safety, and well-being of all citizens. It is in this context that children are provided a free public education.

COMPULSORY ATTENDANCE

Every state requires children between certain ages, usually 6 or 7 through 16 or 17 years old, to attend public, private, or home school. States operating under the doctrine of *parens patriae,* which literally means the state has sovereign powers over persons such as minors, was enacted during the years 1852 through 1918 and was designed to protect children from unlawful labor abuse. Today, parents who willfully fail to comply with compulsory attendance laws face criminal charges. Thus, compulsory attendance laws today are enacted to ensure that students receive a suitable education. Students who violate compulsory attendance requirements may be suspended or expelled, depending on the severity of their absenteeism. Compulsory attendance is based on the common law responsibility that the parent has an obligation to the child and the state to ensure that the child receives an appropriate education. Therefore, parents do not have a right to be totally free from state laws affecting the upbringing of their children.

In an early case, the U.S. Supreme Court affirmed the right of a state to require compulsory attendance but indicated that school attendance may be met through attending private schools. In 1922, Oregon voters amended their state constitution, which required all residents to send their children between the ages of 8 and 16 to public schools only. A statute was subsequently passed which declared violating this act to be a misdemeanor, and which was to take effect in 1926. A Catholic school corporation and a military school that operated academies in the state sued state officials in a federal district court under the federal Constitution, seeking an injunction to prohibit enforcement of the act. The court ruled for the schools. State officials appealed to the U.S. Supreme Court. The Court ruled that the Oregon statute unreasonably interfered with parental liberty rights to direct the upbringing and education of their children. "The fundamental theory of liberty on which all governments in this Union repose excludes any general power of the state to standardize its children by forcing them to accept instruction from public teachers only." The Court noted that the schools could not claim this liberty guarantee for themselves, in as much as they were corporations. However, the schools sued to vindicate their own business and property interests, and were clearly threatened by arbitrary and unlawful interference by the statute. Because of the immediate threat of harm to the two schools, they were entitled to relief in the form of a court order preventing state officials from enforcing the invalid statute. The Court affirmed the district court's order for the schools.[3]

In a New York case, the school's policy required students to attend 90 percent of all classes in each course to receive credit. The policy also required schools to drop students from any course in which they had been deliberately absent. A group of students brought action against the district challenging the constitutionality of the attendance policy.

Students claimed that the denial of credit for a class is tantamount to dropping a student from enrollment, which is contrary to New York law. The school district filed a motion for summary judgment, which was granted by the court. The students appealed to the New York Supreme Court, Appellate Division. The court rejected the students' arguments and held that the denial of credit was not equivalent to being dropped from enrollment, since it did not prevent a student from attending class or attending make-up classes. The court upheld the lower court's entry of summary on behalf of the school.[4]

Compulsory Attendance Exceptions

The state's right to require school attendance was the subject of considerable controversy during the twentieth century. In *Wisconsin v. Yoder,* the U.S. Supreme Court reversed its earlier position by stating that the state's interest regarding universal and compulsory education is by no means absolute to the exclusion or subordination of all other interests.[5] The plaintiffs in this case challenged Wisconsin's compulsory education statute, which required children between the ages of 7 and 16 to attend school on a regular basis. Parents of one child challenged the statute by refusing to send their child to school after reaching the eighth grade. They believed that continuation in school violated the basic tenets of their Amish religion. The parents were convicted of violating the state's compulsory law. They appealed the conviction by stating that the statute infringed on their free exercise of religion rights. The Wisconsin Supreme Court held for the parents. The U.S. Supreme Court affirmed this decision in holding that the First Amendment prohibits state action that interferes with a parent's right to control the religious upbringing of his or her child. It is important to note that this decision did not invalidate compulsory attendance requirements beyond the eighth grade—it only suggested minimum literacy as a compelling state interest, which does not have to be manifested by completing high school. Furthermore, only students who have strong religious beliefs that conflict with a continuing public school education are permitted to be exempted from compulsory attendance beyond the eighth grade.

A number of states also makes provisions for exemptions to their compulsory attendance laws for married students who are emancipated and are no longer under their parents' care.

Home Schools

Increasingly, parents who are not satisfied with public schools are electing to provide instruction for their children at home. It is estimated that roughly 1.3 million students receive home schooling. Virtually every state in the nation makes provisions for home schooling. Minimum standards for home schooling vary among the states based on the individual state's compulsory attendance laws. Minimal standards for curriculum and instruction, length of instruction time, and the number of days in which instruction should be provided are generally prescribed by state statute or state board of education policies. All such requirements must be met by parents offering home instruction.

Parents who fail to comply with state statutes regarding home schooling may be brought to trial for failure to comply. In most cases, the burden of proof rests with the parents to demonstrate that home instruction is essentially equivalent to instruction offered in public schools. In fact, in *New Jersey v. Massa,* a New Jersey Supreme Court held that equivalent education other than that which is offered in public schools only requires a showing of academic equivalence.[6]

A home schooling challenge emerged in South Carolina when a group of parents brought suit to enjoin the enforcement of a state law requiring parents who only possessed a high school diploma to pass a basic skills examination to be approved for home schooling. The examination in question had been used to test entry-level education students in areas of reading, writing, and mathematics. This examination did not assess teaching ability. The district engaged a company to evaluate the test's suitability to assess home-schooling instructors. A 33-member panel consisting of home schoolers, public school teachers, and college professors was formed to determine whether the knowledge needed to succeed on the basic skills examination was a necessary prerequisite to offering home schooling. Although there was a wide range of opinion among the panelists regarding suitability of the examination, it was validated for use. A trial court found the test to be properly validated. The parents appealed. The state appellate court disagreed, finding that the validation process was unreasonable based on disparities among panelists. The court noted further that 16 panel members were not familiar or experienced with home schooling and found that it was manifestly unreasonable to rely on their evaluation. Lastly, home schoolers had a high pass rate on state tests. Consequently, they should not be required to pass a test as a prerequisite.

The following cases reflect the requirements imposed by various states regarding home schooling:

1. Michigan passed a law requiring home schools to comply with teacher certification requirements. Parents who objected to the law based on religious grounds were exempted.[7]
2. In West Virginia a statute was passed by the legislature making children ineligible for home school if their national standardized test scores fell below the fortieth percentile and did not improve after having remedial home instruction.[8]
3. A Virginia court upheld the state's compulsory attendance law requiring home schoolers to be "tutors or teachers" but did not require private instructors to meet similar qualifications.[9]
4. A Maryland law was upheld that required the state to monitor home education when a parent challenged the required curriculum by arguing that it promoted atheism, paganism, and evolutionism by diminishing the importance of Christian holidays.[10]
5. In North Dakota, the State Supreme Court allowed parents to choose home-based instruction exception rather than a private school exception to comply with state compulsory attendance laws and minimum state standards. The private school exception required compliance with health, fire, and safety laws applicable to private buildings.[11]

A home-schooling case arose in Michigan when several parents decided to educate their children at home using a home-based education program, which they had purchased from a private-school corporation. These parents were charged with truancy. They, along with the private-school corporation, sued the superintendent of public instruction and various school officials, claiming that their constitutional rights had been violated. Specifically, they stated that they had a constitutional right to educate their children at home and that they had been denied due process of law.

The case was heard before a federal district court. The district court held that the private-school corporation could not bring the lawsuit because it had not demonstrated economic loss. The corporation also was not considered an association of members, but rather a business, marketing a service to customers. The court stated that because the parents were able to assert their own rights, the corporation need not bring an action on their behalf. The court ruled further that the right to educate children at home is not a fundamental right guaranteed to parents. While parents have a constitutional right to send their children to private schools and to choose private schools that offer specialized instruction, private school education can be regulated by the state so long as it is reasonable. Because the state merely required that a certified teacher provide instruction in courses comparable to those offered in the public schools, the court ruled that the regulation was reasonable. Finally, the court held that the parents were not "members of a class of people federal discrimination statutes were enacted to protect. They were merely a group of people who wished to educate their children at home. The court denied the parents' claims.[12]

HEALTH REQUIREMENTS

States typically require medical examinations and certain immunizations as a prerequisite for school admission. Since the state, through its police powers, shares a primary responsibility to protect the health and safety of students enrolled in public schools, they have been supported by the courts in establishing health requirements for public school students.

The most common challenge faced by school districts involved First Amendment objections by parents who claimed that mandatory immunization violates their rights to a free exercise of religion. However, courts have been fairly consistent in supporting the state in requiring specific immunizations to prevent communicable disease and have viewed the state interest to be more compelling than parents' interest. Parents have been convicted and fined for failure to have their children vaccinated as a condition for admission to public schools. Some states provide for certain exemptions so long as the health and welfare of other students are not jeopardized, while others have not been quite as lenient.

For example, a court refused to grant religious exemption from school immunizations in New York when a New York couple refused to comply with the school district's enforcement of the state's health law regarding immunization. This case arose when a rural New York couple who were members of the Universal Life Church, which advocated a natural existence, refused to comply with the state's immunization requirements. They claimed their son was entitled to a religious exemption from immunization under New York law. The exemption required affiliation with a bona fide religious organization. The school district found no conflict between the family's religious beliefs and vaccination. The couple unsuccessfully appealed to the state education commissioner. They then filed a lawsuit in a federal district court for a declaration that their beliefs were within the religious exemption, plus $1 million for civil rights violations. The court ruled that their beliefs did not exempt them from immunization.

On appeal to the U.S. Court of Appeals, Second Circuit, the couple argued that their beliefs were sincere and that the term "religious" expanded beyond belief in a deity. The court held for the school district, finding that the couple's belief was not essentially religious but primarily scientific in nature. Strong conviction did not convert their scientific beliefs into religion. The court affirmed the refusal to grant the religious exemption. Because there was no violation of the couple's First Amendment rights, there was no basis for any damage claim.[13]

In *Brown v. Stone,* a religious exemption also was disallowed. The court in this case held that an exemption based on religious grounds would discriminate against the vast majority of children whose parents did not subscribe to their religious convictions.[14] In a rather unusual case, *Lewis v. Sobel,* the court held that a state law requiring a student whose parents' religious convictions conflicted with state health requirements be provided an exemption. Although the parents were not members of an organized church, their beliefs caused them to reject preventive medicine. The court found that the parents' beliefs were sincere in that these beliefs permeated every facet of their lives and the immunization requirement placed a burden on their religious beliefs even though they had on one occasion relinquished their opposition to immunization. The district was ordered to admit the child to school. In a very rare move, the court awarded monetary damages to the family for emotional distress.[15]

RESIDENCE

Public schools generally are required to educate students who reside within the district's boundaries. Residence is a student's actual dwelling place. A student may also have a domicile which is where the student intends to remain indefinitely. It is conceivable that a student may have a number of residences but only one domicile. At one time, common law suggested that a student's domicile be associated with his or her father. In recent years, this view has changed. A student's domicile follows that of his or her legal guardian. If the child is emancipated (free of parental control) his or her domicile is determined by where the student intends to remain indefinitely. Domicile is basically determined by intent. When a student intends to remain in a certain location, domicile is established. Courts have taken the position that public school officials are required to educate school age students who reside within their district with the intent to remain. In the past, a student was not allowed to establish residence within a district for the primary purpose of attending a school within the district. This practice is highly questionable today if there is evidence that the student has an intent to establish permanent residence and is actually living within the district with a degree of permanency. The student is entitled to a public school education even though his or her parent or guardian may live elsewhere. School districts may impose reasonable tuition costs when a student attends school within a district in which he or she has not established legal residence.

A case arose involving proper residence when the grandmothers of three young children filed a lawsuit against a Texas school district seeking an order that the children be allowed to attend public schools. A federal district court issued an order to compel their enrollment. The children had resided with their grandmothers for considerable time periods, but not for the primary purpose of attending public school in the local school district. The grandmothers were not the legal guardians of the children. Texas laws require that the presence of the child in the school district not be for the primary purpose of attending their free public schools.

The school district took the position that children could not establish residency apart from their parents or legal guardians, and that persons having lawful control or custody of children must initiate some type of judicial proceeding. The district court issued a permanent order instructing the school district to allow the children to enroll in their schools. The court ruled that these children living apart from their parents or legal guardians must be admitted to school to prevent violation of the federal constitution. The children had established their residence by physical presence and an intention to remain in the district.[16]

Another case involving residence arose in New York. A New York State law has a provision that allows a homeowner whose property or dwelling intersects adjoining school districts to choose either district in which to send his or her children. A homeowner who desired to send his children to a school in another district purchased a small parcel of land adjoining his lot in order to meet the law's intersection provision. The other school district sued the homeowner, seeking tuition payment. A trial court held for the school district, concluding that the homeowner's motivation in purchasing the parcel disqualified him from using the other school district tuition-free. The homeowner appealed to an appellate division court, which reversed the trial court decision. The homeowner's motivation in purchasing the adjoining parcel was immaterial and his children could attend the new district school without paying tuition.[17]

In a significant case regarding nonresidence for homeless children, the court held that homeless children must be provided a right to be educated under New York law. This case arose when Diane Harrison and her two school-age children had been homeless since 1986 after a fire destroyed their apartment. They moved to a motel and later to various residences. At one point, the children lived with their father in Peekskill and enrolled in the district. In October of 1987, they were required to leave his residence by the landlord, and they moved back with their mother at the hotel in which they had lived previously. The hotel was not located in the Peekskill district. Harrison was notified that her children could no longer attend Peekskill schools unless they found an apartment in Peekskill. She received no written notice detailing factual or legal grounds for the expulsion. She also was not notified of any right to a hearing pursuant to New York Education Law § 301. The court held that the expulsion clearly denied children their right to an education under New York law. In the case of a homeless child, the New York Commissioner of Education had previously found that, for the purpose of residence, children are entitled to continue to attend in their previous home district. Since the children had resided in Peekskill and enrolled in their schools, Peekskill represented their previous home district. Additionally, the court observed that after the suit was filed and prior to rendering a decision, a new regulation was implemented allowing parents of homeless children to designate either the school district in which the child resided at the time he or she became homeless or the district where the child was temporarily living. Under this regulation, districts that deny a child admission based on nonresidence must provide written notification to parents and allow parents to produce evidence that the child has a right to attend school.[18]

CURRICULUM STANDARDS

Minimal curriculum standards in public schools are established by state statute and policy. In almost all cases, certain courses and minimum achievement standards are determined through state policy. Local school districts may establish other standards so long as they do not contradict state requirements. Federal aid programs such as Title I, Goals 2000, Educate America Act of 1994, Education for Disabled Students, and most recently the No Child Left Behind Act specify certain standards that must be met to receive federal funds. Also, under the Goals 2000 and Educate America Act of 1994, states receive funds if they agree to develop plans to meet certain national goals. Generally, courts are very reluctant to intervene in matters involving public school curricula based on the view that states retain the authority to establish curriculum standards so long as there is no federal constitutional infringement involved. State legislation requires that certain subjects be included in school curricula throughout the state and that instruction be provided in subjects such as American history, state government, civics, and U.S. and state constitutions. State legislatures generally prescribe broad guidelines and delegate authority to determine the specifics of the curriculum to the state board of education and local school districts. Except for issues involving religious matters, courts are reluctant to interfere with school officials' authority to prescribe curriculum. School officials tend to develop a common secular curriculum to avoid the assertion that the curriculum advances a particular or specialized sectarian interest to the exclusion of others.

Most conflicts involving curriculum center around special interest groups that register objections to the school's use of certain textbooks, courses, or programs. Courts have generally supported schools as they advocate knowledge expansion rather than knowledge restriction. While school boards have generally prevailed in matters regarding curriculum disputes with parents, their powers are not absolute. If legitimate constitutional issues emerge, the courts will intervene to determine the constitutionality of the issue under review and will rule appropriately based on the facts involved in the case.

As an example, in *Mozert v. Hawkins County Board of Education* the plaintiff, Vicki Frost, as a born-again Christian, objected to her daughter's sixth-grade Holt reader that contained content on mental telepathy. Reading further, Frost found other themes in the text to which she had objections. After discussing her concerns with other parents, she met with the principal of Church Hill Middle School, who agreed that the school could use an alternative reading program for students whose parents objected to the assigned reader. Students who elected the alternative program left the classroom during reading sessions and worked on assignments from another textbook series. The Hawkins County Board of Education voted later to eliminate all alternative reading programs and required every student to attend classes using the Holt series. The plaintiff's children refused to read the Holt series or attend reading classes where the series was taught.

Frost filed suit contending that her religious beliefs were contrary to the values taught in the Holt series, and that requiring her children to read it violated her religious beliefs. She cited 17 categories, ranging from evolution to secular humanism, as violations of her religious convictions. The plaintiff focused on the textbook rather than teaching methods. The plaintiff was unable to provide evidence by a teacher or student that anyone was required to affirm his or her belief or disbelief on any idea or practice mentioned in the book. Had the plaintiff's student been required to participate beyond reading the material or been disciplined for disputing assigned materials, a free exercise clause violation might have been implicated because the element of compulsion would have been present. Since this was not the case, there was no evidence that the conduct required of these students was forbidden by their religious beliefs. A claim that the content might lead students to develop beliefs contrary to those of their parents was insufficient to establish an unconstitutional burden.

The U.S. Court of Appeals held for the school district.[19]

Over the past decade, the federal government has taken a more active role in public education through the passage of major acts designed to improve K–16 public education such as Title I and Goals 2000, and the Educate America Act of 1994. Perhaps the most comprehensive and sweeping act passed in the last three decades is the No Child Left Behind Act.

NO CHILD LEFT BEHIND ACT OF 2001

On January 8, 2002, President Bush signed into law the No Child Left Behind Act of 2001 (NCLB). This act is considered to be the most sweeping reform since the Elementary and Secondary School act was passed in 1965. This new act redefines the federal government's role in K–12 education and is designed to close the achievement gap between disadvantaged and minority students and their peers. It is based on four principles:

- Stronger accountability for results
- Increased flexibility and local control
- Expanded options for parents
- An emphasis on teaching methods that have been proven to work

Increased Accountability

The NCLB Act will strengthen Title I accountability by requiring states to implement statewide accountability systems covering all public schools and students. These systems must be based on challenging state standards in reading and mathematics, annual testing for all students in grades 3–8, and annual statewide progress objectives ensuring that all groups of students reach proficiency within 12 years. Assessment results and state progress objectives must be broken out by income, race, ethnicity, disability, and limited English proficiency to ensure that no group is left behind. School districts and schools that fail to make adequate yearly progress (AYP) toward statewide proficiency goals will, over time, be subject to improvement, corrective action, and restructuring measures aimed at getting them back on course to meet state standards. Schools that meet or exceed AYP objectives or close achievement gaps will be eligible for state academic achievement awards.

More Choices for Parents and Students

The NCLB Act significantly increases the choices available to the parents of students attending Title I schools that fail to meet state standards, including immediate relief, beginning with the 2002–2003 school year, for students in schools that were previously identified for improvement or corrective action under the 1994 ESEA reauthorization.

LEAs must give students attending schools identified for improvement, corrective action, or restructuring, the opportunity to attend a better public school, which may include a public charter school, within the school district. The district must provide transportation to the new school, and must use at least 5 percent of its Title I funds for this purpose, if needed.

For students attending persistently failing schools (those that have failed to meet state standards for at least three of the four preceding years), LEAs must permit low-income students to use Title I funds to obtain supplemental educational services from the public- or private-sector provider selected by the students and their parents. Providers must meet state standards and offer services tailored to help participating students meet challenging state academic standards.

To help ensure that LEAs offer meaningful choices, the new law requires school districts to spend up to 20 percent of their Title I allocations to provide school choice and supplemental educational services to eligible students.

In addition to helping ensure that no child loses the opportunity for a quality education because he or she is trapped in a failing school, the choice and supplemental service requirements provide a substantial incentive for low-performing schools to improve. Schools that wish to avoid losing students, along with the portion of their annual budgets typically associated with those students, will have to improve or, if they fail to make annual progress for five years, run the risk of reconstitution under a restructuring plan.

Greater Flexibility for States, School Districts, and Schools

One important goal of the No Child Left Behind Act was to breathe new life into the "flexibility for accountability" bargain with states first struck by President George H. W. Bush during his 1989 education summit with the nation's governors at Charlottesville, Virginia. Prior flexibility efforts have focused on the waiver of program requirements; the NCLB Act moves beyond this limited approach to provide states and school districts with unprecedented flexibility in the use of federal education funds in exchange for strong accountability for results.

New flexibility provisions in the NCLB Act include authority for states and LEAs to transfer up to 50 percent of the funding they receive under four major state grant programs to any one of the programs or to Title I. The covered programs include Teacher Quality state grants, Educational Technology state grants, Innovative Programs, and Safe and Drug-Free Schools.

The new law also includes a competitive state flexibility demonstration program that permits up to seven states to consolidate the state share of nearly all federal state grant programs, including Title I, Part A grants to local educational agencies, while providing additional flexibility in their use of Title V innovation funds. Participating states must enter into five-year performance agreements with the Secretary of Education, covering the use of the consolidated funds, which may be used for any educational purpose authorized under the ESEA. As part of their plans, states also must enter into up to ten local performance agreements with LEAs, which will enjoy the same level of flexibility granted under the separate Local Flexibility Demonstration Program.

The new competitive Local Flexibility Demonstration Program would allow up to 80 LEAs, in addition to the 70 LEAs under the State Flexibility Demonstration Program, to consolidate funds received under Teacher Quality state grants, Educational Technology state grants, Innovative Programs, and Safe and Drug-Free Schools. Participating LEAs would enter into performance agreements with the Secretary of Education and would be able to use the consolidated funds for any ESEA-authorized purpose.

Summary and Implications

Accountability.   Each state will implement a statewide accountability system that will be effective in ensuring that all districts and schools make adequate progress. The accountability system includes rewards and sanctions. Students cannot be left behind based on

- Race/ethnicity
- Disabilities
- Limited English proficiency
- Economic status (disadvantaged)

Participation

- Students with disabilities who take alternative assessment must participate.
- Schools and districts must have a 95 percent participation rate for all students.

Adequate Yearly Progress

- The same high academic achievement standards will be applied to all students.
- There should be continuous and demonstrated academic improvement for all students.
- Separate measures and annual achievement objectives may be used for all students including those in racial and ethnic groups, the economically disadvantaged, students with disabilities, and students with limited English proficiency.

Teacher Quality

- All core academic teachers must be highly qualified by 2005–2006.
- Core academics include
  a. English, reading, or languages
  b. Mathematics, science, foreign languages, civics, and government
  c. Economics, the arts, history, and geography

Qualified Teachers. The following measures will be used in part to assess qualified teachers:

- A teacher's license
- Success in passing a test
- Content area knowledge:
  a. Academic major or graduate degree in content area
  b. Credits equivalent of academic major (24 hours)
  c. Success in passing test such as Praxis

Paraprofessionals. Paraprofessionals must meet the following requirements:

- Two years of higher education
- Associates degree
- Test (Parapro through ETS)
- High school diploma or its equivalent
- Translators and parent liaisons

Each group of students should meet or exceed annual objectives, except as follows:

- The number of students who are below proficiency standards should be reduced by 10 percent from the prior year.
- Other indicators may be used to measure progress for subgroups.

Restructuring (Corrective Action). If a school fails to make adequate yearly progress after one full year of corrective action, the district must

- Continue to make public school choice available
- Continue to make supplemental services available
- Prepare a plan to restructure the school

Alternative Governance.   By the beginning of the following school year, the district must implement one of the following alternatives:

- Reopen the school as a public charter school
- Replace all or most of school staff including the principal
- Enter into a contract with an entity, such as a private management company with a proven record of effectiveness to operate the school
- State takeover
- Any other major restructuring of the school's governance plan

USE OF THE INTERNET FOR INSTRUCTION

Another important component of the instructional program is the use of electronic technology. Information technology has drastically altered teaching and learning as well as the school's administrative processes. It has changed the fabric of school operations. Internet access has increased by almost 70 percent in public schools and roughly 80 percent in public school classrooms during the period between 1994 and 2000, as illustrated in Figure 11.1. Given the widespread use and application of the Internet and the potential for abuse, students and parents should be required to review and agree on rules governing access and use of the Internet.

School Officials' Responsibility

School officials should include procedures for accessing the Internet and identify resources that are well suited to the school's learning objectives. These components may be included under "student acceptable use for electronic network." Filtering software should be used to block access to visual images that are obscene, pornographic, or otherwise deemed unsuitable for children. The software is required under the Children's Internet Protection Act of 2000, which will be discussed later. Students should be expected to exhibit good behavior on school-owned computer networks. Furthermore, they should be made aware that communications on the network most often are public. School officials must stress that access to the school's information network is not a right but a privilege. Parental consent should be required for minors to access the school's network. School officials should clearly communicate by policy, which acts are permissible and which are not. Specific disciplinary action should be clearly defined and communicated to students and parents alike when violations occur. Millions of pages of information, have been posted to the Internet by all types of individual and organizations, so students must be cautioned that many of these pages contain offensive, sexually explicit, and inappropriate materials.

Children's Internet Protection Act

School officials also must understand their responsibilities under the Children's Internet Protection Act (CIPA). This act was enacted by Congress at the end of 2000 as part of the

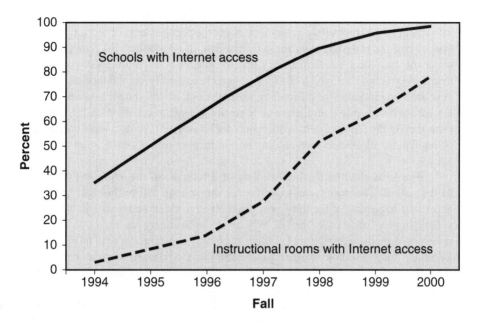

FIGURE 11.1 Percent of all public schools and instructional rooms having Internet access: Fall 1994 to Fall 2000

Source: U.S. Department of Education, National Center for Education Statistics, Fast Response Survey System, *Internet Access in Public Schools and Classrooms: 1994–2000.*

House Appropriations Bill H.R. 4577. Under this law, schools and libraries are required to adopt an Internet safety policy and install filtering technology if they are to receive certain federal funds. This law applied to all schools and libraries that receive discounted rates for the purchase of equipment and services used to access the Internet under the E-Rate Program or through the Library Services and Technology Act (LSTA) or Title III of the Elementary and Secondary Education Act (ESEA). Although the act required libraries to install filtering technology, this requirement has been *ruled unconstitutional* by a special three-judge district court. The court held that filtering technology erroneously blocks a massive amount of speech that is protected by the First Amendment. *This ruling only affects libraries.* The portion of the law that applies to schools remains intact. Section 1703 of the act requires the National Telecommunication and Information Administration no later than 18 months after its enactment to initiate a notice and comment proceeding for the purpose of (1) evaluating whether current available technology protection measures, including commercial Internet blocking and filtering software, adequately addresses the needs of educational institutions, (2) making recommendations on how to foster the development of measures that meet such needs, and (3) evaluating the development and effectiveness of local Internet safety policies that are currently in operation after community input. A LEA covered under the act shall certify its compliance during each annual program application cycle.

Schools without Internet safety policies and technology for the first program year after the effective date of the act in which the agency is applying for funds shall certify that it is undertaking such actions, including any necessary procurement and procedures to implement an Internet safety policy that meets the requirements of the act. During the second year of the program, after the effective date in which the LEA is applying for funds under the act, The LEA shall certify that the school is in compliance with such requirements. Any school for which the LEA is unable to certify compliance during the second year shall be ineligible for all funding under the act, in this and all subsequent years, until the school comes into compliance. Any school subject to certification for which the LEA cannot make the required certification may seek a waiver if state or local procurement rules or regulations or competitive bidding requirements prevent certification required by the act.

The LEA shall notify the Secretary of Education of the applicability of that clause to the school. The notice shall certify that the school will be brought into compliance before the beginning of the third year program after the effective date in which the school is applying for funds under the act. Whenever the Secretary has reason to believe that any recipient of funds under the act is failing to comply substantially with its requirements, the Secretary may withhold further payments, issue a complaint to compel compliance through a cease and desist order, or enter into a compliance agreement to bring the school into compliance with the requirements of the act.

The primary focus of the act is to protect children from undesirable content accessed through the Internet. An administrator, supervisor, or other person authorized by the certifying authority may disable the technology protection measure during use by an adult to enable access for bona fide research or other lawful purpose. The determination regarding subject matter that is inappropriate for minors shall be made by the school board, LEA, library, or other authority responsible for making the determination. Each Internet safety ruling adopted by LEAs shall be made available on request to the Federal Communications Commission for review.

School or District Responsibility

Schools or school districts should develop and enforce an acceptable use policy. This policy should govern all electronic programming such as e-mail and general access to the Internet by students and employees. The board of education will generally not incur liability if it has filtering software installed that may inadvertently fail. However, measures must be taken to correct the failure. By standard practice, each district or school should establish a process for modifying the filtering system or defiltering Internet access for students when it is educationally appropriate.

At a minimum, the filtering system should restrict access to Internet sites or chatrooms that contain

- Offensive messages
- Obscene language
- Sexuality
- Sexual acts
- Violence
- Sexual attire
- Crime
- Nudity

- Intolerance
- Harassing messages

Students or employees who violate board policy may be banned for using the Internet. Students who are banned should not be otherwise excluded from participation in the educational program. Minimal due process requirements should be met if a student or employee is banned from Internet use. These procedures should be communicated to students, parents, and employees. Disciplinary actions for students should be tailored to the severity of the violation and to further assist the student in gaining knowledge and developing reasonable judgment in the use of the Internet. Employee violations resulting in disciplinary action should be based on defensible policy.

Teacher's Responsibility

Teachers have a responsibility to select material that is appropriate based on the age and maturity of students and consistent with course objectives. Consequently, teachers must preview material and sites that students are required to access to determine the appropriateness of material contained on the site. Teachers should also provide guidance by identifying and listing resources to assist students in their learning activities. They should monitor content that students access on the Internet and follow approved procedures when student violations occur.

Parent's Responsibility

Parents should be aware of guidelines and instructions for student protection while using the Internet. Although the board or school acceptable-use policy will restrict access to inappropriate material, there is a wide range of material available to students on the Internet. Parents must assume a leadership role in instilling proper values to their children and instructing their children regarding which materials are acceptable and which are not acceptable. Parents should also monitor Internet use at home to ensure that their children are following their directives. Home monitoring by parents will reinforce acceptable use policies implemented by school officials. Cooperation and coordination of Internet use between parents and the school will generally yield more favorable results regarding Internet use by students.

■ ■ ■ ■ ■

ADMINISTRATIVE GUIDE

USE OF THE INTERNET

1. Involve parents and students in drafting Internet use policies.
2. Make certain that Internet use policy is clearly written and communicated to parents and students.
3. Policies should inform teachers, students, and parents of their responsibilities regarding enforcement of Internet use policies.

(continued)

■ ■ ■ ■ ■

ADMINISTRATIVE GUIDE (*continued*)

4. Due process and fundamental fairness should be observed in enforcing Internet use policies.
5. School districts have a responsibility to develop acceptable use policies regarding the use of the Internet by students and employees.
6. Specific disciplinary measures for inappropriate use of the Internet should be spelled out in the district's acceptable-use policy.
7. Students should be cautioned that personal contact information about themselves or others should not be posted on the Internet without prior written consent from the parent or legal guardian.
8. Students should be informed that they should promptly disclose inappropriate messages they receive on the Internet to their teachers.
9. Users should be informed by policy that the following activities are prohibited:
   a. Subverting network security
   b. Bypassing restrictions established by school officials
   c. Using the Internet for illegal purposes such as drug transactions, obtaining alcohol for minors, and gang-related activities
   d. Seeking information about passwords of others
   e. Using obscene, vulgar, rude, threatening, or abusive language
   f. Taking writings of others and presenting them without prior written permission (plagiarizing)
   g. Using the Internet to promote personal or commercial enterprises

GRADING AND ACADEMIC REQUIREMENTS

As stated previously, courts traditionally have been reluctant to interfere in cases involving academic matters. The prevailing view held by the courts is that professional educators are better prepared to make decisions regarding student evaluation. Requirements regarding progress from one grade to another typically are not reviewable by the courts unless there is substantial evidence of unreasonableness. For example, the Fourth Circuit Court of Appeals refused to intervene in the failure of a school district to promote to the third-grade students who failed to pass a reading level test.[20] The court respected the educational judgment of professional educators even though the students' intelligence indicated that they were capable of reading at the third-grade level; the students could not be promoted until they had demonstrated mastery of the requisite reading skill. One court observed that academic matters by their very nature are more subjective and evaluative than typical issues presented in disciplinary decisions and that such academic judgments should be left to professional educators.[21]

Student Testing

It is well established that the state has the authority to promulgate promotion and graduation requirements. Often, standardized tests are used to determine student competencies. If the measures are reasonable and nondiscriminatory, they will generally be supported by the courts. School officials are provided considerable discretion in matters relating to appropriate academic requirements. By and large, courts do not feel equipped to evaluate academic performance issues.[22] Because courts are not equipped to evaluate academic performance issues, they limit themselves to addressing issues relating to due process, discriminatory impact, or arbitrary or capricious acts by school officials. Therefore, the state's authority to develop and assess student performance standards is not debatable. However, challenges may be raised regarding the fairness of certain assessment programs. These challenges most frequently involve minimal competency tests used to determine whether students met requirements for high school graduation.

In an early challenge, the State of Florida was unable to demonstrate that the school's curriculum actually reflected concepts included on the test and whether the literacy test actually covered material taught in the classrooms. Tests also cannot be defended if there is a showing of discrimination based on race. The most common challenge regarding testing programs is whether tests are used to track students, which results in discrimination and a violation of the Fourteenth Amendment's equal protection clause. The issue becomes more profound when there are little or no opportunities for students to move from one track to another. The key issue involves intent. Tests will not be supported by the courts if there is discriminatory intent. Therefore, school officials must be able to demonstrate a compelling state interest to support tests if they resulted in separation of students by race. Testing programs must be fair and equitable to all students. There must be a regard for due process rights of students. Special areas such as inadequate phase-in periods, inadequate matches between tests and instructional materials, racially discriminatory tests, and other arbitrary and capricious practices should be given special consideration to ensure that individual rights of students are not violated.

Oregon was the first state to establish minimum competency requirements for graduation. In the fall of 1975, New York administered to its ninth graders the first statewide competency test. Arizona was the first state to formulate minimum competency standards as a condition of graduation for its senior class of 1976. Florida was the first state to provide major funding for remedial programs for students who did not achieve the minimum score required for passage of the test. Florida's minimal competency program met legal challenges in the mid 1970s. In 1976, the Florida legislature passed the Educational Accountability Act of 1976, and based on an analysis of minimum competency programs, stated the following in regard to the act:

> [The Act] directs the State Commissioner of Education to develop and administer in the public schools a uniform, statewide program of assessment to determine periodically, educational status and progress and the degree of achievement of approved minimum performance standards. The uniform statewide program shall consist of testing in grades three, five, eight, and eleven and may include testing of additional grades and skill areas as specified by the Commissioner.

The law also specifies that each school district "shall periodically assess student performance and achievement in each school." Particular emphasis must be placed "upon the pupil's mastery of basic skills, especially reading, before he/she is promoted from the third, fifth, eighth, and eleventh grades."

The literacy test graduation requirement stems from a section of the 1976 law which stated

Beginning with the 1978–79 school year, each district school board shall establish standards for graduation from its secondary schools. Such standards shall include, but not be limited to, mastery of the basic skills and satisfactory performance in functional literacy as determined by the State Board of Education and the completion of the minimum number of credits required by the district school board.

   Each district shall develop procedures for the remediation of the deficiencies of those students who are unable to meet such standards."

As pointed out by a study panel that examined the Florida program under sponsorship of the National Education Association and the Florida Teaching Profession–NEA, the word *test* is not used in the functional literacy requirements, although testing is specified as the method of assessing basic skills. The law actually does not specify the method of assessing functional literacy performance.

   In enforcing the law, the Florida State Board of Education and State Department of Education developed basic skills tests to be administered each October to students in grades three, five, eight, and eleven. Eleventh graders also were given the State Student Assessment Test, Part II (formerly the functional literacy test, the name of which was changed to remove the stigma that failure inferred illiteracy). The multiple-choice test included practical applications of skills in reading, writing, and mathematics, and was divided into two parts: communications and mathematics. A passing score of 70 was required on each section. A student was required to retake any section of the test not passed. Three additional opportunities for retest were provided prior to graduation (1978–1979). Seniors were allowed two additional opportunities to retake the test. If a student did not pass, he or she would receive a certificate of completion in lieu of a diploma.

   In response to litigation against the act, a Florida federal court ruled that imposing minimum competency testing too hastily can result in a court order compelling the awarding of a diploma. Black students who failed Florida's 1978 minimum competency test alleged that they were denied equal protection and due process of law under the Fourteenth Amendment by imposition of the Florida minimum competency requirements. In *Debra P. v. Turlington,* the federal district court agreed with the students and ordered that the diploma be awarded to those students who had failed the examination but had otherwise qualified for graduation. The court determined that inadequacy of notice was a violation of due process. Students were not adequately notified during their instruction of the required skills and that graduation would depend on the mastery of those skills.[23] As a practical matter, six years must pass before Florida's minimal competency test legislation, enacted in 1977, could be used to deny the diploma.

   Courts do tend to allow for some degree of subjectivity by school officials regarding criteria for graduation and test items with respect to levels of difficulty. Substantive due process challenges typically do not apply to subjective standards. However, there are objective standards in which substantive due process will apply. In *Debra P. v. Turlington,* cited previously, the courts were not only concerned with the timely notice to students regarding graduation requirements but also with the validity and reliability of the tests.

   A related challenge involving graduate exit exams arose in *Rankins v. Louisiana State Board of Elementary and Secondary Education* when five public school students challenged a state law requiring graduating seniors to pass a graduate exit examination to receive their diplomas. These five students had completed their coursework but failed the graduate exit examination. They sued the state board seeking a declaration that the policy was invalid and an order requiring the district to award them their diplomas. The trial court issues a preliminary order prohibiting the board from withholding the diplomas. The board appealed to the Fifth Circuit Court of Appeals. The court found the graduate exit examination to be permissible under the board's broad discretion. The policy was found not to violate the U.S. Constitution's equal protection clause, even though the test was not required in private schools. Although public and private school students were treated differently, the court upheld the testing requirement because it was rationally related to the goal of ensuring minimal competency in public school graduates.[24]

Grade Reductions for Absences

Excessive absenteeism by students poses a challenge for school officials who oftentimes resort to grade reductions as a means of limiting excessive absences. Courts will generally support reasonable policies regarding grade reduction for excessive absences if they do not conflict with state statute, as illustrated by a case in Michigan. A Michigan high school student was absent from school for five days during the first of six grading periods for the school year. Her absences were due to an injury and were thus excused. The local board of education's policy required that any student with more than three excused absences in a grading period make up the missed time at after-school study sessions, failure to comply would result in a reduction in the student's letter grade. The plaintiff attended only one of the five required make-up sessions. Consequently, her grades were lowered by one full letter grade.

The student filed suit against the school board, claiming that the grading policy was beyond the scope of the board's authority and that the policy violated her due process rights. The circuit court dismissed the case. The student appealed to the Michigan Court of Appeals. The court held that the grading policy was not beyond the board's scope of authority because the attendance policy was impliedly authorized by statute and was not arbitrary or unreasonable. The court also held that due process protections require a property right. The court ruled that the student's right to due process was not violated since the student had no vested property interest in any grade higher than those she actually received. The court of appeals affirmed the trial court's decision.[25]

Grade Reduction for Unexcused Absences

School rules that penalize students academically for unexcused absences, or truancy, are not uncommon. Courts have been more supportive of schools on this type of rule than on one that mandates grade reduction based on general misconduct. In fact, since the mid 1970s courts have been quite consistent in ruling against school districts for grade reduction related to misconduct. Thus, school districts must be certain that their rules in this area are carefully drawn. The following cases illustrate this point.

In a New Jersey school district, school board policy mandated that a student receive a zero in all subjects on those days he or she was truant from school. The student could make up any tests missed on such days, but the zero had to be used when grades were averaged for the term. In ruling for a student who challenged the rule, the New Jersey Commissioner of Education found the penalty to be excessive.[26] In some instances a student could receive a failing grade in a class for even a single absence. A major reason the school board lost its case appears to be related to the severity of the penalty, rather than the policy of grade reduction in general.

In a Colorado school district, students who had more than seven absences for any reason from a given class were denied academic credit. The court ruled against the school district in this case because the school board regulations violated the state's attendance statute.[27] State law specified that students should be in attendance at school for a minimum of 172 days. Days of absence because of illness or suspension were to be counted as days of attendance for the purpose of meeting the requirement of 172 days. On the basis of the state statute, the court concluded that a school district was prohibited from imposing sanctions on students who were absent from school based on illness or school suspension.

In Illinois a school district was upheld in a case in which a student's grades were lowered as a result of his having unexcused absences.[28] The school board's policy mandated that grades be lowered one letter grade per class for unexcused absences. Kevin Knight was truant two days. Thus, his grades were reduced in accordance with the rule. In one of his classes his grade was not reduced, and in three of his other classes the grade reductions were less than the one letter grade required by the board's policy. These inconsistencies apparently had a bearing on the court's decision. The board of education rescinded the rule that had been applied to Kevin. The court, after expressing its reluctance to interfere with the school's judgment regarding grades, held that the rule, as applied to Kevin Knight, was not so harsh as to deprive him of substantive due process of law. The court pointed out that the rule was not fully applied to Knight. The court also noted that the possibility of damage to Knight was remote, because the following year he was admitted to a junior college. It would have been interesting to observe what the court might have decided had the rule been applied fully and Kevin Knight had been unable to enter college.

In a related case, Roberta Raymon, a high school student, was penalized for an unexcused absence from class by the deduction of three points from her six-weeks algebra grade. This penalty did not alter her grade point average significantly and did not change her class standing. She remained second in her class. Arguing that the penalty was arbitrarily imposed in violation of the Fifth and Fourteenth Amendments, her parents brought this action for damages and injunctive relief under 42 U.S.C. § 1983. The district court, without deciding the federal constitutional issue, exercised jurisdiction over state law claims and ordered the three points restored to Raymon's algebra grade. The court refused to award attorneys' fees and plaintiffs appealed that denial to the Fifth Circuit Court of Appeals.[29]

In its ruling The Fifth Circuit Court of Appeals stated that federal courts are proper forums for the resolution of serious and substantial federal claims. They are frequently the last and oftentimes the only resort for those who are oppressed by the denial of the rights afforded them by the Constitution and laws of the United States. Fulfilling this mission and the other jurisdiction conferred by acts of Congress has imposed on the federal courts a work load that taxes their capacity. Each litigant who improperly seeks federal judicial relief for a petty claim forces other litigants with more serious claims to wait for their day in court. When litigants improperly invoke the aid of a federal court to redress what is patently a trifling claim, the district court should not attempt to ascertain who was right or who was wrong in provoking the quarrel but should dispatch the matter quickly.

Accordingly, the court reversed the judgment and ordered the district court to dismiss the complaint for lack of subject matter jurisdiction. The Fifth Circuit Court considered the plaintiff's claim to be petty and a misuse of the court's time given the litigation of more serious cases before the court.

Grade Reduction for Academic Misconduct

A number of school districts has formulated policies requiring grade reductions for misconduct. An example of the courts' position regarding this was illustrated in the following case.[30] Shaun Dunn and Bill McCullough were both fine musicians who participated as guitar players in the high school band program at Fairfield Community High School. Fairfield prohibited its band members from departing from the planned musical program during band performances, and it specifically forbade guitar solos during the performances. In direct defiance of those rules and their teacher's explicit orders, Dunn and McCullough played two unauthorized guitar pieces at a February 10, 1995, band program. The discipline they received for this infraction caused them both to receive an F for the band course, and that F prevented McCullough from graduating with honors. Dunn and McCullough appealed the district court's decision to grant summary judgment for Fairfield. The court concluded that the schools actions violated no right under the federal civil rights statutes.

Every rehearsal and concert were assigned a point value. Points were awarded for presence at the event, appropriate dress, and appropriate conduct. Additionally, there were at least two playing evaluations per quarter for points. The point scale worked as follows:

Daily rehearsal: 5 points
Performances: 20 points
Playing evaluations: 25 points

The policy also warned that conduct at performances had to be professional and that conduct not meeting that standard would give rise to serious consequences.

The court rejected the students' contentions, noting also that they had failed to address the Eighth Amendment component of their case in their summary judgment motion. The disciplinary action in question, the court concluded, bore a rational relation to the school's interest in maintaining order and providing an education. The court also commented that if the plaintiffs were to prevail, "almost every disciplinary action could become a federal case." The court then considered the students' claim that Fairfield had violated Illinois state law. Because the complaint did not invoke the court's supplemental jurisdiction under 28 U.S.C. § 1367, the court expressed doubt that the claim was properly before it. The court decided that the undisputed facts showed that no violation of Illinois law had taken place.

A different case arose in Indiana in which a student's grade was reduced as punishment for alcohol-related misconduct. The student's parents brought suit against the district and moved for summary judgment. The district court held that a high school rule mandating a 4 percent reduction in grades for each day a student had been suspended for alcohol use during school hours was invalid and a violation of substantive due process. The court stated further that the policy was arbitrary and the school failed to demonstrate a reasonable relationship between the use of alcohol during school hours and a reduction in grades.[31]

Physical Punishment for Poor Academic Performance

Physical punishment of public school students for failure to maintain acceptable academic standards has not received support by the courts. Courts have consistently ruled against school officials for the use of physical punishment when the student's behavior did not involve improper conduct. For example, one court ruled against physical punishment of a student who failed to perform athletically at a desired level even though the coach considered the punishment to be instructive and a source of encouragement to the student.[32]

A teacher in Iowa was found guilty of assault and battery when he inflicted punishment on a child who was unable to complete studies in algebra.[33] The courts have also held that it was improper to physically punish a student who was unable to solve a mathematics problem at the blackboard.[34] U.S. courts have consistently held that public school students should not be physically punished for conduct not related to disciplinary infractions. An Indiana court held that it was not proper to physically punish a child for accidentally breaking school objects and for failure to pay for such damages. The court reasoned that students must rely on their parents for financial resources. Consequently, if parents refused to pay or were not able to pay, the student then would be punished for not having met an obligation he or she had no power to meet.[35] School officials would be ill-advised to physically punish a child for not paying school debts. Furthermore, students should not be physically punished for failure to complete homework or other assignments. School officials may adopt policies calling for academic penalties such as a loss of credit for failure to meet academic assignments, but under no circumstances should physical punishment be inflicted in cases involving academic matters.

Withholding Diplomas

School officials are delegated the authority to determine when a student has completed the required curriculum entitling him or her to be awarded a diploma. It is well established that when a student has met prescribed academic requirements for graduation, he or she must be awarded a diploma. However, a student may be denied participation in the graduation ceremony if his or her conduct significantly deviates from acceptable standards of behavior. There is no direct relationship between earning a diploma and participation in the graduation ceremony. The awarding of a diploma is a ministerial act which must be performed by school officials. There have been instances in which a student has been denied a diploma for nonacademic reasons, primarily misconduct. The courts have been very consistent in ruling that the student must be granted his or her diploma if all academic requirements have been met.

An early court case, which is most often cited, regarding withholding a diploma is *Valentine v. Independent School District of Casey.*[36] This case involved students who refused to wear the caps and gowns required for participation in the ceremony. These students indicated that the gowns smelled, even though they had been cleaned. They were denied diplomas based on their refusal to wear the prescribed dress. The court, in holding for the students, stated that these particular students had earned their diplomas based on their academic performance. Consequently, participation in the actual ceremony was not prerequisite to receiving a diploma. The court further stated

> that a diploma, therefore is *prima facie* evidence of educational worth, and is the goal of the matriculate. . . . The issuance of a diploma by the school board to a pupil who satisfactorily completes the prescribed course of study and who is otherwise qualified is mandatory, and, although such duty is not expressly enjoined upon the board by statute, it does arise by necessary and reasonable implication. . . . This Plaintiff. . . having complied with

all the rules and regulations precedent to graduation, may not be denied her diploma by the arbitrary action of the school board subsequent to her being made the recipient of the honors of graduation.

EDUCATIONAL MALPRACTICE

Over the last two decades, educational malpractice has emerged as a formidable threat to educators. Increasingly, parents have brought suits on behalf of their children, alleging that teachers were either negligent or incapable of providing competent instruction and proper placement and classification of their children. In these cases, students have charged that they suffered academic injury by being denied the full benefits of a proper education.

Although numerous suits have been filed in the past, to date no case has been won by parents or students. However, with the emergence of school-based management, national teaching standards, greater teacher accountability, and an emphasis on professionalism in education, the prospect of a successful malpractice challenge is greatly heightened. There is little doubt that somewhere in the foreseeable future a malpractice suit will be won by a student who has suffered academic injury.

Educational malpractice generally is considered to be any unprofessional conduct or lack of sufficient skill in the performance of professional duties. It represents a new kind of injury to students. This new type of injury is not physical but emotional, psychological, or educational, resulting from poor teaching, improper placement, or inappropriate testing procedures.

Since the courts have long established legal duties for teachers to instruct, to supervise, and to provide for the safety of children, a breach of these duties resulting in injury to students may form adequate grounds for a liability suit. Increasingly, students are claiming *academic injury* in cases where teachers allegedly failed or were unable to meet minimal standards of instructional competency.

In cases involving alleged academic injury to students, courts have faced the very difficult task of determining exactly where actual fault lies. Does the alleged injury rest with the student's inability to acquire basic or minimal skills due to the student's lack of ability or motivation? Or does the alleged injury rest with the teacher's inability to meet minimal standards of teaching? Further, if the teacher is determined to be at fault, is it a single teacher, a select few, or all teachers involved in a child's educational experiences who are to be blamed? Because of these difficulties, courts have failed to support charges of malpractice. Also, because teachers historically have had no direct influence over school policies, curriculum, working conditions, or resource acquisition, they could not reasonably be held to a strict standard of liability. However, with the emergence of teacher empowerment, school-based management, and national teaching and certification standards, the courts may be better able to determine if liability has occurred and precisely where it occurred.

Professionalism in Education

The development of national teaching standards involves the establishment of quality indicators and standards of practice that should drive the instructional program. There seems to be a view that judges, who are members of a profession themselves, would understand that any program sequence ought to include certain professional standards of quality to which the instructional program subscribes.

As national standards are embraced by educators and policymakers across the nation, the prevailing question in malpractice suits would likely be whether a certain teacher's practice or the school's program meets these professional standards. If either does not, it will then be easier to identify the particular aspect of the curriculum or the particular teacher or teachers who failed to meet required standards. By doing so, the courts may be able to unravel the complexities surrounding the teaching-learning process. This resolution by the courts would remove the ambiguity traditionally associated with malpractice cases because clearly developed professional standards would be used as a basis for allowing the courts to make proper judgments in malpractice cases.

The teacher as a professional would then be viewed as one who sets standards, exhibits competency and creativity, and conveys subject matter effectively in a variety of ways to all students. In short, teachers would be expected to know the subject they teach, how to teach students effectively, how to organize instructional settings and to model various modes of inquiry, how to use curricular materials, and how to plan and execute instruction. Strengthening the intellectual and methodological foundation of teaching certainly would be one of the products of professionalism in education.

School-Based Management

As school-based management has emerged across the nation as a prevalent organizational structure, teachers have more direct involvement and decision-making authority in matters affecting school policies, curriculum design, program delivery, textbook selection, and governance and overall management of the school. However, with this increased involvement comes greater expectations for accountability regarding student outcomes. Thus, teachers will no longer be totally insulated from threats of malpractice, because they will be exerting considerably more influence over school factors that affect student achievement.

This new level of involvement by teachers may allow courts to determine more precisely where the accountability rests in future cases involving academic injury to students. Teachers may no longer be protected by what the courts commonly have referred to as "public policy grounds" in cases where educational malpractice claims have been brought against school districts. As illustrated by the following cases, courts have been uncomfortable in attempting to apportion liability, because of the absence of professional standards and the multiple factors affecting a student's progress.

Educational Malpractice Cases

In perhaps the earliest malpractice case, *Peter W. v. San Francisco Unified School District,* "plaintiffs brought suit alleging that the school district negligently failed to provide an effective education, and in doing so, violated its professional duty to educate, at least to a minimum standard." The California court, in refusing to recognize educational malpractice as an appropriate course of action, stated that the issue was a "novel and troublesome question." The *Peter W.* suit was originally filed in 1973, but was not decided until 1976. The parents filed suit against the San Francisco Unified School District, its agents, and its employees. The suit alleged intentional misrepresentation, negligence, and a violation of statutory and constitutional duties owed students and parents. The defendant school district was charged with negligently failing to use reasonable care in the discharge of its duties and failing to exercise that degree of professional skill required of an ordinary prudent educator under the same circumstances.[37]

After high school graduation, Peter W. was not able to read above a fifth-grade level. Teachers had systematically promoted him each year and had told the parents he was performing at or near grade level.

The court of appeals refused to recognize a legal duty of care and decided in favor of the school district on public policy considerations. The court reasoned that it could not establish standards of care for classroom instruction and that California's education code had been "structured to afford optimum educational results, not to guard against risk of injury."

In perhaps the most revealing case, *Hoffman v. Board of Education,* the court held for the student, stating that he had experienced diminished intellectual development and psychological injury as a result of inappropriate placement. At age 6, Danny Hoffman had a speech defect. He was given a verbal abilities test by his school to determine placement. He scored 74, one point below normal. That one point resulted in his being placed, for 11 years, in programs for the mentally retarded. At age 17, Danny took an intelligence test required by the Social Security Administration and scored an IQ of 94. He then sued. The trial court held for Hoffman by stating

> Had [the] plaintiff been improperly diagnosed or treated by medical or psychological personnel in a municipal hospital, the municipality would be liable for the ensuing injuries. There is no reason for any different rule here because the personnel were employed by a government entity other than a hospital. Negligence is negligence, even if a defendant . . . prefer(s) semantically to call it educational malpractice.[38]

This case demonstrates one court's willingness to rule on the merits of the case rather than on public policy grounds. The lower court in this case refused to make an exception merely because a governmental entity was involved or because a new theory of educational malpractice would be created. The appellate court upheld the lower court's decision, but lowered the damages to $500,000. The New York Court of Appeals, however, reversed and held for the board of education. The appeals court in New York reached the same decision as the appellate court in California. It stated that the plaintiff had failed to establish that the school board had breached its duty, and such a cause of action should not, as a matter of public policy, be entertained by the courts of New York.

As illustrated in this case, the courts have taken a rather liberal view regarding malpractice in education. However, this position by the courts will not deter future malpractice threats. Increasingly, parents will be inclined to seek damages for injury that they conclude has resulted from poor pedagogy, particularly when educators have a legal duty to provide competent instruction.

A more recent malpractice claim involved a senior high school student in Ohio enrolled in a psychology course to complete a graduation requirement. She failed the course and was unable to graduate with her class. She filed a suit against her psychology teacher seeking damages for negligence, breach of an implied contract, and reckless breach of duty. She claimed that her teacher had not followed guidelines established by the school board. Among these was the requirement that the teacher assign and grade five assignments each semester. The teacher had only assigned three up until the last day of class. During the final class period, a final examination and three quizzes were administered. The student also claimed that the teacher had failed to notify her parents that she was in danger of failing. The teacher moved to dismiss the student's claims. The trial court granted the teacher's motion regarding the negligence and breach of contract claim but did not dismiss the reckless breach of duty claim. The teacher then filed a motion for summary judgment on the remaining claim, which was granted by the trial court. The student appealed to the Ohio Appellate Court.

On review, the appeals court had to determine whether the teacher had sovereign immunity, whether the student had produced sufficient facts to demonstrate that the teacher's actions were the proximate cause of her failing grades, and whether public policy precluded a cause of action for educational malpractice. The court noted that sovereign immunity applied unless the public employee's actions were malicious, in bad faith, or in a wanton or reckless manner. The court held that the student had failed to establish that the teacher's conduct was reckless. The facts alleged by the student also failed to demonstrate that the teacher's actions were the proximate cause of her failure in the class. Although the teacher's omissions contributed to the student's problems in the psychology class, they were not considered to be the proximate cause of her failing the course. The court upheld the trial court's grant of summary judgment and noted that public policy does not favor the court's interference with the professional judgment of educators in determining appropriate methods of teaching.[39]

■ ■ ■ ■ ■ ▬▬

ADMINISTRATIVE GUIDE

EDUCATIONAL MALPRACTICE

1. Develop quality standards of practice as a means to guide the instructional program within schools.
2. Make certain that instructional personnel are well prepared and highly focused on their instructional duties.
3. Ensure that all required competencies and skills are taught in the classroom.
4. Provide systemwide remediation for students who fail to master required skills and competencies or for those who have difficulty learning.
5. Make informed decisions regarding the appropriateness of curriculum, textbooks and instructional policies.
6. Develop flexible and varied instructional strategies and techniques to meet individual needs of students.
7. Use well-prepared promotion and retention standards as guides to decisions affecting student progress.
8. Make certain that curricula objectives are translated into topics actually taught in the classroom.
9. Avoid inappropriate testing procedures that could result in misclassification or inappropriate placement of students.
10. Develop proper means to monitor instructional practices to improve the overall educational delivery system.

ADMINISTRATIVE GUIDE

INSTRUCTIONAL PROGRAM

1. The state legislature has a responsibility to provide schooling for all children within the state at public expense.
2. The legal authority for defining curriculum resides with the legislature.
3. Courts typically do not intervene in curriculum matters because each state retains the authority to establish curriculum standards. They will only intervene if legitimate constitutional issues emerge.
4. Secular curricula are developed by school officials to avoid First Amendment religious conflicts involving church and state.
5. All schools should be held accountable for ensuring that the achievement gap between disadvantaged and minority students is close to that of their peers under the No Child Left Behind Act.
6. Competency tests are supported by the courts where there is no evidence of discriminatory intent.
7. Students may be penalized academically for unexcused absences or truancy if state statute permits. However, policies in this area should be carefully drawn to ensure fairness.
8. Compulsory attendance policies are legally defensible. Parents are accountable and may be penalized for failure to comply with compulsory attendance laws.
9. Exceptions to compulsory attendance policies may be justified based on religious grounds.
10. Home schooling is generally permissible as long as minimal state requirements are met. However, parents do not have a fundamental right to educate their children at home.
11. Public schools generally are required to educate students who reside within their boundaries if the students establish a degree of permanency.
12. Reasonable tuition fees may be imposed on students who attend school outside of their legal residence.
13. Students who are emancipated (not under parental control) are not subject to compulsory attendance requirements.
14. School districts may establish mandatory immunization requirements under the state's police powers, even over parents' religious objections.

IMMUNIZATION AND RELIGION

Tom Banks is the principal of a large elementary school in an urban district. The school includes students from kindergarten through sixth grade. The district requires all students to be immunized before enrolling in school. Two kindergarten children, whose parents hold sincere and genuine religious beliefs against immunization were not allowed to enroll. The parents, who were Jewish, based their belief on a passage from the Bible which they interpreted as forbidding immunization. The parents requested an exemption. Based on information Banks received from a local rabbi, nothing in Jewish teaching prohibits immunization for children.

DISCUSSION QUESTIONS

1. Is an exemption warranted? If so, why? If not, Why?
2. How should Banks respond to the parents' request?
3. The parents have a sincere and genuine religious beliefs against immunization for their children. Should the school or district respect their beliefs?
4. What is the relative weight of parental rights versus the powers of the school or district?
5. If you were facing this issue, how would you respond?
6. How do you think the court would view this issue?
7. How should this issue be resolved?

INSTRUCTIONAL PROGRAM AND QUESTIONABLE CURRICULUM CONTENT

Gary Stone is the principal of a middle school in a steel mill town in the northeastern United States. The town is small, and parents are united and quite vocal regarding school issues. One issue that has emerged involves the school's use of a series of English and literature books that the parents consider Godless, profane, and inappropriate for use in the school. They have organized boycotts and public prayer meetings calling for the death of the principal and school board members who supported the series.

DISCUSSION QUESTIONS

1. What rights do parents have to determine curriculum or course content?
2. How should Stone respond to these irate parents?
3. Should the superintendent and board intervene on behalf of the school? Why or why not?
4. If you were Gary Stone, how would you attempt to resolve this issue, given the very strong emotional position taken by parents?
5. If the court was called into this conflict, how do you think it would rule?
6. How would you assess the relative value of continuing the use of the series versus the disruptions that have been created by the parents?

ENDNOTES

1. *State v. Harwith,* 23 N.E. 946, 947 (Ind. 1890).
2. *Child Welfare Society of Flint v. Kennedy School District,* 189 N.W. 1002, 1004 (Mich. 10922).
3. *Pierce v. Society of Sisters,* 268 U.S. 510, 45 S.Ct. 571, 69 L. Ed 1080 (1925).
4. *Bitting v. Lee,* 564 N.Y.S. 2d 791 (A.D. 3d Dept. 1990).
5. *Wisconsin v. Yoder,* 406 U.S. 205 (1972).
6. *New Jersey v. Massa,* 231 A. 2d 252 (N.J. Sup. Ct. 1967).
7. *People v. Bennett,* 501 N.W. 2d 1067 (Mich. 1993).
8. *Null v. Board of Education,* 815 F. Supp. 937 (W. Va 1993).
9. *Gregg v. Virginia,* 297, 2. E. 2d 799 (Va. 1982).
10. *Battles v. Anne Arundel County Board of Education,* 904 F. Supp. 471 (Md. 1995).

11. *Birst v. Sanstead*, 493 N.W. 2d 690 (N.D. 1992).
12. *Clonlara v. Runkel*, 722 F. Supp. 1442 (E.D. Mich. 1989).
13. *Mason v. General Brown Cent. School Dist.*, 851 F. 2d 47 (2d Cir. 1988).
14. *Brown v. Stone*, 378 So. 2d 218 (Miss. 1980), cert. denied, 449 U.S. 887 (1980).
15. *Lewis v. Sobel*, 710 F. Supp. 506 (S.D.N.Y. 1989).
16. *Byrd v. Livingston Indep. School Dist.*, 67 F. Supp. 225 (E.D. Tex. 1987).
17. *Crowe v. MacFarland*, 515 N.Y.S. 2d 429 (A.D. 3d Dept. 1988).
18. *Harrison v. Sobol*, 705 F. Supp 870, 52 Ed. Law Rptr. 91 (S.D.N.Y. 1988).
19. *Mozert v. Hawkins County Board of Education*, 827 F. 2d 1058 (1987).
20. *Sandlin v. Johnson*, 643 F. 2d 1027 (4th Cir. 1981).
21. *Board of Curators of the University of Missouri v. Horowitz*, 435 U.S. 78, 985 S.Ct. 948 (1978).
22. Ibid.
23. *Debra P. v. Turlington*, 644 F. 2d 397 (5th Cir. 1981).
24. *Rankins v. Louisiana State Board of Elementary and Secondary Education*, 637 So. 2d 548 (La. App. 5th Cir. 1994).
25. *Slocus v. Holton Board of Education*, 429 N.W. 2d 607 (Mich. App. 1988).
26. *Minorities v. Board of Education of Phillipsburg, N.J. Commissioner of Ed.* (1972).
27. *Gutierrez v. School Dist. R-1*, 585 P. 2d 935 (Colo. App. 1978).
28. *Knight v. Board of Education of Tri-Pt. Comm. Unified School District*, 348 N.E. 2d 299 (Ill. 1976).
29. *Raymon v. Alvord Independent School District*, 639 F. 2d 257 (N. Tex. 1981).
30. *Dunn and McCollough v. Fairfield Community High School District No. 225*, 158 F. 3d 962; U.S. App. (1998).
31. *Smith v. School City of Hobart et al. Defendants*, 811 F. Supp. 391, 80 Ed. Law Rept. 839 (Ind. 1993).
32. *Hogenson v. Williams*, 542 S.W. 2d 256 (Tex. App. 1976).
33. *State v. Mizner*, 50 Iowa 145 (1878) in 89 A.L.R. 2d 457.
34. *Melen v. McLaughlin*, 176 A. 297 (BT. 1935).
35. *State v. Vanderbilt*, 18 N.E. 26 (In. 1888).
36. *Valentine v. Independent School District of Casey*, 191 Iowa 1100, 183 N.W. 434 (1921).
37. *Peter v. San Francisco Unified School District*, 131 Cal. Rptr. 854 (1976).
38. *Hoffman v. Board of Education of New York City*, 64 A.D. 2d, 369 N.Y.S. (1978).
39. *Poe v. Hamilton*, 565 N.E. 2d 887 (Ohio App. 1990).

CHAPTER 12

SCHOOL DESEGREGATION

DE JURE SEGREGATION

Racial segregation sanctioned by law persisted in America until the 1950s and 1960s, when the courts took a firm position that separation of children based on race was constitutionally impermissible. Although the Fourteenth Amendment, passed in 1868, provided for equal protection under the laws, a majority of the schools in America remained segregated. Until the mid to late 1960's most school boards held the view that separate but equal was acceptable, when in reality separate facilities for minorities were not equal to those for nonminorities. This view of separate but equal was reinforced by the 1896 *Plessy v. Ferguson* case, in which the U.S. Supreme Court held that a Louisiana statute providing for "equal but separate" accommodations for the white and "colored" races on passenger trains was not illegal. Plessy, a black passenger, had entered a coach designated for whites and refused to leave. He challenged the constitutionality of the law after he was arrested, claiming that discrimination on the basis of color violated the Fourteenth Amendment. The U.S. Supreme Court affirmed that Louisiana's law was not discriminatory, thereby sanctioning the concept of separate but equal. Although this case did not involve schools, its decision established the legal basis for segregated public facilities that was embraced by most public schools.[1]

In 1954, in the landmark *Brown v. Board of Education* case, the principle of separate but equal was struck down by the U.S. Supreme Court which stated that

> Segregation of white and colored children in public schools has a detrimental effect upon the colored children. The impact is greater when it has the sanction of the law; for the policy of separating the races is usually interpreted as denoting the inferiority of the Negro group. A sense of inferiority affects the motivation of a child to learn. Segregation with the sanction of the law therefore has a tendency to retard the educational and mental development of Negro children and to deprive them of some of the benefits they would receive in a racially integrated school system. We conclude that in the field of education, the doctrine of separate but equal has no place. Separate educational facilities are inherently unequal. Therefore, we hold that plaintiffs and others similarly situated for whom this action has been brought are, by reason of the segregation complained of, deprived of the equal protection of the law guaranteed by the Fourteenth Amendment.

Brown v. Board of Education arose when black children in Kansas, South Carolina, Virginia, and Delaware challenged state statutes requiring racial segregation in public schools. Each group challenged the laws in federal district courts on the basis that these laws violated the equal protection clause of the Fourteenth Amendment. Subsequently, each court affirmed that as long as school facilities for blacks were equal to those of whites, segregation was permissible. The U.S. Supreme Court granted *certiorari*. Plaintiffs argued successfully that segregated public schools were not and could not be made equal because they are separated from white facilities. The court examined the effects of separated facilities on children enrolled in public schools and concluded that separate but equal facilities are inherently unequal. Where the state undertakes to provide education, it must make it available to all persons on an equal basis.

Although *Brown* was a landmark decision rendered by the Supreme Court banning *de jure* segregation, the decision did not provide a remedy for removing the vestiges of segregation in the public schools. It provided no guidance and mandated no time frame to achieve desegregated schools. Specific issues unaddressed in *Brown I* were not clearly addressed in *Brown II* which was decided on May 17, 1954. The prevailing message was that the conversion from a dual to a unitary school system must occur with all deliberate speed. Since very little guidance was provided and virtually no direction regarding a specific timetable in which the conversion should occur, there was wide disparity among school districts across the country in complying with the Court's mandate. The High Court essentially returned the cases to the local federal courts to fashion remedies that would permit desegregation with all deliberate speed, since the Fourteenth Amendment only applies to the states. Consequently, the U.S. Supreme Court ruled on the day of the *Brown* ruling that segregation in the public schools of Washington, D.C. was a denial of due process of law guaranteed by the Fifth Amendment.

BROWN II IMPLEMENTATION

After its ruling in *Brown I,* the Supreme Court ruled in *Brown II* to ensure proper implementation of the ruling in *Brown I.* The Court remanded the cases to the federal district courts because of their close proximity to local school districts. It further held that school authorities should be delegated the primary responsibility for implementing its ruling, in good faith and with all deliberate speed. However, the court stated that each district could, in reviewing implementation plans, consider problems related to administration, transportation, personnel, and other issues that might arise during the transition to a nondiscriminatory school system. District courts were mandated to supervise the transition from dual segregated systems to unitary desegregated school systems.[2]

By the 1960s the Supreme Court recognized that the test of good faith and all deliberate speed was not moving as rapidly as it had mandated. Consequently, the Supreme Court became more aggressive by ordering immediate desegregation of students and facilities in the *Rogers v. Paul* case in 1965 in which a desegregation plan adopted by the school system was a grade-a-year plan. Black students in high school did not have the range of courses offered at white schools because the plan started at the lower grades. The Court ruled that where equal course offerings are not available to black students in grades that have not yet been desegregated under a grade-a-year plan, the black students must be admitted immediately to the white school, which had a superior curriculum.[3] In the *Green v. County School Board of New Kent County,* the High Court held that the school board had a leading responsibility to develop a defensible system of determining admission to public schools on a nonracial basis. The Court placed the burden on school districts to develop realistic and workable plans to achieve desegregated schools.[4] The Supreme Court did not support "freedom of choice plans," which allowed students to choose their own school, because they were not effective in achieving desegregation. The only exception involved a clear demonstration by a school district that proper results were achieved. By and large, freedom of choice plans were not deemed to be appropriate remedies to eliminate segregated facilities. In a leading case, the Supreme Court held that continued operation of segregated schools under a standard allowing all "deliberate speed" for desegregation was no longer constitutionally permissible. An obligation was placed on every school district in America to eliminate dual school systems immediately and thereafter to operate only unitary schools.[5]

The *Swann* case was a leading case in defining the scope of the duty to eliminate *de jure* segregation and a dual school system.[6] Chief Justice Burger delivered the opinion of the Court. This case and those argued with it arose in states having a long history of maintaining two sets of schools in a single school system deliberately operated to carry out a governmental policy to separate pupils in schools solely on the basis of race. That was what *Brown v. Board of Education* was all about. These cases present us with the problem of defining in more precise terms than heretofore the scope of the duty of school authorities and district courts in implementing *Brown I* and the mandate to eliminate dual systems and establish unitary systems at once. Meanwhile, district courts and courts of appeals have struggled in hundreds of cases with a multitude and variety of problems under this Court's general directive. Understandably, in an area of evolving remedies, those courts had to improvise and experiment without detailed or specific guidelines. This Court, in *Brown I,* appropriately dealt with the large constitutional principles; other federal courts had to grapple with the flinty, intractable realities of day-to-day implementation of those constitutional commands. Their efforts, of necessity, embraced a process of "trial and error," and our effort to formulate guidelines must take into account their experience.

Racial Balances or Racial Quotas

Our objective in dealing with the issues presented by these cases is to see that school authorities exclude no pupil of a racial minority from any school, directly or indirectly, on account of race; it does not and cannot embrace all the problems of racial prejudice, even when those problems contribute to disproportionate racial concentrations in some schools.

In this case it is urged that the District Court has imposed a racial balance requirement of 71%–29% on individual schools.***

We see therefore that the use made of mathematical ratios was no more than a starting point in the process of shaping a remedy, rather than an inflexible requirement. From that starting point the District Court proceeded to frame a decree that was within its discretionary powers, as an equitable remedy for the particular circumstances. As we said in Green, a school authority's remedial plan or a district court's remedial decree is to be judged by its effectiveness. Awareness of the racial composition of the whole school system is likely to be a useful starting point in shaping a remedy to correct past constitutional violations. In sum, the very limited use made of mathematical ratios was within the equitable remedial discretion of the District Court.

One-Race Schools

The record in this case reveals the familiar phenomenon that in metropolitan areas minority groups are often found concentrated in one part of the city. In some circumstances certain schools may remain all or largely of one race until new schools can be provided or neighborhood patterns change. Schools all or predominately of one race in a district of mixed population will require close scrutiny to determine that school assignments are not part of state-enforced segregation.

An optional majority-to-minority transfer provision has long been recognized as a useful part of every desegregation plan. Provision for optional transfer of those in the majority racial group of a particular school to other schools where they will be in the minority is an indispensable remedy for those students willing to transfer to other schools in order to lessen the impact on them of the state-imposed stigma of segregation. In order to be effective, such a transfer arrangement must grant the transferring student free transportation and space must be made available in the school to which he desires to move.* * * The court orders in this and the companion *Davis* case now provide such an option.

Remedial Altering of Attendance Zones

The maps submitted in these cases graphically demonstrate that one of the principal tools employed by school planners and by courts to break up the dual school system has been a frank—and sometimes drastic—gerrymandering of school districts and attendance zones. An additional step was pairing, "clustering," or "grouping" of schools with attendance assignments made deliberately to accomplish the transfer of Negro students out of formerly segregated Negro schools and transfer of white students to formerly all-Negro schools. More often than not, these zones are neither compact nor contiguous; indeed they may be on opposite ends of the city. As an interim corrective measure, this cannot be said to be beyond the broad remedial powers of a court.

We hold that the pairing and grouping of noncontiguous school zones is a permissible tool and such action is to be considered in light of the objectives sought. Judicial steps in shaping such zones going beyond combinations of contiguous areas should be examined in light of what is said in subdivisions (1), (2), and (3) of this opinion concerning the objectives to be sought. Maps do not tell the whole story since noncontiguous school zones may be more accessible to each other in terms of the critical travel time, because of traffic patterns and good highways, than schools geographically closer together. Conditions in different localities will vary so widely that no rigid rules can be laid down to govern all situations.

Transportation of Students

The scope of permissible transportation of students as an implement of a remedial decree has never been defined by this Court and by the very nature of the problem it cannot be defined with precision. No rigid guidelines as to student transportation can be given for application to the infinite variety of problems presented in thousands of situations. Bus transportation has been an integral part of the public education system for years, and was perhaps the single most important factor in the transition from the one-room schoolhouse to the consolidated school. Eighteen million of the Nation's public school children, approximately 39%, were transported to their schools by bus in 1969–1970 in all parts of the country.

An objection to transportation of students may have validity when the time or distance of travel is so great as to either risk the health of the children or significantly impinge on the educational process.* * * It hardly needs stating that the limits on time of travel will vary with many factors, but probably with none more than the age of the students. The reconciliation of competing values in a desegregation case is, of course, a difficult task with many sensitive facets but fundamentally no more so than remedial measures courts of equity have traditionally employed.

The Court of Appeals, searching for a term to define the equitable remedial power of the district courts, used the term "reasonableness." In Green, supra, this Court used the term "feasible" and by implication, "workable," "effective," and "realistic" in the mandate to develop "a plan that promises realistically to work, and . . . to work now." On the facts of this case, we are unable to conclude that the order of the District Court is not reasonable, feasible and workable. However, in seeking to define the scope of remedial power or the limits on remedial power of courts in an area as sensitive as we deal with here, words are poor instruments to convey the sense of basic fairness inherent in equity. Substance, not semantics, must govern, and we have sought to suggest the nature of limitations without frustrating the appropriate scope of equity.

It does not follow that the communities served by such systems will remain demographically stable, for in a growing, mobile society, few will do so. Neither school authorities nor district courts are constitutionally required to make year-by-year adjustments of the racial composition of student bodies once the affirmative duty to desegregate has been accomplished and racial discrimination through official action is eliminated from the system. This does not mean that federal courts are without power to deal with future problems; but in the absence of a showing that either the school authorities or some other agency of the State has deliberately attempted to fix or alter demographic patterns to affect the racial composition of the schools, further intervention by a district court should not be necessary.

For the reasons herein set forth, the judgement of the court of appeals is affirmed as to those parts in which it affirmed the judgement of the district court. The order of the district court, dated August 7, 1970 is also affirmed.

It is so ordered.

FREE TRANSFER AND FREEDOM
OF CHOICE PROGRAM

Although some courts had held that free transfers and freedom of choice plans were not effective ways to achieve desegregation, many districts adopted these plans as a means to avoid desegregation. The implementation of free transfers led to students being assigned to racially identifiable schools. School officials were not able to avoid court-ordered desegregation by permitting students to select any school they wish to attend within the district. A number of districts adopted minority-to-majority transfer plans in an effort to avoid desegregation orders. These plans permitted a student to transfer from a school where he or she was in the racial minority to a school where he or she would be in the racial majority. The plan had the effect of resegregating schools, as virtually no students sought transfers. Consequently, these plans were not supported by the courts.

As an example, a group of black children in Tennessee challenged their school board's desegregation plan in a federal district court.[7] The plan provided for rezoning of school districts without reference to race. However, the plan also provided that a student could request to transfer from the school to which he or she was reassigned, back to his or her former segregated school where his or her race would be in the majority. The plan was approved by a federal district court and by the U.S. Court of Appeals, Sixth Circuit. The U.S. Supreme Court granted *certiorari.*

The black children contended that the district's transfer policy perpetuated racial segregation. They pointed out that although transfers were available to those who chose to attend school where their race was in the majority, there was no provision for a student to transfer to a school in which his race was in the minority, unless he or she could show "good cause" for the transfer. The Court agreed and struck the plan down as constitutionally insufficient to fulfill the *Brown* requirements of desegregation. The Court ruled that if the plan had provided for transfer provisions regardless of the students' race or of the schools' racial composition, it would have been constitutional. Classifications on the basis of race for transfer purposes between schools violate the Fourteenth Amendment. The Court invalidated the plan.

Freedom of choice plans met the same resistance by the courts when used to perpetuate segregated schools. Freedom of choice plans resulted in a sparse number of black students attending predominately white schools and no whites attending predominantly black schools. The court held in *Green v. County School Board* that

> The burden on a school board today is to come forward with a plan that promises realistically to work. . . . Now we do not hold that the Freedom of Choice Plan might of itself be unconstitutional. . . rather, all we decide today is that a plan utilizing freedom of choice is not an end in itself. . . If the means prove effective, it is acceptable, but if it fails to undo segregation, other means must be used.[8]
>
> The only school desegregation plan that meets constitutional standards is one that works.[9]

Prior to the passage of *Brown I* and *II,* the equal protection clause of the Fourteenth Amendment was subject to customs and traditions as determined by state legislative interpretation, irrespective of the impact of the law on a particular class of people.

De Jure Segregation

Because the equal protection clause essentially covers state action, it prohibits state-endorsed discrimination. Racial segregation derived from the enforcement of law is called *de jure segregation* and is illegal and unconstitutional. Conversely, segregation or racial imbalance created by housing patterns independent of government influence is called *de facto segregation* and is generally deemed permissible. The following elements are usually present in cases involving *de jure* segregation:

1. It has been initiated or supported by government action
2. With an intent or motive to discriminate, and
3. The action must result in creating or increasing segregation.[10]

While unconstitutional *de jure segregation* may lack a precise definition based on factors that surround each case, it has consistently been held unconstitutional by the courts.

Although the Supreme Court has come under enormous criticism, it has been fairly consistent in approving the *de jure–de facto* distinction in its rulings involving segregated facilities.

> What is or it not a segregated school will necessarily depend on the facts of each particular case. In addition to the . . . composition of a school's student body, other factors such as the racial and ethnic composition of faculty and staff and the community and administration's attitudes toward the school must be taken into consideration.[11]

De Facto Segregation

De facto segregation is present when a substantial number of students enrolled in a school represent a racial or ethnic minority. This situation developed through no action taken by the school district designed to encourage or require it. However, the courts, and especially *Brown,* mandate that corrective actions be taken in instances where school officials gerrymander (alter) school attendance zones to create zones with large concentrations of black students assigned to historically black schools within the district. These actions represent deliberate efforts to create segregated schools by governmental action. While often referred to as *de facto* segregation, it is in reality a form of *covert de jure* segregation.

An example of false *de facto* segregation emerged in New Rochelle, New York. The board of education realigned several school attendance boundaries and permitted transfers only of white students who lived within the boundaries of the school in question. Approximately 90 percent of the students attending the school were black. According to the Second Circuit Court of Appeals, the primary objective of the school redistricting was to produce a substantially segregated school. Such conduct clearly violated the Fourteenth Amendment and the *Brown* holding, and it was deemed to be *de jure* segregation.[12]

A very different case arose in Connecticut when a suit was filed on behalf of public school children alleging denial of equal educational opportunities based on racial and ethnic segregation. The facts suggested that such segregation was *de facto* rather than *de jure* (based on law). Consequently, the defense requested that the case be dismissed. Plaintiffs asserted that their rights under the state constitution were violated because it provided a right to a free public elementary and secondary education as well as a right to protection from segregation. The Supreme Court of Connecticut held for the plaintiffs. The court stated

> We direct the legislature and the executive branch to place the search for appropriate remedial measures at the top of their respective agenda . . . We are confident that with energy and good will, appropriate remedies can be found and implemented in time to make a difference before another generation of children suffers the consequences of a segregated public school education.[13]

Nonetheless, the court mandated a remedy to segregation in this case whether it was based on *de facto* or *de jure* segregation.

It is important to understand that school districts are generally not required to take corrective action in cases where racial imbalances have developed within the schools of the district as a result of housing patterns and the uniform application of school zoning and student transfer policies. However, it also does not mean that the courts will support unequal facilities, programs, and staffs in predominately black schools. These deficiencies will necessitate responsive corrective action to ensure equality of educational opportunity.

The posture of the courts regarding *de facto* segregation has been to correct educational inequalities without requiring racial mixing.

THE CIVIL RIGHTS ACT OF 1964

Congress passed the Civil Rights Act of 1964, specifically Title VI, which prohibits discrimination on the basis of race or color in programs receiving federal funds, making the elimination of segregated schools compliant with maintaining federal financial aid. The U.S. Department of Education issued guidelines to be implemented in determining whether segregated school districts were making sufficient progress toward establishing unitary schools within their districts. Failure to comply with Department of Education guidelines would result in a cessation of federal funds. School districts in the South that were not under court-ordered desegregation plans were required to file compliance plans with the U.S. Office of Education.

The U.S. Department of Justice was charged with enforcing various components of the Civil Rights Act. The U.S. attorney general was granted the authority to initiate suits against school districts to achieve desegregation. The courts gave "great weight" to the Department of Education guidelines in assessing the effectiveness of proposed desegregation plans.[14] However, they emphasized that they were not bound by these guidelines. Federal courts, especially in the South, were overburdened with school desegregation cases. These cases were mixed. Some represented resistance while others attempted to comply with federal guidelines. For example, schools in Little Rock, Arkansas attempted to implement desegregation plans in 1957 but were met with resistance by the Governor Orval Faubus, who ordered the National Guard to prevent black students from entering the schools in which they had been assigned under the district's plan.

Local authorities in some districts sought postponement of implementing desegregation plans by suggesting that public peace would be preserved. The U.S. Supreme Court addressed this issue in *Cooper v. Aaron*[15] by stating that desegregation of schools could not be postponed in spite of the state's effort to hamper the district's good faith efforts to desegregate its schools. Other school districts resorted to more drastic action to avoid desegregating their schools.

Virginia repealed its compulsory education laws, making school attendance a local option. Prince Edward County closed its schools and established private schools for whites only with county and state assistance. The Supreme Court rejected this course of action and ordered the district to levy taxes and generate funds to reopen and operate a nondiscriminatory public school system. The State of Virginia passed laws to close and eliminate funds for public schools that were not desegregated. The legislation was struck down by the Virginia courts. The state then adopted a freedom of choice program and left school attendance to each locality. The U.S. Court of Appeals for the Fourth Circuit held that the practices employed by the district were discriminatory and ordered that they must cease. In response to the court's decision, the county refused to levy taxes for the next school year, resulting in the closing of schools for several years, during which time private schools for whites only were established. These private schools received tuition grants and tax credits from the state. A federal district court held that these actions were explicitly designed to prevent desegregation and ordered that schools be reopened. The county requested that the district court stay proceedings pending a state court suit to determine the validity of the tax breaks and grants and whether schools could be closed under Virginia's constitution. The district court denied, but the court of appeals reversed. The U.S. Supreme Court granted *certiorari*. The High Court reversed the appellate court's decision and reinstated the district court's ruling. It held that black children in Prince Edward County had been denied equal protection of the law because white children could attend private schools, whereas black children had no access to any schools. It concluded that public schools had been closed for the sole purpose of preventing white and black children from attending the same school. The court remanded the case to the district court to enter a decree ensuring that black children would receive an equal education in public schools along with whites.[16]

INTRA-DISTRICT SEGREGATION

Attendance Zones

School officials and courts alike viewed gerrymandering of school districts' attendance zones as a useful tool to alleviate segregated schools. Pairing, clustering, and grouping of noncontiguous school zones were considered to be permissible remedies by the courts to achieve desegregated schools. These initiatives were designed primarily to move black students out of segregated schools and to transfer white students into historically black schools. The objective of zoning plans was to create racially neutral student assignments. However, these plans were not always viewed as acceptable by the courts. For example, if they failed to counteract the continuing effects of past school segregation resulting from the discriminatory location of schools to achieve racial separation, they were not supported. School officials were not permitted to create racially identifiable schools by drawing attendance zones. In cases where school officials created unlawful segregated schools in one segment of the district, the Supreme Court held that the constitutional remedy was limited to that part of the district that produced *de jure* segregation. The courts may order reassignment of teachers and students to remove vestiges of segregation. They also may remedy the adverse effects of past discrimination by ordering segregated districts to implement and fund certain educational programs such as remedial reading and writing as well as staff development training for minority teachers.

A student assignment plan was not acceptable by the courts simply because it appeared to be neutral. Evidence was needed to ensure that the plan counteracted the continuing effects of past school segregation. An example of the court's position arose in an extended case involving intra-district segregation in 1977 when the Kansas City, Missouri School District (KCMSD), its school board, and a group of students who resided within the district sued the state and a number of suburban school districts in U.S. district court. They contended that the state had caused and perpetuated racial segregation in Kansas City schools. Following a realignment of parties to establish KCMSD as a nominal defendant, the district concluded that the state and KCMSD were both liable for an intra-district constitutional violation. Both defendants were ordered to eliminate all vestiges of state-imposed segregation. Because the district's student population was approximately 70 percent black, the district court ordered a wide range of education plans, resulting in magnet schools for all high schools, middle schools, and some elementary schools that were designed to attract white students from the suburbs. The court's action was based on a finding that Kansas City school students' achievement levels still lagged behind national averages in some grades. The state contested its court-ordered responsibility to assist in funding capital improvements for Kansas City schools. It also contested district court orders requiring it to share the cost of teacher salary increases and quality education plans. The U.S. Court of Appeals for the Eighth Circuit affirmed the district court's orders.

On appeal by the state, the U.S. Supreme Court observed that the district's remedial plan had been based on a budget that exceeded the Kansas City schools' authority to tax. There also was no compelling evidence in the district court's records to support the theory that the continuing lack of academic achievement in the district resulted from past segregation. The High Court held that the district court had exceeded its authority by ordering construction of a superior school system to attract white students. Its mandate was to eliminate the racial identity of Kansas City schools. The intra-district remedy exceeded the intra-district violation. The magnet concept could not be supported by the existence of white flight. The district court's orders for state contributions to salary increases, quality education programs, and capital improvement were reversed.[17]

Busing

Historically, the courts have viewed busing as an effective means of achieving desegregated schools. It has met opposition by parents and taxpayers who considered busing to be a threat to the neighborhood school concept, time-consuming for students, and an added expense on taxpayers. Parents and taxpayers advocated that money be expended on improving neighborhood schools rather on busing. Several states passed antibusing legislation to prohibit the use of busing. For example, a North Carolina law prohibited busing children to achieve racial desegregation was passed in the middle of the *Swann* case. Blacks involved with the *Swann* case sought injunctive and declaratory relief against the statute. A three-judge federal district court declared the antibusing law unconstitutional. The state board of education and school officials sought review by the U.S. Supreme Court.

The Court held that busing based on race was a necessary and legitimate manner in which to carry desegregation. Although busing was not required by the district, a blatant prohibition against it conflicted with the obligation of school officials to implement an effective desegregation plan. The district court's decision was upheld.[18]

Federal courts were challenged when their rulings called for busing to remedy segregated schools. For example, California passed Proposition One, barring busing to achieve desegregation and voters in Washington approved legislation restricting busing. However, in *Washington v. Seattle School District No. 1,* the U.S. Supreme Court upheld an appellate court's ruling that mandated the use of busing to achieve a racial balance in schools within the district. The Supreme Court held that an antibusing initiative would result in impermissible racial classification of students for the purpose of achieving segregated schools.[19] However, in a California case, *Crawford v. Board of Education of Los Angeles,* the Supreme Court upheld a state constitutional amendment barring the use of mandatory busing except where there was evidence of Fourteenth Amendment violations. California was not required to adhere to more stringent standards than were mandated by the Fourteenth Amendment because by state law, *de facto* and *de jure* segregation were prohibited.[20]

Involuntary busing emerged as a major issue during the height of the courts' efforts to achieve nonracially identifiable schools. Busing has been imposed by the courts and legislation as one solution to eliminate segregated schools. It has been viewed as an affirmative effort to correct inequities as a result of past discrimination. Consequently, many districts, as a component of their desegregation plan, implemented programs requiring students to be transported to schools outside their neighborhoods. The intent was to create equal educational opportunities for all children regardless of race, national origin, or socioeconomic background. Interestingly, busing was initiated almost as a one-way concept simply because black students were bused to allegedly better schools in white neighborhoods. Busing was opposed by many citizens including parents of minority children. A number of minority parents felt that one-way busing, supported discriminatory attitudes toward black children and that their children were bearing the burden by having to be transported great distances away from their neighborhoods. Similar views were also expressed by non-minority parents whose children were transported away from their neighborhoods.

A number of district courts concluded that allowing students to attend schools near where they lived would not effectively dismantle dual school systems. Busing was considered one viable measure used by the courts to achieve desegregated schools.

Faculty Desegregation

The issue involving faculty desegregation did not surface until the mid to late sixties. Teacher race had not been challenged during the initial desegregation cases. Plans involving desegregation of faculty had not been required by the courts as they addressed plans involving desegregation of students. Then, in 1965, two black students filed suit in a federal district court to enforce pupil and teacher desegregation in an Arkansas school district's high schools.[21] The district court refused to grant the order by holding that the students had no standing to challenge desegregation among faculty. The U.S. Court of Appeals for the Eighth Circuit affirmed that decision. During the proceedings, one of the students had graduated and the other had reached the twelfth grade. Two other black high school students petitioned the U.S. Supreme Court to be added as plaintiffs in the suit. The Court ruled that the students did in fact have legal standing to challenge faculty segregation in the district because it denied them equal educational opportunities. The case was remanded to courts of appeal for further deliberations.

Because desegregation plans involving faculty were not addressed during the height of school desegregation plans, progress came very slowly. To compound the problem, there was no test or standard to be applied to measure racial mix in faculty. The absence of a test made it difficult for the courts to fashion remedies without creating untimely delays. One tangible remedy, ordered by a lower court and upheld by the U.S. Supreme Court, established a goal for each school within the district that called for assigning approximately the same ratio of black and white teachers as was the ratio existing in the school district population as a whole.[22]

The following year this concept was adopted by the Fifth Circuit Court of Appeals as a guide for integrating faculty throughout the circuit.[23] Some district courts had accepted a slow integration of black and white faculty based on the view of boards of education that a rapid pace would result in white flight among their faculties. The court of appeals was not very sympathetic to this view and held that faculty resistance cannot form the basis for not moving ahead to achieve a unitary school system.

Problems arose in integrating faculty with respect to tenure status, especially in cases where a disproportionate number of black faculty were not retained. Courts scrutinized cases where large reductions occurred among black faculty based on a long history of racial discrimination and resistance among districts to move aggressively with the implementation of desegregation plans. Consequently, school boards were required to justify their action with clear evidence when there was an inference of discrimination. School districts were required to formulate nonracial objective criteria for retention and employment of teachers and to apply them equally to all teachers.

Seeking Unitary Status

After years of fashioning remedies for segregated schools, school districts across the country are presently filing for unitary status, in which school officials are claiming that good faith efforts have been initiated to achieve desegregated schools; therefore, they should be relieved of court supervision. Desegregation orders have been lifted in Denver, Colorado; Buffalo, New York; Dallas, Austin (Texas); Indianapolis, Indiana; Savannah, Georgia; and Nashville. Many more districts are currently filing for unitary status. Two U.S. Supreme Court decisions during the 1990s provided some direction in addressing judicial supervision.

In *Board of Education of Oklahoma City Public Schools v. Dowell* in 1972, a federal district court issued an injunction mandating a school desegregation plan for Oklahoma City. In 1977, the court found that the district had achieved unitary status. Consequently, an order was issued by the court terminating the case. In 1984, there was an increase in young black students that necessitated them being bused farther away. Based on this development, the board adopted the Student Reassignment Plan (SRP), which assigned students in grades K–4 to their neighborhood schools and continued busing for grades 5–12. Parents who initiated the desegregation suit filed a motion requesting that the case be reopened because SRP was a return to segregation. The federal district court refused to reopen the case and held that the district was unitary and would not be relitigated. Parents appealed to the Tenth Circuit Court of Appeals, which held that the court's 1977 finding was binding but did not mean that the 1972 injunction should necessarily be lifted. The case was remanded to determine whether the injunction should necessarily be lifted. The trial court, on remand, found that the SRP did not have a discriminatory intent and ordered that the injunction be lifted. The case was again appealed to the U.S. Court of Appeals, which reversed the lower court's decision. The school district petitioned the U.S. Supreme Court for a review.

The High Court held that the 1977 order did not dissolve the desegregation decree. Furthermore, the district court's finding that the district was unitary was too ambiguous to prevent parents from challenging the later actions by the board. The Court emphasized that supervision of the district by federal courts was intended to serve as a temporary remedy to past discrimination. The U.S. Supreme Court remanded the case to the trial court to determine whether the district had shown sufficient compliance with constitutional requirements when it adopted the SRP. The trial court was to determine whether the district had acted in good faith to eliminate vestiges of past discrimination—to the extent possible.[24] In essence, the U.S. Supreme Court held that the federal court's regulatory control over an unlawful segregated district is limited to the necessary time needed to remedy vestiges of past discrimination.

In another case involving unitary status, *Freeman v. Pitts,* the DeKalb County, Georgia school system was cited for unlawful segregated schools in 1969 and placed under supervision by the court. The district implemented a variety of measures to achieve unitary status, then requested that judicial control be removed. A federal district court held that unitary status had been achieved to the extent practicable regarding student assignments, transportation, physical facilities, and extracurricular activities. However, unitary status had not been achieved regarding faculty assignments and resource allocation. The district court relinquished control in the four areas found to be unitary but retained control of the remaining two areas. On appeal, the U.S. Court of Appeals rejected the incremental approach and held that unitary status in some areas could not lead to relinquished judicial control until all areas under review were unitary. On *certiorari,* the U.S. Supreme Court reversed the court of appeals decision in holding that the incremental approach was constitutional. The Court ordered no further remedy in areas found to be unitary, thus allowing the district to focus on areas in need of correction.[25] The implication of this case is that the federal district court, which supervises court-ordered desegregation, has the latitude to order incremental withdrawal of its supervision and control.

The U.S. Court of Appeals for the Tenth Circuit in *Brown v. Board of Education of Topeka* (Brown III) expressed its view of unitariness and the standards for determining whether it has been achieved. It stated that the court must assess what a school district has or has not done in good faith to meet its obligation to desegregate. Once it has been established that the district is intentionally segregated, the burden of proof rests with the district to demonstrate that it has eliminated all vestiges of segregation to the fullest extent possible. Racially identifiable schools must first be present to satisfy the court that segregation exists, which is commonly demonstrated by the assignment of students to one-race schools. However, if one-race schools are present due to no fault of the district but based on shifts in demographics beyond the control of the district, they are not necessarily illegal so long as *de jure* segregation is not present. In such cases, the district is not held accountable. If a district can demonstrate effective results in moving from a segregated district to a desegregated district, it will generally meet the approval of the courts. In cases where there is a substantial record of evidence demonstrating that school officials have acted in good faith to achieve a desegregated school system, the courts are inclined to grant the request. The burden of proof that unitary status has been achieved rests with the school district. Absent proof of a good-faith effort and effective results, many districts have not been relieved of court supervision.

A case challenging removal of court supervision arose in Alabama. The Talladega County school district was under federal court-ordered supervision from 1967 to 1985. A group of black parents contended that after dismissal of the original lawsuit, the district engaged in action that had a disparate impact on black students attending schools in the district. The group alleged that the district closed an all-black school, constructed a new school in the white community, allowed white students to transfer to other public school systems, and ignored the black parents' concerns at school board meetings. Parents filed suit against the school district in the U.S. District Court for the Northern District of Alabama claiming violations of the Fourteenth Amendment, Title VI of the Civil Rights Act of 1964, state laws such as the Open Meeting Act, and a breach of contract of the 1985 stipulation of settlement. When the court dismissed the case the parents appealed.

The U.S. Court of Appeals, Eleventh Circuit ruled that the district court had properly dismissed the constitutional and Title VI complaints based on the failure of the parents to prove that the board's action had been motivated by racial discrimination. The rationale provided by the board for closing and constructing new facilities was supported by substantial evidence that its actions met legitimate educational goals. There was insufficient evidence to support the claim that the board could have taken action against white students who transferred to schools outside the district. The district court had properly dismissed the breach of contract and state law claims, but its decision stated no reason for ruling against the parents regarding their complaint that the board had prohibited recordings of its public meetings. That portion of the district's court decision was vacated and the remainder was affirmed.[26]

ADMINISTRATIVE GUIDE

DE JURE SEGREGATION

1. *De jure* segregation is illegal and will not be supported by the courts.
2. Involuntary segregated schools deny black students equal protection under the law.
3. "Separate but equal" schools for blacks and whites are inherently inequal.
4. Lack of funds cannot be used by school districts as a basis for failure to create a desegregated school district.
5. *Brown* was a pivotal case in establishing the civil rights of black Americans not only in education, but also in public transportation and housing.
6. Court-ordered quota systems and busing have not been totally effective in achieving desegregated schools and may have precipitated white flight.
7. During the late twentieth and early twenty-first centuries, there has been a discernible trend toward resegregated schools where many blacks are attending inferior inner city schools while whites attend more affluent suburban schools.
8. School authorities should be committed to providing an equal educational opportunity for black and white students even in the absence of court-ordered desegregation rulings. Pairing and Clusters are allowable as means of achieving desegregation in the work to remove vestiges of segregated schools.
9. Busing, while not a popular option among parents and citizens, was one remedy by which school officials could affirm desegregated schools.
10. Court supervision may be lifted in part or in whole where a school district can show that it has acted in good faith to remedy past discrimination in its schools.
11. Once unitary status has been achieved by a school district and no deliberate action is taken to recreate segregated schools, The school district *is not required to seek remedies* in situations involving segregation *which may evolve* that are beyond the district's control.
12. Race may be used as a factor in university admissions decisions.
13. Point systems or quotas are disallowed in university admissions decisions and violate the Fourteenth Amendment's equal protection clause.

DESEGREGATION—AN END TO BUSING

An affluent school district was subject to a court-ordered desegregation plan involving busing. After receiving the court order recognizing that the district had achieved unitary status, the district decided to discontinue elementary school busing and move toward a neighborhood plan that would bus sixth-graders to a middle school. Parents and citizens challenged the end of elementary school busing, alleging that it would recreate segregated schools.

DISCUSSION QUESTIONS

1. Do parents and citizens have a valid claim?
2. Are the district's actions designed to create segregated schools?
3. Does the district have a right to discontinue elementary-school busing and implement a neighborhood plan after it has achieved unitary status?
4. Did the district use its new status to engage in *de jure* segregation? Why or why not?
5. How do you think the court would rule in this case? Provide a rationale for your response.
6. What are the administrative implications of this case?

DESEGREGATION AND TEACHER TRANSFER

A board of education in an urban school district of 160,000 students adopted a teacher-transfer policy in each of its schools to establish a racial composition that was within 10 percent of the racial composition of the district population as a whole. This policy was not mandated by the court. Essentially, this policy restricted voluntary transfer of black and white teachers to other schools within the district but also required reassignment of other teachers. The policy was challenged by the teachers' association, which claimed a violation of teachers' Fourteenth Amendment rights.

DISCUSSION QUESTIONS

1. Does the teachers' association have a valid claim? Why or why not?
2. Is the district justified in the formulation of this transfer policy? Why or why not?
3. Can teachers make a valid claim of disparate impact in this case? Why or why not?
4. Should not the policy be race-neutral? Why or why not?
5. Do you feel that such a policy is arbitrary and capricious? Why or why not?
6. How would the court likely view this policy?
7. What are the administrative implications?

ENDNOTES

1. *Plessy v. Ferguson* 163 U.S. 537 (1891).
2. *Brown v. Board of Education,* 349 U.S. 294, 75 S.Ct. 753, 99 L. Ed. 1083 (1955). (*Brown II*)
3. *Rogers v. Paul,* 382 U.S. 198 (1965).
4. *Green v. County Board of New Kent,* 391 U.S. 430 439–40 (1968).
5. *Alexander v. Holmes County Board of Education,* 396 U.S. 1218, 90 S.Ct. 14 (1969).
6. *Swann v. Charlotte Mecklenburg Board of Education,* 402 U.S. 1, 91 S.Ct. 1267, 28 L. Ed. 2d 554 (1970).
7. *Goss v. Board of Education,* 373 U.S. 683, *3 S.Ct. 1405, 10 L. Ed. 2d 632 (1963).
8. Op. cit.
9. *United States v. Jefferson County Board of Education,* 372 F. 2d 836, 847 (5th Cir. 1966).
10. *Alexander v. Youngstown Board of Education,* 675 F. 2d 787, 791 (6th Cir. 1982).
11. *Keyes v. School District No. 1, Denver,* 413 U.S. 189, 196 (1973).
12. *Taylor v. Board of Education of City School District of New Rochelle,* 294 F. 2d 36 (2nd Cir. 1961), cert. den., 368 U.S. 940, 82 S.Ct. 382, 7 L. Ed. 2d 339 (1961).
13. *Sheff v. O'Neill,* 678 A. 2d 1291 (Conn. 1996).
14. *Singleton v. Jackson Municipal Separate School District,* 348 F. 2d 729 (5th Cir. 1965).
15. *Cooper v. Aaron,* 358 U.S. 1; 78 S.Ct. 1401; 3 L. Ed. 2d 19; 1958 U.S. Lexis 1939; 79 Ohio L. Abs. 462.
16. *Griffin v. County School Board,* 377 U.S. 218, 84 S.Ct. 1226, 12 L. Ed. 2d 256 (1964).
17. *Missouri v. Jenkins,* 115 S.Ct. 2038, 132 L. Ed. 2d 63 (1995). (*Jenkins III*).
18. *North Carolina State Board of Education v. Swann,* 402 U.S. 43, 91 S.Ct. 1284 2d L. Ed. 2d 586 (1971).
19. *Washington v. Seattle School District No. 1,* 458 U.S. 457; 102 S.Ct. 3187; 73 L. Ed. 2d 896 (1982).
20. *Crawford v. Board of Education of Los Angeles,* 458 U.S. 457; 102 S.Ct. 3187; 73 L. Ed. 2d 896 (1982).
21. Op. cit., 382 U.S. 198 (1965).
22. *United States v. Montgomery County Board of Education,* 395 U.S. 225, 89 S.Ct. 1670, 23 L. Ed. 2d 263 (1969).
23. *Singleton v. Jackson Municipal Separate School District,* 419 F. 2d 1211 (5th Cir. 1970), cert. den., 396 U.S. 1032, 90 S.Ct. 612, 24 L. Ed. 2d 530 (1970).
24. *Board of Oklahoma City Public Schools v. Dowell,* 498 U.S. 237, 111 S.Ct. 630, 112 L. Ed. 2d 715 (1991).
25. *Freeman v. Pitts,* 503 U.S. 467, 112 S.Ct. 1430, 118 L. Ed. 2d 108 (1992).
26. *Elston v. Talladega County Board of Education,* 997 F. 2d 1394 (11th Cir. 1993).

THE CONSTITUTION OF THE UNITED STATES

Provisions and Amendments Affecting Education

CONSTITUTION OF THE UNITED STATES

We the People of the United States, in Order to form a more perfect Union, establish Justice, insure domestic Tranquility, provide for the common defence, promote the general Welfare, and secure the Blessings of Liberty to ourselves and our Posterity, do ordain and establish this Constitution for the United States of America.

Article I

Section 1. All legislative Powers herein granted shall be vested in a Congress of the United States, which shall consist of a Senate and House of Representatives.

Section 2. The House of Representatives shall be composed of Members chosen every second Year by the People of the several States, and the Electors in each State shall have the Qualifications requisite for Electors of the most numerous Branch of the State Legislature.

***

Section 7. All Bills for raising Revenue shall originate in the House of Representatives; but the Senate may propose or concur with amendments as on other Bills.

Every Bill which shall have passed the House of Representatives and the Senate, shall, before it become a Law, be presented to the President of the United States; If he approve he shall sign it, but if not he shall return it, with his Objections to that House in which it shall have originated, who shall enter the Objections at large on their Journal, and proceed to reconsider it. If after such Reconsideration two thirds of that House shall agree to pass the Bill, it shall be sent, together with the Objections, to the other House, by which it shall likewise be reconsidered, and if approved by two thirds of that House, it shall become a Law. But in all such Cases the Votes of both Houses shall be determined by yeas and Nays, and the Names of the Persons voting for and against the Bill shall be entered on the Journal of each House respectively. If any Bill shall not be returned by the President within ten Days (Sunday excepted) after it shall have been presented to him, the Same shall be a Law, in like Manner as if he had signed it, unless the Congress by their Adjournment prevents its Return, in which Case it shall not be a Law.

***

Article II

Section 1. The executive Power shall be vested in a President of the United States of America. . . .

Section 2. The President shall be Commander in Chief of the Army and Navy of the United States, and of the Militia of the several states, . . .

He shall have Power, by and with the Advice and Consent of the Senate, to make Treaties, provided two thirds of the Senators present concur; and he shall nominate, and by and with the Advice and Consent of the Senate, shall appoint Ambassadors, other public Ministers and Consuls, Judges of the supreme Court, and all other Officers of the United States, whose Appointments are not herein otherwise provided for, and which shall be established by Law: but the Congress may by Law vest the Appointment of such inferior Officers, as they think proper, in the President alone, in the Courts of Law, or in the Heads of Departments. . . .

***

Article III

Section 1. The judicial Power of the United States, shall be vested in one supreme Court, and in such inferior Courts as the Congress may from time to time ordain and establish. The Judges, both of the supreme and inferior Courts, shall hold their Offices during good Behaviour, and shall, at stated Times, receive for their Services, a Compensation, which shall not be diminished during their Continuance in Office.

Section 2. The judicial Power shall extend to all Cases, in Law and Equity, arising under this Constitution, the Laws of the United States, and Treaties made, or which shall be made, under their Authority;—to all Cases affecting Ambassadors, other public Ministers and Consuls;—to all Cases of admiralty and maritime Jurisdiction;—to Controversies to which the United States shall be a Party;—to Controversies between two or more States;—between a State and Citizens of another State;—between Citizens of different States;—between Citizens of the same State claiming Lands under Grants of different States, and between a State, or the Citizens thereof, and foreign States, Citizens or Subjects.

***

The Trial of all Crimes, except in Cases of Impeachment, shall be by Jury; and such Trial shall be held in the State where the said Crimes shall have been committed; but when not committed within any State, the Trial shall be at such Place or Places as the Congress may by Law have directed.

***

Article IV

Section 1.   Full Faith and Credit shall be given in each State to the public Acts, Records, and judicial Proceedings of every other State. And the Congress may by general Laws prescribe the Manner in which such Acts, Records and Proceedings shall be proved, and the Effect thereof.

Section 2.   The Citizens of each State shall be entitled to all Privileges and Immunities of the Citizens in the several States.

***

Section 4.   The United States shall guarantee to every State in this Union a Republican Form of Government, and shall protect each of them against Invasion; and on Application of the Legislature, or of the Executive (when the Legislature cannot be convened) against domestic Violence.

Article V

The Congress, whenever two thirds of both Houses shall deem it necessary, shall propose Amendments to this Constitution, or, on the Application of the Legislatures of two thirds of the several States, shall call a Convention for proposing Amendments, which, in either Case, shall be valid to all Intents and Purposes, as Part of this Constitution, when ratified by the Legislatures of three fourths of the several States, or by Conventions in three fourths thereof, as the one or the other Mode of Ratification may be proposed by the Congress; Provided that no Amendment which may be made prior to the Year One thousand eight hundred and eight shall in any Manner affect the first and fourth Clauses in the Ninth Section of the first Article; and that no State, without its Consent, shall be deprived of its equal Suffrage in the Senate.

***

Article VI

This Constitution, and the Laws of the United States which shall be made in Pursuance thereof; and all Treaties made, or which shall be made, under the Authority of the United States, shall be the supreme Law of the Land; and the Judges in every State shall be bound thereby, any Thing in the Constitution or Laws of any State to the Contrary notwithstanding.

The Senators and Representatives before mentioned, and the Members of the several State Legislatures, and all executive and judicial Officers, both of the United States and of the several States, shall be bound by Oath or Affirmation, to support this Constitution; but no religious Test shall ever be required as a qualification to any office or public trust under the United States.

Article VII

The Ratification of the Conventions of nine States, shall be sufficient for the Establishment of this Constitution between the States so ratifying the Same.

AMENDMENTS TO THE CONSTITUTION
OF THE UNITED STATES OF AMERICA

Articles in Addition to, and Amendment of, the Constitution of the United States of America, Proposed by Congress, and Ratified by the Several States, Pursuant to the Fifth Article of the Original Constitution

Amendment [I] [1791]

Congress shall make no law respecting an establishment of religion, or prohibiting the free exercise of thereof; or abridging the freedom of speech, or of the press; or the right of the people peaceably to assemble, and to petition the Government for a redress of grievances.

Amendment [IV] [1791]

The right of the people to be secure in their persons, houses, papers, and effects, against unreasonable searches and seizures, shall not be violated, and no Warrants shall issue, but upon probable cause, supported by Oath or affirmation, and particularly describing the place to be searched, and the persons or things to be seized.

Amendment [V] [1791]

No person shall be held to answer for a capital, or otherwise infamous crime, unless on a presentment or indictment of a Grand Jury, except in cases arising in the land or naval forces, or in the Militia, when in actual service in time of War or public danger; nor shall any person be subject for the same offence to be twice put in jeopardy of life or limb; nor shall be compelled in any criminal case to be a witness against himself, nor be deprived of life, liberty, or property, without due process of law; nor shall private property be taken for public use, without just compensation.

Amendment [VIII] [1791]

Excessive bail shall not be required, nor excessive fines imposed, nor cruel and unusual punishments inflicted.

Amendment [IX] [1791]

The enumeration in the Constitution, of certain rights, shall not be construed to deny or disparage others retained by the people.

Amendment [X] [1791]

The powers not delegated to the United States by the Constitution, nor prohibited by it to the States, are reserved to the States respectively, or to the people.

Amendment [XIV] [1868]

Section 1.   All persons born or naturalized in the United States, and subject to the jurisdiction thereof, are citizens of the United States and of the State wherein they reside. No State shall make or enforce any law which shall abridge the privileges or immunities of citizens of the United States; nor shall any State deprive any person of life, liberty, or property, without due process of law; nor deny to any person within its jurisdiction the equal protection of the laws.

Section 5.   The Congress shall have power to enforce, by appropriate legislation, the provisions of this article.

SUMMARY OF RELEVANT FEDERAL STATUTES

CIVIL RIGHTS ACTS OF 1866, 1870—42 U.S.C. § 1981

Section 1981 provides: *"All persons* within the jurisdiction of the United States shall have the same right . . . *to make and enforce contracts,* to sue, be parties, give evidence, and to the full and equal benefit of all laws and proceedings for the security of persons and property as is enjoyed by white citizens, and shall be subject to like punishment, pains, penalties, taxes, licenses, and exactions of every kind, and to no other."

CIVIL RIGHTS ACT OF 1871—42 U.S.C. § 1983

Section 1983 provides: "Every person who, under color of any statute, ordinance, regulation, custom, or usage, of any State or Territory or the District of Columbia, subjects, or causes to be subjected, any citizen of the United States or other person within the jurisdiction thereof to the *deprivation of any rights,* privileges, or immunities *secured by the Constitution and laws,* shall be liable to the party injured in an action at law, suit in equity, or other proper proceeding for redress."

CIVIL RIGHTS ACT OF 1871—42 U.S.C. §§ 1985 AND 1986

Section 1985(3) provides in part: "If two or more persons in any State or Territory conspire . . . for the purpose of depriving . . . any person or class of persons of the *equal protection of the laws,* or of equal privileges and immunities under the laws; or . . . of preventing or hindering the constituted authorities of any State . . . from . . . securing to all persons within such State . . . the equal protection of the laws . . . the party so injured . . . may have an action for the recovery of damages . . . against any one or more of the conspirators."

    Section 1986 provides in part: "Every person who, having knowledge that any of the wrongs conspired to be done . . . [under Section 1985] . . . and having power to prevent . . . the . . . same, neglects or refuses so to do . . . shall be liable to the party injured . . . for all damages caused by such wrongful act. . . ."

CIVIL RIGHTS ACTS OF 1866, 1870—42 U.S.C. § 1988

As amended 1980, § 1988 provides in part:

Proceedings in Vindication of Civil Rights In any . . . proceeding to enforce a provision of sections 1981, 1982, 1983, 1985, and 1986 of this title, title IX of Public Law 92-318, or Title VI of the Civil Rights Act of 1964, the court, in its discretion, may allow the prevailing party . . . *a reasonable attorney's fee as part of the costs.* As amended Pub. L. 94-559, § 2, Oct. 19, 1976, 90 Stat. 2641.

CIVIL RIGHTS ACT OF 1964, TITLE VI (SELECTED PARTS) 42 U.S.C.A. §§ 2000D—D—1

Federally Assisted Programs

§ 2000d. **Prohibition against exclusion from participation in, denial of benefits of, and discrimination under Federally assisted programs on ground of race, color, or national origin**

No person in the United States shall, on the ground of race, color, or national origin, be excluded from participation in, be denied the benefits of, or be subjected to discrimination under any program or activity receiving Federal financial assistance.

Pub.L. 88-352, Title VI, § 601, July 2, 1964, 78 Stat. 252.

§ 2000d—1. **Federal authority and financial assistance to programs or activities by way of grant, loan, or contract other than contract of insurance or guaranty; rules and regulations; approval by President; compliance with requirements; reports to Congressional committees; effective date of administrative action**

Each Federal department and agency which is empowered to extend Federal financial assistance to any program or activity, by way of grant, loan, or contract other than a contract of insurance or guaranty, is authorized and directed to effectuate the provisions of section 2000d of this title with respect to such program or activity by issuing rules, regulations, or orders of general applicability which shall be consistent with achievement of the objectives of the statute authorizing the financial assistance in connection with which the action is taken. No such rule, regulation, or order shall become effective unless and until approved by the President. Compliance with any requirement adopted pursuant to this section may be effected (1) by the termination of or refusal to grant or to continue assistance under such program or activity to any recipient as to whom there has been an express finding on the record, after opportunity for hearing, of a failure to comply with such requirement, but such termination or refusal shall be limited to the particular political entity, or part thereof, or other recipient as to whom such a finding has been made and, shall be limited in its effect to the particular program, or part thereof, in which such noncompliance has been so found, or (2) by any other means authorized by law: *Provided, however,* That no such action shall be taken until the department or agency concerned has advised the appropriate person or persons of the failure to comply with the requirement and has determined that compliance cannot be secured by voluntary means. In the case of any action terminating, or refusing to grant to continue, assistance because of failure to comply with a requirement imposed pursuant to this section, the head of the Federal department or agency shall file with the committees of the House and Senate having legislative jurisdiction over the program or activity involved a full written report of the circumstances and grounds for such action. No such action shall become effective until thirty days have elapsed after the filing of such report.

Pub.L. 88-352, Title VI, § 602, July 2, 1964, 78 Stat. 252.

CIVIL RIGHTS ACT OF 1964 TITLE VII (SELECTED PARTS) 42 U.S.C.A. § 2000E—E—2

Equal Employment Opportunities

§ 2000e–2. Unlawful employment practices

Employer Practices

(a) It shall be an unlawful employment practice for an employer—

(1) to fail or refuse to hire or to discharge any individual, or otherwise to discriminate against any individual with respect to his compensation, terms, conditions, or privileges of employment, because of such individual's race, color, religion, sex, or national origin; or

(2) to limit, segregate, or classify his employees or applicants for employment in any way which would deprive or tend to deprive any individual of employment opportunities or otherwise adversely affect his status as an employee, because of such individual's race, color, religion, sex, or national origin.

Employment Agency Practices

(b) It shall be an unlawful employment practice for an employment agency to fail or refuse to refer for employment, or otherwise to discriminate against, any individual because of his race, color, religion, sex, or national origin, or to classify or refer for employment any individual on the basis of his race, color, religions, sex, or national origin. . . .

Training Programs

(d) It shall be an unlawful employment practice for any employer, labor organization, or joint labor-management committee controlling apprenticeship or other training or retraining, including on-the-job training programs to discriminate against any individual because of his race, color, religion, sex, or national origin in admission to, or employment in, any program established to provide apprenticeship or other training.

Business or enterprises with personnel qualified on basis of religion, sex, or national origin; educational institutions with personnel of particular religion

(e) Notwithstanding any other provision of this subchapter, (1) it shall not be an unlawful employment practice for an employer to hire and employ employees, for an employment agency to classify, or refer for employment any individual, for a labor organization to classify its membership or to classify or refer for employment any individual, or for an employer, labor organization, or joint labor-management committee controlling apprenticeship or other training or retraining programs to admit or employ any individual in any such program, on the basis of his religion, sex, or national origin in those certain instances where religion, sex, or national origin is a bona fide occupational qualification reasonably necessary to the normal operation of that particular business or enterprise, and (2) it shall not be an unlawful employment practice for a school, college, university, or other educational institution or institution of learning to hire and employ employees of a particular religion if such school, college, university, or other educational institution or institution of learning is, in whole or in substantial part, owned, supported, controlled, or managed by a particular religion or by a particular religious corporation, association, or society, or if the curriculum of such school, college, university, or other educational institution or institution of learning is directed toward the propagation of a particular religion. . . .

Seniority or merit system; quantity or quality of production; ability tests; compensation based on sex and authorized by minimum wage provisions

(h) Notwithstanding any other provision of this subchapter, it shall not be an unlawful employment practice for an employer to apply different standards of compensation, or different terms, conditions, or privileges of employment pursuant to a bona fide seniority or merit system, or a system which measures earnings by quantity or quality of production or to employees who work in different locations, provided that such differences are not the result of an intention to discriminate because of race, color, religion, sex, or national origin, nor shall it be an unlawful employment practice for an employer to give and to act upon the results of any professionally developed ability test provided that such test, its administration or action upon the results is not designed, intended, or used to discriminate because of race, color, religion, sex or national origin. It shall not be an unlawful employment practice under this subchapter for any employer to differentiate upon the basis of sex in determining the amount of the wages or compensation paid or to be paid to employees of such employer if such differentiation is authorized by the provisions of section 206(d) of Title 29. . . .

Preferential treatment not to be granted on account of existing number or percentage imbalance

(j) Nothing contained in this subchapter shall be interpreted to require any employer, employment agency, labor organization, or joint labor-management committee subject to this subchapter to grant preferential treatment to any individual or to any group because of the race, color, religion, sex, or national origin of such individual or group on account of an imbalance which may exist with respect to the total number or percentage of persons of any race, color, religion, sex, or national origin employed by any employer, referred or classified for employment by any employment agency or labor organization, admitted to membership or classified by any labor organization, or admitted to, or employed in, any apprenticeship or other training program, in comparison with the total number or percentage of persons of such race, color, religion, sex, or national origin in any community, State, section, or other area, or in the available work force in any community, State, section, or other area.

Pub.L. 88-352, Title VII, § 703, July 2, 1964, 78 Stat. 255; Pub.L. 92-261, § 8(a), (b), Mar. 24, 1972, 86 Stat. 109.

Education Amendments of 1972, Title IX—20 U.S.C. § 1681
Section 901 of Title IX provides in part:

(a) *No person* . . . shall, on the basis of *sex,* be excluded from participation in, be denied the benefits of, or be subjected to discrimination under any *education program* or activity receiving Federal financial assistance, except that:

(1) in regard to admissions . . .

(3) this section *shall not apply* to an educational institution which is controlled by a religious organization if the application . . . would not be consistent *with the religious tenets* of such organization . . .

Title IX regulations provide in part:

"discrimination on the Basis of Sex in Education Programs and Activities; Receiving or Benefiting from Federal Financial Assistance" 34 C.F.R. §§ 106.1–106.71

Title IX Regulations, 34 C.F.R. § 106-1 et seq.

Subpart C—Discrimination on the Basis of Sex in Admission and Recruitment Prohibited.

§ 106.21 Admission

(a) *General.* No person shall, on the basis of sex, be denied admission, or be subjected to discrimination in admission. . . .

(b) Specific prohibitions.

(1) [a] recipient . . . shall not:

(i) Give preference to one person over another on the basis of sex, by ranking applicants separately on such basis . . .

(ii) Apply numerical limitations upon the number or proportion of persons of either sex who may be admitted . . .

(2) A recipient shall not administer . . . any test . . . for admission which has a disproportionately adverse effect on persons on the basis of sex unless the use of such test . . . is shown to predict valid success in the education program or activity in question and alternative tests . . . which do not have such a disproportionately adverse effect are shown to be unavailable.

(c) *Prohibitions relating to marital or parental status* . . . A recipient . . . :

(1) Shall not apply any rule concerning . . . parental, family, or marital status . . . which treats persons differently on the basis of sex . . .

***

(3) Shall treat disabilities related to pregnancy, childbirth, termination of pregnancy, or recovery therefrom in the same manner . . . as any other temporary disability . . . and

(4) Shall not make preadmission inquiry as to the marital status of an applicant for admission. . . .

***

Subpart D—Discrimination on the Basis of Sex in Education Programs and Activities Prohibited

§ 106.31 Education Programs and Activities

(a) *General.* Except as provided elsewhere in this part, no person shall, on the basis of sex, be excluded from participation in, be denied the benefits of, or be subjected to discrimination under any academic, extracurricular, research, occupational training, or other education program or activity operated by a recipient which receives or benefits from Federal financial assistance . . .

(b) *Specific prohibitions.* Except as provided in this subpart, in providing any aid, benefit, or service to a student, a recipient shall not on the basis of sex . . .

***

(2) Provide different aid, benefits, or services or provide aid, benefits, or services in a different manner . . .

***

(4) Subject any person to separate or different rules of behavior, sanctions, or other treatment . . .

§ 106.34 Access to Course Offerings

A recipient shall not provide any course or otherwise carry out any of its education program or activity separately on the basis of sex . . .

(b) This section does not prohibit grouping of students in physical education classes and activities by ability as assessed by objective standards of individual performance developed and applied without regard to sex.

(c) This section does not prohibit separation of students by sex within physical education classes or activities during participation in wrestling, boxing, rugby, ice hockey, football, basketball and other sports the purpose or major activity of which involves bodily contact.

(d) Where use of a single standard of measuring skill or progress in a physical education class has an adverse effect on members of one sex, the recipient shall use appropriate standards which do not have such effect.

(e) Portions of classes in elementary and secondary schools which deal exclusively with human sexuality may be conducted in separate sessions for boys and girls.

(f) Recipients may make requirements based on vocal range or quality which may result in a chorus or choruses of one or predominantly one sex.

§ 106.36 Counseling and Use of Appraisal and Counseling Materials

(a) *Counseling.* A recipient shall not discriminate against any person on the basis of sex in the counseling or guidance of students or applicants for admission.

(b) *Use of appraisal and counseling materials.* A recipient which uses testing or other materials for appraising or counseling students shall not use different materials for students on the basis of their sex or use materials which permit or require different treatment of students on such basis unless such different materials cover the same occupations and interest areas and the use of such different materials is shown to be essential to eliminate sex bias. . . . Where the use of a counseling test or other instrument results in a substantially disproportionate number of members of one sex in any particular course of study or classification, the recipient shall take such action as is necessary to assure itself that such disproportion is not the result of discrimination in the instrument or its application.

(c) *Disproportion in classes.* Where a recipient finds that a particular class contains a substantially disproportionate number of individuals of one sex, the recipient shall take such action as is necessary to assure itself that such disproportion is not the result of discrimination on the basis of sex in counseling or appraisal materials or by counselors.

§ 106.40 Marital or Parental Status

(a) *Status generally.* A recipient shall not apply any rule concerning a student's actual or potential parental, family, or marital status which treats students differently on the basis of sex.

(b) *Pregnancy and related conditions.* (1) A recipient shall not discriminate against any student, or exclude any student from its education program or activity, including any class or extracurricular activity, on the basis of such student's pregnancy, childbirth, false pregnancy, termination of pregnancy or recovery therefrom, unless the student requests voluntarily to participate in a separate portion of the program or activity of the recipient.

(2) A recipient may require such a student to obtain the certification of a physician that the student is physically and emotionally able to continue participation in the normal education program or activity . . .

(3) A recipient which operates a portion of its education program or activity separately for pregnant students, admittance to which is completely voluntary on the part of the student . . . shall ensure that the instructional program in the separate program is comparable to that offered to nonpregnant students.

(4) A recipient shall treat pregnancy, childbirth, false pregnancy, termination of pregnancy and recovery therefrom in the same manner and under the same policies as any other temporary disability with respect to any medical or hospital benefit, service, plan or policy which such recipient administers, operates . . . with respect to students . . .

DISCRIMINATION BASED ON SEX TITLE IX (SELECTED PARTS) 20 U.S.C.A. § 1681

§ 1861. Sex

Prohibition Against Discrimination; Exceptions

(a) No person in the United States shall, on the basis of sex, be excluded from participation in, be denied the benefits of, or be subjected to discrimination under any education program or activity receiving Federal financial assistance, except that:

Classes of Educational Institutions Subject to Prohibition

(1) in regard to admissions to educational institutions, this section shall apply only to institutions of vocational education, professional education, and graduate higher education, and to public institutions of undergraduate higher education;

Educational Institutions Commencing Planned Change in Admissions

(2) In regard to admissions to educational institutions, this section shall not apply (A) for one year from June 23, 1972, nor for six years after June 23, 1972, in the case of an educational institution which has begun the process of changing from being an institution which admits only students of one sex to being an institution which admits students of both sexes, but only if it is carrying out a plan for such a change which is approved by the Commissioner of Education or (B) for seven years from the date an educational institution begins the process of changing from being an institution which admits only students of one sex to being an institution which admits students of both sexes, but only if it is carrying out a plan for such a change which is approved by the Commissioner of Education, whichever is the later;

Educational Institutions of Religious Organizations with Contrary Religious Tenets

(3) This section shall not apply to an educational institution which is controlled by a religious organization if the application of this subsection would not be consistent with the religious tenets of such organization;

Educational Institutions Training Individuals for Military Services or Merchant Marine

(4) This section shall not apply to an educational institution whose primary purpose is the training of individuals for the military services of the United States, or the merchant marine;

Public Educational Institutions with Traditional and Continuing Admissions Policy

(5) In regard to admissions this section shall not apply to any public institution of undergraduate higher education which is an institution that traditionally and continually from its establishment has had a policy of admitting only students of one sex;

Social Fraternities or Sororities; Voluntary Youth Service Organizations

(6) This section shall not apply to membership practices—

(a) of a social fraternity or social sorority which is exempt from taxation under section 501(a) of Title 26, the active membership of which consists primarily of students in attendance at an institution of higher education, or

(b) of the Young Men's Christian Association, Young Women's Christian Association, Girl Scouts, Boy Scouts, Camp Fire Girls, and voluntary youth service organizations which are so exempt, the membership of which has traditionally been limited to persons of one sex and principally to persons of less than nineteen years of age;

Boy or Girl Conferences

(7) This section shall not apply to—

(a) any program or activity of the American Legion undertaken in connection with the organization or operation of any Boys State conference, Boys Nation conference, Girls State conference, or Girls Nation conference; or

(b) any program or activity of any secondary school or educational institution specifically for—

(i) the promotion of any Boys State conference, Boys Nation conference, Girls State conference, or Girls Nation conference; or

(ii) the selection of students to attend any such conference;

Father-Son or Mother-Daughter Activities at Educational Institutions

(8) This section shall not preclude father-son or mother-daughter activities at an educational institution, but if such activities are provided for students of one sex, opportunities for reasonably comparable activities shall be provided for students of the other sex; and

Institution of Higher Education Scholarship Awards in "Beauty" Pageants

(9) This section shall not apply with respect to any scholarship or other financial assistance awarded by an institution of higher education to any individual because such individual has received such award in any pageant in which the attainment of such award is based upon a combination of factors related to the personal appearance, poise, and talent of such individual and in which participation is limited to individuals of one sex only, so long as such pageant is in compliance with other nondiscrimination provisions of Federal law.

Preferential or Disparate Treatment Because of Imbalance in Participation or Receipt of Federal Benefits; Statistical Evidence of Imbalance

(b) Nothing contained in subsection (a) of this section shall be interpreted to require any educational institution to grant preferential or disparate treatment to the members of one sex on account of an imbalance which may exist with respect to the total number of percentage of persons of that sex participating in or receiving the benefits of any federally supported program or activity, in comparison with the total number or percentage of persons of that sex in any community, State, section, or other area: *Provided,* That this subsection shall not be construed to prevent the consideration in any hearing or proceeding under this chapter of statistical evidence tending to show that such an imbalance exists with respect to the participation in, or receipt of the benefits of, any such program or activity by the members of one sex.

Educational Institution Defined

(c) For purposes of this chapter an educational institution means any public or private preschool, elementary, or secondary school, or any institution of vocational, professional, or higher education, except that in the case of an educational institution composed of more than one school, college, or department which are administratively separate units, such term means each such school, college, or department.

Pub.L. 92-318, Title IX, § 901, June 23, 1972, 86 Stat. 373; Pub.L. 93-568, § 3(a), Dec. 31, 1974, 88 Stat. 1862; Pub.L. 94-482, Title IV, § 412(a), Oct. 12, 1976, 90 Stat. 2234.

FAMILY RIGHTS AND PRIVACY ACT (BUCKLEY AMENDMENT) (SELECTED PARTS) 20 U.S.C.A. § 1232G

§ 1232G. Family educational and privacy rights

Conditions for availability of funds to educational agencies or institutions; inspection and review of education records; specific information to be made available; procedure for access to education records; reasonableness of time for such access; hearings; written explanations by parents; definitions

(a)(1)(A) No funds shall be made available under any applicable program to any educational agency or institution which has a policy of denying, or which effectively prevents, the parents of students who are or have been in attendance at a school of such agency or at such institution, as the case may be, the right to inspect and review the education records of their children. If any material or document in the education record of a student includes information on more than one student, the parents of one of such students shall have the right to inspect and review only such part of such material or document as relates to such student or to be informed of the specific information contained in such part of such material. Each educational agency or institution shall establish appropriate procedures for the granting of a request by parents for access to the education records of their children within a reasonable period of time, but in no case more than forty-five days after the request has been made. . . .

(2) No funds shall be made available under any applicable program to any educational agency or institution unless the parents of students who are or have been in attendance at a school of such agency or at such institution are provided an opportunity for a hearing by such agency or institution, in accordance with regulations of the Secretary, to challenge the content of such student's education records, in order to insure that the records are not inaccurate, misleading, or otherwise in violation of the privacy or other rights of students, and to provide an opportunity for the correction or deletion of any such inaccurate, misleading, or otherwise inappropriate data contained therein and to insert into such records a written explanation of

the parents respecting the content of such records. . . .

Release of education records; parental consent requirement; exceptions; compliance with judicial orders and subpoenas; audit and evaluation of Federally-supported education programs; record-keeping

(b)(1) No funds shall be made available under any applicable program to any educational agency or institution which has a policy or practice of permitting the release of education records (or personally identifiable information contained therein other than directory information, as defined in paragraph (5) of subsection (a) of this section) of students without the written consent of their parents to any individual, agency, or organization, other than to the following—

(A) other school officials, including teachers within the educational institution or local educational agency who have been determined by such agency or institution to have legitimate educational interests;

(B) officials of other schools or school systems in which the student seeks or intends to enroll, upon condition that the student's parents be notified of the transfer, receive a copy of the record if desired, and have an opportunity for a hearing to challenge the content of the record;

(C) authorized representatives of (i) the Comptroller General of the United States, (ii) the Secretary, (iii) an administrative head of an education agency (as defined in section 1221e–3(c) of this title), or (iv) State educational authorities, under the conditions set forth in paragraph (3) of this subsection;

(D) in connection with a student's application for, or receipt of, financial aid;

(E) State and local officials or authorities to whom such information is specifically required to be reported or disclosed pursuant to state statute adopted prior to November 19, 1974;

(F) organizations conducting studies for, or on behalf of, educational agencies or institutions for the purpose of developing, validating, or administering predictive tests, administering student aid programs, and improving instruction, if such studies are conducted in such a manner as will not permit the personal identification of students and their parents by persons other than representatives of such organizations and such information will be destroyed when no longer needed for the purpose for which it is conducted;

(G) accrediting organizations in order to carry out their accrediting functions;

(H) parents of a dependent student of such parents, as defined in section 152 of Title 26; and

(I) subject to regulations of the Secretary, in connection with an emergency, appropriate persons if the knowledge of such information is necessary to protect the health or safety of the student or other persons.

Nothing in clause (E) of this paragraph shall prevent a State from further limiting the number or type of State or local officials who will continue to have access thereunder.

(2) No funds shall be made available under any applicable program to any educational agency or institution which has a policy or practice of releasing, or providing access to, any personally identifiable information in education records other than directory information, or as is permitted under paragraph (1) of this subsection unless—

(A) there is written consent from the student's parents specifying records to be released, the reasons for such release, and to whom, and with a copy of the records to be released to the student's parents and the student if desired by the parents, or

(B) such information is furnished in compliance with judicial order, or pursuant to any lawfully issued subpoena, upon condition that parents and the students are notified of all such orders or subpoenas in advance of the compliance therewith by the educational institution or agency. . . .

(C) With respect to this subsection, personal information shall only be transferred to a third party on the condition that such party will not permit any other party to have access to such information without the written consent of the parents of the student. . . .

Students' rather than parents' permission or consent

(d) For the purposes of this section, whenever a student has attained eighteen years of age, or is attending an institution of postsecondary education the permission or consent required of and the rights accorded to the parents of the student shall thereafter only be required of and accorded to the student. . . .

Pub.L. 90-247, Title IV, § 438, as added Pub.L. 93-380, Title V. § 513(a), Aug. 21, 1974, 88 Stat. 572, and amended Pub.L. 93-568 § 2(a), Dec. 31, 1974, 88 Stat. 1858.

§ 1232h. Protection of pupil rights

Inspection by parents or guardians of instructional material

(a) All instructional material, including teacher's manuals, films, tapes, or other supplementary instructional material which will be used in connection with any research or experimentation program or project shall be available for inspection by the parents or guardians of the children engaged in such program or project. For the purpose of this section "research or experimentation program or project": research means any program or project in any applicable program designed to explore or develop new or unproven teaching methods or techniques.

Psychiatric or psychological examinations, testing, or treatment

(b) No student shall be required, as part of any applicable program, to submit to psychiatric examination, testing, or treatment, or psychological examination, testing, or treatment, in which the primary purpose is to reveal information concerning:

(1) political affiliations;

(2) mental and psychological problems potentially embarrassing to the student or his family;

(3) sex behavior and attitudes;

(4) illegal, anti-social, self-incriminating, and demeaning behavior;

(5) critical appraisals of other individuals with whom respondents have close family relationships;

(6) legally recognized privileged and analogous relationships, such as those of lawyers, physicians, and ministers; or;

(7) income (other than that required by law to determine eligibility for participation in a program or for receiving financial assistance under such program), without the prior consent of the student (if the student is an adult or emancipated minor), or in the case of unemancipated minor, without the prior written consent of the parent.

Jan. 2, 1968, P.L. 90-247, Title IV, Part C, Subpart 2, § 439, as added Aug. 21, 1974, P.L. 93-380, Title V, § 514 (a), 88 Stat. 574; Nov. 1, 1978, P.L. 95-561, Title XII, Part D, § 1250, 92 Stat. 2355.

AMERICANS WITH DISABILITIES ACT OF 1990 (SELECTED PARTS), PUBLIC LAW 101-336, 42 U.S.C. § 12101

Title I—Employment

§ 101. Definitions
As used in this title:

(1) Commission.—The term "Commission" means the Equal Employment Opportunity Commission established by section 705 of the Civil Rights Act of 1964 (42 U.S.C. 2000e–4).

(2) Covered entity.—The term "covered entity" means an employer, employment agency, labor organization, or joint labor-management committee.

(3) Direct threat.—The term "direct threat" means a significant risk to the health or safety of others that cannot be eliminated by reasonable accommodation.

(4) Employee.—The term "employee" means an individual employed by an employer.

(5) Employer.—

(A) In general.—The term "employer" means a person engaged in an industry affecting commerce who has 15 or more employees for each working day in each of 20 or more calendar weeks in the current or preceding calendar year, and any agent of such person, except that, for two years following the effective date of this title, an employer means a person engaged in an industry affecting commerce who has 25 or more employees for each working day in each of 20 or more calendar weeks in the current or preceding year, and any agent of such person.

(B) Exceptions.—The term "employer" does not include—

(i) the United States, a corporation wholly owned by the government of the United States, or an Indian tribe; or

(ii) a bona fide private membership club (other than a labor organization) that is exempt from taxation under section 501(c) of the Internal Revenue Code of 1986.

(7) Person, etc.—The terms "person," "labor organization," "employment agency," "commerce," and "industry affecting commerce," shall have the same meaning given such terms in section 701 of the Civil Rights Act of 1964 (42 U.S.C. 2000e).

(8) Qualified individual with a disability.—The term "qualified individual with a disability" means an individual with a disability who, with or without reasonable accommodation, can perform the essential functions of the employment position that such individual holds or desires. For the purposes of this title, consideration shall be given to the employer's judgment as to what functions of a job are essential, and if an employer has prepared a written description before advertising or interviewing applicants for the job, this description shall be considered evidence of the essential functions of the job.

(9) Reasonable accommodation.—The term "reasonable accommodation" may include—

(A) making existing facilities used by employees readily accessible to and usable by individuals with disabilities; and

(B) job restructuring, part-time or modified work schedules, reassignment to a vacant position, acquisition or modification of equipment or devices, appropriate adjustment or modifications of examinations, training materials or policies, the provision of qualified readers or interpreters, and other similar accommodations for individuals with disabilities.

(10) Undue hardship.—

(A) In general.—The term "undue hardship" means an action requiring significant difficulty or expense, when considered in light of the factors set forth in subparagraph (B).

(B) Factors to be considered.—In determining whether an accommodation would impose an undue hardship on a covered entity, factors to be considered include—

(i) the nature and cost of the accommodation needed under this Act;

(ii) the overall financial resources of the facility or facilities involved in the provision of the reasonable accommodation; the number of persons employed at such facility; the effect on expenses and resources, or the impact otherwise of such accommodation upon the operation of the facility;

(iii) the overall financial resources of the covered entity; the overall size of the business of a covered entity with respect to the number of its employees; the number, type, and location of its facilities; and

(iv) the type of operation or operations of the covered entity, including the composition, structure, and functions of the workforce of such entity; the geographic separateness, administrative, or fiscal relationship of the facility or facilities in question to the covered entity.

INDIVIDUALS WITH DISABILITIES EDUCATION ACT (SELECTED PARTS), 20 U.S.C. SECS. 1400–1485

Purpose

It is the purpose of this chapter to assure that all children with disabilities have available to them, within the time periods specified in section 1412(2)(B) of this title, a free appropriate public education which emphasizes special education and related services designed to meet their unique needs, to assure that the rights of children with disabilities and their parents or guardians are protected, to assist States and localities to provide for the education of all children with disabilities, and to assess and assure the effectiveness of efforts to educate children with disabilities.

§ 1401. Definitions

(1) The term "children with disabilities" means children—

(A) with mental retardation, hearing impairments including deafness, speech or language impairments, visual impairments including blindness, serious emotional disturbance, orthopedic impairments, autism, traumatic brain injury, other health impairments, or specific learning disabilities; and

(B) who, by reason thereof need special education and related services. . . .

***

(15) The term "children with specific learning disabilities" means those children who have a disorder in one or more of the basic psychological processes involved in understanding or in using language, spoken or written, which disorder may manifest itself in imperfect ability to listen, think, speak, read, write, spell, or do mathematical calculations. Such disorders include such conditions as perceptual disabilities, brain injury, minimal

brain dysfunction, dyslexia, and developmental aphasia. Such term does not include children who have learning problems which are primarily the result of visual, hearing, or motor disabilities, of mental retardation, of emotional disturbance, or of environmental, cultural, or economic disadvantage.

(16) The term "special education" means specially designed instruction, at no cost to parents or guardians, to meet the unique needs of a child with a disability, including—

(A) instruction conducted in the classroom, in the home, in hospitals and institutions, and in other settings; and

(B) instruction in physical education.

(17) The term "related services" means transportation, and such developmental, corrective, and other supportive services (including speech pathology and audiology, psychological services, physical and occupational therapy, recreation, including therapeutic recreation and social work services, and medical and counseling services, including rehabilitation counseling, except that such medical services shall be for diagnostic and evaluation purposes only) as may be required to assist a child with a disability to benefit from special education, and includes the early identification and assessment of disabling conditions in children.

(18) The term "free appropriate public education" means special education and related services that—

(A) have been provided at public expense, under public supervision and direction, and without charge,

(B) meet the standards of the State educational agency,

(C) include an appropriate preschool, elementary, or secondary school education in the State involved, and

(D) are provided in conformity with the individualized education program required under section 1414(a)(5) of this title.

(19) The term "transition services" means a coordinated set of activities for a student, designed within an outcome-oriented process, which promotes movement from school to post-school activities, including post-secondary education, vocational training, integrated employment (including supported employment), continuing and adult education, adult services, independent living, or community participation. The coordinated set of activities shall be based upon the individual student's needs, taking into account the student's preferences and interests, and shall include instruction, community experiences, the development of employment and other post-school adult living objectives, and, when appropriate, acquisition of daily living skills and functional vocational evaluation.

(20) The term "individualized education program" means a written statement for each child with a disability developed in any meeting by a representative of the local educational agency or an intermediate educational unit who shall be qualified to provide, or supervise the provision of, specially designed instruction to meet the unique needs of children with disabilities, the teacher, the parents or guardian of such child, and, whenever appropriate, such child, which statement shall include—

(A) a statement of the present levels of educational performance of such child,

(B) a statement of annual goals, including short-term instructional objectives,

(C) a statement of the specific educational services to be provided to such child, and the extent to which such child will be able to participate in regular educational programs,

(D) a statement of the needed transition services for students beginning no later than age 16 and annually thereafter (and, when determined appropriate for the individual, beginning at age 14 or younger), including, when appropriate, a statement of the interagency responsibilities or linkages (or both) before the student leaves the school setting.

(E) the projected date for initiation and anticipated duration of such services, and

(F) appropriate objective criteria and evaluation procedures and schedules for determining, on at least an annual basis, whether instructional objectives are being achieved. In the case where a participating agency, other than the educational agency, fails to provide agreed upon services, the educational agency shall reconvene the IEP team to identify alternative strategies to meet the transition objectives.

AGE DISCRIMINATION ACT—29 U.S.C. § 621 (§ 623)

(a) It shall be unlawful for an employer—

(1) to fail or refuse to hire or to discharge any individual or otherwise discriminate against any individual with respect to his compensation, terms, conditions, or privileges of employment, because of such individual's age. . . .

(c) It shall be unlawful for a labor organization—

(1) to exclude or to expel from its membership, or otherwise to discriminate against, any individual because of his age. . . .

(3) to cause or attempt to cause an employer to discriminate against an individual in violation of this section. . . .

(f) It shall not be unlawful for an employer, employment agency, or labor organization—

(1) to take any action otherwise prohibited under subsections (a), (b), (c), or (e) of this section where age is a bona fide occupational qualification reasonably necessary to the normal operation of the particular business, or where the differentiation is based on reasonable factors other than age. . . .

(3) to discharge or otherwise discipline an individual for good cause. . . .

REHABILITATION ACT OF 1973—29 U.S.C. § 794 (§ 504)

The Act provides in part:

" otherwise qualified handicapped individual . . . shall, solely by reason of his handicap, be excluded from the participation in, be denied the benefits of, or be subjected to discrimination under any program or activity receiving Federal financial assistance."

EQUAL EDUCATION OPPORTUNITIES ACT 20 U.S.C. § 1703

§ 1703 provides:

No State shall deny equal educational opportunity to an individual on account of his or her race, color, sex, or national origin, by—

(a) the deliberate segregation by an educational agency of students on the basis of race, color, or national origin among or within schools. . . .

(c) the assignment by an educational agency of a student to a school, other than the one closest to his or her place of residence within the school district in which he or she resides, if the assignment results in a greater degree of segregation of students on the basis of race, color, sex, or national origin.

***

(d) discrimination by an educational agency on the basis of race, color, or national origin in the employment, employment conditions, or assignment to schools of its faculty or staff, except to fulfill the purposes of subsection (f) below. . . .

(e) the transfer by an educational agency, whether voluntary or otherwise, of a student from one school to another if the purpose and effect of such transfer is to increase segregation of students on the basis of race, color, or national origin among the schools of such agency; or

(f) the failure by an educational agency to take appropriate action to overcome language barriers that impede equal participation by its students in its instructional programs.

PREGNANCY DISCRIMINATION ACT OF 1978—
P.L. 95-555

Be it enacted by the Senate and House of Representatives of the United States of America in Congress assembled, That section 701 of the Civil Rights Act of 1964 is amended by adding at the end thereof the following new subsection:

(k) The Terms "because of sex" or "on the basis of sex" include, but are not limited to, because of or on the basis of pregnancy, childbirth, or related medical conditions; and women affected by pregnancy, childbirth, or related medical conditions shall be treated the same for all employment-related purposes, including the receipt of benefits under fringe benefit programs, as other persons not so affected but similar in their ability or inability to work, and nothing in section 703(h) of this title shall be interpreted to permit otherwise. This subsection shall not require an employer to pay for health insurance benefits for abortion, except where the life of the mother would be endangered if the fetus were carried to term, or except where medical complications have arisen from an abortion: *Provided,* That nothing herein shall preclude an employer from providing abortion benefits or otherwise affect bargaining agreements in regard to abortion.

SEC. 2 (a) Except as provided in subsection (b), the amendment made by this Act shall be effective on the date of enactment.

(b) The provisions of the amendment made by the first section of this Act shall not apply to any fringe benefit program or fund, or insurance program which is in effect on the date of enactment of this Act until 30 days after enactment of this Act.

SEC. 3 Until the expiration of a period of one year from the date of enactment of this Act or, if there is an applicable collective-bargaining agreement in effect on the date of enactment of this Act, until the termination of that agreement, no person who, on the date of enactment of this act is providing either by direct payment or by making contributions to a fringe benefit fund or insurance program, benefits in violation with this act shall, in order to come into compliance with this Act, reduce the benefits or the compensation provided any employee on the date of enactment of this Act, either directly or by failing to provide sufficient contributions to a fringe benefit fund or insurance program: *Provided,* That where the costs of such benefits on the date of enactment of this Act are apportioned between employers and employees, the payments or contributions required to comply with this Act may be made by employers and employees in the same proportion: *And provided further,* That nothing in this section shall prevent the readjustment of benefits or compensation for reasons unrelated to compliance with this Act.

GLOSSARY OF RELEVANT
LEGAL TERMS

abatement   Termination of a lawsuit.

action   A lawsuit proceeding in a court of law.

advisory opinion   An opinion generally rendered by a lower court when no actual case is before it.

affidavit   A written statement made under oath.

affirm   To uphold a lower court's decision or ruling.

allegation   A statement in the pleadings of a case, which is expected to be proven, usually brought by the plaintiff.

amicus curiae   A friend of the court. A party that does not have a direct interest in a case who is requested or offers information to the court to clarify an issue before the court.

appeal   An application to a higher court to amend or rectify a lower court's ruling.

appellant   One who causes an appeal to a higher court. The appellant may be the plaintiff or the defendant.

appellate court   A higher court that hears cases on appeal from a lower court.

appellee   A person or party against whom an appeal is brought.

arbitrary   An act or action taken without a fair and substantial cause.

assault   An offer to use physical force in a hostile manner.

battery   Making physical contact with another person in a rude and hostile fashion.

bona fide   Acting honestly and in good faith.

breach   Failure to execute a legal duty.

brief   A written argument presented to a court by attorneys.

busing   The transporting of students across school-district boundaries, usually court-ordered, to create more racially balanced schools.

case law   A body of law created by decisions of the judicial branch.

cause of action   The basis for a legal challenge.

certiorari   A judicial process whereby a case is moved from a lower court to a higher one for review. The record of all proceedings at the lower court is sent to the higher court.

civil action   An action in court with the expressed purpose of gaining or recovering individual or civil rights.

civil rights   The personal freedoms of citizens guaranteed by the thirteenth and fourteenth amendments to the U.S. Constitution.

class action   Legal action brought by one or more individuals on behalf of themselves and others who are affected by a particular issue.

code   A systematic compilation of statutes usually arranged into chapters and headings for convenient access.

common law   A system of law in which legal principles are derived from usage and custom, as expressed by the courts.

compensatory damages Damages awarded to compensate an injured party for actual losses incurred.

complaint A formal plea to a court seeking relief and informing the defendant on the basis for a legal challenge.

concurring opinion An opinion written by a judge expressing the will of the majority in a court ruling.

consent decree Agreement by parties to a dispute and the admission by parties that the decree is a just determination of their rights based on facts related to the case.

contract A legal agreement between parties involving an offer and acceptance to perform certain duties that are enforceable by courts of law.

contributory negligence Negligence by the injured party which, when combined with the negligence of the defendant resulted in the proximate cause of the injury.

court of record A court that maintains permanent records of its proceedings.

damages Compensation or indemnity claimed by the plaintiff or ordered by the courts for injuries sustained resulting from wrongful acts of the defendant.

declaratory relief An opinion expressed by the court without ordering that anything be done; it recognizes the rights of the parties involved.

de facto In fact, in reality. A state of affairs that is accepted without the sanction of law.

decree An order issued by a court in an equity suit.

defamation Scandalous words or expression, written or spoken, that result in damages to another's reputation, for which legal action may be taken by the damaged party.

defendant The party against whom a legal action is brought.

de jure Sanctioned by law.

de minimis Something that is so insignificant that it does not warrant judicial attention.

demurrer Objection to a pleading that is viewed as legally insufficient.

de nova New. A preceding that ignores all previous proceedings. It is usually associated with a second trial mandated by a higher court to a lower court for a new trial.

deposition A statement of a witness taken under oath obtained before the actual trial.

desegregation The ending of the separation of people of one race from people of another race.

dicta Statements in a judicial opinion that have no bearing on the decision of the case.

dictum An opinion expressed by a judge in a proceeding that is not relevant in reaching a court's decision.

discretionary power The exercise of judgment in deciding whether to take action in a certain situation.

discrimination The unfair treatment of a group of people by another because of race, gender, religion, culture, or national origin.

dissenting opinion An opinion written by a judge in disagreement with the decision of the majority hearing a case.

due process A course of legal proceedings in accordance with principles of law designed to protect individual rights.

emancipation Legal release from another's control (e.g., a married child from its parents').

en banc By all judges of the court.

enjoin To require an individual by writ of injunction to perform or refrain from a certain act.

et. al And others. Unnamed parties involved in legal proceedings.

et seq. And those following.

ex parte A proceeding for the benefit of one party.

ex rel On behalf of.

felony A crime that is punishable by imprisonment or death.

fiduciary A special relationship between individuals in which one person acts for another in a position of trust.

finding The conclusion reached by a court regarding a factual question.

functional exclusion   Disabled students who are provided equal access without special provisions that will enable them to benefit from instruction although they are physically exposed to the same experience as nondisabled students.

governmental function   One which is required of an agency for the protection and welfare of the general public.

hearing   An examination of a legal or factual issue by a court.

holding   A ruling or decision by the courts on a question or issue properly raised in a case.

implied   Inferred; not expressed.

in loco parentis   In place of parents.

infra   Following; below.

injunction   A court order prohibiting a person from committing an act that threatens or may result in injury to another.

integration   The process of bringing together different races of students so that all may enjoy the same educational benefits.

inter alia   Among other things.

invitee   A person who is on the property of another by expressed invitation.

ipso facto   In and of itself.

judgment   A decision reached by a court.

liable   Bound or obligated by law; responsible for actions that may involve restitution.

licensee   A person granted the privilege to enter into property by actual or implied consent for his or her own purpose rather than the purpose of the one who owns the property.

litigation   Formal challenge involving a dispute in a court, a lawsuit.

malfeasance   Commission of an unlawful act.

malice   The intentional commission of a wrongful act without justification.

mandate   A legal command.

material   Important to a case.

ministerial acts   Required usually by public officials in which there is no discretion.

misfeasance   Improper performance of a lawful act.

motion   A request for a court ruling.

negligence   A lack of proper care; failure to exercise prudence which may result in injury to another.

nolens volens   With or without consent.

nuisance   A condition that restricts the use of property or creates a potentially dangerous situation for the user.

original jurisdiction   The legal capacity of a court to accept a case at its inception.

parens patriae   The state's guardsmanship over those unable to direct their own affairs, such as minors.

per curiam   An opinion rendered by an entire court rather than by any one of several justices.

petition   A written application to a court for the redress of a wrong or the grant of a privilege or license.

plaintiff   The party who brings action by filing a complaint.

pleadings   Formal documents filed in court containing the plaintiff's contention and the defendant's response.

plenary   Full; complete.

police powers   The inherent power of the government to impose restrictions to protect the health, safety and welfare of its citizens.

precedent   A decision relied on for subsequent decisions in addressing similar or identical questions of law.

prima facie   At first view. A fact presumed to be true if not rebutted or proven untrue.

proprietary function   Those functions not normally required by statutes or law and usually involving a state or governmental agent.

punitive damages   An award intended to punish the wrongdoer.

quid pro quo   A consideration; giving one valuable thing in exchange for another.

ratio decidendi   Reasoning applied by a court regarding crucial facts related to the case in rendering a judgment.

relief   Legal redress sought in the court by the plaintiff.

remand   To send back. The act of an appellate court when it sends a case back to the lower court for further proceedings.

remedy   A court's enforcement of a right or the prevention of the violation of such right.

respondeat superior   The responsibility of a master for the acts of his servants.

respondent   The party against whom an appeal is taken; the defendant.

restrain   To prevent or prohibit from action.

segregation   The separation of one group of people from another through laws or personal discrimination.

"separate but equal"   A concept that gave states the right to segregate people of different races in public transportation. This idea was extended to allow races to have separate but similar-quality schools. It was subsequently ruled unconstitutional.

sin qua non   A thing that is indispensable.

slander   Oral defamation.

sovereign immunity   A doctrine providing immunity from suit of a governmental body without its expressed consent.

standing   The right to raise an issue in a lawsuit.

stare decisis   To stand by a decided case.

statute   An act of the state or federal legislative body; a law.

statute of limitations   A statute that established the time period in which litigation may be initiated in a particular cause of action.

substantive law   The proper law of rights and duties.

suit   A proceeding in a court of law initiated by the plaintiff.

summary judgment   A court's decision to settle a dispute or dispose of a case promptly without conducting full legal proceedings.

tenure   A security measure for those who successfully perform duties and meet statutory or contractual requirements; a continuous service contract.

tort   An actionable wrong committed against another independent of contract; a civil wrong.

trespass   The unauthorized entry upon the property of another; taking or interfering with the property of another.

ultra vires   Outside of the legal power of an individual or body; exceeding the power of authority.

vacate   To rescind a court decision.

vested   Fixed. Not subject to any contingency.

vicarious liability   A form of liability in which school districts are held liable for negligent or intentional wrongdoing of their employees when the act is committed within the scope of the district employment position, even though the district may not be directly at fault.

void   Null. Without force or a binding effect.

waiver   To forego, renounce, or relinquish a legal right.

warrant   A written order of the court; arrest order.

white flight   A term used to describe the trend of white families to move out of neighborhoods that black families have moved into.

writ of mandamus   A command from a court directing a court, officer, or body to perform a certain act.

zoning   A strategy used by school districts to create desegregated schools.

INDEX

Please remember that this is a library book,
and that it belongs only temporarily to each
person who uses it. Be considerate. Do
not write in this, or any, library book.